Taming the Cycles of Finance?

Macro-prudential regulation is a set of economic and policy tools that aim to mitigate risk in the financial and banking systems. It was largely developed in response to the financial crisis of 2007–8, turning central banks into de facto financial police officers. *Taming the Cycles of Finance?* traces the post-crisis rise of macro-prudential regulation and argues that, despite its original aims, it typically supports finance in times of crisis but fails to curb it in times of booms. Investigating how different macro-prudential frameworks developed in the UK, the USA and the Eurozone, the book explains how central bank economists went about building early warning systems to identify fragilities in the financial system. It then shows how administrative and political constraints limited the effects of this shift, as central banks were wary of intervening in a discretionary manner and policymakers were opposed to measures to limit credit growth.

MATTHIAS THIEMANN is Associate Professor of European Public Policy at Sciences Po's Center for European Studies. His work focuses on the ideational underpinnings of financial regulation and its policy effects. His book *The Growth of Shadow Banking: A Comparative Institutional Analysis* (2018) was published by Cambridge University Press.

Taming the Cycles of Finance?

Central Banks and the Macro-prudential Shift in Financial Regulation

MATTHIAS THIEMANN

Sciences Po Center for European Studies and Comparative Politics

CAMBRIDGE
UNIVERSITY PRESS

Shaftesbury Road, Cambridge CB2 8EA, United Kingdom

One Liberty Plaza, 20th Floor, New York, NY 10006, USA

477 Williamstown Road, Port Melbourne, VIC 3207, Australia

314–321, 3rd Floor, Plot 3, Splendor Forum, Jasola District Centre, New Delhi – 110025, India

103 Penang Road, #05–06/07, Visioncrest Commercial, Singapore 238467

Cambridge University Press is part of Cambridge University Press & Assessment, a department of the University of Cambridge.

We share the University's mission to contribute to society through the pursuit of education, learning and research at the highest international levels of excellence.

www.cambridge.org
Information on this title: www.cambridge.org/9781009233132

DOI: 10.1017/9781009233125

First published 2024

A catalogue record for this publication is available from the British Library

Library of Congress Cataloging-in-Publication Data
Names: Thiemann, Matthias, author.
Title: Taming the cycles of finance? : central banks and the macro-prudential shift in financial regulation / Matthias Thiemann.
Description: Cambridge, United Kingdom ; New York, NY : Cambridge University Press, 2023. | Includes bibliographical references and index.
Identifiers: LCCN 2023024032 (print) | LCCN 2023024033 (ebook) | ISBN 9781009233132 (hardback) | ISBN 9781009233149 (paperback) | ISBN 9781009233125 (ebook)
Subjects: LCSH: Banks and banking, Central.
Classification: LCC HG1811 .T45 2023 (print) | LCC HG1811 (ebook) | DDC 332.1–dc23/eng/20230720
LC record available at https://lccn.loc.gov/2023024032
LC ebook record available at https://lccn.loc.gov/2023024033

ISBN 978-1-009-23313-2 Hardback

Contents

Figures

Tables

Prologue

In the last fifteen years, Western societies have learned about the fragility of finance the hard way.[1] Few if any today would doubt the statement that financial markets are inherently fragile and that stability might give way to sudden and unexpected fluctuations, which in turn might lead to bank-runs and panics. And few if any would doubt that such ructions in the financial system could spill over into the "real economy" of production, employment and income. In that sense, the transatlantic financial crisis of 2008 and the subsequent reverberations have generated a deep public distrust in financial markets, leaving us to ask policymakers to protect us from financial instability. And, indeed, central banks around the world today hold a more or less explicit financial stability mandate, pledging to intervene should such dynamics threaten to unfold.

At the same time that we have become convinced of the dangers inherent in finance, every year we observe the expansion of finance – of debt obligations both traded in financial markets and held on the balance sheets of financial institutions. And not only that; from 2015 onwards we have observed the continued rise of house prices, the increase of mortgage volumes, the increase in indebtedness of both private households and corporations – in other words, an increase in the same debt obligations we have become convinced carry with them the possible grains of future destruction. How, in such a world of ever-rising debt and fragile finance, one might ask, could we argue that we have learned anything at all from the events of 2008? What, if anything, did we learn? And if we learned something, what measures did we take and why do they translate into such an unhemmed expansion of finance?

---

[1] These lessons were already learned several decades ago in developing countries, with the frequency of financial crises increasing markedly from the 1980s onwards (Kaminsky and Reinhart 1999).

These are the questions this book sets out to explore. It does so by following the policymakers that were charged with learning the lessons of the crisis and their attempt to translate a new idea set into practical policy devices, which could allow for "taming the cycles of finance." Localized mostly within central banks, these technocrats aimed to reconfigure the financial system and to build the early warning systems that could allow discretionary intervention ahead of disaster unfolding, limiting the damages finance could generate in the downswing. Tracing and telling this story, this book brings into relief the creative practical agency of these groups, which belie the accusation of the "nothing has happened" and "nothing has changed" accounts one so often hears. Yet, while showcasing the production of a set of policy devices in central banks these applied economists generated, the book at the same time tells a story of mostly political defeat, incremental change and limited regulatory successes, which seem so disproportionate to the growing volume of financial assets circulating in the global financial system.

So, then, has all this activity been in vain? Were all the conferences on financial stability, all the hard work on assembling large-scale data sets and "making the data speak," conducted for little purpose other than to keep technocrats busy in their pursuit of careers within central banks? Such a statement seems unjust and also very much contradicts our understanding of knowledge production and its effects. Today's world has a much clearer, better-documented and better-theorized understanding of financial instability, which will make claims of surprise the next time disaster strikes largely non-credible attempts at cover-ups, hence easily discerned as efforts to protect the status quo from increasing regulatory interventions.

Yet, if such knowledge exists within technocratic circles in central banks, then what is holding this knowledge back from becoming performative, actively curtailing the expansion of fragile finance? As this book will seek to show, it is the manner in which this knowledge is applied in the realm of regulatory debates, where concerns over the buildup of risks requiring action are separated from mere hypothetical yet unproven dangers, that is limiting its potential. In this realm of "regulatory science," regulators are facing a very high burden of proof to show the dangers inherent in finance before any regulatory action is taken. What I will show is that during these debates, again and again, their concerns based on the causal understandings of inherent financial fragilities are transformed from programs of action into programs of research, asking for definite evidence before any action can be undertaken. It is this modus operandi of financial regulation, which is sustaining and sustained by the power of finance, that is holding back the translation of new knowledge into action. Evidence-based policies have become a mainstay of our democracies, seeking to protect citizens from unwarranted statist interventions, yet the manner in which this form of policymaking plays out currently is protecting finance and its expansion. Such a burden of proof is required both to convince skeptical regulators, adherent to different understandings of the world, and to overcome the resistance by finance, entrenched as these understandings are in the circles of policymakers.

At the same time that these technocrats face this daunting task of overcoming the power of finance to resist regulation, their newly gained understanding of the dangers of finance and the policy devices created to showcase pending dangers become tools in the emergency lending operations of central banks, enacted to prevent these deleterious dynamics of finance from unfolding. In this way, the technocrats of financial stability with very limited capabilities and mandate to intervene in the procyclical upswings of finance have become the guardians of financial stability in the downswing, cushioning any disruptive developments that might transpire in the financial system.

Through these now seemingly perennial actions of market-makers of last resort, which provide financial systems with a liquidity backstop, central banks in their interventions validate the fragile financial structures responsible for the threat of systemic illiquidity, furthering the expansion of finance rather than limiting it. In this sense, the technocrats of financial stability, much to the contrary of what they might have desired, become stabilizing agents of the ever-continuing expansion of finance. Rather than taming the cycles of finance, they install an asymmetric regime in which the procyclical dynamics of finance are mitigated in the downswing but are largely left unchecked in the upswing.

For this state of affairs, we cannot solely blame them, given the structural situation they were facing since 2008. Seeking to bring about change based on their new macro-prudential mandate, they were confronted with skeptical market regulators and financial market operations departments in central banks busy with nothing else but keeping the financial system afloat (in particular in the Eurozone). They hence often found their efforts hemmed in by the need for coordination with other actors less willing and convinced of the need to act, by the lack of data to prove their point and by the dependence of political systems on the ever-flowing production of credit. These context conditions made their proposed constraints based on their newly won economic expertise hardly viable in terms of bureaucratic and political action. The goal of this book is not to decry their failure but instead to depict their work and point to the situation within which the expertise they developed over the last fifteen years cannot but largely be impotent. If anything, it is an attempt to contribute to a change in this situation by politicizing the status quo and empowering these agents seeking to act upon the excesses of finance and to reduce the systemic risks central banks have to face in their daily work.

Acknowledgments

This book is the outcome of a ten-year journey. I had finished my dissertation about the growth of shadow banking in Europe in 2012 when I was struck by the importance of economic concepts such as the notion of liquidity for the configuration of financial regulation post-crisis. I hence decided to embark on a study almost in real time of the ideational changes the financial crisis brought about and their impact on actual regulation. I could not have begun this journey at a better place than Frankfurt, with the Bundesbank and European Central Bank around the corner and the Center for Sustainable Architecture for Finance in Europe on-campus at Goethe University Frankfurt. It was there that I encountered many of the financial economists working on the topic who took the time to talk to me about their research, most notably Jan-Pieter Krahnen and Loriana Pellizon. There were also (former) practitioners, such as former Vice President of the Bundesbank Hans Helmut Kotz, responsible for financial stability at the Bundesbank, who was central in orienting my first steps. I would like to thank them very much for the deep insights they provided, as well as the more than eighty practitioners of financial regulation, central bankers and economists who shared with me their time and understanding of contemporary regulatory dynamics.

Equally important were the exchanges and engagement with academic colleagues, first at Goethe University Frankfurt and then in the broader context of the German scene working on the sociology of economics and financial regulation. Here, the deeply insightful Mohamed Aldegwy, humble and erudite, was a great inspiration. Colleagues such as Daniel Mertens, Andreas Noelke and Patrick Sachweh always had an open ear, willing to listen and engage. Most important, though, was a group of young MA and doctoral students, willing to engage this vast topic with me and nurturing the effort with their enthusiasm and curiosity: Marius Birk, Vanessa Endrejat, Jan Friedrich, Edin Ibrocevic, Max Nagel and Slavek Sivagrakau (now Roller), many of whom became my coauthors and good friends. Without their tireless work, much of this book could not have been written.

The project moved to a new level thanks to a semester stay in spring 2017 at the Institute for Advanced Studies in Paris, a setting that provided the calm for contemplation as well as the pleasure of intellectual engagement with other fellows from disciplines far from my own. From there, I moved to Sciences Po, Paris in fall 2017 where I encountered a group of colleagues who were both supportive and challenging. Cyril Benoit, Patrick Le Gales, Colin Hay, Laura Morales, Bruno Palier and Cornelia Woll were always listening and providing thoughtful feedback, while also pushing me to finish the project. A first version of this book was defended as my habilitation in June 2020, in the midst of COVID-19 via Zoom, with internationally renowned colleagues Ben Clift as well as Bruce Carruthers providing additional feedback. Further feedback was provided by Cornel Ban, Nathan Coombs, Len Seabrooke and in particular Bart Stellinga, who has proven to be an indefatigable conversation partner on these issues.

In addition, I would like to thank the anonymous reviewers who commented on the manuscript and on papers that provided an initial foundation for this book. Their insightful, often challenging feedback has helped me to further sharpen my arguments. Chapter 5 draws on ideas first presented in "Is Resilience Enough? The Macroprudential Reform Agenda and the Lack of Smoothing of the Cycle," which appeared in *Public Administration* 97 (2019) (pp. 561–575), while Chapter 7 draws on joint work with Marius Birk and Jan Friedrich, which was published in 2018 as "Much Ado about Nothing? Macro-Prudential Ideas and the Post-Crisis Regulation of Shadow Banking," in *Koelner Zeitschrift fuer Soziologie und Sozialpsychologie* 70 (pp. 259–286). Chapter 10 draws on a paper that appeared in 2021 under the title "The Asymmetric Relationship of Central Banks to Market-Based Finance: Weighing Financial Stability Implications in the Light of Covid Events" in *Revue d'economie financiere* 144 (4) (pp. 191–201).

Lastly, my thanks go to my family. In particular during the COVID-19 lockdowns, my family more than ever became the backbone of my work, keeping me sane in somewhat frightening circumstances. My parents Martina and Wolfgang, my brothers André and Stephan and in particular my sister Anna allowed me to maintain a notion of normalcy, even if we were only connected via Zoom. Alina, my wife, was my rock during this time and provided me with the calm and determination to see the project through, and without her understanding and encouragement this book would not have seen the light of day. At the same time, my kids Karl and Katharina adapted as well as possible to the new situation and showed understanding for my leaves of absence in my office. I dedicate this book to them, hoping that the next years of this decade will be less tumultuous than the first three.

1 | *Introduction*

How do policy frameworks change as a result of crises and policy failures? Are societies able to learn from these failures and modify regulatory ideas, incorporating these lessons into policies that allow us to address the main policy shortcomings? Or are we doomed to keep repeating the same mistakes, barred by vested interests and policy inertia from reforming the system? In our current era, characterized by the "poly-crisis" of environmental degradation, financial market turmoil and political unrest, such questions gain increasing prominence (Tooze 2022). One cannot help feeling that such inertia is indeed one of the reasons why such policy problems fester and become entrenched, in turn aggravating problems in other areas. Engaged in permanent emergency measures for crisis fighting, policymakers seem largely incapable of addressing the underlying trends (Tooze 2022).

In few areas do such problems manifest themselves more glaringly than in the realm of financial markets and their regulation. Despite massive policy interventions since the Global Financial Crisis of 2007–8, these markets continue to be a permanent source of instability and concern for policymakers, leading to one emergency liquidity intervention by central banks after another. As central banks continue to act as firefighters, seeking to quell any financial instability before it threatens to turn into a systemic crisis (Bernanke et al. 2019b), the question is whether the regulatory interventions in the aftermath of the last financial cataclysm have been futile.

After all, in the crisis aftermath of 2008, G20 leaders formulated the hope that central banks would in the future intervene ex ante, addressing financial fragilities before they require interventions (G20 2009a). They asked central banks and financial regulators to develop a forward-looking systemic approach to financial regulation, widely known as macro-prudential regulation. In contrast to the pre-crisis micro-prudential approach, which focused on safeguarding the stability of individual banks, this new approach was supposed to take developments within

1

the financial system as a whole into account, intervening to remove and attenuate the fragilities that might cause systemic financial distress. In particular, macro-prudential regulation was supposed to mitigate and reduce the impact of cyclical developments in financial markets, which moved from booms to busts to new booms (Blyth 2008). These new tasks required central banks to manage and foresee financial market developments and intervene in them if they were deemed to threaten financial stability. These new responsibilities challenged the non-political status of central banks, which had already come under pressure because of their persistent crisis-fighting role. In a sense, this new task set was challenging the role of central banks in contemporary financial systems.

The Role of Central Banks in Contemporary Financial Systems

The evolution of financial practices must be guided to reduce the likelihood that fragile situations conducive to financial instability will develop. Central banks are the institutions that are responsible for containing and offsetting financial instability and, by extension, they have a responsibility to prevent it.

(Minsky 1986, 358)

With these simple words the eminent economist of financial instability Hyman Minsky summed up the position and tasks of central banks. As the main institutions capable of ending financial panics, based on their ability to provide emergency funding to financial markets and institutions, central banks have taken on a pivotal role in today's financialized capitalism, stabilizing financial markets that seem ever more volatile and fragile. Their role as the final liquidity backstop of the system came to the fore during the tumultuous years of the Global Financial Crisis (2007–8), when Western central banks, with the Federal Reserve at its helm, injected trillions of dollars to stabilize a financial system. At that moment, the system was essentially facing a systemic bank-run on the shadow banking system after a financial boom in the 2000s had led to the accumulation of bad mortgage debt in an increasingly interconnected and fragile financial system.

Since then, central banks have been at the forefront of stabilizing financialized capitalism (Langley 2014) and permitting a return to economic growth. They have used their balance sheets as a tool to meet their inflation targets and stimulate asset growth through quantitative easing[1] and to stabilize financial markets whenever liquidity dried up and turbulences in financial markets threatened to impact the real economy (see Figures 1.1 and 1.2). By intervening in money markets during the financial crisis in 2007–8 and in short-term secured

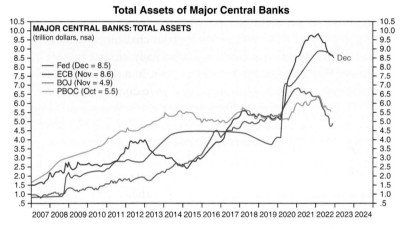

Figure 1.1 Growth of major central banks' total assets (Yardeni 2023, 1, monthly balance sheets [yardeni.com]).

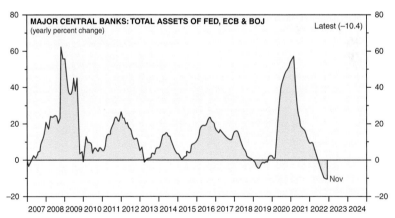

Figure 1.2 Annual growth of major central banks' balance sheets (Yardeni 2023, 2, monthly balance sheets [yardeni.com]).

[1] Quantitative easing is the name for a transaction by a central bank using freshly created central bank money to buy up assets in financial markets.

repo-markets[2] and bond markets in 2019 and 2020, central banks have taken on a much more active role in offsetting and containing financial instability. This trend to an increasingly present role of central banks to contain and offset financial instability is universal among Western central banks. As these figures demonstrate, central banks in the last fifteen years have been engaged in a system-stabilizing role of historical proportions (Tucker and Cecchetti 2021).

In the context of this new historic function, the question arises as to how far central banks have been empowered to intervene ex ante in the structure of financial markets in order to prevent such episodes of financial instability, guiding financial practices "to reduce the likelihood that fragile situations conducive to financial instability will develop" (Minsky 1986, 358). This question poses itself in the context of a secular growth of financial markets, which since the financial crisis of 2007–8 has continued unabated rather than reversing itself, growing from 150 trillion dollars in

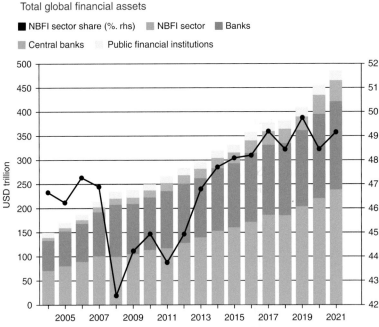

Figure 1.3 Growth of total global financial assets by sector (FSB 2022, 7).

---

[2] The repo-market is a secured short-term market for loans, mainly between banks, but also hedge funds and other financial market players (see Chapter 7).

2004 to 450 trillion dollars in 2021 (see Figure 1.3). And not only have total global financial assets tripled in the last eighteen years, they have also done so in a manner that has seen non-bank financial institutions grow more rapidly than the banking sector. Formerly known as the "shadow banking sector," these non-bank financial institutions that engage in bank-like activity are particularly prone to "bank-run dynamics" and hence financial instability. These developments hence make the capacity for such a preventive approach a crucial issue of our time.

The Rise of Macro-Prudential Policy

A policy program for such preventive action was introduced in the wake of the 2007–8 financial crisis, charging central banks and prudential authorities around the world with taking a systemic view on the financial system and installing macro-prudential regulation capable of preventing financial imbalances from rising to such a degree as to threaten financial instability (G20 2009a). Developing largely outside of the mainstream of Western regulatory thinking before the crisis (Borio 2003b), macro-prudential thinking experienced a sudden and unexpected rise after the failure of Lehman and the ensuing recession (Baker 2013a). Rhetorically embraced by the G20 at the 2009 summit as the political answer to the crisis (Lombardi and Moschella 2017), macro-prudential thinking was to complement the focus on the risk management of individual institutions of the micro-prudential approach. Employing a systemic view, it aimed to increase the resilience of the system as a whole and to lean against the wind as credit booms accelerate (Baker 2013a, b, 2014; IMF, FSB and BIS 2016), empowering macro-prudential central bankers to act as "a risk manager to the financial system" as a whole (Persaud 2014, 161).

Once agreed upon in 2009, this macro-prudential shift was presented by the G20 as the answer to the financial crisis, a necessary correction to a micro-prudential focus on banking institutions alone, which had failed to consider the larger changes in the financial system that had led to greater interconnectedness and hence greater fragilities. It furthermore had ignored the procyclical character of the financial system, which amplified a boom-and-bust cycle. In this vein, the prescriptions, much like the analysis of the financial crisis according to the official G20 discourse, were in line with Minsky's recommendations. In 1986 Minsky had already insisted that such preventive central bank action could no longer only be limited to banks and the setting of interest rates, but needed to include the money markets, which by then had taken on a large role in US financial capitalism (Minsky 1986, 359).

Macro-prudential regulation was hence supposed to extend beyond the realm of banking regulation and include the shadow banking sector, seeking to preventively reduce financial fragilities before they could threaten a systemic financial crisis. These actions were to limit the cross-sectoral fragilities, which had emerged from the increasing inter-linkages of banks and non-bank financial institutions. They were also to limit the endogenous buildup of systemic risks over time, which in turn gave rise to the boom-and-bust cycles: the acceleration of asset prices in the boom phase followed by the quick deceleration of such prices in the bust (Borio 2009). Both tasks required a massive expansion of supervisory capabilities at central banks to enable them to analyze and capture the buildup of systemic risks that required macro-prudential intervention. They also required an increase in the coordination of supervisory tasks between central banks and market regulators to expand these macro-prudential regulations to shadow banks in capital markets, thus establishing, if possible, "prudential market regulation" (Tarullo 2015) that would limit the fragilities in that sector.

In short, what was required was nothing less than the buildup of an entirely new analytical and bureaucratic policy apparatus, implying a massive expansion of discretionary interventions by central banks to preventively ensure financial stability. To enact this, central banks had to not only generate a commonly agreed definition of systemic risks and the indicators to measure them but also agree on the macro-prudential policy goals they were to pursue and the macro-prudential toolkit best able to achieve them. Furthermore, they needed to set up monitoring frameworks in line with these decisions and decide if and under which conditions they were to activate the tools they had newly installed. All this occurred in the context of little academic guidance on these issues (Adrian 2018) and with little to no prior experience by Western central banks as to how such interventions should be calibrated (CGFS 2010b). The challenging tasks related to the set-up of macro-prudential regulation regarding concepts, measures, interventions and monitoring are depicted in Figure 1.4.

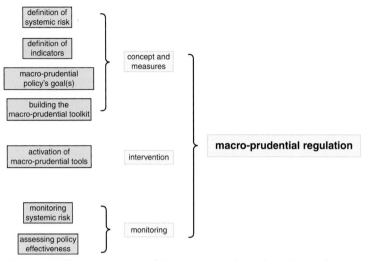

Figure 1.4 The components of the macro-prudential regulatory framework.

The Status Quo Crisis?

How far has this policy program, initiated after the 2007–8 financial crisis, transformed the financial system and its impact on capitalist economies? In particular, how far have post-crisis reforms reduced the procyclical character of the financial system, which has been characterized as a system of compounding bubbles, moving from boom to bust to the next boom (Blyth 2008)? Rarely if ever have the conditions for policy change been more favorable than after the complete failure of the pre-crisis policy paradigm governing financial markets (see, e.g., FSA 2009), as the huge costs of bail-outs and recessions caused by the crisis (Woll 2014) spurred a radical rhetoric by policymakers and politicians at the global level. Diagnosing the need for fundamental change to financial regulation, they were pledging to install the new macro-prudential paradigm to tame the financial cycles shaking the world economy (Moschella and Lombardi 2017).

And yet, despite the evident failure of the reigning policy paradigm (Langley 2014) and its subsequent disavowal by policymakers, the political science literature comes to a sobering assessment: rather than the radical transformation some had hoped for or expected

(Baker 2013a, b), the regulatory developments post-crisis are largely seen as incremental, engaging in paradigm repair rather than fundamental change (Kessler 2012; Mirowski 2013; Moschella and Tsingou 2013; Muegge 2013; Eichengreen 2014; Helleiner 2014; Gabor 2015, 2016a; Baker 2018; for an outlier, see Wilf 2016).

Categorizing the occurring regulatory changes post-crisis as a "status quo crisis" some identified the macro-prudential shift as a largely discursive branding exercise (Helleiner 2014) that led to little meaningful change. Even more optimistic observers, who acknowledged the potential for paradigmatic change inherent in macro-prudential regulation (Baker 2013a, b), were sobered by the limited institutional change following the "grandiose" announcements by the G20 (Baker 2013c). They soon came to see the actually implemented measures as too weak to actively manage the cyclical tendencies of the system (Baker 2018). Whereas initial discussions were structured around the question whether macro-prudential regulation could save the "neo-liberal growth model" of Anglo-Saxon capitalism (Casey 2015) or whether it fundamentally contradicted it (Baker and Widmaier 2015), subsequent research saw little in terms of path-breaking regulatory changes (Baker 2018), a finding that was linked to the adverse selection of radical ideas in a context that favored the interests of financial capital (Underhill 2015). Based on a binary logic of either a full paradigm shift or no paradigm shift at all, the political science literature largely sided with the no-paradigm-shift interpretation, thus seemingly closing the subject.

This stance, I argue, is premature as it pays insufficient attention to the different temporalities inherent in the maturation process of new regulatory frameworks (cf. Braun 2014). Meaningful policy change requires a translation from ideas to new policy devices to policy frameworks in action, and this takes time (see also Kaya and Reay 2019). By treating the macro-prudential framework as a full-fledged policy paradigm from its inception, these analyses overlook the immense efforts of applied central bank economists necessary to transform a set of loose discursive commitments into a viable policy framework. The central dynamics of this process remain hidden to date as most analyses have focused on the discursive commitments to the new macro-prudential approach at the top of the political and technocratic levels (Baker 2013a, b, 2015) and their limited translation into new policies (Stellinga and Muegge 2017; Stellinga 2019).

These analyses, however, neglect the substantiation of these discursive commitments through the practical work of applied economists over time and its effects.

Fragmented Policy Change: Actionable Knowledge and the Enactment of a Policy Program

This book seeks to provide a more nuanced understanding of the effects of macro-prudential reform efforts by "following the practical life of ideas – the messy and material process of their production and circulation" (Best 2020, 596). It emphasizes that a central pillar in the strength of policy paradigms resides in the socio-technical policy devices that policymakers use to perceive the issues they want to govern and that help them choose their preferred way to act (Hirschman and Popp-Berman 2014). It is these models, systems of risk measurements and their metrics (such as early warning systems) – embedded in the routine of policymaking – that have undergone tremendous development over the last fifteen years. The binary approach to policy change risks missing these substantive changes, not in the least in the outlook of central banks on financial markets, as encapsulated in the newly installed macro-prudential monitoring frameworks. In contrast to the pre-crisis period, these metrics now clearly signal the buildup of cyclical systemic risks in financial markets, standing in potential contradiction to existing regulatory measures and pushing for anti-cyclical regulatory measures for central banks and others to enact.

In order to capture these tensions and provide a more detailed view of the macro-prudential regulatory movement and its effects, the book employs the concept of "fragmented policy change" (Kaya and Reay 2019). This allows us to see substantial and rapid changes in some areas, such as the ideational underpinnings or institutional set-ups of regulation, whereas other areas see limited or no change (Kaya and Reay 2019, 386). It thereby pays attention to the different spatial and temporal dynamics inherent in the maturation process of new regulatory frameworks in different jurisdictions (cf. Braun 2014), from ideas to new policy devices to policy frameworks in action (see Kaya and Reay 2019). Such a different perspective allows us to identify the changes that have occurred without dismissing them ex ante as non-important, pointing to the potential buildup of contradictions between the knowledge base of regulation on the one hand and the regulatory action it incites on the other. It also allows for an identification of the structural obstacles that prevent the macro-prudential approach from coming fully into its own. Such an assessment of change thus acknowledges the analytical and operational work by central banks over the course of the last fifteen years in making such a macro-prudential framework work, all the while remaining alert to its current shortcomings in terms of policy implementation.

To provide such an assessment, the book is based on the viability framework of economic ideas as developed by Hall (1989b). He distinguishes between the economic, bureaucratic and political viability of economic ideas to understand how such "new ideas acquire influence over policy-making" (Hall 1989b, 362) and why their spread and implementation differ across jurisdictions. Based on a careful study of the spread and ascendancy of Keynesian macroeconomic ideas in the wake of World War II, Hall maintained that economic ideas do not only need to be seen to convincingly address the contemporary economic problems in order to become politically powerful (economic viability). They also need to be in line with the "long-standing administrative biases of the officials responsible for implementing [policy]" (Hall 1989b, 371), as well as the structural capacities for implementation (bureaucratic viability). Lastly, they need to be politically viable, appealing to the "interests of the political entrepreneurs who would have to put them into action" (Hall 1989b, 375) and potential coalition partners, which could forge an alliance strong enough to implement these ideas (political viability).

This book enriches this approach with social-constructivist understandings of the role and power of economic ideas. These understandings point to the hidden "politics" of economic ideas within technocratic institutions (Clift 2018, 2019) and the preconditions that such ideas need to fulfill in order to be accepted and used in policymaking. Most importantly, to be turned into practice, such ideas needed to be translated into actionable knowledge and take the shape of "policy devices," which allow policymakers to see, observe and intervene in economic affairs (Hirschman and Popp-Berman 2014). Before such ideas could be acted upon, they needed to be hardened by the epistemological assurances technocratic policymaking requires, generating credible "risk objects" whose behavior is sufficiently understood in order to justify technocratic intervention. It is at this level that this book identifies the greatest change, observing the work of applied economists within central banks and international organizations. Jointly with certain groups of academic economists, they have built the ideational infrastructure that could allow central banks to monitor financial stability conditions and detect the evolution of systemic risks that require intervention.

Such monitoring frameworks, providing actionable knowledge, had to be implemented in central banks based on their "long standing administrative biases" and their structural capacities to implement them (Hall 1989b, 373). These factors, based on administrative traditions and the centralization of decision-making, were shaping the set-up and orientation of domestic macro-prudential frameworks, guided by the reflexive leadership of central banks all too wary of exposing their institution to politicization. As actors in the space between the academic field of economics, the bureaucratic field of macroeconomic governance and the political field of interest politics (Coombs and Thiemann 2022), these central bankers carefully weighed their ambitions with respect to this policy program in the light of structural and cultural constraints.

As macro-prudential policies extend beyond the boundaries of depoliticized central bank activities (particularly monetary policy), central banks were forced to recalibrate their activities and their relationship to "the political," as they included this new scope of duties (Tucker 2018). The intervention of central banks based on their macro-prudential frameworks was thereby shaped by the political viability of their proposals; that is, the degree to which they could enroll the political actors involved in the decision-making process, ensuring the legitimacy of their discretionary macro-prudential interventions. Given the distributional character of macro-prudential interventions, this implied a heightened need for scientific objectivity upon which central bankers could base themselves to depoliticize and justify their interventions. The prophylactic dampening character of these measures, in contrast to measures of quantitative easing, which were supposed to enliven them, made this need for scientific underpinning even more necessary, in particular in countries where the legal system provides strong protections for business from arbitrary infringements on their business activities.[3]

---

[3] Paradigmatic here is the case of the USA, with its administrative rule-making procedures, which enshrine a due process amid a legal adversarial style. This approach emphasizes the role of scientific evidence as an important precondition for regulatory action.

Table 1.1 *The creation, stabilization and use of macro-prudential policy devices*

Process	Creation of policy devices	Stabilization of policy devices	Use of policy devices
Field of occurrence	Transnational field of economics	Administrative field: interaction national and transnational (International Monetary Fund, Bank for International Settlements)	Field of politics, national interaction of technocrats/ politicians
Dimension	Economic viability	Administrative viability	Political viability
Unit of analysis/ analytical focus	Regulatory science: interaction of applied and academic economists creating devices	Creation of policy frameworks, organizational transformation, central banks	Policy actions taken to mitigate systemic risk, interaction of political actors and technocrats

As Table 1.1 shows, this analytical framework combines an analysis of the creation of macro-prudential policy devices in the transnational field of regulatory science with their stabilization in national administrative fields and their subsequent use, decided in the interaction between politicians and technocrats.

The objective of the framework then is to unfold the different levels involved in changes in policy paradigms and analyze their multidimensional character. Doing so, I investigate the sequencing and feedback loops between three different fields: (1) the field of transnational economics, (2) the national administrative field, which includes central banks, ministries of finance and supervisory agencies in their interaction with relevant transnational organizations and (3) the field of domestic politics. This more complex approach is needed because the field of economics develops the devices for measuring and mitigating systemic risks, bestowing upon them economic viability. But it is in the administrative field that these devices are calibrated and linked to actual policy instruments, gaining administrative viability (or not). And it is in the interaction with the political field that final decisions on how to constrain financial activities often have to be approved, and where the political power of these ideas, now embedded in policy devices and instruments, resides.

Case Selection, Method and Data

To investigate the creation, stabilization and implementation of these policy devices, I focus on three substantially different cases: the Eurozone, the USA and the UK. All three cases have a high centrality in the realm of financial markets and were all, albeit to different degrees, directly involved in the transatlantic crisis of 2007–8 (Bell and Hindmoore 2015). They were also active in the subsequent creation and diffusion of macro-prudential frameworks. And yet, because of substantially different governance traditions and the different political economy surrounding central bank independence, they arrived at very different institutionalized frameworks for macro-prudential policies regarding both the centralization of decision-making and the involvement of politicians versus mere technocratic decision-making. As these cases have substantially different governance traditions and very different institutionalized frameworks for macro-prudential policies, they represent a most diverse case study, allowing me to contrast the different pathways to countercyclical action (Seawright and Gering 2008). These differences allow me to inquire into the translation of the transnational discourse on systemic risks and macro-prudential regulation into local bureaucratic and political requirements, capturing which economic ideas became politically powerful, how and why.

To trace these processes, I have used an innovative methodology, triangulating findings from cutting-edge quantitative methods with more traditional qualitative methods for process tracing. I have used quantitative methods for large-scale textual analysis (including structural and author topic modelling) to identify the evolution of themes in economic discourse regarding the systemic risks inherent in the financial system from 1995 to 2017. I have then used the generated data to sample expert interviews with the leading economists both in central banks and academia on these themes. These interviews were used to understand the process of transformation of these ideas into policy devices and how they have been integrated into central banks' policy frameworks. Document analysis helped to establish how exactly these new institutional frameworks to govern finance were set up and what were the motivations of technocratic policymakers. Lastly, exploiting the variance in the use of the policy recommendations for policy action, the methodology traces the institutional and political obstacles policies might face in their implementation.

In addition to qualitative and quantitative document analysis, I conducted seventy-seven on-the-record expert interviews with eighty-two central bank economists between the summer of 2014 and June 2022 – regulators and academics working on the topic of financial instability (Table 1.2 displays the categories; see the Appendix for a list of the interviews). These interviews, which lasted between 20 minutes (two interviews) and 2 hours, were recorded and subsequently transcribed. Matching the deeply interconnected space of knowledge production I am studying, most of the interviewed academic economists also had experience working in or collaborating with central banks. Furthermore, some International Monetary Fund economists worked before at the Federal Reserve, several European Central Bank (ECB) economists at the Bundesbank and those of the Bundesbank at the ECB. Some of the interviewees were also seconded from their home institution to other central banks, allowing me to draw on their experience to learn more about the differences in these institutions.

To supplement these interviews, I attended several conferences in central banks to observe the interaction between central bankers and academic economists as they debated issues of financial stability. Among these, four conferences at the ECB (three on macro-prudential regulation in 2016 and one on the interplay between monetary policy and macro-prudential regulation in 2019) were particularly important. I furthermore attended several conferences at the Bundesbank as well as numerous conferences at the Center for Sustainable Architecture of Finance in Europe at Goethe University (such as the conference on macro-prudential regulation by the International Group of Central Bankers in 2015). These conferences allowed me to participate in and observe the interaction between these two communities over questions of the validity of assumptions and presumed effects of these measures.

Table 1.2 *Number of interviews according to different categories of interviewees*

Institutional affiliation of economist/policymaker	European Central Bank/European Systemic Risk Board	Bundesbank/BaFin	European Securities and Markets Authority (European Union)/Securities and Exchange Commission (USA)/Financial Services Authority (UK)	Other European central banks	Bank for International Settlements/Financial Stability Board	International Monetary Fund	Federal Reserve	Bank of England/Financial Services Authority	Private bank/central counterparty economists	Academics	Total
Number of interviews	11	16	4	9	4	2	8	7	4	12	77

Such a mixed-methods approach allows for an encompassing, cumulative view on policy change that connects the immense academic and bureaucratic work flowing into the ideational infrastructure of policy frameworks with the administrative and political viability of these ideas. This multidimensional view pays attention to the professional preconditions for economic ideas to gain prominence and the pathways for their translation into the bureaucratic and political space. It permits both a cumulative account of when and where paradigm shifts do occur and a nuanced understanding of where change is occurring and where it is not, which also allows for an understanding of in which dimension a paradigm change might be stuck.

Contributions of the Book

Based on this multidimensional view and this empirical material, I improve on the current literature on the macro-prudential paradigm shift in three ways. Regarding the origins and creation of anti-cyclical policy devices, my analysis shows how the idea of endogenous financial cycles originated from a group of central bankers, who from the 1980s onwards were worried about the increasing fusion of banks and capital markets. By the time of the financial crisis, this idea had gained some traction in central bank circles but was missing the epistemic backing of academia. This limited economic viability severely hampered its immediate implementation after the crisis and was only overcome through the massive research efforts of applied central bank economists post-crisis, who sought to develop monitoring frameworks to detect such cyclical upswings.

Regarding the stabilization of these policy devices in macro-prudential policy frameworks, I show how concerns over the politicization of central banks due to the discretionary nature of anti-cyclical tools and the high requirements for accurate monitoring frameworks shaped their implementation. These concerns interacted with the administrative biases and the legal and cultural embedding of central banks to produce a somewhat muted embrace of the anti-cyclical component in the USA, a pragmatic engagement in the UK and a much greater emphasis in the Eurozone. It furthermore shows that concerns over politicization, which were particularly acute in the USA, could increasingly be overcome with time, as anti-cyclical tools were linked to stress tests, thus operating outside of the public domain. The different administrative viability of these ideas in the three jurisdictions thus shaped their translation into policy devices.

Finally, regarding the actual use of anti-cyclical policies, I show that while we do see some (albeit limited) action on banking systems in the context of overheating housing markets, there is little to no action with respect to the shadow banking system. Here, any attempt to expand macro-prudential regulation to this sector is opposed by market regulators, powerful lobby interests and politicians, marking the lacking political viability as the Achilles's heel of anti-cyclical policy interventions. This puts central banks in a bind: they know that these markets are crucial for financial stability and implementing monetary policy and they have a heightened awareness of the stability risks arising from this sector, yet they have limited power to implement precautionary measures. When problems do emerge, central banks see no other option but to intervene with large-scale emergency liquidity measures.

In this way, the book reveals the substantive changes and unintended consequences the macro-prudential reform efforts have brought about. It shows that the 2007–8 crisis did not maintain the status quo, as it substantially transformed the dominant view of central banks on financial markets and their capacity to self-govern. Yet, paradoxically, this insight did not lead to major anti-cyclical restraints but rather to an infrastructure supporting and sustaining financial markets' expansion, coupled with some minor discretionary interventions to the contrary.

For the academic literature on knowledge-based regulation, the book hence points to the inherent paradox of seeking to govern future potential crises based on conclusive evidence, which combined with the opposition from vested interests and politicians severely limits public agencies' capacity for decisive precautionary action. For the academic literature on policy change, the book demonstrates the fruitfulness of using the concept of multidimensional fragmented policy change rather than the binary paradigm-shift view. Rather than being dismissive of non-fundamental change, this concept allows scholars to trace the construction of risk objects and its possibly unintended side effects. This allows for a productive engagement with the complex, messy world of regulation in a way that does justice to its cognitive, bureaucratic and political dimensions.

Outline of the Chapters

In order to make these arguments, Chapter 2 in a first step provides the reader with a state of the art on the political science literature on paradigm shifts and their failure to materialize post-crisis. It seeks to nuance this binary view by using the social-constructivist approach to the political power of economic ideas, emphasizing the preconditions the new idea set needed to fulfill to become operational. It combines these arguments with the sociology of economics and science and technology studies, which focus on the modalities of regulatory science and its interaction with academia. It insists that for economic ideas to become politically powerful, they need to be able to construct "risk objects" about which sufficient secured knowledge exists to justify public intervention.

Chapter 3 then traces the history of the macro-prudential thought collective before the crisis of 2007–8. It shows how it was driven by concerns over the deregulation of financial systems in the context of the breakdown of Bretton Woods, and how this community of central bankers was pushed aside by the micro-prudential expert network that crystallized in the Basel Committee for Banking Supervision. It shows how despite the active attempts of the latter to silence these systemic concerns over the increasing integration of capital markets and banking business, this community forged a nascent alliance with academics to systematize and theorize the systemic implications of financial system changes. This expert network was then further empowered by the increasing bouts of financial instability as they occurred from the 1990s onwards, leading to the installation of the Financial Stability Forum in 1999, which became a central locus for the formulation of macro-prudential thought.

Chapter 4 then zooms in on the attempt of this expert network to shape the post-crisis financial regulatory agenda from the beginning of the crisis in 2007 to 2009. While central to the crisis analysis right from the beginning, the chapter shows how most of the macro-prudential regulatory reform efforts were not able to impose themselves, in particular the installation of anti-cyclical policy tools for the shadow banking sector. While efforts seeking to address the interconnectedness of the financial system and increase its resilience by raising capital buffers of systemically important banks were agreed upon at the international level, efforts to address the procyclical character of the financial system were largely transformed into research projects, seeking to prove the existence of such procyclical phenomena. The chapter links these developments to the immaturity of the idea of the financial cycle, which up to that point had remained marginal in academic and regulatory science. Rather than being agreed on at the global level, the installation of monitoring frameworks and anti-cyclical tools was then delegated to the national level, where central banks were placed in charge.

In Chapter 5, I show how reflexive central bank leaders sought to adapt the new policy paradigm in a way that was compatible with the institutional context. This involved both the political economy within which their central bank was embedded (both with respect to the way that central bank independence was installed and with respect to the industry relationships they had to entertain) and the way that central bank accountability was secured. I unearth a muted embrace of the new macro-prudential mandate, in particular the discretionary anti-cyclical part, owing to the lack of scientific legitimacy of these new ideas and the fear of politicization inherent in this new regulatory approach. Overall, I find that the bureaucratic work to adapt and operationalize the macro-prudential mandate led to a prioritization of the goal to increase the resilience of the system, whereas the anti-cyclical goal became a secondary element, although the studied countries differed in their emphasis on anti-cyclical action. Such anti-cyclical action exposed central banks to the risk of agonizing both political elites and the financial industry, making reflexive agency leaders shy away from its full enforcement.

Nevertheless, some anti-cyclical elements made it into the global regulatory overhaul post-crisis. This applies in particular to the countercyclical capital buffer, the only anti-cyclical regulatory tool in the global Basel III regulation. As I show in Chapter 6, operationalizing this tool and executing the countercyclical mandate required the creation of robust early warning systems, which could detect and signal the buildup of cyclical systemic risks sufficiently ahead of time in order to enable timely preventive action. The chapter traces the work of applied economists in the three central banks under study, showing how their decade-long research effort provided such monitoring frameworks, which not only provided robust signals but also shifted the academic scientific discourse on this issue, providing the stylized facts that challenged a sanguine view of financial markets. The study at the same time finds that these early warning frameworks were often implemented in the design of stress tests, allowing central bank policymakers to engage in discretionary countercyclical action without overtly exposing themselves to the politicization of these acts.

Central bank attempts to expand their regulatory remit and apply similar anti-cyclical measures to the shadow banking sector faced a less successful fate, as I show in Chapter 7. Seeking to translate their newly gained insights into the cyclical risks emanating from the shadow banking sector, in particular the repo-market, central banks faced opposition from both market regulators and the financial industry. This transformed their attempts at regulation into a mere large-scale research endeavor, being required to prove the procyclical behavior of these markets based on extensive data collection before any action could be taken. Frustrated in their attempts to control this general procyclical behavior of these short-term funding markets, central bank actors used their control over the final implementation of Basel III regulations to impose frictions on this market. Imposing regulatory charges on the activity of banks' broker-dealers in these markets, these change agents sought to limit the procyclical expansion of short-term liquidity in the upswing, thus limiting its expansionary tendencies. Occurring by stealth, this structural regulation allowed critical central bankers to overcome the political opposition to these acts. At the same time, it imposed a continuous drag on the liquidity provision by broker-dealers in these markets, imposing a fragility that central banks would have to offset in future emergency lending programs.

Chapter 8 then follows these newly implemented measures and their effects into the upswing phase of the cycle, which occurred from 2013 onwards. I find that while the early warning frameworks detected a cyclical credit expansion to corporations and to the housing sector, anti-cyclical measures were often hemmed in by the political resistance, both by ministries of finance and the financial industry. This opposition slowed and reduced the degree of anti-cyclical action taken, limiting its mitigating effect. Similarly, I show how the macroprudential concerns over the growth and transformation of the shadow banking sector from 2013 onwards led to attempts to limit the sector's growth and remove the structural fragilities that threatened the financial system with both a procyclical expansion in good times and its potentially calamitous decline in bad times. Fueling this procyclical upswing with their massive quantitative easing programs, central banks found themselves unable to rein in these structural frailties, facing once more extensive opposition to any regulatory changes. In turn, these structural frailties, which materialized episodically in bouts of illiquidity, forced central banks repeatedly to backstop these markets. Unable to change the structure, central banks nevertheless found it necessary to stabilize it.

This tendency to backstop the shadow banking system, amid its procyclical expansion, found its most glaring expression during the beginning of the COVID-19 crisis in March 2020 (the focus of Chapter 9), when central banks around the globe, in particular the Federal Reserve, the Bank of England and the ECB, engaged in massive asset purchases to stabilize the financial system. Within a few weeks, these central banks purchased more than a trillion dollars of assets in order to stem an incipient run on the shadow banking system. Seeing themselves forced to backstop the short-term money markets in this manner in order to contain financial instability, central banks subsequently engaged in attempts to remove the risks inherent in that part of the shadow banking sector, yet, as the research shows, to little to no avail. Having contained financial instability in a way that largely escaped the attention of the public and hence without arousing political censure, central banks have been incapable of overcoming the resistance by powerful financial actors, such as BlackRock, to any further regulation. That is to say, central banks containing financial instability find themselves incapable of removing the underlying structural frailties that make their intervention necessary in the first place.

This finding leads me to the conclusion of the book in Chapter 10. As a result of the work of applied economists within central banks, economic knowledge about financial instability grew impressively after the crisis. Yet this new knowledge is applied asymmetrically. Whereas it has become the foundation for quick intervention to contain financial instability as it unfolds, requiring little to no additional evidence to become effective, the very same knowledge faces substantial hurdles when it seeks to intervene in financial markets in a precautionary manner, making such ad hoc interventions necessary in the first place. This asymmetry reveals the paradox of evidence-based macro-prudential regulation. Whereas conclusive evidence beyond any doubt is necessary to intervene and constrain financial actors in the upswing, such evidence becomes unnecessary when procyclical amplifications of financial stress threaten to undo the entire web of the interconnected financial system. Herein resides, I argue, the tragedy of the macro-prudential reform efforts, which, while producing knowledge about the dangers and mechanisms of financial instability, are incapable of mustering the political will to engage in preventive action.

2 | The Changing Regulation of Finance after the Crisis
The State of the Art and Beyond

Prior accounts of post-crisis financial regulation have noted macro-prudential regulation as a major point of departure from pre-crisis regulation (Baker 2013a, b; Underhill 2015). And yet, they have quickly been disappointed by the only incremental shifts occurring after the crisis (Baker 2015). In so doing, they have underestimated the time it takes for a new policy approach to come to fruition, including its scientific underpinnings and then observing the conditions for the use of these devices by policymakers. In short, they have expected results too quickly, underestimating the time and effort it takes to build a new policy framework. In doing so, they have arguably looked at the wrong places to detect change.

To make this point, this chapter proceeds as follows. I first review the political science literature on the rise of macro-prudential policy after the crisis and its subsequent implementation. This literature is characterized by a strong bifurcation. On one hand, it places the emphasis on the large-scale ideational shift occurring in regulatory circles post-crisis. On the other hand, it provides accounts of largely minimal, ineffectual regulatory changes that this ideational shift has brought about. I trace this somewhat paradoxical finding to an overemphasis on statements by the proponents of the ideational shift and an under-appreciation of the need for the backing of policy measures by regulatory science for them to come into effect. To overcome these shortcomings of prior studies, I present a new theoretical approach based on the literature on regulatory science.

The Status Quo Crisis?

The financial crisis of 2007–9 and the ensuing Eurozone crisis have arguably been major crises of the policy paradigm that saw a guarantee for the optimal allocation of capital in the increasing self-regulation of financial markets (Skidelsky 2010; Kotz 2015). This paradigm emerged through the interplay of market actors, academics and policymakers (Tsingou 2004; Seabrooke and Tsingou 2009; Konings 2011; Krippner 2011). It was based on a new statecraft after Keynesian interventionism, where states increasingly retreated from intervening in economic activity directly and instead chose to engage in market-making regulatory policies (Vogel 1996; Majone 1997; Levi-Faur 2005). This was undergirded in macroeconomics by the "rational expectations" revolution in the 1970s (Lucas 1972; Kydland and Prescott 1977; Helgadottir 2021) and the connected Lucas critique, which implied that all macroeconomic state interventions to govern the business cycle, such as stimulus programs, were futile as rational agents would anticipate future tax hikes (Lucas and Sargent 1979).

Embedded in this ideology of the futility of direct macroeconomic state intervention, financial economics in general and the efficient (financial) market hypothesis in particular have been the "boundary object" (Star and Griesemer 1989)[1] that brought together technocrats, academics and market participants in the construction of the regulatory paradigm of financial markets pre-crisis (Whitley 1986; MacKenzie 2006; Seabrooke and Tsingou 2009). As a positive theory, the Efficient Market Hypothesis influenced much of the policymaking since the 1970s, striving for increasingly complete markets that were supposed to permit the realization of welfare gains (Whitley 1986). These views of the world were engrained in market devices (such as the Black–Scholes formula and its calculation spreadsheets; MacKenzie 2006), which have allowed increased trading on derivatives markets, making the future subject to calculated, hedged speculation (Esposito 2011).[2] Based on this belief that financial markets are able to efficiently price risks, policymakers delegated the evaluation of risk-taking to the internal risk management systems of banks themselves (Tsingou 2004), which in turn depoliticized the risk-taking of these institutions (Lockwood 2015).

---

[1] "Boundary objects" are concepts that are sufficiently defined to provide a common point of coordination, allowing different groups to collaborate, yet at the same time permitting sufficient interpretive flexibility for each group to pursue their own interests.

[2] In these models, financial markets are assumed to always be liquid and to price risks correctly, leading to "market discipline" that punishes excessive risk-taking and leads to an efficient allocation of capital.

The financial crisis shook this intellectual edifice, which underlay the policy paradigm in its foundations (Turner 2012; Langley 2014; Weyl 2017). It made plainly and painfully evident that financial market participants had not been able to properly price risks, in particular those that have come to be known as cyclical systemic risks, which extend beyond the risk-taking of individual institutions and regard the risk-taking of the financial system as a whole (Crockett 2000; Persaud 2010). Furthermore, the crisis demonstrated that the efficient allocation of capital had not been achieved, irrational herd behavior on markets seemed pervasive and liquidity could vanish quickly (Shin 2011).

And yet, despite these failures of the reigning policy paradigm and the ensuing rhetoric of policymakers about the need for radical change, there was no immediate fundamental break with this pre-crisis mode of regulation, neither in political discourse (Muegge 2013; Moschella and Tsingou 2013; Underhill 2015), nor in financial economics (Mirowski 2013), nor in the regulation of those parts of the financial markets most affected, such as derivatives (Pagliari 2012).[3] Instead, the large-scale attempt to re-regulate finance in a macro-prudential way that was initiated by the G20 in 2009 can be most fruitfully analyzed as an act of "symbolic politics," seeking to assure the general public that answers to the glaring policy failures that were revealed by the financial crisis would be found (Lombardi and Moschella 2017).

Pointing to the vague project of macro-prudential policies to secure financial stability (Hellwig 2014), the G20 delegated the work to technocratic circles in the newly formed Financial Stability Board, the prudential supervisors assembled in the Basel Committee for Banking Supervision (Baker 2013a; Lombardi and Moschella 2017) and national macro-prudential authorities to be established. Technocrats in these bodies were tasked not only with increasing the resilience of the system (e.g. through increasing the capital buffers of large institutions) but also with intervening in the cyclical buildup of booms that turn into busts (Baker 2013a, b, 2014). Central to their work on these macro-prudential policies, including its concerns over financial fragilities and its impact on the macroeconomy, was the rise of the notion of systemic

---

[3] The ambiguity in the field of economics was on full display in the Nobel Memorial Prize in Economic Sciences of 2013, granted to both Eugene Fama, a staunch defender of the efficient financial market hypothesis, and Robert Shiller, pointing to irrational exuberance in financial markets.

risk (for the history of the term, see Ozgode 2022). Macro-prudential regulation was to go beyond a look at the aggregated individual risks of financial institutions (fallacy of composition) to also include the risks of common exposures and interconnectedness (often mediated through markets and market risks).

The task of macro-prudential policymakers was to complement the individual risk management systems of banks with regulatory metrics of systemic risk, which would allow them to see, know and regulate systemic risks (Black 2013; for the failure of pre-crisis cognitive schemes inherent in central bank models, see Fligstein et al. 2017). In its most ambitious version, regulators were to become the systemic risk managers of the financial system as a whole (Persaud 2014), reversing the pre-crisis delegation of risk management to market actors, with all the attendant uncertainties for regulators (Stellinga and Muegge 2017). In this endeavor, there was both little in terms of mainstream academic work that they could draw upon and little in terms of support by private actors that had been so consequential in the development of private individual risk management systems (Adrian 2018). Regulators were hence largely thrown back upon themselves and their own research capabilities to generate the insights that could justify their interventions, drawing in allied academics in the process.

Analyzing the ensuing changes to the regulation of financial markets post-crisis, the political science literature has come to a sobering assessment (for an outlier, see Wilf 2016): rather than the radical change some had expected post-crisis, following a diagnosed "third-order ideational shift" to financial regulation (Baker 2013a[4]), the regulatory changes post-crisis are largely seen as incremental (Moschella and Tsingou 2013). While there has been a significant expansion of public authority over markets, the content and purpose of public interventions in the immediate aftermath of the crisis were seen to remain constant, in line with the pre-crisis paradigm (Pagliari 2012, 61). In this analysis, neo-liberal ideas – that is, a faith in markets' self-disciplining capacities – have not been rebuked but have merely seen an ordoliberal amendment, whereby regulatory activity after the crisis was driven by the insight that beneficial markets do not emerge naturally but need to be harnessed

---

[4] Baker describes the developments, using Kuhnian language, as a "Gestaltswitch," whereby regulators after the crisis had come to see financial markets and the risks that emanate from them as completely different from the way they saw them pre-crisis.

through regulatory intervention (Biebricher 2012), leading regulators to adjust markets to make them function as they ideally should (Birk and Thiemann 2020). These interventions are therefore interpreted as paradigm repair, leading Helleiner (2014) to call it a "status quo crisis."

This revisionist rather than radical approach to policy change has been explained by the lack of alternative economic ideas (Mirowski 2013; Muegge 2013), in particular in the USA, and the ensuing difficulties of international coordination (Helleiner 2014). One identified factor is the inclusion of private financial actors in the rule-making process, which block alternative idea sets such as macro-prudential regulation (Underhill 2015). Another is the success of central bankers in limiting the worst fallout from the crisis due to aggressive interventions. Having learned the lessons from the Great Depression (Eichengreen 2015), they were hesitant to introduce drastic new measures, fearing the unknown consequences of these interventions (Stellinga and Muegge 2017; Stellinga 2019). For these reasons, macro-prudential reform efforts have been identified as incremental projects, which, while challenging the epistemic authority of the market, lagged far behind initial expectations (Underhill 2015; Baker 2018). At their worst, macro-prudential reform efforts are merely seen as a continuation of neoliberalism because of their focus on increasing the resilience of the system (Walker and Cooper 2011; Casey 2015; Konings 2016).

While this correctly depicts the often timid attempts at re-regulation in the immediate aftermath of the financial crisis, in particular with respect to shadow banking (see Thiemann 2018; Thiemann et al. 2018b; Endrejat and Thiemann 2020), it risks missing a bigger, yet largely subliminal change. This change has occurred in the translation of a changed general perspective on financial markets into new metrics and models of systemic risk (which developed in the ten years after the financial crisis in technocratic and economic circles), which are only currently reaching their full potential in terms of the regulation of finance. In this respect, it is important to emphasize the speed with which judgment was cast by political scientists upon regulatory initiatives.[5]

---

[5] Muegge's (2013) insightful essay on the lack of alternative idea sets, challenging neoliberal ideas, was written in 2012, as was Mirowski's (2013) intervention. Helleiner (2014), giving a verdict on the effects of the crisis, was written in 2013 (for a related critique, see Tooze 2018, 20). In all fairness, Helleiner (2014) does point out that a proper assessment of macro-prudential regulation will only be possible after about ten years.

In the short time span of five years, when these judgments were pronounced, it was arguably difficult for economists to operationalize this new idea set and see it accepted in the mainstream of academic and regulatory opinion, such that it could legitimately inform regulatory activity. But this was arguably the task for economists in central banks and academia if they wanted to enact truly novel "macro-prudential" regulation, which would seek not only to increase the cross-sectional resilience of the financial systems to shocks through raising capital requirements for different financial institutions but also to mitigate the boom–bust cycles of finance. As Muegge (2013) rightly points out, the former is completely justifiable within the pre-crisis approach, whereby agents are practically facing difficulties in assessing their mutual exposures and where the structural fact of banks being "too big to fail" is leading to excessive risk-taking.[6] In contrast, the idea of governments intervening during excessive booms in financial markets, seeking to mitigate the latter's propensity for boom–bust cycles, was arguably new and radically different.

To do so, macroeconomic change agents needed to convince their fellow regulators that they had the capacity to detect these excesses and the tools to mitigate them, and while economists at the Bank for International Settlements had done some work on these issues pre-crisis (Borio and Drehmann 2009), it was by no means a consensus that government agencies had the capacity to do so (see, e.g., Tarullo 2013a, b). Reaching that consensus was especially difficult after "thirty years of spectacular returns and pseudo-stability ... had convinced every recognized authority, from the Organisation of Economic Co-operation and Development to the ECB [European Central Bank] ... from the Swedish Riksbank to the U.S. Federal Reserve, that markets were rational, prices were right, and their policies were optimal" (Blyth 2013, 210). This expectation of quick policy change after a big financial crisis or the assessment of the lack of such change, seemingly precluding any change in the future, hence ignores the different temporality inherent in the maturation process of new regulatory frameworks, from ideas in regulatory science to new policy devices to overall frameworks (cf. Moschella and Tsingou 2013; Braun 2014).

---

[6] As he puts it, "[t]hus derived, the need for macroprudential regulation can be directly derived from an orthodox approach to financial markets and it complements, rather than challenges, a neoliberal take on financial governance" (Muegge 2013, 215).

This expectation of rapid paradigm changes has been created in the political science literature through the importation of the concept of a paradigm shift by the historian of science Thomas Kuhn into policy arenas. This import was achieved in two seminal articles by Hall (1992, 1993), which can be seen at the beginning of this trend, focalizing analysts' attention on processes within the state apparatus. The ensuing literature unfortunately has come to locate the factors responsible for such a shift almost exclusively within the arena of policymaking itself, largely excluding developments in other fields, such as economics, from the analysis. By foregrounding discursive shifts and power struggles in the political and technocratic realm itself to detect these shifts, changes in economic reasoning have been placed in the background, which is ironic given Hall's more nuanced earlier work on the different factors that account for the variegated rise of Keynesianism in different national political economies after World War II (Hall 1989a, b), including the acceptance or not of Keynesianism by leading economists. The following analysis will hence seek to unearth from this literature the importance of economics itself and hence the need for a multilevel analysis, all the while being attentive to the important conceptual distinctions that literature has developed.

The Literature on Policy Paradigm Change after Hall: Losing Sight of Economics

In his classic 1993 article, Peter Hall uses the case of the ascendancy of monetarism in the UK in the 1980s, after its first, failed attempt in the 1970s, to theorize how such new policy paradigms can come about. To do so, he combines the analytical framework Kuhn had developed for paradigm changes in the natural sciences with Hugh Heclo's notion of policymaking as social learning, a mixture of puzzling and powering, to explain what he terms shifts in policy paradigms. These policy paradigms are defined by Hall as

a framework of ideas and standards that specifies not only the goals of policy and the kind of instruments that can be used to attain them, but also the very nature of the problems they are meant to be addressing. Like a Gestalt, this framework is embedded in the very terminology through which policymakers communicate about their work, and it is influential precisely because so much of it is taken for granted and unamenable to scrutiny as a whole. (Hall 1993, 279)

This definition gave pride of place to the discursive universe of ideas within which policymakers operate, often in an unreflected manner, much as in the famous statement by John Maynard Keynes at the end of his *General Theory of Employment, Interest and Money* that practical people, such as policymakers, are often the "slaves of some defunct economist" (Keynes 1936, 383). It observed the change from Keynesianism to monetarism as a sudden shift in 1980, which was preceded by gradual, incremental change on the level of instruments and tools by the Bank of England in their fight with the anomaly of stagflation in the 1970s (what Hall called first- and second-order change). This gradual change in the 1970s prepared the ground for the abrupt shift to monetarism with the ascension to power by Margaret Thatcher, which he analyzes as a third-order ideational shift, a "Gestaltswitch," which repurposed these changed policy tools and policy settings based on a completely different and new understanding of the economy, with new goals for policy interventions.

Through his intervention, Hall sought not only to condense the new state-centric approach in political science but also to provide an analytical conception of how changes in policymaking occur as an outcome of variables inside the state apparatus (Berman 2013, 219f.). In his historical narrative, he therefore points out how the anomaly of stagflation severely damaged both the epistemic authority of Keynesianism as a policy paradigm and the treasury as its institutional carrier (Hall 1993, 287), which had repeatedly emitted inaccurate forecasts and taken ineffective policy actions. Unable to explain stagflation, the treasury was not only forced to reveal the intricacies of its models, thereby making itself and the model subject to more critique, but it also increasingly lost authority over policymaking decisions to the Bank of England, which positioned itself as the bulwark against the problem of inflation. As Hall insists in his analytical summary, "such shifts are likely to be more sociological than scientific, because while there are different opinions among experts, the choice of paradigms can rarely be made based on scientific grounds alone." Instead, it is driven by a set of judgments "more political in tone, and the outcome will depend, not only on arguments of competing factions, but on their positional advantages within a broader institutional framework, on ancillary resources and on external circumstances" (Hall 1993, 281).

Despite the occasional reference to the coherence of an economic paradigm as an important causal factor, the focus of this approach has been on the institutional configurations within the technocratic and bureaucratic realm that shape how idea sets are adopted into policy (Wilder and Howlett 2014; Christensen 2017), seeing economists largely as carriers of ideas imbued during education and in the organization (see Chwieroth 2010) rather than as creators of new economic ideas (but see Ban 2015 and Clift 2018, noting the bricolage International Monetary Fund economists are engaged in). Social learning is squarely placed within the realm of policymaking and technocratic organizations, largely excluding changes in economic paradigms or the capacity of applied economists to create new economic thinking itself from the focus of their analysis. Hall's emphasis on developments within the state apparatus therefore led to a reduced emphasis on developments within the economic field, both by applied and academic economists and its interaction with policy changes.[7]

However, Hall's historical analysis of the policy paradigm shift toward monetarism had included the comparison between the Conservative leader Edward Heath in the early 1970s versus Thatcher in the early 1980s, and had pointed out that while Heath had a jerry-built structure of arguments to push for the fight against inflation, Thatcher could draw on a much more fully elaborated monetarist paradigm (see Hall 1992, 97f., 1993, 290). This is analyzed as an instance of the power of a coherent paradigm, which grants the capacity to resist some societal demands while giving in to others. Crucially, without such a paradigm Prime Minister Heath, while pursuing the same goals as Thatcher, had to fall back upon Keynesianism when the first negative consequences of his policies materialized. He simply lacked an alternative coherent narrative that he could point to in order to face his opponents.

The literature that ensued on shifts in policy paradigms after these major contributions by Hall has been very good at analyzing the factors that affect policy shifts internal to the field of politics and policymaking (Howlett and Wilder 2014), pointing to the emergence of consensus among policy elites as an important factor (e.g. Schmidt 2008, 2011), but has been largely silent on the boundary-crossing activities of economic ideas into administrations and into politics (but see Mudge and

---

[7]   In this spirit, Hall, for example, acknowledges the importance of the carriers of new economic ideas among civil servants (1993, 291), then at the same time deemphasizes it as a necessary but not a sufficient condition for policy change.

Vauchez 2012). Instead, the Kuhnian concept of paradigm shifts has been applied to policymakers, who, when confronted with enough anomalies that cannot be explained by the dominant analytical frame, question the latter and experiment with competing policy paradigms (Hay 2001; for a more refined version, see Hay 2016).[8]

Zooming in on the dynamics of social learning within the realm of (technocratic) policymaking, the focus in this literature is on the contest between carriers of certain idea sets, whose jockeying for power is juxtaposed with shifting institutional configurations of authority (e.g. Chwieroth 2010; Mandelkern and Shalev 2010). However, as Mudge and Vauchez (2012) point out, this literature does not pay attention to the professional preconditions for economic ideas to gain prominence and the dynamic pathways for their translation into the bureaucratic and political space (see also Mudge 2018). It can trace the fate of economic ideas within the policy space, yet it cannot specify where these ideas come from or how they gain professional approval. And yet, such new idea sets were needed to bring about the creation of new policy devices (Hirschmann and Popp-Berman 2014), permitting policymakers to see, know and regulate systemic risks (Black 2013). It is this blackboxing of the process of the creation of new models and their translation into policy devices that this book seeks to address.

More recent social-constructivist scholarship has refined this analysis, yet it still largely remains within the realm of politics and policymaking, blackboxing the realm of economics proper and its interaction with policymaking. Processes of persuasion inside policy networks are at the center of this analysis, which involves the struggle over the appropriate diagnosis of the crisis and the necessary steps that follow from it (Blyth 2002, 2013; Widmaier et al. 2007; Chwieroth 2010; Baker 2013a). This strand has hence emphasized the importance of the narrative framing of these crises to explain when a series of anomalies comes to be perceived as a problem and what the likely responses will be (Hay 2001), as well as pointing to the sequential role of ideas in reducing uncertainty in those moments of crisis (Blyth 2002). It has furthermore challenged the view of policymakers as dogmatic actors who cling to internalized idea sets.

[8]   Hay (2001) thereby presumes that alternative idea sets are simply out there for policymakers to choose from, ignoring the differential endowment of these ideas with professional approval or the temporal processes that might be involved in the generation of such validity for alternative idea sets in the realm of economic discourse.

Instead, it points to their creative efforts to amalgamate new policy proposals from a set of preexisting ideas (Carstensen 2011). It has focused on the activities of policy entrepreneurs – creative change agents who recombine ideas in a manner comparable to bricolage (Carstensen 2011; Carstensen and Schmidt 2016) to strategically outmaneuver their opponents and gain acceptance of their ideas (Blyth 2013).

Discursive institutionalists have furthermore pointed out that new policy paradigms are co-constructed by politicians crafting communicative discourses to the public, as well as by technocrats engaging in the search for a new discourse to coordinate among themselves (Schmidt 2008). Whereas in communicative discourses the simplicity of ideas and their fit with overarching economic paradigms and public sentiment are important elements (Campbell 1998), coordinative discourse is characterized by a focus on evidence-based propositions and an attempt to avoid politicization (Schmidt 2008, 2011). Differentiating policy statements in terms of their level of abstraction, discursive institutionalism points out that very general philosophical statements and more concrete programmatic statements of what goals a policy program should pursue are more present in communicative discourse, whereas concrete policy proposals, based on evidence, are more likely to occur in technocratic discourse. This literature thereby establishes that the way in which ideas are presented, in which form and in which context can be as important as the content of these ideas itself.

In this way, social learning is now understood as a communicative process that is riveted more by power structures than by Bayesian updating, powering rather than puzzling (Blyth 2013), with an ongoing contestation over the scientific legitimacy of ideas (or epistemic authority) and battles for the reputation of their authors (Blyth 2013; Ban 2015). One implication of this stance is that the professional standing, prominence and positioning of carriers of these new ideas within state apparatuses (Hall 1989a; Chwieroth 2010; Baker 2013a) are seen to be very influential for shifts in policy. Yet, while very insightful to understand the institutional context within the state apparatus in which economic ideas can thrive, this research still largely ignores the process of production of new economic ideas and the preconditions for these new economic idea sets to become viable in the economic field in the first place, a precondition that bestows highly prized "objectivity" on these idea sets (for a similar critique, see Campbell and Pedersen 2014, 11 and Braun 2014; for a contribution attentive to their role, see Clift 2018).

As Mudge and Vauchez (2012, 454) put it eloquently, this "non-differentiation of ideas and inattention to their scholarly and professional origins" has caused "difficulty moving beyond the basic proposition that 'ideas matter' to an understanding of the interconnected processes by which ideas are produced, imported into political and bureaucratic spaces, and translated into categories of perception and programs of action." The neglect of these questions is on full display in the recent scholarship on post-crisis regulatory change in the realm of macro-prudential regulation. If this scholarship has focused on ideational change, it has mostly looked at discursive changes at the top of the political and technocratic levels (cf. Baker 2013a, 2014) and commitments to a new macro-prudential approach to the regulation of finance; only little has it studied the substantiation of these promises through the practical work of economists. However, to understand the final shape of the macro-prudential paradigm, it is at the level of interaction between politics, policymaking and the world of applied economics that analytical attention needs to be placed.

Whereas macro-prudential ideas were formulated at the Bank for International Settlement (BIS) and by some academics pre-crisis, these views were far from being the mainstream view at the time (Baker 2013a; Lombardi and Siklo 2016); indeed, the lack of use of mathematical models and advanced econometric techniques largely placed these ideas outside of the mainstream view (interview, former Bundesbank economist, August 19, 2014). This effectively meant that the format within which they were expressed did not meet the epistemic requirements of academic economic discourse. Since the crisis, economists in central banks and international organizations tasked with developing systemic risk frameworks have spent much time and energy formalizing these ideas about the causes and mechanisms of financial cycles and other fragilities, making them live up to these standards. Jointly with some academics, they have been able to propose metrics and overarching frameworks for monitoring systemic risks that only recently have come into full use by central banks and international organizations (Ibrocevic and Thiemann 2018; Thiemann 2022), a fact that has largely escaped the post-crisis literature (but see Coombs 2020, 2022).

Bringing Economics Back In: Toward a Multidimensional Understanding of Regulatory Change

Recent scholarship in the tradition of constructivist institutionalism (Ban 2015; Clift 2018, 2019; Kaya and Reay 2019) has been a welcome improvement in how it treats ideas and their potential for impacting policymaking, as it places emphasis on the form in which these ideas need to be expressed to exert influence. In his work on the International Monetary Fund's (IMF's) post-crisis rediscovery of Keynesian ideas on financial and fiscal policies, Clift identifies four mechanisms that are at play as technocratic organizations interact with a broad array of what is deemed acceptable mainstream economic ideas to react to crises (Clift 2018; see also Ban 2015).[9] In order to become part of the toolkit of such an organization, these new ideas need to be corroborated with evidence and reconciled with old thinking by the organization that embraces them;[10] they have to be operationalized into metrics for actual policymaking and require the authoritative endorsement of academic authorities. Leaning on historical institutionalist insights, these mechanisms imply the distinct possibility that large crises can lead to only incremental policy changes (Clift 2018, 7, 32; see also Wilder and Howlett 2014).

In contrast to historical institutionalists, however, Clift emphasizes the "contingent and open-ended nature of institutional change and the crucial role of its ideational mediation" (Clift 2018, 32), where the "packaging and framing of new thinking in light of salient cognitive filters is the stuff of, as well as major terrain for, the politics of economic ideas" (Clift 2018, 41). This openness to either radical or incremental change after a crisis points to the role of applied economists within technocratic organizations that act as reflexive agents that seek to shift "the legitimate policy space," mindful of the "conditions their ideas need to fulfill to bring about change" (Clift 2018, 54).[11] Clift thereby clarifies that while the "economic mainstream" is

---

[9] In this line of work, what is economic mainstream is assumed to be both historically contingent and socially constructed.

[10] These institutions can also abandon old policies; however, they can only do so rarely in order not to lose epistemic authority (Clift 2018, citing chief economist Blanchard).

[11] Clift mentions the increasing trend for IMF economists to publish academic papers, corroborating their new approach (2018, 59), but he does not pursue this approach any further.

historically contingent and socially constructed within the technocratic organizations that seek to define the "policy space," it nevertheless imposes upon change agents the need to live up to epistemic standards and robustness tests established by academic economic discourse.

These new insights can be integrated into recent theorizing of policy change as fragmented, "whereby a crisis may induce rapid change in one specific dimension of a paradigm . . . at some point, while another dimension develops slowly in response to cumulative gradual pressures" (Kaya and Reay 2019, 392). As Kaya and Reay emphasize, "when analysing shifts in a major ideational framework over an extended period of time, fragmented change cautions against looking exclusively for either rapid or gradual change, via a single dominant institutional route" (2019, 386). In contrast to the dichotomy of radical and abrupt shifts on the one hand and slow, gradual change on the other, they argue that "fragmented change offers a distinct possibility for institutional and ideational alterations in that it cannot be reduced to either type of change" (2019, 403). Change does not have to occur in a hierarchical manner but can occur in a more "diffused manner, given that radical change is not the final culmination, but rather a component of varied types of change." In that sense, competing policy paradigms can coexist for a longer period of time (Campbell and Pedersen 2014, 11). While one is ascending, the other one might still exert influence, even if in decline.[12]

This attention to the required characteristics of policy ideas to become performative in a technocratic space and the concept of fragmented change, including radical change at one level but not at others, can help us to capture the current state of development of macroprudential regulation. It can be fruitfully applied to the incremental change Baker and others are observing regarding macro-prudential regulation after the crisis (Baker 2013b, 2014; Moschella and Tsingou 2013; Thiemann et al. 2018a), as technocrats internally to central banks first needed to be convinced of the merits of the new

---

[12] This idea of coexistence of policy paradigms matches very well with the suggestion by Latour to perceive of the "relative existence of facts" (1999, 155), whereby certain facts might be held up and affirmed in one network of humans and nonhumans, whereas opposite facts might be held to be true in different networks. The question becomes: which network is expanding and powerful and which one is not, which one is ascending, and which one is declining in membership and reach?

approach before espousing it. It also fits very well with the analysis of macro-prudential regulation as a broad ideational shift without operational consensus (Baker 2013a) as these new ideas needed to be reconciled with existing and acknowledged methods and thinking.

However, because the concept of fragmented change no longer operates in the dichotomy of radical or incremental change, but instead is able to perceive of these two occurring jointly in different dimensions, we can thereby perceive of the possibility of continued development of the macro-prudential agenda in the scientific dimension, while observing a momentary blockage in execution, rather than seeing it as completely stuck in the thicket of evidence-based technocracies (Baker 2018). In this vein, macro-prudential thinking can be seen to open a space for policy experimentation for central bankers, much like it did for the IMF (Moschella 2015). It also allows us to consider the possibility that old techniques are repurposed and suddenly come to serve new functions; for example, processes of incremental bricolage to govern the crisis (Langley 2014) can then exert a path-shaping influence on the new governance framework that will govern financial stability, as was the case for stress-tests in the post-crisis environment (Langley 2014; Coombs 2020, 2022).

The Path-Shaping Power of Technocratic Economists: Creating Robust Policy Devices

This book follows up on these accounts by focusing on the work of technocratic economists within central banks and other agencies to establish the validity of new ideas and their translation into new policy devices, which prepares the ground for changes in the policy apparatus. In a bureaucratic environment characterized by scientization, these new ideas had to be operationalized, reconciled with existing thinking and models and corroborated by evidence (Clift 2018, 39f.) before they could serve as the foundation for regulatory devices that allow regulators to visualize systemic risks and act on them. However, they add an important element to these social-constructivist accounts, namely the idea that these applied economists themselves, together with academic economists or on their own, can be creative and generative of new ideas. They can design new models and measurement devices to provide ways to their central bank to legitimately exercise the new tasks that have been imposed upon them, namely macro-prudential regulation.

I argue that it is these technocratic economists, allied with academic economists well disposed toward the project of "rethinking financial markets as instable," that have generated the metrics and models that established macro-prudential risks as "risk objects" (Hilgartner 1992) with clearly identified linkages to harm. Their work thereby not only establishes the need to act against these risks but also provides the policy devices to control them (Hilgartner 1992, 50f.).[13] Hilgartner's crucial contribution has been to point social scientists to the work of these technical experts as crucial agents driving the construction of "risk objects" and their linkage to harm (Hilgartner 1992, 52f.). These agents thereby have been able to deliver the decisive input for macro-prudential policy frameworks that structure the action of policymakers.

In the words of Power (2007), their work has been to "organize uncertainty" over systemic dangers that can build up in the financial systems into the notion of systemic risk, seeking "to produce decidability and actionability. Knightian uncertainties become risks when they enter into management systems for their identification, assessment and mitigation" (Power 2007, 5).[14] These economists hence engaged in the construction of systemic risk as a "risk object" that can be subjugated to a "management process" (Power 2007, 8). As Power points out in his study on operational risk, such uncertainties do not exist sui generis "but must of necessity be organized, ordered, rendered thinkable, and made amenable to processes and practice of intervention" (Power 2007, 8). The work of these economists then guides the attention of their employers, central banks, to what they perceive to be the most crucial elements in the buildup of these risks. At the same time, these economists engage in establishing the optimal tools to react to these threats, seeking to establish trade-offs between positive and negative events but also making the macro-prudential governance framework itself auditable and transparent, allowing the interested public to follow and evaluate the macro-prudential policy decisions taken. By focusing on the work of these economists, we can take into view the

[13] In Hilgartner's language, these policy devices are placed in the network of control for these risks.

[14] Prior ideational scholarship in political economy has pointed to the role of ideas in organizing such uncertainty (cf. Blyth 2002, 44f.) but it has failed to specify the locus and the agents of this work, in my case applied economists in central banks.

"catalytic role of ideas and new descriptive categories in changing conceptions of practice and risk management in particular" (Breslau 1997a, b; Power 2007, 6).

Doing research on this kind of boundary-spanning work between regulation and science in the realm of "regulatory science" (Jasanoff 1990, 2004) requires focusing less on the spokespersons/promoters of certain economic and regulatory paradigms and more on model builders or those generating statistical evidence that supports such a shift (Eyal and Buchholz 2010, 131).[15] In other words, it requires more attention to "economists in the wild" (Callon 2007); that is, economists in bureaucratic settings and how they interact with academic research and researchers to combine theory, methods of measurement and data to frame the negative externalities that require regulatory intervention (Callon 1998b; Eyal 2013, 175f.). In their efforts to translate abstract concepts into actionable indicators and models that can guide policymaking (Callon et al. 2007), economists in technocratic bureaucracies enroll academic allies (Callon 1986; Eyal 2013) and engage in "regulatory science": a process of negotiation over the stock of scientific knowledge deemed sufficiently objective to provide the basis for regulatory action (Jasanoff 1990; Jasanoff 2011a, 2012).[16]

Regulatory science is boundary work in "a space between fields" (Eyal 2013), negotiated over where science ends and politics begins (Gieryn 1983, 1995; Weingart 1999), seeking to establish what science can state with certainty and what is subject to political decision-making because of a lack of conclusive evidence (Jasanoff 1990, 14, 237). It is the iterative boundary work of science against politics (Gieryn 1983, 1999) but also the boundary crossing that it enables, moving a claim from the realm of the political into the realm of the scientific that establishes the knowledge base of regulatory tools. This space of regulatory science operates on epistemic standards of proof that deviate from academic standards because of politically perceived needs for action and time pressure, potentially following the principle of

---

[15] For the power of statistics in hardwiring certain normative valuations of finance into our outlook on the world, see Christophers (2011, 2013).

[16] The current era of evidence-based policy (Strasheimer 2015) can in general be characterized as an era of regulatory science, where policymakers seek to avoid personal judgment and instead aim to base themselves on hard-won scientific objectivity.

precaution rather than unequivocal evidence (Jasanoff 1990, 250, 2012, 109). This means that regulatory science, unfolding in a "boundary space between the economic field, the bureaucratic field and the academic field" and "carried out by actors, who have a foot in each of these, but by the same token are also somewhat marginal to each" (Eyal 2013, 176), might precede science proper.[17] As experts, it is these actors in the space of regulatory science

> who govern the production and evaluation of policy-relevant science. And unlike scientists, whose primary mission is fact-making, experts are by definition boundary-crossers whose job it is to link scientific knowledge to matters of social significance: they are the diagnosticians of public problems, the explorers of solutions and the providers of remedies. (Jasanoff 2011b, 24)

It is in these discussions among experts that the appropriate answers to the regulatory challenges are determined, including the validity of their quasi-scientific underpinnings.[18] Their work then transforms new policy ideas into socio-technical devices, becoming an "agencement" of regulators that both reshapes their vision of the economy and the capacity to intervene in it (Callon 1998b; Callon et al. 2007; Hirschman and Popp-Berman 2014, 782). In these discussions, newly developed regulatory devices for detecting risks are linked to possible remedies, which in turn are subjected to attempted analysis of trade-offs in terms of costs and benefits to frame the discussion over the desirability of public intervention (Callon 1998b, 261f.). Adopting a certain set of measures in the end then co-constitutes the assumed nature of the object to be regulated, but the assumed responsibilities and capabilities of the regulating subject, knowledge objects and social orders are also co-produced (Hilgartner 1992, 47; Jasanoff 2004, 275f., 2005, 92). As Luhmann put it, framing uncertainties in terms of risk implies calculability and hence allocates responsibility for the (regulating) actor that can know and react to these calculable risks (as cited in Power 2007, 6). In other words, by co-constituting the

---

[17] Jasanoff's early work on the regulation of carcinogenic elements by the Food and Drug Administration and the Environmental Protection Agency (Jasanoff 1990) shows well why this is the case. The principle of precaution led these agencies to forbid certain chemical elements, even if the proof of their carcinogenic effect was not yet fully established.

[18] I use "quasi-scientific" to clarify that regulatory science operates based on standards close but not equivalent to academic research (Jasanoff 2011a).

knowledge object of systemic risk and the world within which it unfolds, this work also creates the responsibility for regulators to act to mitigate it.

It is this process of translation of (new) economic ideas into an actionable policy framework and policy devices by experts in the space of regulatory science that is of utmost importance for an actual shift in policy orientation to occur. For this reason, I pay special attention to the analytical debates of economists working in central banks, as these are operating at the intersection of economics as a research endeavor and policy action. Their interaction both with academic economists and with economists in international organizations, such as the BIS and IMF, on these issues is seen as crucial, as it shapes the technocratic coordinative discourse regarding which policy programs to adopt based on which models and measurement devices to answer these policy challenges. As this book documents, it took about ten years following the crisis for this translation process from ideas into measurement devices and policy recommendations, embedded in macro-prudential policy frameworks, to come to a (preliminary) conclusion.

Lessons from History

These linkages between economics as a scientific discourse and economics as a bureaucratic practice raise the question of when, how and under which conditions changes in the intellectual field of economics lead to changes in policymaking, and under which conditions changes in policymaking impact the intellectual field of economics. Which ideas are institutionalized and lead to changes in practice and which ideas are discarded? Which new scientific objects subsumed under the risks to be regulated are accepted and what are the implications in terms of regulation? To answer these questions, we need to observe changes in economic discourse emanating from the intellectual field, including both applied and academic economists, and changes in political discourse jointly and sequentially, postulating that changes in economics facilitate shifts in policies (see Braun 2014, 52 for the shift from Keynesianism to neoliberalism) and that changes in policies facilitate shifts in economics (Hall 1989a).[19]

---

[19] For example, the installation of a policy device based on a change in politics can generate the data/evidence needed to change an economic view.

Such thinking in sequences in no way means that the relationship is unidirectional; indeed, it might better be conceptualized as cycles, whereby demands emanating from politics after crises are answered by the economic discourse[20] and in turn can transform policy and politics (Fourcade 2009). Following this perspective established by Fourcade's work (2001, 2009), the call for macro-prudential policies in 2008–9 is interpreted in this book as a demand by politics to economics to provide answers as to how finance could be better regulated to prevent a reoccurrence of the events of the financial crisis, which in the past set in motion a process of re-envisioning the economy (Mitchell 2005).

Such an emphasis on the work of applied economists and the policy devices they produce is borne out by a comparison with prior paradigm shifts in policymaking after crises that acted as watershed moments. Before its ascendance to dominance as a policy paradigm, Keynesianism required the installation of extensive statistics and the invention of econometric techniques by Tinbergen and others to generate a representation of the economy that policymakers felt they could use to legitimately intervene in (Mitchell 2002; Breslau 2003); that is, actionable knowledge.[21] Similarly, the new macroeconomic consensus on limited fiscal policy and focus on monetary policy (Clift 2018, 79), linked to the rational expectations revolution, gained its full policy influence only when it was included in the workhorse models for economic forecasting of all major central banks in the 1990s (Helgadottir 2021, 1), a model now called the Dynamic Stochastic General Equilibrium (DSGE) model.[22]

These prior historical experiences also point to the fact that with regard to fundamental shifts in economic policy paradigms, there are different temporalities at play in the realm of economics, administrative activities and political action in the gestation, transfer and embrace of these ideas (see Hall 1989b; Blyth 2002; Helleiner 2010). When we look at the history of the evolution of macroeconomic governance

[20] Langley's (2014, 9) reference to economics as the administrative art of establishing order through concepts that make governance possible is most apt here.

[21] Tinbergen and his econometric work was arguably as important to Keynesianism as was Keynes (Braun 2014, 57f.). He produced the powerful indicators (Muegge 2016) that Keynesianism was based upon.

[22] Its proclaimed "scientificity" was one of the main elements that undergirded the claim to central bank independence, which underlay the rising power of both the Federal Reserve and the ECB in the decade before the crisis (McNamara 2002).

paradigms, such as Keynesianism or the rational expectations revolution of the 1970s, which undergirds current neoliberalism, we find a pattern of sequential co-evolution, whereby policy experimentation and economic theory co-evolve.[23] There is hence a need to focus on the interaction of these different fields and their different temporalities to understand the emergence and implementation of new policy paradigms (Mudge 2008, 707; Vauchez and Mudge 2012; Mudge 2018).

Transferring the historical insights into the present day, we can see certain similarities: just as in the 1930s and 1970s, we are finding ourselves in the wake of a crisis both of the economy in the Western world and in current economics (see, e.g., Mirowski 2013; Romer 2016), where the economic profession seeks to identify ways to understand and incorporate the lessons of the crisis. At the forefront of these developments are applied economists within international organizations such as the IMF or central banks, seeking to incorporate finance and its potential for negative feedback loops with the real economy in their models of the macroeconomy (see, e.g., IMF chief economist Blanchard, as cited in Clift 2018, 81). The question is whether and how this work of applied economists, in seeking to adapt their (macro) economic models, leads to changes in the policy paradigm of financial market regulation and central bank action (Henriksen 2013; Braun 2014). Does a view that sees the role of finance as much less benign and in need of constraint result in actual policy actions through the translation of these concerns into metrics of risks that are posed to the real economy by the financial system? The installation of such a paradigm, which intervenes in the evolution of booms and busts in financial markets, would be a fundamental shift to the pre-crisis paradigm.

To construct such a new paradigm of the governance of financial markets at the macro level required fundamental change: first, formulating a new vision of the economy; second, formalizing and operationalizing this vision in model economies; and third, seeking ways to

---

[23] Keynes's *General Theory* was published in 1936, seven years after the beginning of the Great Depression, and became influential as a blueprint for policy action on a global scale only after 1945, with prior experimental engagements in aggregate demand management in western Europe and the USA in the late 1930s. And even then, at no point was Keynesianism a universally shared paradigm; instead, the openness of the policy apparatus to the new Keynesian ideas as well as prevalent political coalitions shaped variegated Keynesianisms around the Western world (Hall 1986; Weir 1989).

measure, estimate and predict the associated variables in these models (Braun 2014, 50; see also Widmaier 2016). The first level – the different visions of the economy – contains fundamental concepts, such as the cyclical nature of financial markets or the assumption that they operate efficiently. These concepts give rise to economic models formulated according to the rules of academia, which function "as artificial economic systems that can serve as laboratories" (Lucas 1980, 696, as cited in Braun 2014, 54), which serve to produce forecasts and act as narrative devices to explain what is going on in the economy (Braun 2014, 54).

Once such inherently coherent models of the economy are produced, they then need to be able to "fit the data," reproduce data patterns from the past and correctly predict future developments. It is at this point that the development of governability paradigms is "inextricably bound up with developments in econometrics. Problems such as aggregation from micro-data, identification and measurement of variables, model calibration, and model uncertainty all fall under this third requirement of empirical fit" (Braun 2014, 54). Once these three phases are concluded, this work can give rise to a governability paradigm, a clear and relatively coherent framework, which, based on reliably identified causal relationships, proscribes certain policy actions. This was the case for Keynesian models of aggregate demand post-World War II, which crystallized in hydraulic models of the economy and the New Keynesian synthesis of the 1980s, focusing almost exclusively on setting monetary policy and exemplified in DSGE models.[24]

Put in these terms, the intellectual challenges posed for the construction of a macro-prudential framework that could be part of such a new governability paradigm were stark in 2008. The new vision, as formulated by Crockett (2000) and Borio (2003b), among others, maintained that finance was endogenously unstable and operated in cycles, in turn threatening economic growth (Borio 2012). Such a view was diametrically opposed to the pre-crisis vision, which, based on the efficient

---

[24] As Braun (2014) points out, there are weakening effects of these policy apparatuses once installed and used over time. He suggests that their success might generate a certain overconfidence in identified relationships that would lead to an undermining of the capacity of such a macro-paradigm to generate the desired results, as problems outside of the framework accumulate (see also Widmaier 2016). However, these issues are not yet a concern to a macro-prudential governability paradigm in the making, as this apparatus first has to become operational.

Table 2.1 *Different visions of finance and their different related policy devices*

Vision of finance	Pre-crisis: efficient market hypothesis (Fama)	Macro-prudential vision (Kindleberger, Minsky)
Nature of finance	Finance follows a random route	Finance is cyclical
Capital allocation	Optimal capital allocation	Misallocation due to manias
Epistemic authority	Markets	Regulators/state officials
Policy devices for seeing and knowing risks	Bottom-up, private risk management systems integrated into public risk management	Public systemic risk measurements; top-down assessment by regulators
Policy tools for interventions to alleviate risks	Rules based; interventions only in case of individual failures, interventions regarding individual risk management systems, "benchmarking"	Discretionary, ex ante intervention by regulators in markets and institutions based on public systemic risk measurements

For a related table, see Baker (2013a, 117).

market hypothesis and the rational expectations framework, advocated for a structural deregulation of finance (Mirowski 2013; Braun 2014). Based on an uncritical acceptance of efficient market assumption, macroeconomic models had no banking systems (Clift 2018, 72). Financial variables, such as short-term credit flows, were largely outside of the mainstream analytical focus (cf. Mirowski 2013; Braun 2014). Table 2.1 details in an ideal-typical fashion the fundamental departure that the vision of financial markets that underlies macro-prudential regulation represents with respect to the pre-crisis vision, based on the efficient market hypothesis, which was central in the way regulators envisioned financial markets (FSA 2009, 11; see also Baker 2013a, 118). The fundamental difference in the vision of these two approaches lies in the assumed nature of finance.

In the macro-prudential vision of finance that can be traced to thinkers such as Minsky (1986) or Kindleberger (1988), finance is seen as subject to boom-and-bust cycles, which are sufficiently predictable to allow forecasts and hence policy actions (see, e.g., Greenwood et al. 2019). In the efficient market hypothesis view, it is seen to follow a random route, where all available information is already priced in (cf. Fama 1970). This view makes a prediction of future developments by an agent external or internal to the market impossible, as future information will arrive randomly and cannot be guessed by anybody (Fama 1970). Based on this different conception of the nature of finance, a different understanding of the effects for capital allocation follows, which in the case of frantic markets might well lead to a misallocation of capital, whereas capital allocation is deemed optimal in efficient markets, at least in its strong version (Aglietta 2018, 26). Hence, this different vision implies, in its extremes, a very different allocation of epistemic authority with respect to financial market dynamics, including investment decisions, with one making the correcting intervention of state agents in financial market excesses a duty and the other making the extraction of hindering state regulation a primary goal of state activity.

Assuming cyclical financial markets, there is a role for regulators/state officials to assess developments in financial markets with respect to their tendencies to become self-reflexive, either in the boom phase, when speculation drives prices upwards beyond their fundamental values, or in the bust phase, when expectations of gloom worsen price dynamics below what their fundamentals would justify (Orlean 2011). Their role is to intervene before these dynamics unfold, to mitigate these trends and to make the system more resilient, allowing it to withstand the repercussions once these booms go bust. On the other hand, assuming that financial markets themselves are optimal at processing information implies the exact opposite for the role of regulators. Instead of intervening in financial markets, they should seek to extricate themselves from the market in order not to distort its capacity to amalgamate information (Riles 2011). Furthermore, they should seek to reduce transaction costs, allowing trading on all possible kinds of financial contracts in order to maximize the information-processing power of financial markets (de Goede 2001).[25]

---

[25] De Goede notes this implication of the Black–Scholes formula for derivatives pricing, which made the theory highly appealing to practitioners, who were all in favor of more trading (de Goede 2001, 130f.). The implications of this theory and its capacity to place derivatives trading in the realm of productive speculation rather than gambling are that pursuing market completion and an expansion of trading became a goal of policymaking.

These different visions also require different policy devices for seeing and knowing risks, as well as for different policy tools to intervene in those markets and secure financial stability.

Whereas a view that ascribes epistemic authority to markets could content itself with copying the most up-to-date risk management systems of private institutions, namely value-at-risk systems,[26] this is not an option for a view that sees private agents as prone to succumbing to the underpricing of risks in the boom times and overpricing of risks in the bust times (Crockett 2000; Borio 2003b). Such a view requires new policy devices to track the buildup of systemic risks from a regulatory perspective and the mechanisms to discretionarily intervene when imbalances are building up before the boom.

As this book documents, this new vision of financial markets as posing a repeated, cyclical threat to economic growth that can be predicted based on developments within financial markets was established in economic discourse in the decade after the crisis through a long and arduous process. While not uncontested, the formalization and operationalization of this vision can currently be observed both in the most prestigious academic journals (see, e.g., Adrian and Brunnermeier 2016; Adrian et al. 2019; Greenwood et al. 2020) and in recent publications by the IMF, the BIS and central banks.[27] Because of the ongoing "scientization" of central banks (Marcussen 2009a; Mudge and Vauchez 2016), based on a decades-long investment in economic expertise in in-house research departments, central banks are at the center of this reorientation, which (re-)perceives finance as fragile and which hence sees the need for inclusion of credit and finance in models of the economy, using these insights to inform policymaking. In this role, central bank economists have become central producers of knowledge about the issues pertaining to money, banking and credit (Mirowski 2013, 193; Jacobs and King 2016; Mudge and Vauchez 2016; Claveau and Dion 2018).

---

[26] For how these became integrated in Basel II, see Tsingou (2004) and Seabrooke and Tsingou (2009); for an extended critique of the risk-management tool and its depoliticizing effect, see de Goede (2004) and Lockwood (2015).

[27] These new works published in the most prestigious economic journals, including the flagship *American Economic Review*, emphasize the linkages between finance and the macroeconomy both on the global and the national level (Mian and Sufi 2011, 2018; Schularick and Taylor 2012; Rey 2013; Brunnermeier and Sannikov 2014; Jordà et al. 2015, 2017b; Miranda-Aggripino and Rey 2015; Knoll et al. 2017; Mian et al. 2017; Adrian et al. 2019).

As in prior policy shifts (Fourcade-Gourinchas and Babb 2002; Fourcade 2006; Babb 2013), the development of ideas and policy blueprints at the transnational level has been crucial in this reorientation (Muegge and Perry 2014; Grabel 2018). The reason for the centrality of this transnational debate is, on the one hand, that international organizations, such as the IMF, the Organisation for Economic Co-operation and Development and the BIS, compete in generating ideas to meet policy challenges and promoting policy blueprints they deem desirable for their constituents (Kranke and Yarrow 2019).[28] On the other hand, economists employed in national technocratic institutions, most prominently central banks, are actively participating in these transnational debates (among others, Haas 1992; Marcussen 2009b; Johnson 2016), where they enter their input to justify their domestic choices as well as drawing inspiration for the development of new policy programs domestically (Clift 2018; Thiemann 2019).

To date, the existence of prominent challenger discourses in the technocratic discourses, which advocate to constrain and limit the role of financial markets globally (for an analysis of these debates, see Nagel and Thiemann 2019) and domestically (Baker 2018), represents a moment of discursive openness (de Goede 2004), of productive incoherence (Grabel 2018) in which the path of the future policy paradigm of macro-prudential regulation and its links to monetary policy and fiscal policy is forged (for central banks, see Johnson et al. 2019; for first effects on the IMF, see Gallagher 2016). As we currently witness the formalization and testing of this new paradigm, it is simultaneously entering the implementation phase, which differs from jurisdiction to jurisdiction (see Lombardi and Moschella 2017; Hungin and James 2019; Thiemann 2019). What we therefore observe post-crisis is the simultaneous organizational and institutional work of implementing these ideas by reconfiguring state–society relations (Hall 1986) at the same time that these ideas were developed.[29] Crucial questions in

---

[28] Sometimes described as think tanks (Westermeier 2018), one of their main activities is to establish the epistemic authority of their institution by providing policy proposals that are widely accepted and/or by providing warnings on impending dangers that subsequently materialize.

[29] Because of the emasculation of ministries of finance after Keynesianism and the resultant centrality of independent central banks in the current governance architecture of finance (McNamara 2002; Watson 2002; Mandelkern 2021), this work crystallizes mostly in central banks tasked with macro-prudential regulation.

these debates are how macro-prudential policy is institutionalized in central banks and how the monetary policy framework should interact with the new goals regarding financial stability (see, e.g., Stein 2013a; Johnson et al. 2019). But before we turn to these questions, we shall first investigate the slow consolidation and rise of the expert network pushing for these ideas pre-crisis.

3 | The Evolution of Systemic Risk Thinking Pre-crisis
An Expert Network in the Making

The macro-prudential perspective involves a holistic view on financial system developments and an emphasis on endogenously created systemic risks. This perspective was marginal in the community of technocrats concerned with banking regulation until the mid-2000s (Baker 2013a). The dominant understanding at the time of how to achieve financial stability in the banking sector was a micro-prudential approach, which focused on the risk management of individual institutions rather than developments at the system level. This pre-crisis regulatory approach excluded macro-prudential problems of liquidity risks and the procyclical tendencies of the financial system (Stellinga and Muegge 2017, 17). Instead, ensuring the safety and soundness of the banking system meant ensuring the prudent risk management of banking institutions, which increasingly was delegated to the large banks themselves.

This rise to dominance of this particular micro-prudential understanding of how to achieve financial stability in the 1990s has been traced to an alliance of bank regulators, academics and private risk management officials. This alliance was centered on private risk management techniques (Seabrooke and Tsingou 2009, 16), which allowed private bankers to portray themselves as responsible and reliable risk managers (de Goede 2004; Lockwood 2015). To explain the formation of this alliance, they have pointed to the endorsement of financial innovation by high-level regulators such as Greenspan (Tsingou 2004), which was constraining the capacity of regulators to intervene in financial markets. Given their lack of data and understanding of the systemic consequences of innovation, regulators then increasingly placed hopes for containing systemic risks on market discipline and market-based supervision (Tsingou 2004), embracing both private risk transfer and private risk management techniques. While this account successfully explains the integration of private risk management techniques in public regulation, it tends to underplay the tensions and the opposing voices to this development within the regulatory community, which were coalescing around the concept of macro-prudential regulation and the intellectual challenges to this dominant view this thought collective produced.

In this chapter, I thus revisit these findings by looking at them through the lens of two competing networks of expertise: one that formed around the concept of systemic risk and macro-prudential regulation and one that formed around the concept of micro-level risk management by banks based on modern financial economics and micro-prudential supervision. Focusing on "networks of expertise" means reconstructing how networks of "devices, actors, institutions and concepts" are assembled in time, which are competing over "how to handle unknowns" by "converting them into calculable risks, or into non-numerical forms of calculation" (Eyal and Pok 2015, 38). These two networks then engaged in a jurisdictional struggle over the right approach to financial stability from the late 1970s onwards, when both groups were first institutionalized at the transnational level as a reaction to the reemergence of financial instability after the demise of Bretton Woods (Helleiner 1994) and the new form of central bank cooperation required. Tracing their fate over time will help us to better understand how the micro-prudential viewpoint and the link it developed to private risk management systems became dominant, and how it in turn was instigating an increasingly fervent critique by the macro-prudential network of expertise largely located within central banks.

In this vein, the chapter documents the uneasy coexistence of the macro-prudential network of expertise, first institutionalized at the international level in the Euro-Currency Standing Committee with the dominant network of expertise on banking regulation centered on the Basel Committee for Banking Supervision (BCBS) from the 1970s. The latter persistently sought to silence the former's macro-prudential concerns regarding the risks stemming from the increasing internationalization of financial flows and the merger of banking and capital markets business. In its own response to these financial innovations and the challenges they might pose, the BCBS then formed in the 1990s with private finance and academia based on the common inclusion of financial risk management techniques. This embrace of private risk management in turn instigated a debate on systemic risk and its measurement in central banking circles, seeking to formalize both the notion of systemic risk and necessary macro-prudential responses. In this process, the notion of systemic risk itself became subject to deepened economic scrutiny, beginning its transformation from a pragmatic notion used by practitioners to justify their actions (see Brimmer 1989) into an abstract economic concept that potentially could guide preventive action.

Historical Beginnings: The 1970s and 1980s

The network of expertise preoccupied by macro-prudential concerns began to crystallize around the Euro-Currency Standing Group, a standing group of the central bank governors of the G10 countries established at the Bank for International Settlements (BIS) from 1971 onwards. The Euro-Currency Standing Committee was renamed the Committee for the Global Financial System (CGFS) in 1999, with all its published documents rebranded as products of the CGFS, a convention I follow in this book. Born of the "epistemic uncertainty" that surrounded the functioning of the financial system in the context of the demise of Bretton Woods (Braun et al. 2021, 804), it united a group of central bankers to study macro-international financial developments and the increasing role of international banking in it. In particular, the rising importance of the Euro–dollar market was a major preoccupation, as it implicated large internationally active banks in new forms of business, bringing about risks of contagion and banking crises beyond national boundaries.

According to Goodhart (2011, 465), the CGFS was the "premier macroeconomic forum for the discussion of international tensions/imbalances," with "the BIS economic adviser (Chief Economist) playing a central role, providing much of the input to its discussions." Institutionally anchored at the BIS, it was motivated by concerns over the need for lender-of-last-resort action by central banks in the context of globalizing finance (Braun et al. 2021). In the context of these concerns, this group started to popularize the term "macro-prudential" in the late 1970s (Clement 2010, 58).

On the other hand, the kernel of the network of expertise that was preoccupied with the micro-prudential consequences of these changes crystallized around the second standing group of the G10 central bank governors, the BCBS. Bringing together banking supervisors from the G10 countries and Luxembourg, it was planned in 1974 and constituted in February 1975. It aimed to place the interaction of bank supervisors on a more permanent level after the bankruptcy of the small German bank Herstatt, active in the Euro–dollar market. The contagion effects of the unexpected default in the US banking system had demonstrated the dangers of the newly liberalized financial markets. Built upon prior informal exchanges of banking supervisors in the European Community,[1] this committee brought together prudential experts, often employed outside of central banks in supervisory authorities, and foreign exchange experts of central banks (Goodhart 2011, 41). Its focus was on micro-economic questions of a prudential nature, coupling concerns over host- and home-country responsibilities with concerns for a level playing field.[2]

The BCBS was hence dominated by supervisors and their practical concerns, which, as Goodhart points out, meant little to no engagement with the concerns of central banks or economics, with no particular economic theory underlying regulations or actual empirical analysis to better understand its consequences (Goodhart 2011, 195f., 574).[3] Instead, practical issues of a micro-prudential nature dominated the group, based on surveys regarding existing practices. As such, the group focused on payment and settlement systems and the responsibilities of host- and home-country regulators and supervisors in this new, more complex world of banking. These concerns and the pragmatic approach at the same time were the strength of the group, leading to the two greatest achievements of the BCBS, the Concordat (1975) and the Basel Accords (1988). But they were also the reasons why they rejected the macro-prudential approach, as we will see shortly.

This comparison shows that the concerns and foci of these two groups, facing the consequences of globalizing capital flows and increasing interconnectedness that characterized the post-Bretton Woods era (Helleiner 1994), diverged, with the groups reacting to similar problems from distinctly different angles. On the one hand, the increasing cross-border activities of banks raised issues of

---

[1] "La groupe de contacte," established in 1972.
[2] Initially set up to develop an early warning system for international financial crises by the central bank governors at the G10, the committee quickly disavowed this task after a few attempts (Goodhart 2011, 129, 141) and instead worked on practical supervisory problems.
[3] Goodhart, himself an economist who had attempted an economic critique of Basel II that was largely ignored, is certainly a biased observer. And even he acknowledges that the mainstream financial economics pre-crisis did not really have much to offer to regulators, a situation that changed post-crisis.

controlling credit extension domestically and the need for lender-of-last-resort actions by central banks for foreign banks (Konings 2009). On the other hand, the increased presence of foreign banks in domestic territory and the financial stability implications this implied raised questions about how to treat these entities in terms of national regulation and supervision. These different preoccupations also emerged from the different composition in terms of membership and professional preoccupations, where the BCBS group consisted of delegates from ministries of finance and supervisory agencies, focusing on the safety of individual banks. The Euro-Currency Standing Group, on the other hand, was manned by central bankers concerned over monetary policy and the lender-of-last-resort function of central banks, performing macro-analyses of changes to the financial system regarding these risks (Braun et al. 2021).

The Struggle over the Jurisdiction of How to Achieve Financial Stability

This difference in set-up and composition led almost from the beginning to struggles over jurisdictional authority, as different viewpoints arising from these different strands of financial expertise clashed. This began in the late 1970s, when the chair of the Euro-Currency Standing Group, Alexandre Lamfalussy, after studying the growth of international bank lending, started to push for an increasing focus on funding risks and hence the market as a whole rather than individual banks (see Maes 2009; Clement 2010). The Standing Group thus suggested imposing increased capital weights for international lending as well as forcing banks to increase their provisions for non-defaulting loans (Goodhart 2011, 138f.).

The BCBS, which was working in parallel on the harmonization of international banking regulation, was discussing this idea but opposed the public communication of these macro-prudential measures, thereby preventing its public recommendation (Clement 2010, 60). As Goodhart puts it, the BCBS "effectively killed off" the two proposals of the Euro-Currency Standing Group, pointing to the lack "of sound prudential reasons" for such measures that would "pose problems of conflict between macro-economic and prudential aims" (Goodhart 2011, 138f.). This clash already foreshadowed the cleavage between the two groups in the coming decades.

Because of this oppression of the work of the Standing Group, it was only in 1986 that the concept "macro-prudential regulation" was first mentioned in an official document, the work on which was initiated by the Euro-Currency Standing Committee (Clement 2010; Goodhart 2011, 353). In the report of a study group instituted by the Central Banks of the Group of Ten at the BIS, which was called "Recent Innovations in international banking" (also known as the Cross Report), macro-prudential regulation is first mentioned as "the safety and soundness of the broad financial system and payments mechanism" (CGFS 1986, 2). The report notes the increasing use of derivatives and off-balance-sheet business to problematize the increasing interlinkages and lack of transparency these trends bring about. Seeking to clearly distinguish itself from the micro-prudential work of the Basel Committee on the same issues happening at the same time, the report avoids drawing conclusions for micro-prudential rules and instead seeks to develop a macro-prudential rationale for regulation and to assess the implications of these trends for monetary policy (Goodhart 2011, 353). In this vein, the report notices the increasing entanglement of banks and capital markets and the potentially grave consequence of interlinkages and risks of contagion, also aggravated by off-balance-sheet activities in financial markets. It was hence asking whether, in order to protect the financial system and the payment functions it exerts, an expansion of regulation to quasi-banks and other financial institutions might be necessary (CGFS 1986, 240f.).

This stance explicitly criticized a narrow view on banking supervision and regulation, which only focuses on protecting deposits of individual banks rather than the financial system as a whole (CGFS 1986). Instead, concerns by the Euro-Currency Standing Committee (ECSC) were based on the macroeconomic view of the crucial importance of banks in the financial system, "being based not only on their deposit-taking and payment activities, but also on their role as a backstop source of liquidity and as channels through which the conduct of monetary and credit policy is conducted" (CGFS 1986, 240f.). Based on this importance, a rationale for macro-prudential regulation was derived that includes "protection against development of systemic risks and limiting the degree of moral hazard risks to central banks arising from the safety nets." The report was hence motivated by a concern over central banks' lender-of-last-resort function in the context of the increasing entanglement of banks and capital markets.

Similar concerns were also present among central bankers within the BCBS, yet they were deemed outside of the supervisory remit of the Committee, which instead focused on the proper inclusion of off-balance-sheet exposure of banks in terms of capital requirements (a micro-prudential response; see Goodhart 2011, 354ff.).

The fact that the BCBS veered in the direction of prudential supervision rather than larger central bank concerns can be clearly seen in the evaluation of new banking practices in the late 1980s. When the BCBS prepared for a dialogue with the International Organization of Securities Commissions in 1988, the BCBS initially expressed a strong interest in the "systemic or macro-prudential issues arising from the process of securitisation, such as questions relating to the lender of last resort." However, they then

agreed that the systemic issues, while of great importance to the central-bank members of the committee in particular, are not particularly supervisory in nature, and that they should not be the particular focus of any initial discussions with securities regulators. In its own work, of course, the Committee will continue to bear them in mind, particularly the question of settlement risk. (Notes of the Working Party, 1988, as printed in Goodhart 2011, 481)

Hence, while these concerns over the ongoing entanglement of banks and capital markets were present in the BCBS, they were persistently suppressed by its main concern for harmonizing the micro-prudential supervision of banks.

This continued exclusion of macro-prudential concerns from the focus of the BCBS became consequential, as the BCBS rose in importance during the 1980s, moving from a committee seeking to exchange on best supervisory practices to a body seeking to engender a harmonization of practices by proposing global rules for international banks, a goal it achieved with the conclusion of the first Basel Accord in 1988 (Kapstein 1992). This rising importance of the BCBS in global banking regulation also strengthened the claims of the BCBS to the jurisdiction over prudential concerns at a global level, keeping a close eye on any interventions by the Euro-Currency Standing Committee or the BIS in prudential matters.

A particularly pertinent example of this can be found in the notes the chairman of the BCBS in 1994, Tommaso Padoa-Schioppa, made following a meeting he had with the Euro-Currency Standing Committee, where he stated, "I made the point that in areas where so-called macro and micro-prudential issues may overlap proposals should not be brought to the Governors unless agreed with the Basle Committee" (as cited in Goodhart 2011, 466f.). Similarly, in frank exchanges between the BIS and the BCBS on matters of prudential regulation in 1996, the BCBS told the BIS staff (Andrew Crockett and William White) who wanted to publish studies on (macro-) prudential questions that they could not communicate these ideas because of the possibility that people might infer that they reflect the thinking of the BCBS, thereby constraining the latter's actions (Goodhart 2011, 468). Concerned over its freedom of action, the BCBS kept macro-prudential concerns of the central banking community at bay, in particular regarding the increasing capital market activities of banks, which was fueling both the expansion of credit and the vulnerabilities of the banking system to sudden liquidity shocks, halting the discussions on their implication for the regulation of the financial system during the late 1980s and early 1990s.

The Rising Complexity of Bank–Capital Market Interactions

The jurisdictional struggle over the character of prudential regulation in the context of changing banking practices was hence largely won by the BCBS in the 1990s, as it arduously defended its claim to prudential regulation and supervision against any intrusion both by the Euro-Currency Standing Committee and the BIS. At the same time that the BCBS kept the expression of these macro-prudential concerns over the increasing integration of banks and capital markets at bay, the BCBS itself had to get to grips with its regulatory implications. Following complaints by the large banks about the clumsiness of its initial capital risk weightings, which operated in three simple risk buckets, the BCBS deemed it necessary to update banking regulation to reflect the modalities of this engagement. In particular, the initial framework Basel I, based on three conventional buckets of risks and risk weighting used, for example, by the Dutch Central Bank, had been fueling regulatory arbitrage reaction by banks, in turn furthering the engagement with wholesale financial markets (Gabor 2016b; Gabor and Vestergaard 2016; Thiemann 2018).[4]

---

[4] This practice in particular regarded securitization (offloading credit risks of assets into financial markets) but also the use of repo-markets as refinancing their activities cheaply and outside of the constraints of central bank reserves (Gabor 2016b; Gabor and Vestergaard 2016).

To properly reflect the risks banks took in financial markets, the BCBS proposed to undertake an amendment to these risk buckets for market risks. When publishing the consultative paper on market risk in 1994, however, the BCBS had to realize that its proposals were not at the level of international banks' internal risk models, harming their epistemic authority (Tsingou 2004; Goodhart 2011). With no help forthcoming from securities regulators, which were refusing to collaborate on capital standards for investment houses, the BCBS realized that it was out of its depth in terms of expertise. In response, it set up an internal risk model task force in 1994 and embraced private banks' expertise to get to grips with these latest technical developments (Goodhart 2011, 414ff.). This new tactic led to cooperation with large international banks; in particular, their largest lobby group, the Institute for International Finance, in the mid-1990s, with the BCBS endorsing full cooperation in 1996, the moment that the Market Risk Amendment was published (Tsingou 2004, 2015; Goodhart 2011, 414f.). This embrace of the new risk modelling techniques developed by large internationally active banks then set the path for the revisions of Basel II, whereby a coalition of supervisors, private finance and academia worked on incorporating advanced private risk management practices into the heart of global banking regulations (Tsingou 2015; Seabrooke and Tsingou 2021).

The mid-1990s thus witnessed the formation of a powerful hinge between private banks and their risk management professionals, banking supervisors and academics that supported the micro-prudential approach to banking regulation, which had at its center banks' risk management systems (Seabrooke and Tsingou 2009). Enamored with advanced risk management systems, which were seen as superior to public capabilities and infused with the idea of the beneficial effects of credit risk transfers, this expert network was dominating the debate, much superior to the macro-prudential network because of its internal coherency and external support. It was further strengthened by the weakening of the grip of central banks over banking supervision, as central banks either lost control over banking supervision (such as the Bank of England in 1997) or were founded without any supervisory responsibilities (such as the European Central Bank [ECB] in 1999). Effectively upending the "single composite" of monetary policy, financial stability and banking supervision that was located at central banks, these developments were leading to the question whether financial stability, "the land in between," was still a responsibility of central banks (Padoa-Schioppa 2003, 270).

The Formation of a Central Bank Community Debating the Measurement of Systemic Risk

This hinge based on modern risk management practices, however, was not simply embraced in an uncritical manner in the central banking community. Instead, it fueled a sustained debate about issues of systemic risk, linked to an increasing worry among technocratic economists within central banks about the systemic consequences of the increasing fusion of wholesale financial markets and banks, which was concentrated in the Euro-Currency Standing Committee (cf. CGFS 1995). This worry, which centered on the increasing engagement of banks with derivative markets, often using over-the-counter products, and the increasing links it created between banks, was first expressed in a report from the Euro-Currency Standing Committee working on "Recent Developments in International Interbank Relations" (known as the Promisel Report; CGFS 1992).

Tasked by the G10 central bank governors with investigating these developments, the group noted the increasing fusion between interbank and wholesale markets, the increasing concentration among very few players and the heightened systemic risks this might bring about (CGFS 1992, 19). Strikingly, the report also notes, based on interview data, the widely held belief by market participants that central banks would quell any financial instability before it reached systemic proportions, a conviction generally deemed beneficial by market participants for the stability of financial markets (CGFS 1992). Based on these findings, the report expressed the need for much better data collection but also "a deepening and broadening of collective understanding of these markets" (CGFS 1992, 39). It was clear to this expert network that central bank expertise needed an update in the light of these developments with respect to derivatives markets and their consequences for financial stability, seeking to also involve private sector expertise (CGFS 1992).

The final report of the Euro-Currency Standing Committee focusing on the financial stability implications of this development was called "Issues of Measurement Related to Market Size and Macroprudential Risks in Derivatives Markets" (known as the Brockmeijer Report; CGFS 1995). This report made the "macroprudential concerns" of the central banking community with respect to the in-transparent derivatives markets very explicit (CGFS 1995, 2), seeking to bring about a harmonized collection of data at the international level that would allow central bankers to better understand the financial stability risks building up in derivatives markets. In addition, the question arose whether these developments did not require a new monitoring apparatus of systemic risks on the side of central banks, as central banks were acting as the lender of last resort for this system (CGFS 1995, 3). Engaging in such efforts, the report was not, however, able to come up with a unified framework for measuring the systemic consequences of these developments for financial stability. For this reason, the Euro-Currency Standing Committee suggested "*that central banks support further research in this field through collaborative efforts*" (CGFS 1995, 4; emphasis mine). By involving both collaborative central bank research and interaction with academics and private risk managers on these topics, the hope was to generate such measures.

In order to engender such collaboration on the definition and measurement of systemic risks arising from this fusion of banks and wholesale financial markets, the CGFS suggested to finance conferences on these themes at central banks (CGFS 1995). The most visible of these central bank-sponsored encounters occurred in the "triannual conferences on risk management and systemic risk," which were set up in response to this call for central bank collaboration by the Euro-Currency Standing Group (Board of Governors 1996, 10) and held from 1995 until 2005 at four different central banks (Federal Reserve, Bank of Japan, BIS, ECB). The conference proceedings of these conferences, which were held in collaboration with the Euro-Currency Standing Group, provide a good understanding of the evolution of these concerns and the systemic risk thinking, which, as we will see, were shaped as much by real-life events as by advances in theory.[5]

---

[5] The notion of systemic risk in the context of the financial system was not created at that moment in time. Instead, Ozgode's insightful analysis of the rise of the concept "systemic risk" suggests it originated in the late 1970s to justify the use of the Emergency Credit Assistance program of the Federal Reserve to protect the economy from liquidity crunches (Ozgode 2022, 21f.). He hence suggests that "systemic risk" as a concept was invented by the Federal Reserve to shield its persistent interventions from criticism by the public, pointing to the dangers of chain reactions in money markets, which could lead to the unraveling of the financial system. Based on this notion, the Federal Reserve had already pursued several interventions since the 1970s to stabilize money markets in pursuit of larger financial stability, justifying them by the goal of "diminishing the systemic risks faced by capital markets" and its implication for banks (Brimmer 1989, 15; Ozgode 2022). This system of ex post containment, which was accompanied by the ex ante reduction of some vulnerabilities, mainly in payment systems, was to be strained by the increasing mixing of banks and financial markets from the 1980s onwards.

The Struggle to Conceptualize and Measure Systemic Risks Pre-crisis

The ambivalence of the central banking community regarding the increasing engagement of banks with wholesale financial markets and the connected increase in the leverage of the financial system is well captured in Alan Greenspan's luncheon address at the first triannual conference on risk measurement and systemic risk in November 1995. In this speech, Greenspan reflects on the "catastrophic financial insurance coverage" central banks provide to leveraged financial markets (Greenspan 1996), which, according to him, is the cost a society has to pay "to operate a leveraged financial system" that contributes positively to economic growth (Greenspan 1996, 4). As central banks were the only ones able to stem panics that threatened the unraveling of such a system, the proper measurement of systemic risk was seen to be of primary importance for central banks in order to inform their lender-of-last-resort policies.

However, this new risk management task for central banks, directly linked to their lender-of-last-resort function, was seen as distinct from private risk management systems. As Greenspan put it, "With central banks taking on the risks of serving as lenders of last resort, research on financial risk that is done by central banks properly places disproportionate focus on the most extreme outcomes. Conversely, financial risk analysis in the private sector rationally concentrates on outcomes other than the most extreme" (Greenspan 1996, 5). Hence, while "the concerns of central banks and the private financial community generally intersect in a preoccupation with the analysis of risk in general and in an interest in the development of risk management models" (Greenspan 1996, 5), their particular focus differs. For central bankers, the "characterization of the distribution of extreme values" on the left-hand side of the distribution, known as the left tail of the distribution, is "of paramount concern" (Greenspan 1996, 6) as it serves both to guide lender-of-last-resort policies and to inform structural and policy changes to reduce systemic risks. And yet, to Greenspan, this exercise in risk management of the tail distribution faced a fundamental problem of definition. As Greenspan pointed out, while "it would be useful to central banks to be able to measure systemic risk accurately ... its very definition is still somewhat unsettled." This is why, "until we have a common theoretical paradigm for the causes of systemic stress, any consensus on how to measure systemic risk will be difficult to achieve" (Greenspan 1996, 7).

In line with this lacking theoretical paradigm of systemic risk, this first conference, which mentioned the monitoring of global systemic risk as a particular goal, featured an "eclectic and wide ranging collection of topics covered in the program" (Board of Governors of the Federal Reserve System 1995, 1). Summarizing the state of research on these issues in the second luncheon address of the event, Charles Taylor, head of the G30, a body of industry experts and former central bankers, pointed to the lack of maturity in this area of research. In the speech, he notes the large chasm between highly abstract academic research and central bank practitioners' worries, which fuels central bankers' own policy-related investigations regarding this issue. With respect to the latter, he lauds the "incremental" research undertaken by practitioners at the BIS and other bodies as rich in institutional detail, but then points to its largely atheoretical nature as a serious drawback (Taylor 1996, 19). On the other hand, he described the academic research, with its assumption of homogeneous agents operating in equilibrium, as largely incapable of addressing issues of systemic risk, which by their very nature are driven by disequilibrium and heterogeneous agents (Taylor 1996, 18).

To him, this chasm between practitioners' worries and academic research, which was to characterize the next decade, was furthered by the low incidence of systemic events, which made the analyses of system behavior in normal times largely useless for such considerations. Furthermore, he pointed to the rapid evolution of the system, which meant that it was likely that systemic risks would migrate and mutate before research could identify them, which was the cause of much worry in the central banking community. He nevertheless expressed hope for a confluence of research at the intersection of academic and the central banking community, similar to that experienced regarding the area of micro-level risk management. As he stated, a "similar confluence of factors could be about to launch a similar flowering in our understanding of financial risk at a systemic level: global financial integration, new theoretical insights, yet more raw computer power and the increasingly urgent need for policymakers to address systemic issues" (Taylor 1996, 23).

The interventions by Taylor and others at the conference clarify the early conceptual stages of the work on systemic risk at this moment in time – an almost embryonic status. The contrast with the other hinge that had developed with respect to the possibilities for general risk management, which had brought together academics, regulators and private industry, was particularly stark. And yet, despite this difficulty to grasp issues of systemic risk, practicing central bankers at this conference, such as Iwao Kuroda from the Bank of Japan (BoJ), insisted on the very existence of systemic risks and the necessity for central bankers to face them, a feat they had achieved in the past and that required more work on this issue, despite the insistence of academics that systemic risks were reduced by the better distribution of risks with the help of new tools for risk management.

The cautious ambivalence over the risks of contagion and market illiquidity would transform into a stance of much greater concern at the next triannual conference at the BoJ in fall 1998, a conference that was marked by the East Asian financial crisis in 1997 and its reverberations in Japan. In this context, BoJ president Masaaki Shirakawa (Japan), when introducing the conference, emphasized the need for more research on liquidity risks and contagion to face these real-world events. What one can observe at this conference is a deeply unsettled epistemic community of central bankers who are looking for models to help them grapple with these developments. Taking into account the volatility of financial markets and their spillovers into the real economy, as well as the micro-structure of financial markets, the discussion sought to come to terms with the observed "wobbly" nature of financial markets in a way that would allow these events to be accommodated by economic models of financial markets. Along these lines, the academic Kenneth Singleton at the end of the conference made a call for more research that is able to model the observed dynamics "and that draws out the potential roles for policy action" (Bank of Japan 1998, 16).

In this struggle to gain theoretical orientation for policy action, the fight over how systemic risk should be conceptualized and understood was central. It was hence no coincidence that the conference began with a paper seeking to provide a general definition of systemic risk as a negative externality (Bandt and Hartmann 1998, published as Bandt and Hartmann 2000), a crucial contribution in the early discourse on systemic risk (Thiemann et al. 2018b). It was immediately attacked by its discussant, the economist Jeffrey Lacker from the Federal Reserve, for its undue boldness of proposing such a definition. As Lacker put it, "a definition of systemic risk should not be put forth unless one has complete and well-articulated models that display systemic risk." He then argued that "advancement of knowledge can only be achieved by one of the two following methods: one is to seek plausible models which display the same empirically observed phenomenon, and the other is to seek the phenomenon which has been identified by the theoretical models" (Bank of Japan 1998, 1). In this view, models were seen as the "obligatory passage point" (Callon 1986) to make any claims regarding the real world, whereby definitions needed to be validated by theoretical models.[6]

This debate at the conference over the definition of "systemic risk" thus shows the strong orientation toward formal economics by a significant bloc of actors in the regulatory space. In particular, the Federal Reserve economists attending were engaging in boundary work (Gieryn 1983), policing what could count as sound regulatory science. They were insisting on the need to have a model that could explain issues of systemic risk before one could even proceed to define it. And yet, despite this very cautious stance, empirical events were requiring theoretical clarification. It is in this sense that at the same event, other conference participants were seeking to process the Japanese experience of the East Asian financial crisis, pointing to institutional specificities of different national financial systems that have a particular impact upon crises and how they unfold. The practical experience of central bankers, which were caught by surprise by the unfolding financial instability, which could not be accommodated in financial models, had an increasing presence in this conference in 1998 compared to the first one in 1995.

The East Asian Financial Crisis and the Strengthening of the Macro-Prudential Network of Expertise

It was in fact this real-life event that would bring about a reconfiguration of the regulatory debate, leading to a much more sustained discussion of systemic risks and how to control them through macro-prudential regulation among central banks and international organizations. Overall, the unfolding financial instability in the 1990s did

---

[6] For similar findings on the general discourse on banking regulation and systemic risk at that time, see Thiemann et al. (2018a).

a lot to vindicate the preoccupation of the central banking community with these macro-prudential concerns linked to large internationally active banks. Starting with the failure of Barings Bank in 1992, the Mexican peso crisis in 1995, the East Asian financial crisis in 1997 and the linked financial crisis in Russia in 1998, which led to the near collapse of the highly leveraged hedge fund Long Term Capital Management (LTCM), events were pointing to the risks of increasing interconnectedness. This heightened occurrence of bouts of instability led to an explicit institutionalization of these concerns at central banks and international organization in the second half of the 1990s, strengthening the growing macro-prudential expert network.[7]

The rising practical importance of macro-prudential concerns over financial instability after the East Asian financial crisis was reflected in the reorientation of the Euro-Currency Standing Committee. Renamed as the Committee for the Global Financial System (CGFS) in February 1999, it received a revised mandate, its goal now being to provide policy analysis to "support the central banks in the fulfilment of their responsibilities for monetary and financial stability."[8] This expansion of macro-prudential analysis was further supported by the reaction of the International Monetary Fund (IMF) to the East Asian financial crisis in 1997, with the IMF for the first time employing the language of macro-prudential regulation in January 1998 (Clement 2010, 63) and engaging from 1999 onwards in the development of a policy

---

[7] A first effect of these bouts of instability was the institutional anchoring of increased intellectual efforts within central banks, with the Bank of England in 1996 becoming the first central bank to publish a quarterly financial stability report. Following the recommendations of its new chief economist, Mervyn King, who insisted that securing financial stability was the second main function of central banks next to monetary policy, the economic staff of the bank analytically engaged the risks from new bank practices (Acosta et al. 2020). While the Bank of England would lose its supervisory mandate the next year, relegating the concern over financial stability to second rank (Acosta et al. 2020), the practice of financial stability reports would diffuse in the coming ten years, rising from one to forty central banks from 1996 to 2005 (Osterloo et al. 2007, 340), a crucial event for their diffusion being the East Asian crisis that unfolded from 1997 onwards.

[8] In the coming years, the committee was discussing, inter alia, credit risk transfer mechanisms (CGFS 2003) and the subprime housing market in the USA (CGFS 2006). In that sense, the "analysis of problems was there; what was missing was regulatory action" (interview, Bundesbank, July 22, 2016).

program of macro-prudential analysis for its Financial Sector Assessment Program (Sundarajan 2002, 1).[9]

This work received additional institutional support when, as a response to the East Asian financial crisis and the near collapse of LTCM (Clarke 2014, 197), the G7 agreed in 1999 to set up the Financial Stability Forum (FSF). This forum, which was to be located at the BIS, was envisioned by Bundesbank president Hans Tietmeyer, charged by the G7 to set up this forum. In his report to that group, Tietmeyer named the "identification of incipient vulnerabilities and concerted efforts to mitigate systemic risk" (Tietmeyer 1999, 4) as the most important shortcoming of the current supervisory structure of the global financial architecture. The report hence called for the development of early macro-warning indicators and the pooling of data available at international financial institutions (IFIs) "in order to overcome the separate treatment of micro-prudential and macro-prudential issues" (Tietmeyer 1999, 3). To effectively integrate these macro-prudential concerns, Tietmeyer suggested a body whose inner core would be formed by the international organizations (IMF, the World Bank, BIS, the International Organization of Securities Commissions, BCBS and the International Association of Insurance Supervisors) that were to be endowed with decision-making powers at the global level.

However, the USA refused to hand over any regulatory powers and instead shifted the set-up of the FSF to a mere discussion forum, focusing on the improvement of emerging markets financial market governance (Reisenbichler 2015, 1013). Set up in April 1999, the FSF hence only had the function to serve as a discussion forum for best standards, bringing together central bankers, finance ministries and regulators of the member states, in addition to the IFIs and international standard-setting bodies. While the forum did not deliver on any early warning measures of incipient vulnerabilities or provide any visible integration of micro- and macro-prudential concerns in its work until 2007, it nevertheless proved to be a forum of exchange, where several of the incipient vulnerabilities, such as the housing boom in the USA and information asymmetries regarding credit risk transfers, were discussed

---

[9] As Sundarajan et al. from the IMF put it, "A broad search for tools and techniques to detect and prevent financial crises was prompted by the international financial turmoil of the late 1990s. More recent episodes of instability have further highlighted the importance of continuous monitoring of financial systems as a crisis prevention tool" (Sundarajan et al. 2002, 1).

before the financial crisis (Blustein 2012). Its inauguration would also provide an opportunity for the group of macro-prudential thinkers at the BIS to publicly challenge the procyclical aspects of the incipient Basel II regulations and push for a macro-prudential approach that would take heed of the cyclical risks inherent in financial systems.

Cyclical Macro-Prudential Concerns Come to the Fore

Andrew Crockett, chair of the BIS from 1994 to 2003, and from 1999 onwards also the first chair of the FSF, used the new-found prominence of the macro-prudential discourse to challenge the BCBS's work on Basel II, which by June 1999 had generated a first proposal to replace Basel I. Crockett did so first in private, writing a letter to the head of the BCBS in October 1999 pointing to the dangers of procyclical capital standards and the possibility of countering these tendencies through countercyclical capital weights. The response in March 2000 from the BCBS clarified that while these concerns were noted, they were not taken seriously. Rather, as summarized by Baker (2020, 144), the BCBS emphasized that "the softening of market discipline and the resulting moral hazard implied by a countercyclical framework was a far greater danger. At this point, the BCBS essentially opposed a countercyclical capital regime and instead focused on incentives facing individual institutions, rather than systemic patterns that might induce financial instability."

Following up on this exchange and emboldened by the recent shift in the global discourse on the need for macro-prudential regulation, Crockett publicly doubled down on the macro-prudential approach in 2000, giving several speeches on the theme. He did so most notably in the speech "Marrying the Micro- and Macro-Prudential Approach" in September in front of the Eleventh International Conference of Banking Supervisors held in Basel (Crockett 2000),[10] where he spelled out the principles of macro-prudential regulation in his view. Doing so, he introduced the concept of the financial cycle as the focal point of macro-prudential regulation.

---

[10] Later recollections by policy makers, such as Tarullo would argue that it was this speech which put macro-prudential regulation on the policy agenda (Tarullo 2013b).

Described as wasteful in the upswing (when surging asset prices feed and are fed by credit expansion) and painful in the downswing, the problem with financial cycles, according to him, was that they are evident only ex post to micro-prudential risk management systems of banks (Crockett 2000, 6). Individual market agents, he argued, could only evaluate differential but not overall risks related to the financial cycle, providing the basis for a clear mandate for macro-prudential regulators to mitigate the financial cycle. As he famously stated,

In terms of the measurement and mitigation of risk over time, *the key challenge is to take better account of the financial cycle that underlies financial instability.* If risk increases in upswings and materialises in recessions, it stands to reason *that defences should be built up in upswings so as to be relied upon when the rough times arrive.* This would strengthen institutions' ability to weather deteriorating economic conditions, when access to external financing becomes more costly and constrained. *Moreover, by leaning against the wind, it could reduce the amplitude of the financial cycle, thereby limiting the risk of financial distress in the first place.* (Crockett 2000, 6; emphasis mine)

Such programmatic pronouncements were followed up by work from the in-house economists at the BIS, seeking to measure and operationalize the notion of the financial cycle (Borio et al. 2001; Borio 2003a), suggesting indicators for it as well as potential mitigating policy tools (Borio and Lowe 2002). In this quest, they sought to develop an encompassing policy framework to mitigate systemic risks, pointing to interventions both in the cross-sectional dimension of systemic risk and the time dimension. Their focus was on the procyclical character of private risk management systems, which focused only on relative risk, not on absolute risk, and implicitly assumed that risks go down during booms and up during busts. This means that financial market participants are likely to get absolute risks wrong, leading to a procyclical financial system (Borio et al. 2001). Notable about their interventions at that point in time is how cautiously they themselves treat the notion of the financial cycle, pointing out that their policy measures still applied if the concept of the endogenous financial cycle was rejected. Their data merely "suggests" these things, and their "slightly more formal treatment of basic hypotheses" (Borio and Lowe 2002, 5) is a simple logical exposition of the argument, with a few flow charts to suggest these trends. However, without a single formula, much less a model, the impact of these interventions on the overall regulatory discourse was severely hampered (interview, former high-ranking Bundesbank official, August 19, 2014). Nevertheless, the BIS would continue its push for such a cyclical perception of the financial system in the years to come, holding conferences on the topic (e.g. BIS 2001). Fittingly, the next triannual conference on risk measurement and systemic risk in 2002 took place at the BIS, organized on behalf of the CGFS. Influenced by the banking and currency crises of the preceding years, the conference laid particular emphasis on the discussion of sources of financial instability and how to prevent stress in financial markets from becoming systemic. In the introduction to the conference, Crockett emphasized the evolution of thinking about systemic risk in the context of the East Asian financial crisis and the liquidity and contagion risks it laid bare, postulating a "new focus on market liquidity risks, contagion across regions and sources of banking crises" (Crockett 2002, 1).[11] The biggest advance to Crockett, however, was that

risk is now seen as endogenous. The environment is not given, but is the product of actions of individual agents. As a result, systemic stability is critically determined by the collective behaviour of individual market players. Under this "new view," strategies of market participants, including policymakers and regulators, need to take account of any feedback of their collective actions on the conditions under which individual market participants operate. (Crockett 2002, 2)

Linking these insights to the "game-theoretic contributions of recent years,"[12] Crockett points to the mismatch between locally rational action and their potential to aggravate systemic outcomes. Expanding on such deleterious macro-consequences derived from rational micro-action, Crockett points in particular to the potential systemic consequences of value-at-risk models, which could lead to fire-sale dynamics

---

[11] "In his remarks at the first joint conference in 1995, Alan Greenspan referred to risk measurement and systemic risk as parts of a newly evolving area of research in finance and economics. He foresaw that such research would influence the way business would be done in both the private and public sectors. Research on risk measurement-related issues indeed strongly influenced the character of regulatory and policy initiatives as well as of industry practice during recent years" (Crockett 2002, 1).

[12] Crockett is pointing here to research on strategic action by actors under limited information, for example situations of noisy signals, which could lead to herd behavior (see Morris and Shin 2003), a theme followed up at the conference itself.

as market participants seek "to cut exposures as market prices fall to match their 'value-at-risk' to their diminished capital position," leading to further market price decline "and a vicious circle that could end in a drying-up of market liquidity and a spreading of financial stress" (Crockett 2002, 3). He ends his speech with a call for more research into these market interactions in times of crises, where the "focus, of course, is on the practical implications, for both financial regulators and market practitioners, of such research." Practical implications of research efforts were hence the primary goal of Crockett and the macro-prudential thought collective at large.

Based on the conference papers and the reported discussions at this conference, we can observe an epistemic community in the process of expanding the understanding of systemic risk from a focus on individual institutions and the deleterious consequences of their failures to include market structures and market interactions (Yamaguchi 2002). Participants continued the search for models that might help them to understand contagion dynamics in financial markets, which at that point in time had come to the center of systemic risk discussions (BIS 2002, 3). However, despite recent advances in endogenizing the sources of the spreading of disturbances,[13] no paper on financial cycles or their monitoring is presented. Hence, while many papers are "paying attention to what creates stress and how stress is contagious" in the short term (Yamaguchi 2002 in BIS 2002, 17), none of the papers embraces the concept of the financial cycle that sought to endogenize systemic risk as a conceptual feature of the financial system.

This new concept of the financial cycle that Crockett sought to promulgate instead found its clearest programmatic expression through the work of Claudio Borio at the BIS (cf. Borio 2003b). Critical of the dominant way of seeing systemic risks prevalent in mainstream academia and the central banking community at the time, Borio sought to outline a new vision. Distinguishing the "cross-sectional dimension of risk" (across industries and financial institutions) and the "time dimension of risk" (e.g. amplification mechanisms, cyclical elements based on the endogeneity of risk), he claimed that the then dominant systemic risk thinking was mostly cross-sectional with a

---

[13] In this respect, a new model by Allen and Gale (1998) that endogenized fire-sale dynamics in financial markets was celebrated as a strong advancement beyond the classical Diamond and Dybvig (1983, 1ff.) model of banking, which could only model the dynamics of bank-runs caused by depositors' cash withdrawal.

very limited intertemporal dimension that focused only on the impact of exogenous shocks on the system. This static conception led to a micro-prudential focus on the resilience of individual firms to withstand sudden, unexpected short-term shocks and a willingness to reduce second-round effects by limiting interconnectedness and contagion (Borio 2003b, 5).

In contrast, his proposed "new systemic risk thinking" took a fundamentally different vantage point. Stemming from Hyman Minsky's "Financial Instability Hypothesis" (Minsky 1977), systemic risk here is understood to grow endogenously in the financial system over time. Instability or the system's vulnerabilities seen on a longer time scale, then, become far less static and turn from something external to a variable that builds up over time. Systemic risk thereby becomes an inevitable feature of the system, a genuinely endogenous element of the financial system – "[t]he boom sows the seeds of the subsequent bust" (Borio 2003b, 7). Rather than focusing on short-term problems of individual banks linked to illiquidity, his suggested focus is on "instances ... where systemic risk arises primarily through *common exposures* to macroeconomic risk factors across institutions" (Borio 2003b, 6; italics in original). The focus is hence not on individual institutions but on the cyclical tendencies of the system. It is this understanding of the relevance of time and, ultimately, cyclicality that, according to Borio, the new "macroprudential perspective comes into its own" (2003b, 11).

The concept of a financial cycle thereby directly and fundamentally opposed the then dominant regulatory paradigm in that it urged regulators to move away from a micro-level approach and toward the premise that there are effects on the macro level that warrant a different approach to regulation. In this "new view," vulnerabilities and risks were seen to continuously build up over time as the cycle progresses. While conceptual thinkers at the IMF (cf. Schinasi 2004) were pointing in the same direction, emphasizing the need to integrate the endogenous capacity of financial markets to create systemic risks (Schinasi 2004, 11), economics was of little help in this endeavor as the analysis of financial stability was still in "its infant stage" (Schinasi 2004, 5). This fact can well be observed during the fourth and last triannual conference on risk measurement and systemic risk, which took place at the ECB in November 2005.

A Community between Doubt and Admiration

At this meeting, the ambivalence of the central banking community regarding financial innovations was once more on full display, nurtured by bouts of financial instability. Financial innovation, liberalization and development, by completing markets and improving risk-sharing opportunities, should be good news for financial stability, yet the markets showed signs of instability, leading to the bigger questions of whether these trends might or might not increase resilience. The biggest worry was that the financial system itself had changed in the course of these innovations, giving greater importance to non-banks and market liquidity. This could pose contagion problems, which might be aggravated by recent tools to transfer credit risks. As the summary of the conference put it: "Against this background, the aim of this conference was to provide a comprehensive analysis of current developments in risk measurement and systemic risk with a particular emphasis on the effect of new financial instruments and non-bank financial institutions" (ECB 2007, 1).

A critical perspective on these developments was provided in the dinner speech by Andre Icard, deputy general manager of the BIS and former member of the Committee on the Global Financial System, who reflected upon the transformations of financial markets and systemic risks over the course of his career (ECB 2007, 23). He points out that while in the 1980s, systemic risk was synonymous with the default of single institutions, systemic risks were now seen to have migrated outside of the banking system. As he states,

> The consensus view, therefore, is that systemic disturbances are now more likely than in the past to erupt outside the international banking system and to spread through market linkages rather than lending relationships. … The concept of systemic risk has thus been broadened along several dimensions: (1) it has come to explicitly include non-banks along with banks; (2) the concept has moved beyond traditional lending to include all sorts of financial activities and resulting exposures … while (3) the focus is now firmly on interdependencies between market participants as well as their exposures to common risk factors, including institutions' reliance on core parts of market infrastructure. (Icard 2005, 28)

This summary describes well the broadening of the concept of systemic risks from 1995 to 2005, which now included non-banks, non-lending activities by banks and the interdependencies between market participants and critical market infrastructure this creates.

This analytical focus was driven by recent market developments in risk transfer markets and the worries they raised. In line with these concerns, Lucrezia Reichlin, the director of research at the ECB and organizer of the conference, in her concluding speech points to the "pricing, trading and transfer of credit risk, particularly through so-called structured products, as an area that deserves particular attention" (Reichlin 2007, 2). Further research is needed, she argued, as "central banks need to have a deep understanding of vulnerabilities in banking, in particular credit risk, and other parts of the financial system that could lead to a systemic crisis" (Reichlin 2007, 4f.). The debates over the implications of these recent financial innovations for systemic risk was hence characterized by worried observations of central bank practitioners, noting the dangers of increasing interconnectedness created by financial innovations, while not holding sufficient tools for measurement or even sufficient data to inquire into these issues.

What also comes to the fore when analyzing the conference proceedings is that, while issues of systemic risk of large banks' engagement with credit risk transfer and the increased interconnectedness of the financial system were primary concerns, the notion of the procyclical developments of the financial system itself was largely avoided by this community of researchers pre-crisis. In Borio's language, the emphasis was on the cross-sectional dimension of systemic risks, with little to no work on the time dimension. This differentiated emphasis would have important implications for the global regulatory agenda in the wake of the Global Financial Crisis, as the next chapter will show.

Conclusion

The warnings voiced by members of the expert network on systemic risk would be validated by the crisis, when first the freezing of liquidity in summer 2007 and subsequently the failure of Lehman Brothers in fall 2008 brought the entire financial system to a halt (Gorton 2009). Risk management systems, rather than making the world a safer place, had indeed made the world riskier. These developments were furthermore linked to the cyclical rise of an asset class, as predicted by Borio (2003b), as a sustained housing boom in the USA from 2000 onwards had come to a halt in 2006, leading to a chain reaction that revealed exactly the fragility of the financial system that the macro-prudential expert community had feared. Created by the interlinkages between banks and capital markets that had become increasingly interwoven, this fragility would require massive interventions by central banks and governments around the world to unclog the financial system.[14] The unfolding chain of crisis events in 2007 and 2008 thereby undermined the position of the expert network that had formed around the hinge of private risk management systems, including the BCBS, and it gave a boost to the community of organizations and professionals that had formed around the notion of systemic risk and macro-prudential regulation. In particular, its organizational position was strengthened as the FSF was upgraded by the G20 to become the Financial Stability Board in 2009 and was given the power not only to coordinate but also to initiate global regulatory initiatives (Pagliari 2013), the installation of a macro-prudential approach being a prime element (see next chapter).

However, if the financial crisis can be understood as the moment of ascendance of macro-prudential thinking into the mainstream of regulatory policymaking (see next chapter), it did so in a rather immature phase. As I have shown, discussions in the network of expertise forming around systemic risk and macro-prudential regulation were still divided on the goals of this particular policy program, as well as suffering from a lack of data and models to properly analyze it. Particularly difficult for this expert network was the inclusion of the financial cycle in models that would allow central bankers to model and observe these dynamics properly (see also the quantitative text analysis in the next chapter). Given this rather embryonic status of macro-prudential thinking, not all technocrats, policymakers and economists were convinced of this new macro-prudential vision of financial regulation, as the next chapters will show. The question that hence arises is if and how far this network of macro-prudential experts managed to place

---

[14] To be clear: every single one of these aspects had been noticed by the critical community of central bankers and international organization economists, and yet few if any had joined the dots. For example, the IMF Global Financial Stability Report in April 2007 noticed the cooling of the US housing market and the deterioration of credit risks, and introduced the reader to the "alphabet soup" of subprime mortgage origination. Furthermore, when weighing the potential for spillover of credit risks, it listed all the possible chains of contagion, a prediction that was to prove highly accurate in the next eighteen months. And yet, at the end, the report states that "major dislocation still appears to be a low probability event" (IMF 2007, 10), revealing the dangers to expertise of estimating probabilities publicly.

their core concepts, such as the financial cycle, at the core of the regulatory agenda and make it acceptable for international regulation. To provide an answer to this question, the next chapter traces the installation of the macro-prudential idea set within the transnational regulatory community during and shortly after the financial crisis, focusing in particular on the fate of countercyclical regulation.

4 | The Selective Rise of Macro-prudential Ideas in the Wake of the Crisis

The rise of macro-prudential thinking to the heights of the regulatory agenda in the immediate aftermath of the crisis of 2007–8 was as sudden as it was unexpected (Baker 2013a; Helleiner 2014). Having largely developed outside of and often in direct opposition to mainstream academic and regulatory thinking, macro-prudential regulation was presented at the G20 summit in April 2009 as the regulatory answer to the glaring regulatory shortcomings revealed by the crisis. Rather than focusing on individual institutions, it was to install a system-wide top-down perspective that sought to limit the chain reactions and feedback loops that had brought the financial system to a standstill in 2008. Macro-prudential thinking was to be transferred from broad-based proposals into concrete regulatory tools, pursuing the two goals macro-prudential regulation had set out for itself: raising the resilience of the financial system and reducing its cyclical character by intervening in the upswing and releasing capital in the downswing (Crockett 2000; Borio 2003b). So confident was Claudio Borio, one of the main proponents of macro-prudential thinking pre-crisis, that, paraphrasing Milton Friedman, he stated in April 2009 that "we are all macroprudentialists now" (Borio 2009).

However, looking at the macro-prudential regulatory changes installed at the international level in the immediate aftermath of the financial crisis casts doubt on this wholehearted embrace of macro-prudential thinking. Most of the measures installed can be characterized as increasing the resilience of the international financial system, while not addressing its cyclical tendencies (Tucker 2016). Instead, structural measures that seek to tackle the potential negative externalities of too-big-to-fail banks through capital surcharges for global systemically important financial institutions, as well as measures of bank recovery and resolution, have been prominent throughout the reform process, as have been measures that seek to reduce interconnectedness, opacity and the threat of contagion in financial markets, such as through the mandatory clearing of standard derivatives through central counterparties (CCPs) (Tucker 2014b, 3).

To make sense of this differential development, one can point to the fact that much of the regulatory response was driven by the direct crisis experience. For example, much of the immediate regulatory work on securitization was driven by the realization of risks of securitization that lurked off-balance-sheet, the opacity of securitization procedures and the fact that much of the risk supposedly transferred off the balance sheet of banks actually remained with them (Thiemann 2018). Similarly, both the work on over-the-counter (OTC) derivatives as well as the G-SIFI designation were driven by the impact of the default of Lehman Brothers, whose default had proven to have systemic consequences, even despite Lehman's somewhat limited balance-sheet size. In that immediacy of experiences, the longer-term threats of the cyclical buildup of financial fragilities that had taken hold because of an asset-price boom in the housing market must have been seen as less imminent, even if acknowledged by a number of observers (cf. Borio 2009).

However, this chapter argues that more was at play in the regulatory dynamics post-crisis than these immediate crisis-driven experiences, which can be linked to the state of debate on the definition and operationalization of systemic risks. As I will show in the following, procyclical aspects of financial market developments that contributed to the crisis were discussed right from the beginning of the financial crisis and were indeed crucial to the initial framing of the macro-prudential reform project (FSF 2008). So the question arises as to why the reform projects linked to the cross-sectional dimension of systemic risk were advanced, whereas those seeking to intervene in the cyclical dimension of systemic risk were largely not addressed. To answer this question, the chapter first traces the immediate debate of regulators at the international level during and after the financial crisis (from 2007 to 2010), as they were discussing what the (macro-prudential) regulatory response should look like. Here, we will trace if and how far the view of a cyclical financial system managed to insert itself into these debates and thereby become integrated in the pending regulatory overhaul.

As we will see, the final impact of the cyclical view of the financial system in the immediate post-crisis situation was rather limited, and was very much linked to the lack of economic research on the cyclical tendencies of the financial system as a whole, in particular the non-bank system of credit mediation. To substantiate this point, the second part of the chapter engages in a quantitative analysis of the literature on systemic risk and macro-prudential regulation, as it was available to regulators during that period. The analysis shows that the regulatory themes that were implemented immediately post-crisis had been issues that were subjected to substantial intellectual scrutiny by both academic and central bank economists, whereas works focusing on the cyclical dimension of systemic risk were few and largely shunned by academia. This finding, in line with the analysis of the regulatory debates, points to the differential academic backing and scientific consensus as an important factor influencing the course of the international regulatory agenda.

The Immediate Crisis Phase (September 2007 to April 2009)

As the first ramifications of the financial crisis of 2007 roiled financial markets, the August 2007 halt of valuation by certain funds of BNP Paribas being noted by many as the beginning of the crisis (Acharya and Schnabel 2012), the Financial Stability Forum (FSF) was tasked by the G7 treasury deputies in September 2007 with forming a working group to discuss the response to the unfolding turmoil, "comprising national authorities, the chairs of international supervisory, regulatory and central bank bodies and the relevant international institutions as members" (FSF 2007, 2). This working group on "enhancing the resilience of financial institutions and markets," headed by FSF chairman Mario Draghi, then president of the Banca d'Italia, did not include delegates from finance ministries, a fact that allowed for a quicker, more technocratic and less political treatment of issues (interview, member of the FSF working group, October 29, 2021).[1] Bringing together the heads of the Basel Committee on Banking Supervision (BCBS), the Committee for the Global Financial System (CGFS), the Bank for International Settlements (BIS) and the International Monetary Fund (IMF), as well as the International Organization of Securities Commission (IOSCO) and the International Accounting Standards Board (IASB), it would become the kernel of regulatory initiatives post-crisis, in turn raising the epistemic authority of the FSF to such a degree that it would be

[1] It consisted of nine national central bankers and seven regulatory officials, as well as three representatives of international organizations.

upgraded to the Financial Stability Board (FSB) in April 2009 (Blustein 2012; Pagliari 2013; Helleiner 2014).

The group initially operated under the assumption that the events in financial markets represented a liquidity crisis in particular markets, but by no means an existential crisis of the entire financial system (interview, member of the task force, December 7, 2021; Langley 2014, 56).[2] In line with this diagnosis of a liquidity crisis, the group worked on issues of central bank interventions to provide liquidity and focused on off-balance-sheet securitization, which the crisis revealed to be dangerous (Langley 2014, 60ff.). This reading of the 2007 events would prove incorrect, as the turbulence dragged on and transformed into a full-blown banking crisis, which came to a first peak in March 2008 when the investment bank Bear Stearns neared bankruptcy because of troubles with two internal hedge funds that owned "toxic" mortgages. Its pending bankruptcy forced the Federal Reserve and Treasury to set up a first bad bank (Maiden Lane LLC) and arrange a merger with JP Morgan over a weekend in mid-March (see Eichengreen 2015, 188f.).

Shortly thereafter, in April 2008, the working group at the FSF sent off a first set of recommendations to the G7. While their report was still very much caught up with the financial risks lurking off-balance-sheet and how to structure the imminent crisis response, they already at that point noted that the "forces that contribute to procyclicality in the financial system" require further study. They therefore decided to "examine the drivers of such procyclical behaviour and possible options for mitigating it ... to strengthen the efficiency and resilience of the system, without hindering the processes of market discipline and innovation that are essential to the financial system's contribution to economic growth" (FSF 2008, 2). As is evident from the quote, the group at this point still displayed deference to market discipline and innovation, yet recent developments in financial markets pointed to the need to consider detrimental feedback mechanisms. This stance reflected the fact that it was simply no longer possible to speak of "a subprime shock," as was the case in fall 2007. Instead, it had become more appropriate to speak of the subprime crisis, in which feedback

---

[2]   In line with this focus, its first letter to the G7 on October 15, 2007 (FSF 2007) speaks of "turbulences in financial markets," which were linked to problems of the subprime mortgage market but reinforced by channels of valuation uncertainty and loss of confidence in ratings (FSF 2007, 1).

loops and second-round effects were showing their detrimental impact (interview, member of the FSF group on Enhancing Resilience of Markets and Institutions, October 29, 2021).

In particular, the group noted the *"feedback effects between valuation and risk-taking,"* which proved particularly detrimental, arguing that "the turbulence revealed the potential for adverse interactions between high leverage, market liquidity, valuation losses and financial institutions' capital. For example, write-downs of assets for which markets were thin or buyers were lacking raised questions about the adequacy of capital buffers, leading to asset sales, deleveraging and further pressure on asset prices" (FSF 2008, 9; emphasis mine). Overall, the report noted that "a striking aspect of the turmoil has been the extent of risk management weaknesses and failings at regulated and sophisticated firms" (FSF 2008, 10). These quotes show the degree to which the pre-crisis hegemonic views on private risk management linked to market valuations as the optimal pathway to achieve financial stability were shattered in the regulatory community by the events unfolding during the financial crisis, casting into the spotlight the feedback effects between valuation and risk-taking.

The FSF began its work on the procyclical aspects of financial regulation but also of the financial system at large shortly thereafter, dividing the work into three working groups. The first group was concerned with bank capital issues, and was led by the head of the BCBS, Nout Wellink; the second working group on accounting rules for loan loss provisioning was led by K. Casey (Securities and Exchange Commission [SEC]); and the third group working on valuation and leverage was led by the CGFS under the leadership of Jean Pierre Landau (Banque de France). In the context of the start of these workstreams, the BIS handed in a conceptual framework on September 1, 2008 to the FSF, spelling out ways to approach the topic of procyclicality in financial markets. In this very cautious submission, which was to serve as background material to the discussion, the cyclical view on financial markets is introduced as one of the two possible views on the procyclicality of the financial system. This view sees "financial strains as the natural result of excessive risk-taking during the expansion, which leads to the build-up in vulnerabilities. They also regard amplifying feedback mechanisms during the expansion as a significant contributing factor" (BIS 2008, 1). Yet, the report duly notes the opposing view, which sees these procyclical feedback loops only at work during downswings, insisting on unrelated shocks as the origin of financial instability rather than the endogenous buildup of vulnerabilities.[3]

While this intervention by the BIS hence acknowledged the controversial status that the cyclical view occupied in regulatory circles at this moment in time, it nevertheless sought to assert two fundamental reasons for the procyclicality view independent of these different underlying concepts. Procyclicality, understood as a positive feedback loop between developments in financial markets and the real economy, was seen to arise from limitations in risk management and misaligned incentives (BIS 2008, 2). In addition to these fundamental sources of procyclicality, linked to the short-term horizons of financial actors, the regulatory framework may act as an additional source of procyclicality (BIS 2008, 3), including the procyclical measurements of risks embedded in regulation as well as fair-value accounting.

To stem these procyclical tendencies, measures should seek to "(i) limit the costs of financial distress in the contraction phase and, *possibly*, (ii) restrain the build-up of risk-taking during the expansion phase" (BIS 2008, 3; emphasis mine). This formulation, which points once more to the uncertain and contested status of the measures seeking to address the upswing, is followed by a suggestion for a measure that links these two. Through the buildup of resources in the buildup phase of risks, the system's resilience to shocks could be increased, as well as possibly reducing the buildup of risk-taking (BIS 2008), a formulation that was anticipating the countercyclical capital buffer to be introduced in 2010.

It was two weeks later, on September 15, 2008, that the regulatory community entered full crisis mode when the failure of Lehman led to a downward spiral in financial markets. This spiral could only be stopped through drastic measures of central banks, backstopping insurers and large banks, as well as opening up and/or expanding emergency liquidity facilities to backstop entire segments of the financial markets (Mehrling 2010; Langley 2014). It is in the context of these quickly deteriorating financial market conditions that, on the initiative of the USA, the first ever G20 meeting at the leader level was summoned on November 15, 2008 in Washington, DC. In the communiqué

---

[3] In the words of the report: "Others play down these statistical regularities and see financial sector strains as possibly independent of the expansion phase. They stress the role of shocks external to the financial system and the inherent unpredictability of these crisis episodes" (BIS 2008, 1f.).

published at this summit (G20 2008), the work on mitigating the procyclicality of the financial system was endorsed by the G20 and delegated to the IMF and FSF. In addition, the reform of derivatives markets to reduce their systemic risks was envisioned, including the strengthening of the infrastructure of OTC markets, as is the definition of systemically important financial institutions and their appropriate oversight (G20 2008). Notably, despite the centrality of the notion of systemic risk and the work on procyclicality, the term "macro-pruden-tial regulation" is not mentioned once in the G20 communiques of 2008.

The Macro-Prudential Pivot of April 2009

Instead, this macro-prudential orientation would gain a much more prominent place six months later at the G20 summit in London in April 2009 (Baker 2013a). This summit was a pivotal moment in terms of post-crisis regulation, including the announcement that transformed the FSF into the FSB, placing it on a stronger institutional footing in the process (G20 2009a, 3). It is also in the communiqué of this summit that a macro-prudential orientation of financial regulation is endorsed for the first time in an encompassing way, extending beyond the banking system and including the idea of the buildup of systemic risk over time as an essential justification for macro-prudential action. As the G20 put it,

We have agreed that all systemically important financial institutions, mar-kets, and instruments should be subject to an appropriate degree of regula-tion and oversight. In particular: we will amend our regulatory systems to ensure authorities are able to identify and take account of *macro-prudential risks* across the financial system *including in the case of regulated banks, shadow banks, and private pools of capital to limit the build up of systemic risk*. (G20 2009a, 3; emphasis mine)

On that same day of the G20 meeting, the working group of the FSF on "Enhancing Market and Institutional Resilience" presented its "Recommendations for Addressing Procyclicality in the Financial System" (FSF 2009a), summarizing the suggestions of its three working groups. Seeking to inform "macro-prudential supervision and regula-tion," the FSF insisted that "addressing procyclicality in the financial system is an essential component of strengthening the macro-prudential orientation of regulatory and supervisory frameworks" (FSF 2009a, 1). The document is an impressive discursive embrace of the macro-prudential rhetoric of Crockett's (2000) speech, pointing to the procyclicality of the system both in the up- and downswing (p. 8) and proclaiming the need to limit both the inherent procyclicality of private risk management systems and the procyclicality of regulatory tools themselves. In this spirit, it suggests that policy tools were supposed to aim at limiting the procyclical aspects of these two elements both in the downswing and in the upswing, thereby limiting "the costs of financial distress in the contraction phase and (ii) restrain[ing] the build-up of risk during the expansion phase" (FSF 2009a, 10).

Yet, while strongly acknowledging these two goals of macro-prudential regulation, the report also pointed to four additional criteria against which any such measures needed to be evaluated, namely "simplicity, transparency, fairness and low implementation costs" (FSF 2009a, 10), de facto excluding several of the measures envisioned to counter the procyclical tendencies of the financial system, which were deemed either too costly, too opaque or too complex, such as the imposition of haircuts in the repo-market (see FSF 2009a). As a consequence of this overall orientation that sought to balance costs and benefits, the FSF recommended that the BCBS should increase the overall quality of capital available, install a countercyclical capital buffer that should be built up during boom times and drawn down during crises, install a simple leverage ratio and seek to reduce the procyclical impact of Value-at-Risk (VaR) in the calculation of these capital requirements. The final recommendation thereby retained the idea of the buildup of capital in good times, as proposed by the BIS in September 2008, but no other measures to directly address the procyclicality of the financial system were agreed.

These measures represented a sort of minimal consensus, which was shaped by the preferences of the US, UK and Swiss authorities, which had had coalesced around these measures as the most appropriate way forward (interview, member of the FSF, October 29, 2021). Tellingly, the USA already had a simple leverage ratio in place before the crisis. As one member of the group put it, these criteria and the overall unfolding of the work on procyclicality in the groups were shaped in such a way as to support the introduction of the simple leverage ratio, which these regulatory authorities had decided was the optimal way forward (interview, member of the FSF, October 29, 2021).

Other proposals for regulatory change, which were proposed by central bankers, were blocked by prudential regulators as well as accounting and market regulators. These other possible measures were seeking to address the procyclical impact of market valuations and the issue of fair-value accounting as well as the procyclical tendencies of initial margin practices for derivatives and haircut practices for repo-markets, yet they had proven much more contentious within the regulatory community. Neither market regulators nor accounting regulators or the US Federal Reserve were intent on intervening in these markets or these practices, and hence blocked any further debate (interview, member of the FSF, October 29, 2021).[4]

The least impactful of the three reports, despite being the closest to the initial problem identified by the FSF (2008), was the report on "The Role of Valuation and Leverage in Procyclicality" (CGFS 2009).[5] Written under the leadership of the Committee for the Global Financial System, the report led to no other direct policy recommendation than the use of a quantitative leverage indicator for banks, which was already agreed upon by the BCBS (FSF 2009, 5). Other proposals of the report had no immediate regulatory implications, as they were merely suggestions to review possible anti-cyclical regulatory interventions in the future (e.g. in the repo-market), as well as setting out venues for future research.[6] This anodyne stance was not the outcome of a perceived lack of urgency or a lack of ideas regarding how issues of procyclicality could be addressed (interview, FSF member, December 7, 2021). Rather, it was the impossibility of agreeing on any concrete measures, which led to timid language regarding policy proposals, transforming many initially proposed policy measures into proposals for future research (interview, FSF member, October 29, 2021).

---

[4]   In this vein, the recommendations by the working group on loan loss provisioning, headed by accounting regulators, were much less committed to immediate regulatory change, merely suggesting reviewing the accounting model for loan loss provisioning and adjusting it in a more forward-looking manner, but not committing to any changes in the short term.

[5]   The FSF had identified the "increased direct and embedded leverage, leverage funded with short-term debt, more marketable assets, and extensive application of fair value accounting" as having contributed to an increase in the procyclicality of the system (FSF 2008, 5).

[6]   In this vein, regulators are asked to "*review* enforcing minimum initial margins and haircuts for OTC derivatives and securities financing transactions to limit the cyclical variations of these tools used for increasing leverage" (emphasis mine).

In this vein, the report recommended that "regulators and supervisors should obtain a clear and comprehensive picture of aggregate leverage and liquidity and have the necessary tools to trigger enhanced surveillance if necessary" (FSF 2009, 5). The CGFS and the BCBS should furthermore launch a joint research program to "measure funding and liquidity risk attached to maturity transformation, enabling the pricing of liquidity risk in the financial system" (FSF 2009, 6). This research program should enable them to "define robust measures of funding and liquidity risk, which could assist assessments and pricing of liquidity risk by the private sector." Based on this research program, the BIS and IMF "could make available to authorities information on leverage and on maturity mismatches on a system-wide basis" (FSF 2009, 6), allowing for a system-wide surveillance of buildup of risks linked to liquidity and leverage. Lastly, accounting standard setters and prudential regulators were asked to examine the procyclical effects "*potentially* associated" with fair-value accounting (FSF 2009, 6; emphasis mine), representing yet again an issue upon which no agreement could be generated between central bankers and either prudential or accounting regulators (interview, FSF group member, December 7, 2021; see also Muegge and Stellinga 2015).

These formulations portray the weakness of the macro-prudential thought collective located at the CGFS to impose itself on either market regulators or the prudential supervisors in the BCBS. This blockade was indeed one of the reasons for these ambiguous formulations, leading to a call for research rather than regulation, as no consensus for political action was deemed feasible at the time (interview, one author of the report, October 29, 2021). In the words of one of the authors involved: "this question of procyclicality was still in its infancy, it was very contentious" (interview, October 29, 2021), in contrast to the issue of leverage around which the regulators had coalesced. This "infancy" was largely related to the lack of existing research on this matter. As another member of the group put it,

the report was both too early and too late. Too early, because … it wanted to anticipate developments which only much later would be substantiated by research and too late because it came at a moment when sectoral standard setters, IOSCO, banking and market supervisors already had worked on their own measures, Basel III in particular, which meant their interest in taking a new point of view in light of their own advanced process was not so developed. (Interview, second group member, December 7, 2021; my translation)

Overall, these debates on the need for anti-cyclical time-varying tools to address the procyclical nature of the financial system unfolded within a lively general regulatory debate over the merits of time-varying versus structural, cross-sectional measures of macro-prudential regulation. While adherents of the new macro-prudential idea set were pointing to such measures as the new venue for regulatory action, opponents of time-varying measures were pointing to the difficulties in operationalizing such an approach and the fact that "the credit cycle was an artefact, a construct that is empirically not well founded, and upon which no proper policy could be built" (interview, FSF member, December 7, 2021).[7] In this debate, the change agents within the CGFS faced an "uphill battle" to insert their concerns regarding valuation practices in financial markets. The capacity of this report to exert influence was hence limited, leading primarily to follow-up research work at the CGFS and the BIS, which in turn would have no or minimal effects on the regulation of the procyclical behavior of capital markets (see the next section and Chapter 7).

The Turning Tide: From Procyclicality to Resiliency-Enhancing Measures

The G20 meeting in April 2009 in London formulated many follow-up requests to the IMF, the FSB and the BIS in terms of macro-prudential regulation and supervision (G20 2009b). One request was to develop guidelines to make sure that all systemically important financial institutions, markets and instruments were subject to proper oversight. To do so, they were tasked with identifying systemically important markets, institutions and instruments. They were also tasked with following up on the recommendations by the FSF regarding the procyclical aspects of the financial system and regulation. They commanded that "the FSB, BCBS, and CGFS, working with accounting standard setters, should take forward, with a deadline of end 2009, implementation of the recommendations published today to mitigate procyclicality, including a requirement for banks to build buffers of resources in good times that they can draw down when conditions deteriorate"

---

[7] At that point in time, papers such as Schularick and Taylor (2012) in the *American Economic Review*, which showed the persistence of cycles of credit in the economy over 140 years, were still not published.

(G20 2009b, 2). With this decision the G20 enshrined the goal of a countercyclical capital buffer in the global regulatory agenda, which led to the only inclusion of procyclical concerns in the final revisions of Basel III (Repullo and Saurina 2011).

With this decision to introduce a countercyclical element in Basel III at the G20 summit in London April 2009, the anti-cyclical dimension of macro-prudential regulation reached its height in terms of its influence on the international agenda. From then onwards, the focus was on furthering the resilience of the global financial system rather than the capacity of regulators to engage in anti-cyclical regulation.[8] By the next G20 meeting in Pittsburgh in September 2009, the world leaders embraced the envisioned revisions of Basel III and furthermore paid lip service to the need "to ensure an adequate balance between macro-prudential and micro-prudential regulation to control risks, and to develop the tools necessary to monitor and assess the buildup of macro-prudential risks in the financial system" (G20 2009c, 7). While this statement seemingly endorses the need to assess the buildup of risks, it merely points to the need to develop the monitoring tools, which at that point in time were largely nonexistent. Yet, no other regulatory tools to engage the cyclical character of the financial system were on the agenda, which would allow regulators to react if they detected such a buildup (such as anti-cyclical haircuts for the repo-market).

In contrast, at that same G20 meeting in Pittsburgh in the fall of 2009, the goal of improving the resilience of the OTC market had already been concretized, leading to the goal that all "standardized OTC derivative contracts should be traded on exchanges or electronic trading platforms, where appropriate, and cleared through central counterparties by end-2012 at the latest. OTC derivative contracts should be reported to trade repositories. Non-centrally cleared contracts should be subject to higher capital requirements" (G20 2009c, 7). Furthermore, regulators were tasked with "address[ing] cross-border resolutions and systemically important financial institutions by end-2010" by making sure that "prudential standards for systemically important institutions should be commensurate with the costs of their failure. The FSB should propose by the end of October 2010 possible measures including more intensive

---

[8] Tools not pursued were, for example, the setting of anti-cyclical haircut and margin requirements for repo-markets and derivatives in order to limit credit growth.

supervision and specific additional capital, liquidity, and other prudential requirements" (G20 2009c, 7).

This work, which would lead to the designation of globally systemic
important financial institutions, required the translation of the notion
of systemic risk into a clear attribution of such systemic risk to individual institutions (Kranke and Yarrow 2019; Thiemann et al. 2021).
These concerns would dominate the work of regulators in the months
to come, pushing other macro-prudential concerns, such as the procyclical character of the financial system, aside.[9]

Whereas the G-SIFI reforms and OTC reforms were advancing at a
rapid pace, regulatory work addressing the cyclical properties of the
financial system was at a much more embryonic stage. As the FSB
report points out, "further work is underway that covers the analysis
and measurement of systemic liquidity risk, margins and haircuts, and
other system-wide indicators, including leverage" (FSB 2009, 11).

Such research work at the CGFS, collaborating with the BCBS on
assessing system-wide liquidity risks as well as the work on margins
and haircuts and on developing indicators for early warning exercises,
was much more tentative and unrelated to actually initiated regulatory
projects. This can best be seen in the fate of the follow-up working
group on the procyclical aspects of margin and haircut practices in the
repo-markets at the CGFS, which began its work in March 2009 and
issued a first progress report to the G20 finance ministries in November
2009. The group, while documenting the procyclical aspects of these
practices in financial markets, only recommended measures to enhance

---

[9] That this work was dominating the agenda in terms of macro-prudential
regulation can be seen when analyzing the progress report of the FSB to G20
ministries of finance in November 2009 (FSB 2009). After detailing the extensive
work on the designation of Systemically Important Financial Institutions (SIFIs),
the theme of macro-prudential regulation is placed under the rubric "other
issues." There, the linked 2009 IMF–FSB–BIS report on "how national
authorities can assess the systemic importance of financial institutions, markets,
or instruments ('Guidance to Assess the Systemic Importance of Financial
Institutions, Markets, and Instruments: Initial Considerations')" (p. 10) is
mentioned as a first major step in the task to measure systemic risks, as a working
definition of systemic risk was generated. This definition focused on the "risk of
disruption to financial services that is (i) caused by an impairment of all or parts
of the financial system and (ii) has the potential to have serious negative
consequences for the real economy" (IMF, FSB and BIS 2009, 2). This definition,
based on "the notion of negative externalities" arising from the fact that
institutions were optimizing individual returns, not societal ones, had little to
nothing to say about the cyclical properties of the financial system.

market practices, leaving the hard work on macro-prudential measures, such as through cycle haircuts and countercyclical haircuts, for
possible future consideration (CGFS 2010a, 15f.; see Chapter 7). These
works, while possibly important in the long run, were hence unlikely to
yield any meaningful outcomes soon, leaving the installation of the
countercyclical capital buffer as the only post-crisis regulation with a
clear anti-cyclical aspect (CGFS 2010b).

The Battle over the Installation of the Countercyclical Capital Buffer within Basel III

Even the countercyclical capital buffer (CCyB) faced serious hurdles in
the regulatory community due to the lack of measurements and indicators that would lend themselves to its implementation, which is visible
in the first proposal for the revisions to the Basel rules (called Basel III)
published by the BCBS in December 2009 (BCBS 2009).

While the first draft of Basel III prominently mentioned the newly
introduced macro-prudential orientation of the revisions of Basel,
which includes a focus on "the build-up of system wide risks during the
upswing" (BCBS 2009, 2), the text was still undecided regarding the
actual implementation of this countercyclical dimension. While other
elements to address the procyclical character of regulation, such as a
change in the methods to calculate risk-weights, were clearly specified,
the statements on the countercyclical dimension of capital standards were
still very ambiguous (BCBS 2009, 9f.). Developing the idea of capital
conservation buffers at length, the document noted drily the need to
account for excessive credit growth in good times in a way that could
be aligned with the proposed capital conservation buffers. However, the
BCBS was not yet ready to outline how this could be achieved.

The reticence to outline the actual operationalization of the CCyB can
be linked to the debates within the BCBS as to which indicators to use to
operationalize the countercyclical element. As these could not be quickly
resolved, these issues were delegated to a newly instituted macro-variables
task force founded in spring 2009, after the London summit, which was to
report a final solution to the BCBS in July 2010 (BCBS 2010, 1).[10]

---

[10] The final Basel III document states: "The Macro Variables Task Force (MVTF)
was formed to further develop a proposal to address the fourth objective with
the goal of providing a fully detailed proposal for review by the Basel Committee
at its July 2010 meeting. The proposal takes into consideration the formal

The group was composed of applied economists from member states' central banks and financial regulators, as well as the BIS, most notably the BIS economist Drehmann, who jointly with Borio had proposed measurements of the financial cycle (Borio and Drehmann 2009). Many members of the group, particularly the more "theoretically" inclined, believed in market discipline and were doubtful as to how regulators were supposed to know better than markets (interview, member of the task force, December 30, 2019). Given this doubt, they pursued the idea of basing the calibration of the tool directly on market signals, exploring whether the pricing of risk could not inform the buildup and release of the buffer. However, their attempts to link it to market indicators failed for several reasons, the most important being that such market-based measures were not available in developing countries.

On the other hand, advocates of economic indicators for the counter-cyclical capital standard were strengthened by encouraging results of a paper by the BIS (Drehmann et al. 2010), which suggested that early warning indicators, based on credit measures, were able to signal the buildup of systemic risks one to four years ahead of time. This work was built on the preliminary studies by Borio and his colleagues at the BIS (Borio and Lowe 2002; Borio and Drehmann 2009), in which they had tested the possibility of building effective early warning systems (Borio and Lowe 2002), finding the credit-to-GDP gap as well as time series on house price developments to be particularly powerful predictors of future systemic crises (Borio and Drehmann 2009). These results, coupled with the willingness of the majority of the members of the group to signal that the crisis required a new approach, in the end swayed the decision in favor of using economic early warning systems for the CCyB (interview, member of the task force, December 30, 2019).

The group hence tested these measures for the member states of the BCBS and found the credit-to-GDP gap to be the best single predictor of pending systemic distress (BCBS 2010). It hence suggested to make it the cornerstone for the setting of countercyclical capital buffers, a choice that was also motivated by the lack of reliable time series on real estate price developments in all countries, which had been found to also have good predictive qualities (Drehmann et al. 2010). Whenever the credit-to-GDP gap was beyond 2, the CCyB was to be activated and

feedback on a summary of the broad concept of a countercyclical buffer contained in the December Consultative Document" (BCBS 2010, 1).

accelerated in line with the rising gap. At the same time, the report emphasized the need for guided discretion by policymakers, which were to take into account a bundle of other variables and qualitative judgment when setting the buffer.

In the end, the CCyB was enshrined in this way in the Basel III Accord (BCBS 2010), setting out to "achieve the broader macro-prudential goal of protecting the banking sector from periods of excess credit growth" (p. 1). It was "designed to ensure that banking sector capital requirements take account of the macro-financial environment in which banks operate." To achieve that, national authorities were tasked with varying capital requirements cyclically "when excess aggregate credit growth is judged to be associated with a build-up of system-wide risk" (p. 1). And yet, because of the lack of reliability regarding these measurements, discretionary judgment coupled with sound principles was seen as the only way forward. As the BCBS put it in its revised proposal in July 2010,

[i]n developing the proposal, the Basel Committee saw problems with a hard rules-based approach as it would require a very high degree of confidence that the variables used to calculate the buffer requirement would always correctly perform as intended and would not send out false signals .... Rather than rely mechanistically on the credit/GDP guide, authorities are expected to apply judgment in the setting of the buffer in their jurisdiction after using the best information available to gauge the build-up of system-wide risk. (BCBS 2010, 7)

This stance clarifies the epistemic uncertainty regarding measures of the financial cycle, which hindered an unambivalent embrace of these measures by prudential regulators.

Work to increase the resilience of the system to short-term contagion and to reduce the threat posed by systemically important institutions, in contrast, was well advancing. The entire increase in core capital requirements as well as the development of systemic liquidity requirements for large banks (the Liquidity Coverage Ratio) in the Basel III proposal announced by the end of 2009 can be read as belonging to this attempt to reduce cross-sectional systemic risk (see IMF, FSB and BIS 2011, 7f.). Similarly, the commitment to impose mandatory clearing on all simple derivatives through central counterparties in order to limit the risks of contagion (G20 2010a) and the designation of global systemically important financial institutions were well advanced by 2010, with the proposals of the FSB to designate such institutions approved at the G20 summit in Seoul in November 2010 (G20 2010b).

The Debate over the Anti-cyclical Set-Up of Macro-Prudential Frameworks

This situation meant that the newly embraced macro-prudential vision of financial regulation was largely left without discretionary tools to address cyclical exaggerations, at least as agreed at the international level.[11] Instead, this aspect of the approach was to be developed over the course of the next years, both by the international bodies (IMF, FSB, BIS) and by national macro-prudential authorities that were to be designated in due course (FSB–IMF–BIS 2011, 2). The installation of such macro-prudential regulatory frameworks was placed on the agenda at the G20 meeting in Pittsburgh in fall 2009 (G20 2009b), but it faced the hurdle that such macro-prudential ideas were not very well undergirded by academic research at that point (CGFS 2010b) and that Western central bankers were not well experienced in using anti-cyclical tools (interview, former CGFS member, April 16, 2021).

In order to gain some clarity on the international experience with such macro-prudential frameworks and to further the debate, the CGFS in November 2009 commissioned a report on the experiences with macro-prudential regulation that would draw on both internal discussions and survey data (interview, former CGFS member, April 15, 2021).

Introducing the distinction between increasing the resilience of the financial system and leaning against the cycle as the two distinct goals of macro-prudential regulation, the report once more noted the challenges associated with this policy framework. These included lacking scientific evidence regarding the effectiveness of measures (as contrasted with monetary policy), the absence of early warning indicators and the reputational and political risks for central banks in intervening in the cycle (CGFS 2010b, 16).[12]

---

[11] On the other hand, time-invariant backstops such as the leverage ratio had been introduced, providing a general limit to the expansionary tendencies of the banking system (see Stellinga 2019).

[12] These problems of the literature extended even so far that still no commonly shared definition of financial instability existed, or a commonly defined objective for macroprudential regulation. Underlying these problems, the report points to a deeper underlying issue, namely the lack of models that could help model the interaction between the financial system and the real economy and monetary policy, given the fact that there was limited academic guidance on these issues (CGFS 2010b, 16).

To address some of these issues, the G20 summit in November 2010 in Seoul tasked the FSB, the IMF and the BIS with doing further work "on macro-prudential policy frameworks" (CGFS 2010b, 9f.). The response was a jointly issued IMF–FSB–BIS report of March 2011 on macro-prudential policy tools and frameworks. While finding that major steps had already been taken, it lists the steps still deemed necessary. This daunting list included the need to design and collect better information and data to support systemic risk identification and modelling, better models and techniques to identify and measure systemic risk, as well as the design of effective toolkits, which allow for discretionary calibration of anti-cyclical tools (FSB–IMF–BIS 2011, 1f.). These challenges, they pointed out, applied particularly to measures in the time dimension, of which the report lists the CCyB as the only enacted international measure. This report, as well as the report of the CGFS (2010b), illustrate the infancy of the policy program in terms of leaning into the wind, where both the appropriate data for the measurement of systemic risks and the models themselves still needed to be developed.

The Epistemic Backing of Regulatory Concepts As a Driver of the Regulatory Agenda

This review of the international regulatory agenda from the beginning of 2008 to the end of 2010 suggests that during this period regulatory measures to increase the resilience of the financial system were taken, while measures to reduce the procyclical aspects of financial markets were largely sidestepped and transformed into a research program, seeking to detect good early warning indicators and models that could help policymakers to install these frameworks. This path of reform efforts was driven by several factors, one of them being the decisions by the US regulators as the path-setters for global financial regulation (Helleiner 2011). As the interview material presented earlier suggests, an additional factor was the issue of what was regarded as legitimate and established "economic knowledge" at the time. In this sense, the enactment of reforms was also driven by what was deemed robust knowledge on systemic risk that policymakers could draw upon. To further substantiate this point, in the following I present results based on a large-scale text analysis that details the available models for the conceptualization and measurements of systemic risk that regulators could draw upon by the time the financial crisis hit in 2007.[13]

Based on the 3,716 academic articles and working papers that were published on the topics of systemic risk and macro-prudential regulation between 1995 and 2016, Figure 4.1 displays the general distribution of academic and working papers on the topics of systemic risk and macro-prudential regulation, with the organizational affiliation of authors displayed as well.

The figure reveals that, in general, very few papers were written on these topics pre-crisis, rising strongly only from 2007 onwards. A second result of the analysis is that while academics had engaged with the term "systemic risk" pre-crisis, their engagement with the topic of macro-prudential regulation was minimal, revealing the weakness of the macro-prudential network of expertise to entice academics to apply systemic risk thinking to macro-prudential regulation pre-crisis.

Further investigating the different topics that were treated in the sample, a stark divide between the cross-sectional and the time dimension of systemic risk, as outlined by Borio (2003b), becomes evident. The cross-sectional topics dealing with too-big-to-fail institutions as well as contagion had been worked on by both academics and central bankers pre-crisis (see also Thiemann et al. 2021), whereas issues regarding the cyclical character of the financial system were largely only worked upon by central bankers. This differential distribution is

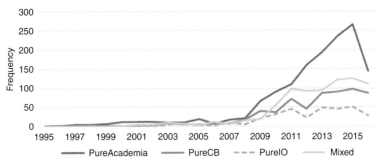

Figure 4.1 Number of publications per affiliation per year (1995–2016).

[13]   These results were first presented in Ibrocevic and Thiemann (2018) and are based on a dataset drawn from RePeC, the largest economic depository in the world. Readers interested in the methodology and data sources are invited to read the paper.

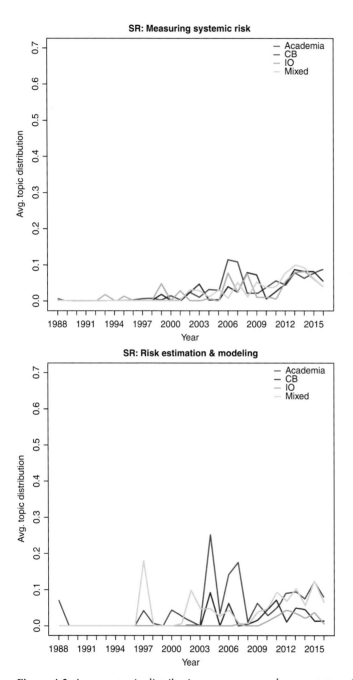

Figure 4.2 Average topic distribution per year per document type for topics regarding "too-big-to-fail."

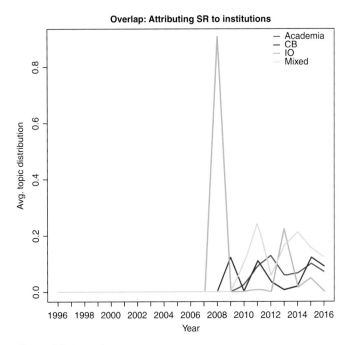

Figure 4.2 (cont.)

particularly stark for topics regarding too-big-to-fail institutions, the biggest regulatory change after the financial crisis (Pagliari and Wilf 2021). As can be seen in the graphs in Figure 4.2, every topic regarding the systemic risks stemming from too-big-to-fail institutions had been engaged with by authors from academia and central banks well before 2008. As becomes evident from the graphs in Figure 4.2, the extensive work of international organizations that occurred in 2008 could draw upon prior work by academics and central bankers.

Similarly, the topics that used concepts regarding networks, contagion and counterparty risk were well developed pre-crisis (see also Chapter 3). In these topics, the relation between financial institutions comes to the fore and, more importantly, the effects the insolvency of one or more financial institution might have on the system as a whole. The graphs in Figure 4.3 display the evolution of topics on interbank contagion and derivatives and counterparty risks. The topic of derivatives and counterparty risks is treated by central bank and academic economists alike already more than a decade before the financial crisis.

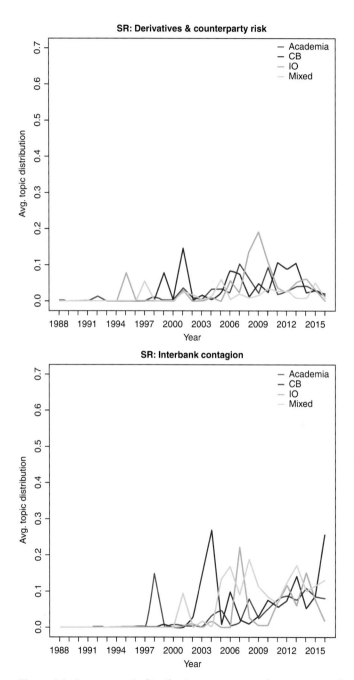

Figure 4.3 Average topic distribution per year per document type for topics on networks and contagion.

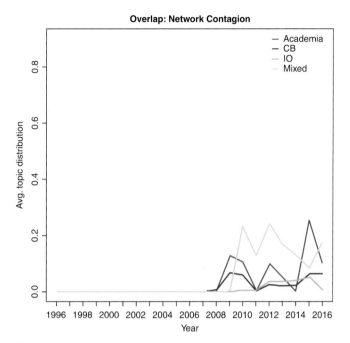

Figure 4.3 (cont.)

Similarly, publications in the topic of interbank contagion begin in the late 1990s, notably begun by academic publications, which then also garner interest from academia and central banks much before the financial crises of 2008. This meant that when central banks and international organizations started to work on this issue in the immediate aftermath of the crisis (see Figure 4.3), they could draw upon these prior works. Notable here is also how academia and mixed publications dominate the topic, providing a strong scientific backing for these measures.

On the other hand, when it comes to topics regarding the cyclical nature of the financial system (the core element of the macro-prudential agenda according to Borio 2003b), only three topics could be identified in the sample, one focusing on countercyclical capital regulation as a macro-prudential tool, one on early warning indicators and on indicators of countercyclical regulation. These topics are dominated by economists from central banks and international organizations, with academic economists only engaging with these topics after the financial

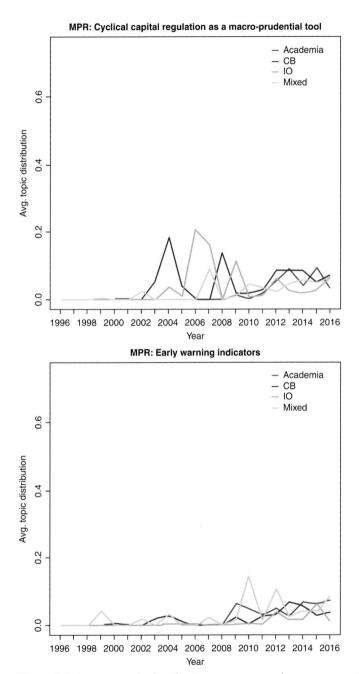

Figure 4.4 Average topic distribution per year per document type for topics regarding cyclicality.

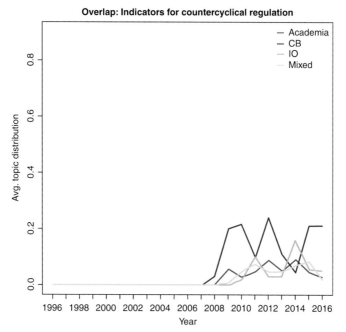

Overlap: Indicators for countercyclical regulation

Figure 4.4 (cont.)

crisis. Furthermore, in all these publications, there is little to no theoretical engagement with the concept of the financial cycle that could explain its unfolding.

For the topic on indicators for countercyclical regulation, the debate starts only after the financial crisis, and is dominated by central bankers. This is because Basel III delegates the implementation of countercyclical capital buffers to national regulators, making this a major intellectual preoccupation. Again, the engagement of academics on this topic is rather minimal and stays that way until 2016. These findings indicate that among the different topics investigated, those regarding the cyclical nature of financial markets received the least attention by academic economists before the crisis. Furthermore, in all these publications, there is little to no theoretical engagement with the concept of the financial cycle in terms of models that could explain its unfolding, further weakening the epistemic backing of this concept.

Discussion and Conclusion

This chapter investigated the installation of macro-prudential tools during the international regulatory actions that ensued during and in the immediate wake of the crisis. It showed how, despite an early concern with the procyclical tendencies of the financial system in the regulatory community (cf. FSF 2008), the actual measures implemented after the crisis sought to increase the resilience of the financial system to withstand shocks, rather than addressing these procyclical mechanisms themselves. While several working groups were set up to investigate and propose policy recommendations that could address these procyclical tendencies, the only countercyclical measure that was finally implemented was the CCyB, which itself aimed more at increasing the resilience of the system than the buildup of excess credit growth (BCBS 2010).

The chapter linked these findings on the one hand to the preferences of the US regulator, the Federal Reserve, as well as the resistance from market and accounting regulators, which were wedded to the notion of efficient financial markets and the sole protection of investors, refusing the engagement with macro-prudential cyclical thinking. The Federal Reserve in turn was worried about the possibilities of regulatory arbitrage with respect to any anti-cyclical measures imposed and was doubtful whether any regulator, based on economic analysis, could anticipate cyclical developments better than market participants. This stance, which advantaged the choice of instruments that focus on resilience rather than the cycle, can furthermore be linked to the lack of reliable measures of the cycle and hence difficulties to impose rules-based standards, which do not require discretionary judgment.

This fact can be linked to the dominant economic discourse on systemic risk at the time, as represented by scholarly work published either as working papers or academic articles. Here, the analysis has shown how the dominant academic writing on topics linked to systemic risk was supporting the focus of regulation on cross-sectional systemic risk as well as short-term contagion. In contrast, issues that focused on the procyclical tendencies of the system and longer-term cyclical upswings were rather marginal in this discourse. These results indicate that it was a mode of analysis and thinking that by 2010 was still largely rejected in academic discourse, which implies that a widely shared academic justification for anti-cyclical regulation was hardly available immediately after the crisis, further impeding the regulatory project of anti-cyclical regulation.

Considering the epistemic standing of the financial cycle in academia and the developing macro-prudential discourse, it is to a certain degree unsurprising that in the early stages of macro-prudential regulations, only the CCyB was implemented to dampen the cycle, while other measures such as anti-cyclical haircuts were discarded. It was the task of central bankers to develop both such discretionary macro-prudential tools that could be used to dampen the cycle as well as the models and indicators that could justify it. It is to this work within central banks, the processes of setting up macro-prudential policy frameworks, the organizational routines and the policy paradigms that drive them that we now turn.

5 | Is Resilience Enough?
The Implementation of the Macro-Prudential Reform Agenda in the USA, the UK and the Eurozone

The development of the intellectual understanding for the need for macro-prudential also overlaps with the institutional peculiarities which are rooted either in the fragmentation of the US regulatory system or the complex maze of the European and Eurozone polity.

(Interview, former UK regulator, February 27, 2015)

Of the two types of social cost ... policy makers have prioritized the costs of financial system collapse over the costs of resource misallocation during financial booms. The assumption is that whatever the inefficiencies during the upswing, the destruction of wealth, jobs and productive capacity during busts matters more ... it is clear that ... the approach adopted by policy makers is not a regime for actively managing the credit cycle.

(Tucker 2016, 31, former deputy governor of the Bank of England, responsible for financial stability)

Introduction

The previous chapter has shown how the internationally agreed macro-prudential measures in the crisis aftermath mainly sought to increase the resilience of the financial system, but only minimally sought to address its cyclical character. This element instead would largely have to be addressed through macro-prudential frameworks at the national level (CGFS 2010b), hence granting national discretion and imposing difficulties of central bank coordination for actions beyond national remits. Central banks, also because of their role as lenders of last resort, saw themselves as having a large role to play in the development of these frameworks (CGFS 2010b, 1; McPhilemy 2016), seeking to formulate their own approach of how to implement the goals of strengthening the resilience of financial systems and controlling its cyclical tendencies. Table 5.1 displays the

Table 5.1 *Resiliency versus anti-cyclical measures*

Macro-prudential objectives/ characteristics	Resiliency	Anti-cyclical
Concept	Cross-sectional/ interconnectedness	Intertemporal/building up of systemic risk over time
Form of regulatory intervention	Time invariant (structural), possibility for due process	Time variant (discretionary), little possibility for due process
Requirement for metrics of systemic risk	Very low, theoretically driven rather than measurement specific, simple over time adjustment (quiet policy learning)	High, need for ex ante warning systems, sufficiently early to allow intervention, sufficiently precise to justify intervention, high likelihood of error
Political exposure of regulator	Limited in the sense that there is due process and calibration, existence of accepted economic analysis	Very high, no due process, no ex ante calibration, limited scientific knowledge

Partially derived from CGFS (2010b).

characteristics of the two intermediate objectives regarding the form of regulatory intervention they require, the demands in terms of risk metrics and the political exposure they imply.

Aware of the dangers inherent in an overly ambitious stance on macro-prudential regulation (see Table 5.1), given the rather immature state of economic knowledge, the macro-prudential change agents within central banks fought for what they deemed to be viable strategies to reduce systemic risks and live up to their newly gained explicit or implicit financial stability mandate. As I will show, all policymakers agreed to increase the resilience of the financial system as a central element of their policy framework, yet differed substantially on the emphasis they would give to the anti-cyclical element. In the following, I trace these pathways to domestic macro-prudential frameworks for the case of the Federal Reserve, the Bank of England and the European System of Central Banks, pointing to the institutional work as well as the technocratic debates that erupted regarding the overall orientation of macro-prudential policies.

In particular, I focus on how the central bank officials that were put in charge of formulating and implementing such an approach sought to shape and interpret this new field of central bank action. Which emphasis they would give to the anti-cyclical aspect of the new policy regime was shaped, as will be shown, by the legal, cultural and administrative context within which these agency leaders were operating, affecting its administrative viability. An important element in their considerations, next to the structural capacities for implementation as well as the administrative biases they held in terms of beliefs, was the culturally specific method of ensuring accountability for regulatory action, including the accepted base of expertise and the variable need for robust scientific backing of the policy ideas guiding regulatory interventions (Jasanoff 2012). Here, the idea of the financial cycle with its relatively new and uncertain ontological status would be viable in some contexts, but not others.

The chapter shows how agency leaders interacted with these legal, administrative and cultural constraints, implementing particular orientations of the macro-prudential framework, from a resolute negation of anti-cyclical tools (in the USA) to a pragmatic embrace (the UK) and a fervent pleading in the case of the European Central Bank (ECB) within the Eurozone. These different stances, developed by reflexive leadership in the context of post-crisis legal and regulatory interventions, sought to adapt the internationally initiated program of macro-prudential regulation to the specificities of the national environment within which these central banks had to operate. These stances would continue to structure central bank action, leading to markedly different approaches to macro-prudential regulation among these central banks.

The Pathway to Macro-Prudential Regulation in the USA

Macro-prudential supervision and regulation in the USA was shaped by administrative and legal considerations as much as it was by the immediate actions undertaken during the crisis, in particular the innovative practice of stress tests. Overall, the particular institutional configuration within which the Federal Reserve had to enact the new policies as well as the intellectual mindset held at the helm of the Federal Reserve meant that the anti-cyclical element of the new macro-prudential framework would be largely muted, hidden away in the stress-testing exercise that would come to dominate macro-prudential action.

While the Federal Reserve Bank of America was no stranger to anti-cyclical interventions, such actions had ended in the 1980s amid an attempt by the Federal Reserve to extricate itself from the complaints and mischief such actions provoked (Krippner 2011).[1] Since then, the Federal Reserve had instead withdrawn to a much more passive stance. While stating that "maintaining the stability of the financial system and containing systemic risk that may arise in financial markets" was one of its four primary duties (FRB 2005, 1), this policy stance in essence was a reactive one with respect to the buildup of financial stability risks. It encompassed the emergency lending assistance programs the Federal Reserve had engaged in from the 1970s onwards, backstopping both financial markets and large banks deemed too big to fail (Brimmer 1989; Ozgode 2022), yet it did not contain any preventive interventions in financial markets aiming at "pricking bubbles" before they burst. Instead, in what came to be known as the "Greenspan doctrine" or the "Greenspan put," the Federal Reserve's role was to use monetary policy to prop up markets when the bubble burst, thereby allowing a quick recovery. Greenspan did so first in 1987 and then in 2001, each time averting a deep recession after an extensive period of stock market exuberances came to a crushing halt.

This reactive stance was discredited after the financial crisis of 2007–8, demonstrating the enormous costs such a strategy could entail. Amid the search for a more proactive approach to guarding financial stability, Federal Reserve chairman Ben Bernanke embraced macro-prudential regulation in a speech at the Jackson Hole in August 2008 (Bernanke 2008). In this speech, Bernanke approved of the need for more macro-prudential supervision, even if he pointed out that it would be difficult to supervise the entire complex financial system of

---

[1] From the 1980 onwards, after President Carter's attempt to control credit growth forced the Federal Reserve to impose constraints on the growth of credit card debt and reserve requirements on money market mutual funds that was aggravating a developing recession (Volcker 1994, 147), the Federal Reserve abstained from implementing any painful anti-cyclical measures (Elliott et al. 2013, 30f.; Krippner 2011).

the USA. To achieve this task, he suggested installing systemic stress tests, systemic horizontal reviews and systemic supervisory guidance. While he even mentioned the need to address the credit cycle in his remarks, this was confined to the procyclicality of regulatory measures themselves, not the procyclical tendencies of the system. His minimal focus on procyclicality was in line with his epistemic positioning, which, in line with his predecessor, insisted that regulators cannot know better than the markets (interview, academic working with the Federal Reserve on issues of financial stability, 2018).

Bernanke's wish for systemic supervision based upon stress tests was about to become reality much sooner than he might have anticipated, becoming the first pillar of the new system of macro-prudential supervision in the USA, even before legislative changes in the USA were enacted. When distrust in financial markets would not dissipate after the disbursal of the Troubled Asset Relief Program (TARP) money in fall 2008, the incoming Treasury secretary Timothy Geithner decided to make a bold move. In his prior work at the International Monetary Fund (IMF), Geithner had become acquainted with the IMF's financial sector assessment program, which implemented a system-wide stress test for emerging markets in the early 2000s (Seabrooke and Tsingou 2009).[2] Against resistance in the administration (Geithner 2014, 288), he announced at the beginning of February 2009 that the Federal Reserve, in close collaboration with the Treasury, would hold a system-wide stress test. Its role was to assess the capital needs of banks and to recapitalize them, should they not be able to do so on their own, thereby removing any doubts about the solvability of the banking system as a whole.[3] The USA thereby became a true innovator, the first country in the West that implemented a broad-based systemic stress test for its banking system (Geithner 2014).

---

[2] Because of his experience at the IMF, Geithner had already placed the topic of financial stability at the center of discussions during his time at the helm of the Federal Reserve New York; that is, before the crisis (interview, academic economist, January 19, 2018, invited to the Federal Reserve New York in 2004 to discuss such matters). At that time, Geithner fostered debate on how to stabilize an ever-expanding financial system (Geithner 2014).

[3] By applying the same reasonably pessimistic scenario to all banks at the same time, the test was to create a commonly shared set of information on the equity position of banks. Subsequently, banks with an equity shortfall would be forced to either build up a sufficient equity basis in the market or receive an infusion of equity by the Treasury.

Named the Supervisory Capital Assessment Program, work on the stress test began on February 25, 2009. Both the novelty of the exercise and the time pressure made this a highly complex and difficult operation. On the one hand, regulators faced the difficulty of generating a stress-test scenario sufficiently severe to be credible without being so severe that it bankrupted the financial system. On the other hand, there was the need to coordinate the collective exercise, which required inter-agency coordination in the collection of the data from banks to guarantee timely and consistent implementation of the test. To coordinate these efforts and devise a coherent stress-test scenario, Bernanke took institutional leadership and installed the Office of Financial Stability Policy and Research in 2009 within the Federal Reserve Board, mandating it to draw on the expertise in the whole of the Federal Reserve system (interview, former Federal Reserve official, January 9, 2018). Strongly supported by Bernanke, this Office would become the organizational hub for the work on financial stability issues within the Federal Reserve system in the years to come, giving an institutional home to an issue that was until then somewhat neglected (interview, former Federal Reserve Board member, April 15, 2021).

Developing the set-up of the systemic stress test, the Office was closely collaborating with the Board and drawing upon expertise in other parts of the Federal Reserve system, in particular the statistics department at the Federal Reserve Board and the New York Federal Reserve. The task required a systemic stress test that could simulate a severe macroeconomic shock and consider the behavior of the banking system as a whole, moving beyond the fate of individual institutions. Despite all the difficulties the Office encountered in devising and implementing this large-scale exercise at such short notice,[4] the stress-test scenario was a success. When its results were announced on May 7, 2009, this measure and the

---

[4] For example, the extremely short time frame in which it had to be put together meant that banks had to calculate their own losses, yet the team at the Federal Reserve at least came to design a common scenario deemed credible. Based on the stress-test scenario, each participating financial institution was instructed to analyze potential firm-wide losses, including in its loan and securities portfolios, as well as from any off-balance-sheet commitments and contingent liabilities/ exposures, under two defined economic scenarios over a two-year time horizon (2009–10). In addition, firms with trading assets of $50 billion or more were asked to estimate potential trading-related losses under the same scenarios.

connected capital infusion calmed financial markets. This success was anchoring this newly devised tool in the system of banking supervision in the long run, becoming one of the strongest pillars of the new macro-prudential regime.

The Dodd–Frank Act

Shortly after the first systemic stress test had been successfully performed by the Federal Reserve, the Obama administration unveiled their first draft for the overhaul of the US system of financial regulation on June 17, 2009. This package, which was most remarkable for its lack of large-scale ambition,[5] pursued the incremental strategy to strengthen the Federal Reserve in the maze of regulatory oversight that characterized the US financial system, fragmented between two market regulators (Securities and Exchange Commission and the Commodities Futures Trading Commission (CFTC)) and four banking regulators (the Federal Reserve, the Federal Deposit Insurance Company, the Office of the Comptroller of the Currency and the Office of Thrift Supervision, the latter being merged with the OCC). This position was also shaped by Federal Reserve officials, which from the very first drafting of the bill had worked closely with the administration to shape the bill in a way that fit its capabilities and interests (see Committee on Financial Services 2009, 58).

Based on these negotiations with members of the Senate and the House, the Federal Reserve was supposed to get an explicit financial stability mandate, as can be clearly seen in the final draft of the Dodd–Frank bill, as submitted to the conference of the two houses on June 10, 2010. There in paragraph 11 it was stated that "The Board of Governors shall identify, measure, monitor, and mitigate risks to the financial stability of the United States" (draft bill, Dodd–Frank Act, p. 1753). However, during the conference between House and Senate members this new mandate was dropped amid anger against the Federal Reserve over the bail-outs approved in Congress that made the delegation of further responsibilities and tasks unpalatable

---

[5] The Obama administration did not envision a big shift in the system of financial regulation comparable to the one after the Great Depression, nor did it envision a clearing up of the fragmented regulatory space that arguably contributed to the failure in supervision before the crisis (interview, Federal Reserve economist, April 2018; former Federal Reserve lawyer, May 20, 2022).

politically (see Eichengreen 2015). Instead, the Federal Reserve was subjected to an audit and its capabilities to provide emergency liquidity assistance under paragraph 13 (3) were severely curtailed, despite the repeated objections by leading actors at the Federal Reserve (Bernanke 2015).

Rather than to the Federal Reserve, the task of monitoring emerging risks to US financial stability and reacting to them by devising new regulation was almost entirely allotted to the Financial Stability Oversight Council, a new committee that was to bring together the four different banking supervisors and the two market supervisory agencies (eight in total), an independent expert plus the Treasury as the chair of the committee, thereby delegating the Federal Reserve to second rank. This committee, unwieldy and complicated to manage to come to an agreement (Edge and Liang 2017), was to be seconded by the Office of Financial Research, which was to support the Financial Stability Oversight Council in terms of research, providing it with the needed data and monitoring to undertake its functions. Its tasks were the designation of Non-Bank Systemically Important Financial Institutions (SIFIs), then to be subjected to oversight by the Federal Reserve (Section 113 of the Dodd–Frank Act) and the formulation of recommendations to the agencies in the committee to address risks to financial stability (Section 120 of the Dodd–Frank Act), which the agency heads as members of the FSOC had a duty to implement.[6]

In terms of macro-prudential tasks assigned to the Federal Reserve, the Dodd–Frank Act, just like the international macro-prudential legislation at the time, had a strong focus on the cross-sectional dimension of systemic risk, coupled with a weak emphasis on the cyclical dimension (interview, former Federal Reserve official, January 9, 2018). While there were two mentions in the bill of the term "countercyclical," charging the Federal Reserve to ensure that large bank holding companies increase their capital in good times to be able to draw it down in bad times, these measures were vague and not linked to any regulatory

---

[6] Yet this direct financial stability mandate only applied to heads of agencies, not the agencies themselves, a fact that could lead to the refusal by agencies to implement FSOC decisions. The detrimental effects of this set-up became evident when members of the SEC refused to implement harsh capital requirements for Money Market Mutual Funds, which would have made them more bank-like, arguing that such measures fell outside of their mandate of protecting investors (see Thiemann 2018).

tools. More important than this new, limited countercyclical task, Section 165 of the Dodd–Frank Act requires the Board to implement heightened capital and liquidity standards, concentration limits and stress testing both for large bank holding companies and non-banks supervised by the Federal Reserve, further addressing the problem of banks deemed too big to fail. It was hence primarily with respect to ensuring the stability of large SIFIs that the financial stability mandate of the Federal Reserve was specified (interview, former Federal Reserve official, January 9, 2018).

Implementing the Limited Macro-Prudential Framework in the Federal Reserve

In order to ensure the proper execution of these tasks and to clarify the importance attached to them, the Dodd–Frank Act installed a powerful new position at the Federal Reserve: the vice-chair responsible for the supervision of large banks. The person put in charge to achieve this task was Daniel Tarullo, a lawyer with expertise in financial regulation and the author of an influential book on Basel II (Tarullo 2008), where he had criticized Basel II for being procyclical and suggested not adopting it for the USA. One of the first picks of the Obama administration, Tarullo was seen as a hardliner on banks, "feared and hated in equal measure" by Wall Street executives for his regulatory interventions (Cohan 2017). While aware of the procyclical tendencies of Basel II, his policy stance cannot be described as acting in a strong anti-cyclical fashion. Instead, he was rather seeking to enact structural measures, a stance that more than anything reflected several practical and administrative problems the Federal Reserve had with respect to the anti-cyclical dimension of a new macro-prudential framework.

First, the Federal Reserve had little to no exclusive say over discretionary measures to address cyclical developments, which if at all were to be decided by inter-agency guidance, the loan-to-value measures being the clearest example.[7] This, in Tarullo's opinion, meant almost by definition that any measure would take a long time to be agreed, in contradiction to the need for speedy action in terms of anti-cyclical measures (interview, former Federal Reserve economist working

---

[7] Loan-to-value ratios for banks, for example, were set by inter-agency guidance in 1993 (see Elliott et al. 2013, 17).

closely with Tarullo, February 2, 2018). Secondly, it reflected the issue
of a lacking clear mandate for such anti-cyclical measures, as the
mandate of the Federal Reserve explicitly only included the need to
ensure the safety and soundness of the financial system, which is a
micro-prudential notion (Adrian et al. 2015, 3). Enacting macro-prudential measures based on systemic risk analysis was difficult to justify
within this constrained mandate of the Federal Reserve, with lawyers at
the Federal Reserve being very concerned with fitting such measures,
based on systemic risk concerns taken in the context of this micro-
prudential mandate (interview, former Federal Reserve economist,
January 9, 2018).

Thirdly, this reticent stance was linked to a philosophical aversion at
the helm of the Federal Reserve Board regarding the capacity of regulators to gauge bubbles in a way that was more accurate than markets.
This administrative bias, which pointed to the difficulty of identifying
and pricing bubbles, was held firmly by Bernanke and other leading
members of the Board (interview, academic working with the Federal
Reserve, January 18, 2018), undergirded by a skepticism regarding the
available academic knowledge on these issues, including leading indicators, as well as a lack of knowledge of the effects of these interventions.[8] In this vein, Governor Tarullo (2013b) in a speech on the appeal
and difficulties of anti-cyclical macro-prudential regulation pointed to
the fact that the financial cycle, while appealing in general terms, is not
yet defensible as an academic concept as it does not have sufficient
scientific backing. This lack of scientific status and the problems of such
discretionary anti-cyclical interventions with due process administrative procedures mandatory in the USA justified a reticent stance to
Tarullo on these measures in contrast to structural measures, as the
following quotes from the speech in 2013 clarify.

In a first rhetorical step, Tarullo admitted that time-varying measures
seeking to tame the cycle are "a conceptually appealing approach." The
problem of the excessive upswing could much better be controlled by
time-varying measures (Tarullo 2013b, 23), while the structural
"through-the-cycle-measures" he advocates would likely be largely ineffective for dealing with increasing leverage or asset prices that raise

---

[8]   This skepticism can be most clearly observed for the case of the countercyclical
      capital buffer, which at least in the early 2010s was seen by Federal Reserve
      economists as plagued by the problem of unreliable indicators and the danger of
      large possible unintended side effects (Edge and Meisenzahl 2011).

macro-prudential concerns. He thus concludes, "well-developed time-varying measures might be effective in slowing the increase in systemic risk to give monetary policymakers more time to evaluate the need for a monetary policy response" (Tarullo 2013b, 23). However, he qualifies this approach that favors time-varying, discretionary measures to temper the cycle as one

> that raises a fair number of significant issues: the *reliability of measures* of excess or systemic risk, the *appropriate officials* to be making macro-pruden-tial decisions, *the speed* with which measures might realistically be imple-mented and take effect, and *the right calibration of measures* that will be effective in damping excesses while not unnecessarily reducing well-under-written credit flows in the economy. (Tarullo 2013b, 15; emphasis mine)

The problems of the reliability of measures, appropriate calibration and the speed of decision-making coupled with the need to identify the competent authority are all issues that are problematic from the point of view of legitimate regulatory decision-making, invoking the need for learning while doing (interview, Dutch central banker, September 21, 2016). They are particularly challenging for the Federal Reserve, as the lack of a clear general macro-prudential mandate for the Federal Reserve and a splintered governance field cobbled together under the umbrella of the Financial Stability Oversight Council proved a chal-lenge for quick and decisive decision-taking (Goodhart 2015, 285; interview, Federal Reserve official, April 6, 2017; interview, former Federal Reserve official, January 9, 2018).[9]

In addition to this problem of inter-agency agreement, the general need for a due process that includes a comment period, to allow the regulated their say and avoid regulatory arbitrariness, was an import-ant second aspect, leading Tarullo to favor structural measures. Structural measures have important advantages in this respect, because while such measures still require judgment, they do not depend on timely measurement of the buildup of risks. As he stated, "unlike real-time measures – where time will presumably be of the essence if those measures are to be effective – the adoption of structural con-straints can proceed with the full opportunity for debate and public

---

[9] For example, when the Federal Reserve sought to design its only countercyclical guidance on leveraged loans in 2013, it first had to get agreement from all banking supervisors, which proved rather difficult.

notice-and-comment that attends the rulemaking process" (Tarullo 2013b, 23).

To these aspects, Tarullo added the penultimate challenge, the lacking scientific proof for the financial cycle, doubting its ontological existence. Directed at the proponents of financial cycle regulation, he points out that the "adoption of consistent terminology does not itself resolve questions of whether ... increases in systemic risk are endogenous to the financial system and thus follow *a somewhat regular cyclical pattern, or are instead somewhat randomized, albeit repeated, phenomena*" (Tarullo 2013b, 2; emphasis mine).[10] He thus points to the uncertain ontological status of the financial cycle as a reason for caution, warning further that because of the concern of macro-prudential regulation with tail events, it is intrinsically difficult to generate sufficient data to test different theories regarding the propagation of systemic risk. This lacking scientific basis is particularly problematic for a US regulator, as regulators in the USA are expected to base their interventions on scientifically backed concepts to support regulatory decision-making (Jasanoff 2012, 12, 37).[11]

Based on implementation problems as well as lacking certainty about the existence of the financial cycle and the appropriate metrics for mitigating it, Tarullo disparaged discretionary measures that seek to lean into the wind and rather favored structural measures, which are non-varying and non-discretionary (Tarullo 2013b, 14).[12] It is the suitability of structural measures to fulfill the procedural requirements of legitimate intervention and their scientific foundation, and not necessarily their adequacy to the task at hand, that to him makes "the task of buffering the financial system against a tail event seem more

---

[10] Tarullo, a former Harvard law professor, is known to reach out to academic economists in the USA to better understand recent developments (interview, European banking regulator, September 26, 2016). US academia in particular has been slow to embrace anti-cyclical thinking (interview, ECB economist, April 21, 2016).

[11] For similar findings concerning the unease at the Federal Reserve with the concepts of systemic risk in general, see Goodhart (2015).

[12] This does not mean that Tarullo categorically denied the usefulness of time-varying measures. Instead, he called for further development "of some well-conceived and well-tested metrics over time" by academia and central bankers (Tarullo 2013b, 14; see also Tarullo 2015a). Until those metrics existed, however, he preferred to rely on static externality analysis, which allows for a due process that "can help identify the points of vulnerability and guide the fashioning of appropriate regulations" (Tarullo 2013b, 23).

tractable than that of moderating the financial cycle" (Tarullo 2013b, 23; see also Kohn 2014, 10).[13] This position, characterized by an attempt to depoliticize macro-prudential interventions in the context of a limited financial stability mandate, led to a very muted embrace of the countercyclical capital buffer, first implemented domestically in 2016 (see next chapter). Instead, and in line with this conviction, Tarullo sought to generate a strong macro-prudential capital cushion for the largest US banks, a course of action much more adapted to the administrative and intellectual context within which it had to unfold.

Seeking to increase the capital cushion for banks, preferably in a dynamic fashion, he found in stress tests a venue that would allow him to address his macro-prudential concerns in the context of the micro-prudential mandate of the Federal Reserve (Tarullo 2012). Basing itself on the mandate of the Federal Reserve to set the capital for large bank holding companies in a countercyclical fashion and to hold annual stress tests, both granted by the Dodd–Frank Act, the Federal Reserve integrated stress tests into an annual Comprehensive Capital Analysis and Review from 2011 onwards. This review, based on an "unlikely but plausible scenario," allowed for "a simultaneous, forward-looking projection of potential losses and revenue effects based on each bank's own portfolio and circumstances" (Tarullo 2012, 3). This projection of losses was the basis to push banks to build up much higher capital cushions, forcing the largest banks to raise 500 billion dollars of equity between 2011 and 2014 (Tarullo 2014a, 6).[14]

These stress tests would also be an element that in the end would allow for some limited form of "leaning against the wind" activity (Tarullo 2014a, 4). While these stress tests initially carried no cyclical elements, persistent work on a financial stability monitoring framework by the Office on Financial Stability and Policy Research, coupled with legal changes in the stress-testing framework in November 2013, would allow for the inclusion of a limited number of anti-cyclical macro-prudential elements in the stress tests from 2014 onwards (see

---

[13] Even in 2020 – that is, after his tenure at the Federal Reserve had come to an end for about three years – Tarullo would insist that "the analytic and governance issues associated with macroprudential policy, especially of the time varying form, remain formidable" (Tarullo 2020, 2).

[14] Key in this respect was the legal capacity of the Federal Reserve to force the large banks to stop dividend payments until they had filled the capital shortcomings the stress tests identified, a provision gained in November 2011.

next chapter). In this way, change agents within the Federal Reserve were able to include "salient risks" based on their analysis of cyclical risks in the stress-testing exercise, thereby circumventing the difficulties of implementing such countercyclical measures in an open administrative process.

Overall, the developing US framework then is primarily characterized by measures to increase the resilience of the banking system, with discretionary anti-cyclical interventions mainly located in its stress-testing exercise. This very limited embrace of anti-cyclical policies was due to the biases of the officials implementing the policy, the structural capacities for implementation and the cultural requirements for regulatory concepts to be backed up by mainstream academic research. A different, somewhat more transparent path for anti-cyclical action was found in the UK.

The UK: A Limited but Active Countercyclical Framework

When the financial crisis hit, the Bank of England (BoE) no longer had any role in banking supervision. Since gaining its official independence in 1997, it was only responsible for monetary policy and for acting as a lender of last resort, two tasks it duly executed from the moment Northern Rock experienced a bank-run in September 2007. Having lost any function in the domain of banking regulation to the newly created Financial Supervisory Authority in the reforms enacted in 1997, it was hence spared the blame regarding the unfolding financial crisis, while it proved itself to be of high value as a crisis manager. The blame for the crisis instead fell squarely on the Financial Services Authority (FSA), which was accused of an overly lenient style of financial regulation and a style of supervision that was too accommodative to the financial industry, charges the FSA itself admitted in an important post-crisis report on the failures pre-crisis (FSA 2009). In this situation, the BoE became a natural contender for the enactment of banking supervision and macro-prudential policies based on a financial stability framework still to be formulated, as politicians were considering how to rearrange the regulatory system in the UK.

In seeking to influence the set-up of such a financial stability framework, technocrats at the BoE could base themselves on more than a decade of in-house work on financial stability, efforts documented in financial stability reports from fall 1996 onwards. These analytical efforts were upgraded in 2005 when a "Systemic Risk Reduction Division" was created and a Financial Stability Board was formed inside the Bank to coordinate this work, including both the governor and the deputy governor. The effects of these pre-crisis efforts were that the BoE was operating at the cutting edge of financial stability monitoring when the crisis hit, with its financial stability reports anticipating many of the problems that were to materialize in the crisis (e.g. on issues of liquidity risks; Wansleben 2021). However, at that point in time the BoE was missing any tools to transform their words into action (Hungin and Scott 2019, 341).

These institutional developments prior to the crisis meant that in 2008 there was a strong in-house voice for a large macro-prudential toolkit, with the division leaders pushing for an extensive and ambitious program of macro-prudential intervention aiming to curb the credit cycle (Aikman et al. 2010; interview, BoE economist, January 13, 2020). Summarizing this expansive stance of the division, despite the uncertainties surrounding the program, Aikman et al. wrote:

> the state of macro-prudential policy today has many similarities with the state of monetary policy just after the second world war. Data is incomplete, theory patchy, policy experience negligible. Monetary policy then was conducted by trial and error. The same will be true of macro-prudential policy now. Mistakes will be made. But as experience with the other arms of macroeconomic policy has taught us, the biggest mistake would be not to try. (Aikman et al. 2010, 25)

This expansive stance of the financial stability division, however, was by no means universal in the Bank. Instead, it was only one side in an extensive debate within the Bank over the appropriate goals for macro-prudential policy at the Bank.

This debate came to a head once the political debate on the regulatory system in the UK started to intensify in 2009. While the then incumbent Labor government was intent on maintaining the tripartite system of governance it had installed, reforming the FSA and installing deeper collaboration between the FSA and the BoE in terms of macro-prudential regulation, the Tories in opposition were weighing the much more radical alternative of suppressing the FSA and returning all its tasks to the BoE. In the context of this pending reorganization of the regulatory structure, the leadership of the BoE took a very proactive stance as it sought to structure the reorganization of the institutional landscape as much as possible in its favor, seeking to make sure that the new powers ascribed to the BoE would not expose it to too many reputational risks (Hungin and Scott 2019).

Anticipating a victory of the Tories and the possibility that macro-prudential powers could be handed to the BoE, the Bank set up a working group in 2009 on the issue of what kind of design of these powers the BoE should want. Inside this group there was a constant battle over whether the Bank should seek an expanded mandate, with the head of the financial stability division Andy Haldane pushing for inclusion of the goal of taming the cycle, whereas Deputy Governor Paul Tucker was pushing to limit it to increasing the financial system's resilience (interview, BoE economist, January 13, 2020), with the latter even willing to give up the macro-prudential powers altogether (interview, former BoE economist, December 20, 2017). The outcome of this debate was a compromise, which would include anti-cyclical policies, yet in a much-diminished role. This position was the one adopted in the ensuing negotiations, where a particular role fell to the BoE governor Mervyn King as well as his deputy Tucker, who early on engaged in talks with both the government and the opposition.

Already before the election in 2010, which would lead to the dismantling of the FSA and the return of micro- and macro-prudential supervision back to the BoE, they negotiated with the Tories over how to reorganize prudential powers, including macro-prudential regulation (interview, BoE economist, January 13, 2020). While the Treasury had intended to chair the new macro-prudential body, BoE governor King prevailed in his opinion to model it based on the Monetary Policy Committee and place it within the BoE, based on an "ex ante mandate, ex-post accountability" (BoE official, as cited in Hungin and Scott 2019, 342). The new Financial Policy Committee (FPC), which was to take over these macro-prudential tasks, was hence established inside the BoE, with the governor of the BoE at its helm. Consisting of twelve voting members (five external experts, the head of the financial service regulator, six BoE staff), it included only a non-voting seat for the Treasury. Rather than being controlled by the Treasury, strict accountability relationships ex post were established with all members due to give reports to Parliament and the Treasury Oversight Committee.

On the side of the BoE, these negotiations were very much driven by the awareness of the risks inherent in anti-cyclical policies. First, the BoE officials, aware of the political dangers inherent in the project of smoothing the cycle because of its discretionary character and its distributional implications, engaged in dialogues with politicians to shape the primary objective of the FPC, the macro-prudential body in the BoE (interview, former BoE official, December 20, 2017). They crafted official language such that it would be primarily focused on the goal of resiliency. This mandate, which was enshrined in the legal remit of the FPC, would charge it to "remove or reduce systemic risk, with a task of protecting and enhancing the resilience of the financial system" (Tucker 2011, 6). In this way, the BoE officials, wary of the political risks involved in anti-cyclical policies, decided to abstain from "fine-tuning the cycle" (Tucker 2013b, 6f.) and instead assigned a secondary role to anti-cyclical policies in the policy regime. Seeking to maintain constant resilience of the system through time-varying measures (Cunliffe 2015, 8f.), they were integrating anti-cyclical policies in their toolkit but explicitly subordinating them to the goal of resilience.

Second, aware that the application of such anti-cyclical measures could have unintended consequences and that learning would have to take place through trial and error, as regulators had no way of knowing ex ante what the impact of these measures would be (Tucker 2013a), the BoE officials insisted on close collaboration with the Treasury and Parliament. Because of the need to learn through mistakes, the unobservable nature of systemic risk for the public and the need for expert judgment, the BoE insisted on the need for legitimacy granted to decision-makers ex ante by Parliament (Dombret and Tucker 2012; Tucker 2012, 2013b). This was seen as important as anti-cyclical policies, "taking away the punchbowl," would be unpopular (Tucker 2012, 7). Institutionally, anti-cyclical measures were hence subjected to persistent parliamentary feedback, an institutional mechanism explicitly endorsed and crafted by the bureaucrats (Tucker 2011, 2012), seeking to gain political legitimacy for central bank action.

The exact powers of the FPC, while already established as an interim body in 2011, were then established in exchange with the Treasury over the course of the next two years (interview, former BoE policymaker, April 15, 2021), with the FPC officially beginning its operations in April 2013. Because of the ongoing debate inside the BoE and the weariness of leadership regarding the political exposure created by anti-cyclical measures, the policymakers only chose to request three binding powers, on which the FPC would gain directing power: to limit the leverage of banks, to set the countercyclical capital buffer and to impose sectoral capital requirements (Bank of England 2013a), powers it was subsequently granted. The FPC did not make any immediate further requests for directing powers, instead seeking powers of recommendation, because it initially feared that direction over more interventionist measures such as loan-to-value and loan-to-income restrictions would directly impinge upon the capacity of citizens to borrow to acquire a home, requiring a level of public acceptability that was not there yet (Bank of England 2012; interview, former BoE economist, December 20, 2017).[15]

This meant that right from the beginning of the FPC and increasingly so as time went on, the macro-prudential toolkit in the UK contained a countercyclical dimension. In line with this strategic orientation, the FPC produced the draft of the policy statement on the countercyclical capital buffer (CCyB) in January 2013 (Bank of England 2013a), which included the credit-to-GDP gap as a leading indicator but made clear that it embraces a wider model of core indicators. As the BoE pointed out, these indicators were to be used in a framework of "guided discretion," whereby the decision would always be taken based on expert judgment, using financial indicators as structuring devices for the discussion.[16] The mechanism of persistent parliamentary feedback was hence coupled with a very pragmatic use of financial cycle measures to structure the expert discussions in the FPC, seeking to achieve shared expert judgment that could be communicated to and understood by the public (Kohn 2016, 3f.). This allowed for communication to the public early on, building the case for anti-cyclical interventions (Kohn 2016, 8). In this way, based on carefully shielding the BoE from the threats to legitimacy immanent in countercyclical policies, policymakers set up a viable, if limited, countercyclical framework.

---

[15] Gradually, as time went on and first experiences were made, the FPC would also request these more interventionist measures in 2014 and 2015, a move that was favored by the shift in governorship from Mervyn King to Mark Carney in June 2013, a governor more open to anti-cyclical thinking and measures (interview, BoE economist, January 13, 2020). When in June 2014 the Treasury announced its intention to grant additional powers to the FPC, the FPC expressed the wish to gain powers over housing market developments and the leverage ratio (Bank of England 2014d). It formulated a framework for loan-to-value and loan-to-income ratios by 2015 (Bank of England 2015b) and finally, after negotiations with the Treasury in 2015, also gained regulatory powers over the buy-to-let market in 2016.

[16] This framework was confirmed in January 2014 (Bank of England 2014a), with the BoE assuming official responsibility for setting the CCyB in May 2014.

The Installation of a Fragmented Macro-Prudential Framework in the Eurozone

The installation of a macro-prudential framework in the European Union (EU), and the Eurozone in particular, is the most complex of the three cases analyzed: it occurred while continuing crises brought about a general transformation of the governance set-up of Eurozone banking supervision (Hennessy 2014). The European System of Central Banks (ESCB), with the ECB at its helm, was only eight years old when the crisis first hit. Its architecture was a tenuous compromise by political leaders in the EU to facilitate the issuance and governance of the Euro by the ECB (Dyson and Featherstone 1999) without granting any additional rights to the ECB to act as either a lender of last resort or an agent in banking supervision, functions jealously guarded by the national central banks.[17]

In this way, the final set-up of the ECB came to closely resemble the ideal typical understanding of an independent central bank at that time that was focusing on price stability, unencumbered by banking supervision and/or lender-of-last-resort functions, let alone an explicit financial stability mandate.[18] But neither did most national central banks in the EU have an explicit financial stability mandate, and while there were some moves pre-crisis to install financial stability departments, these departments yet again were to build up analytic capabilities, not to inform actual policymaking (for the case of the Bundesbank, see Ibrocevic 2022; for the deviant case of the Banco de Espana, see Saurina 2009). Once the transatlantic crisis hit the EU in fall 2008, this set-up of banking regulation and supervision in Europe would be substantially altered, empowering in due course financial stability divisions of both national central banks and in particular the ECB (McPhilemy 2015; Schelkle 2017).

---

[17] In the context of the negotiations of the Maastricht Treaty, the French had argued in favor of a lender-of-last-resort function and an explicit financial stability mandate, yet the German Bundesbank and other national central banks had refused this request (interview, ECB economist, September 4, 2014).

[18] The only faint reference to any such function in the Treaty was a vague paragraph that tasked the ECB with "contribut[ing] to the smooth conduct of policies pursued by competent authorities relating to the prudential supervision of credit institutions and the stability of the financial system" (TFEU Article 127 (5)).

Reform efforts began in earnest with the publication of the de Larosiere report in February 2009, which pointed to the lack of macro-prudential supervision within the EU as one of the main short-comings revealed by the crisis (de Larosiere et al. 2009, 39). While the authors fiercely opposed granting any micro-prudential powers to the ECB for fear of interfering with the setting of monetary policy (inter-view, economist involved in the crafting of the report, March 12, 2018), they advocated to grant it a central role for macro-prudential supervision within the context of the ESCB, seeing the ECB as uniquely positioned to inform such an analysis. The ECB was to chair the European Systemic Risk Council (de Larosiere et al. 2009, 46), which was to develop effective early warning systems for the EU as a whole and for national economies. It was to issue recommendations and warnings to nationally competent authority based on the early warning systems it developed. These proposals were transformed into EU regu-lation in November 2010 and the European Systemic Risk Board (ESRB) was founded on January 1, 2011.[19]

Of all the new European bodies created after the de Larosiere report,[20] the ESRB was arguably the least authoritative and most coordinative (McPhilemy and Roche 2013; Haar 2015, 174). Having sixty-one mem-bers, it was supposed to coordinate the macro-prudential decisions of national competent authorities in the EU (Haar 2015, 175) by issuing non-binding recommendations and warnings, with which National Competent Authorities (NCAs) are expected to comply or explain their deviation. To undertake its work, it was organizationally and

---

[19] To further help with the coordination of macro-prudential decisions in the Eurozone, the Financial Stability Committee of the European System of Central Banks was also installed on January 1, 2011. Chaired by the vice-president of the ECB, who was responsible for financial stability, it was tasked with facilitating exchange between the national central banks, the ECB and national supervisory authorities to support the governing council of the ECB in the fulfillment of its tasks relating to financial stability. This new set-up proved useful as national central banks had become major actors in national macro-prudential frameworks, with fourteen of them designed as the sole macro-prudential authority, and thirteen others gaining at least an important role in the macro-prudential analysis and in making recommendations for policy actions.

[20] The de Larosiere report also suggested the creation of the European Banking Authority (EBA), the European Securities and Markets Authority (ESMA) and the European Insurance and Organizational Pension Authority (EIOPA), which to a certain degree have direct law-making power as well as some direct supervisory functions (Haar 2015).

operationally very closely tied to the ECB, both in terms of its location (within the ECB) and its staff (Mcphilemy 2015, 160) but also with respect to its financial stability analysis. It was to be supported by the financial stability division of the ECB,[21] which from 2010 onwards began to produce country-level specific analyses in addition to analysis for the Euro area as a whole (interview, ECB economist, May 9, 2016).[22]

The de Larosiere report and the regulations that followed hence installed a dispersed distribution of macro-prudential powers. National competent authorities were to take measures in coordination with and supervised by the ESRB, which was to bundle the collective view on developments within the EU held within the ESCB and coordinate it with the different national bodies in charge of prudential supervision. This fragmentation installed at the heart of the European regime for macro-prudential supervision a need for coordination and consensus between different technocratic entities in the EU over cyclical developments (interview, ECB economist, May 9, 2016), as the ECB and the ESRB were largely bound to moral suasion and the attempt to convince policy to engage in macro-prudential measures. It thereby raised the importance of commonly shared frameworks of meaning and measurement to come to a consensual agreement.[23] To respond to this challenge, the ECB under its vice-president Vítor Constâncio, who from 2010 to 2018 was responsible for financial stability, hence substantially expanded the ECB's expertise in this domain. It also engaged in a sustained collective effort within the ESCB to generate new tools and metric devices.[24]

---

[21] See Council Regulation (EU) No 1096/2010 of November 17, 2010 conferring specific tasks on the ECB concerning the functioning of the ESRB.

[22] This change of focus was both due to a specific request to support the emerging ESRB and due to the insight generated by the crisis that financial stability monitoring required national-level analysis.

[23] It is also for that reason that among the three jurisdictions looked at, economists at the ESRB and the ECB have arguably invested the most in the generation of different measurement devices and have embraced most the engineering view on systemic risk, believing in its measurability and clear capacity to instruct action based on science (interview, academic economist, May 30, 2015).

[24] The most vivid incarnation of this trend was the set-up of a Macroprudential Research Network by the European system of central banks with the ECB at its helm in spring 2010, which brought together more than 130 applied central bank researchers as well as three scientific advisers. The network worked for four years, being an important kernel of macro-prudential research efforts in the EU.

Furthermore, after taking up his position in 2010, Constâncio advocated for an expansive, ambitious macro-prudential policy framework based on such newly developed metrics (see, e.g., Constâncio 2010, 2012a). This expansive macro-prudential stance focused its efforts on locating economies in their positioning in the financial cycle and initiating preemptive measures when booms start to accelerate (see, e.g., Constâncio et al. 2019, 32). It was grounded in the peculiar structure of the Eurozone, which combined a European-wide interest rate with national fiscal policy stances and a lack of automatic risk-sharing mechanisms (Schelkle 2017). This structure made the prevention of financial instability, of booms and busts both at the national and European level, a major goal of macro-prudential regulation in the Euro area. As Constâncio put it, "In the euro area context, the relative effectiveness of macro-prudential policy in tackling the build-up of financial stability risks is even more pronounced because, in a monetary union, a single monetary policy is ill-suited to deal with financial imbalances emerging at national level. Such imbalances are better tackled with targeted national macro-prudential measures" (Constâncio 2018; also interview, ECB economist, September 4, 2014).

It was hence an analysis of the danger of the buildup of imbalances in the Eurozone pre-crisis that was key as it underlies the stance on macro-prudential regulation inside the ECB. To the ECB financial stability division, this point was driven home by the Eurozone crisis (2010–12), which was interpreted as an outcome of "sudden stops" of capital flows to the countries in the periphery. These countries had attracted a lot of capital pre-crisis because of an interest rate that overall was too low for the inflationary tendencies of the countries concerned and where much of the money went into real estate bubbles (Constâncio 2018). This critical macro-prudential view by the ECB gained additional supervisory weight within the Eurozone with the political decision in 2012 to install the Banking Union and the Single Supervisory Mechanism (SSM), as the latter granted an explicit supervisory role to the ECB (interview, ECB manager, September 11, 2019). This package of reforms, which was part of the institutional resolution of the Eurozone crisis achieved at the breakthrough summit in summer 2012, occurred in the context of the ECB assuming its new role as lender of last resort, which was coupled with a new role in banking supervision (SSM).

Classification of macro-prudential instruments for the banking sector

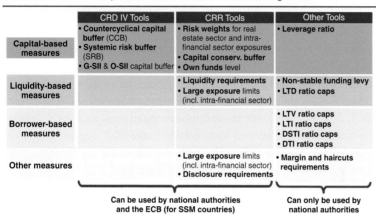

	CRD IV Tools	CRR Tools	Other Tools
Capital-based measures	• **Countercyclical capital buffer** (CCB) • **Systemic risk buffer** (SRB) • **G-SII & O-SII** capital buffer	• **Risk weights** for real estate sector and intra-financial sector exposures • **Capital conserv. buffer** • **Own funds level**	• **Leverage ratio**
Liquidity-based measures		• **Liquidity requirements** • **Large exposure** limits (incl. intra-financial sector)	• **Non-stable funding levy** • **LTD ratio caps**
Borrower-based measures			• **LTV ratio caps** • **LTI ratio caps** • **DSTI ratio caps** • **DTI ratio caps**
Other measures		• **Large exposure** limits (incl. intra-financial sector) • **Disclosure requirements**	• **Margin and haircuts requirements**

Can be used by national authorities and the ECB (for SSM countries)   **Can only be used by national authorities**

Figure 5.1 The distribution of powers to set anti-cyclical macro-prudential policies in the European Banking Union. (From Constâncio et al. 2019, 22.)

Officially taking up this role in November 2014, the ECB engaged in a large expansion of its workforce, an expansion that also included the financial stability division. Most importantly, however, this institutional change also led to an expansion of the ECB's mandate, as since October 2013 the SSM Regulation also allocated supervisory powers and a clear role for macro-prudential policy to the ECB. In this vein, Article 5 of the SSM that was legislated on October 15, 2013 (Council Regulation (EU) No. 1024/2013) bestowed direct macro-prudential powers on the ECB, based on a concern for financial stability formulated in Article 127(5) of the Treaty on the Functioning of the European Union. These institutional developments in the supervisory architecture, in conjunction with the legislative changes enacted in July 2013, led to a new sharing of supervisory powers in the macro-prudential sphere. That month, the EU was the first jurisdiction to transform the entire Basel III package into actual legislation, installing the transnational reform package (and with it the CCyB) at the heart of the European macro-prudential regulation.[25] Several of these newly introduced macro-prudential tools could, at least in theory, be topped up by the ECB, as Figure 5.1 illustrates.

---

[25] The EU included in this adaptation of Basel III several measures, such as the systemic risk buffer, which were unique to the EU (see Stellinga 2021).

Competencies in the Eurozone regarding macro-prudential decisions were now largely shared between nationally competent authorities and the ECB, whereby the ECB had top-up powers for decisions it deemed insufficiently anti-cyclical, including the countercyclical capital buffer (Haar 2015, 183). This installed effectively a co-decision-making process between the ECB and national competent authorities, although the NCAs still were the primary decision-makers (interview, ECB manager, May 9, 2016).[26] While the exact implications of these new legal stipulations were subject to serious legal debate,[27] the ECB in practice mostly sought to increase its epistemic authority in order to persuade and convince NCAs to act, even if they did not want to. In its stance, the ECB was strongly countercyclical, relying on in-house expertise of central bank economists. This position can best be exemplified by several speeches by the vice-chair of the ECB responsible for financial stability between 2012 and 2014, as he was seeking to overcome the skepticism by national central banks. In line with his analysis of the exposure to cyclical risks in the Eurozone and while acknowledging the need to increase the resilience of the system, Constâncio issued passionate pleas that macro-prudential regulation should go beyond that and be strongly anti-cyclical (e.g. Constâncio 2014a, b).

This stance found one of its strongest expressions in 2014, when he was tackling the debate over the two intermediate objectives head on, posing the issue in the following terms: "Macro-prudential policy faces a major test going forward: will there be determination and boldness to try to smooth the financial cycle, or will the authorities just take refuge in building buffers and strengthening financial institutions?" (Constâncio 2014a). His ambitious policy stance is concomitant with a rejection of resilience as the sole policy goal. As he points out,

The aim of macro-prudential policy should definitely be about tempering the cycle, rather than merely enhancing the resilience of the financial sector ahead of crises. ... Admittedly, fully controlling the financial cycle is an unattainable objective, but it would not be worth setting up the macro-prudential policy area if it were to refrain from attempting to fulfil the ambitious goal of influencing the credit cycle. (Constâncio 2014a, 17f.)

---

[26] The ECB is tasked with cooperating closely with them in case it wishes to top up measures (see Council Regulation [EU] No. 1024/2013, article 5, paragraph 4; Alexander 2017, 356).

[27] For example, whether the ECB could activate a measure such as a countercyclical capital buffer or only strengthen it, once it was activated.

Constâncio hence rejected the goal to merely increase resilience because, while much easier to achieve, he deems it to be completely unacceptable from a welfare perspective to observe a housing bubble and asset price growth and to not intervene (Constâncio 2014a, 17f.). He points to the welfare losses incurred because of the cycle and the dangers inherent in simply seeking to raise resilience, as nobody can predict the exact place or the intensity of the next crisis.

In line with this strong stance, he states as a first principle of macro-prudential policy that it should be preemptive and strongly counter-cyclical, based upon the concept of the financial cycle. He further explains that "[t]o effectively tame the financial cycle, a time-varying dimension is crucial in the design of policy instruments – that is, the instruments must be adjustable over the cycle" (Constâncio 2016c). Making his argument for such time-varying tools, he drew on recent academic and in-house contributions by ECB economists that endo-genize boom–bust cycles. However, given the early stages of the research program, he qualifies them as "welcome first steps on the road towards a new framework for the analysis of macro-prudential policy" (Constâncio 2014b), while insisting that policy action cannot wait for scientific breakthroughs. In the next years, he would continu-ously point to recent advances in scientific approaches for measure-ment of the cycle and of simulations portraying possible effects of these measures (Constâncio 2016b, c) to bolster his case for policy actions – advances, however, which were mostly produced by the Bank for International Settlements and in-house by ECB economists.[28]

Constâncio's impatient stance toward the role of science in guiding policy, building partly on in-house research in the making rather than waiting for definite academic results, was contrasted by the skepticism of macro-prudential change agents at European national central banks. The latter, at least initially, found these proposed measures to address the cycle largely unconvincing because of their limited scientific status and their limited scope and applicability (interviews, European banking regulators, July 9, 2016; ESRB, July 19, 2016; Dutch central banker, September 21, 2016). What further differentiated Constâncio's interven-tions, driven by a focus on output legitimacy, from these domestic change agents was the absence of accountability concerns with respect

---

[28] These mostly stem from the major research program (MaRS) initiated by the ESRB in 2012 (cf. Constâncio 2014b).

to Parliament or the European demos in his speeches. This absence, stemming from the uniquely insulated position of the ECB (Jabko 2009) and his belief in the capacity of (in-house) scientific measures to guide anti-cyclical discretionary policies, is what most strongly differentiates the ECB position from his national counterparts, both within the ESCB and with respect to the Federal Reserve and the BoE. His strong anti-cyclical position was in line, one can argue, with the structural position of the ECB within the governance network of macro-prudential regulation and the structural characteristics of the Eurozone.

Discussion

By analyzing the institutional action as well as the public speeches of the officials charged with developing macro-prudential policies at the Federal Reserve, BoE and ECB and the different regulatory stances they expose, we can extract both the common challenges linked to the project of anti-cyclical regulation and the different reactions to it.

What becomes clear is that the ambitious goal of taming the cycle was associated by all policymakers with (exigently) high demands upon metrics and with political dangers inherent in discretionary regulatory decision-taking. On the other hand, the less ambitious goal of structural measures was perceived to coincide with lower demands upon metrics and a process that permits avoiding the impression of unconstrained and arbitrary regulatory power. This shared problem assessment over the demands and risks associated with the goal of smoothing the cycle then interacted with the legitimacy concerns of bureaucrats related to the domestic accountability regimes they were subject to, leading to different, partially orthogonal approaches to the policy goal of combating the financial cycle. Whereas all policymakers agreed on the need to increase the resilience of the system and on the underlying economic concepts (externality analysis), this agreement disappeared with respect to the financial cycle. The USA largely abstained from engaging with the goal and the UK only gave limited endorsement based on a pragmatic approach, while the policymakers in charge of financial stability at the ECB saw it as the primary objective.

This strategic positioning of macro-prudential policymakers can be linked to the institutional constraints that shaped the administrative viability of macro-prudential reforms in these jurisdictions; that is, the administrative biases of officials asked to implement the policies as well

as the structural capacities to implement them. An additional important element were the institutionalized ways in which these societies
ensure the legitimacy of regulatory measures, in particular epistemological and procedural assurances regarding the policy ideas that guide
them (what Sheila Jasanoff calls "civic epistemologies"; see Jasanoff
2005, 2012). In this respect, the uncertain scientific status of the financial cycle and the lack of endorsement by academia, coupled with the
need for discretionary decision-making, structured the stance of central
bankers in the early 2010s (see Table 5.2).

The uncertain scientific status and the lack of endorsement by academia stood in opposition to the distinctive civic epistemology in the
USA, which puts value on scientifically backed, objective decisions
based on expertise outside of the state (academia) and on due process
(Fourcade 2009; Jasanoff 2012). The Federal Reserve subject to oversight by Congress was wary of taking decisions based on an immature
science that might lead to political questioning and hence vastly preferred structural measures, which could be based on (the scientifically
accepted) externality analysis and enacted following a due process.
This position was characterized by an attempt to depoliticize regulatory intervention, bringing it into line with the norms of US regulatory
decision-making. In the case of the BoE, policymakers were also acutely
aware of the political backlash that discretionary policy decisions
might evoke and hence chose to privilege resilience over the anti-
cyclical dimension. There, the immature scientific measurement led to
a pragmatic use of cyclical metrics in the deliberation of the expert
committee, based on common sense.

It is only fitting then that the ECB representative emerges as the most
forceful voice for anti-cyclical intervention, given that in terms of the
accountability regime, the ECB is a unique case among central banks,
with complete independence enshrined in the European treaties and
very limited accountability to politicians (McNamara 2002, 66; Jabko
2009, 400f.). Furthermore, the final responsibility for anti-cyclical
measures mostly resided with national central banks rather than the
ECB itself. Absent these direct accountability concerns, the immature
science did not lead to the abandonment of the project or a subordinated role but to the initiation of an in-house research project, where
central bank economists were given the task to provide the analytics for
central bank intervention. However, in the case of the ECB anti-cyclical
policies need to be orchestrated with national central banks, which in

Table 5.2 *Civic epistemologies and the regulatory stance regarding the financial cycle*

Civic epistemology	USA	UK	ECB
Methods of ensuring accountability	Due process, assumptions of distrust, legal	Assumptions of trust, relational	Interaction between ECB and national central banks
Preferred registers of objectivity	Analytical, economic science/sound science: "view from nowhere"	Expert judgment: negotiated (view from everywhere, i.e. easily comprehensible for all)	Analytical but in-house economists, statist science (view from technocrats)
Accepted bases of expertise	Academia	Experts	Central bank economists
Accountability concerns and their interaction with the goal of smoothening the financial cycle	Input legitimacy: "view from nowhere" cannot be achieved for the financial cycle, discretionary intervention cannot be reconciled with administrative due process	Throughput legitimacy: involve experts with different views, deliberation permits evolution of common-sense judgment by experts, pragmatic use of financial cycle concept	Output legitimacy: danger of welfare losses; technocratic knowledge by central banks to determine financial cycle is capable of guiding regulatory decision-making (at least in the long run)

the 2010s had been largely unimpressed by the scientific progress of the ECB. Constâncio's attempts to re-politicize the issue, pointing to its human-made character and hence its amenability to change, trailed off among a discursive audience that was only too attentive to the political risks such an approach entailed.

In the next chapters, we shall follow the installation of the CCyB, the only discretionary time-varying measure that was installed in Basel III, and that hence had to be implemented by these central banks, both in the EU and the USA, to see if and how far these problems were overcome. As we will see, initial skepticism and a wary stance among technocrats in central banks toward the implementation of this measure, plagued by difficulties in measuring cyclical developments, gave way to an increasingly assertive position of central bank economists regarding their capabilities to detect such trends. This shift was the outgrowth of the continued collective work of these central bankers, who, jointly with interested academics, were developing longitudinal databases and early warning models capable of spotting cyclical swings sufficiently ahead of time in order to inform the setting of the CCyB.

6 | From the Global to the Local

Enacting the Countercyclical Capital Buffer through the Creation of Early Warning Systems

As the last chapter has shown, discretionary anti-cyclical measures were seen to carry substantial political risks for central banks, making the development of sound and reliable early warning systems (EWS) a major precondition for the active use of this measure. The focus of this chapter then is the development of such EWS regarding the buildup of cyclical systemic risks at the Federal Reserve Board, the European Central Bank (ECB) and the Bank of England (BoE) from 2012 to 2017, and how these were to be hardwired into the use of the counter-cyclical measures in these jurisdictions. The chapter thereby probes the construction of macro-prudential policy devices that have been developed post-crisis and the macro-prudential policy decisions they provoke, seeking to trace how the identification of cyclical systemic risks by applied economists within these central banks feeds into the newly installed macro-prudential frameworks.

One particular concern of this work was the calibration of the countercyclical capital buffer (CCyB), the only discretionary time-varying measure to address cyclical fluctuations that had been agreed at the international level (see Chapter 4). Given its internationally enshrined status, no national macro-prudential authority could avoid its operationalization in the long run, forcing central bank economists to address the issue of whether and in how far cyclical upswings could be detected sufficiently ahead of time in order to inform policymaking. In this respect, the framework suggested by the Basel Committee on Banking Supervision (BCBS) could function as a first guide. However, as Chapter 4 has shown, the BCBS's proposal for the calibration of the CCyB had been based on preliminary work that required both further statistical refinement and adaptation to national circumstances (interview, Bundesbank economist, November 6, 2015).

In order to understand the construction of EWS in conjunction with the operationalization of the CCyB, this chapter reflects on the work of applied economists within the ECB, the European System of Central

Banks (ESCB), the Federal Reserve and the BoE. Much like engineers, they were working in research teams, engaging in applied research that sought to detect the buildup of cyclical systemic risk. Conducting their work in parallel, these research teams were seeking to calibrate measurement systems that were appropriate for their particular national context, both in terms of the configuration of their domestic financial system and the set-up of the macro-prudential authority. At the collective level, at the same time, they formed an epistemic community, frequently interacting with each other during research conferences organized in central banks and outside of it, sharing research and experiences (interview, BoE economists, December 12, 2019; BoE economist, January 13, 2020). What we can observe in this case is thus an epistemic community of researchers that engages in regulatory science (Jasanoff 2011a, b), seeking to generate instruments that are robust and reliable enough to guide the macro-prudential actions of their central bank.

Tracing their work, I will first focus on the development of these EWS in the European Union (EU), which was a collaborative exercise between economists from national central banks and the ECB. Second, I will trace how the splintered governance of macro-prudential decisions within the Eurozone, which installed a co-decision-making role for the ECB from 2014 onwards, shaped the development of EWS at the ECB and their use. There, the fact that the assessment of cyclical systemic risks was negotiated between the ECB and national central banks to determine the need for activation of the CCyB led to the set-up of a battery of EWS and the refinement of measurements of the financial cycle at the ECB, driven by the desire to negotiate with national authorities over the appropriate macro-prudential stance.

Third, the chapter contrasts these findings with the case of the Federal Reserve, where economists were operating in a setting where the CCyB found a muted endorsement. Their work therefore rather focused on the attempt to calibrate stress tests and monetary policy in a countercyclical manner. This work produced a coherent framework, which in theory was also seen as a good guide for CCyB calibration. While this analytical work developed in the USA to date had no impact on the setting of the CCyB, it would prove influential internationally and in other jurisdictions, in particular in the UK. The chapter concludes with the UK framework. This framework is the most advanced, drawing upon the work of both US and Eurozone economists, calibrating the CCyB based on anti-cyclical stress test exercises. The latter is analyzed as the synthesis of much of the work of these applied economists over the last decade, emboldening a more proactive anti-cyclical macro-prudential stance.

The Construction of Early Warning Systems in the Eurozone: Assembling Europe

The genesis and character of the financial stability monitoring framework of the ECB can be traced to its coordinating role in a fragmented system of European macro-prudential governance. Rather than a single model, it consists of a battery of probabilistic models that are pragmatically applied to structure the conversation with individual member states (which hold the primary responsibility for macro-prudential decision-making). This battery of models was developed jointly by economists of the ECB and of national central banks in an intense collaborative effort to generate the EWS seen as a necessary prerequisite for the new task of macro-prudential supervision. The coordinating work of the ECB involved the agreement on valid models, valid datasets and to compile the data in a way that allowed comparability across countries, while at the same doing justice to each individual country. This task included first and foremost the calibration of the CCyB.

This coordinating role of the ECB began in January 2011, when the European Systemic Risk Board was officially set up as the new coordinating body for macro-prudential oversight of the entire EU financial system. The ECB was tasked with supporting this body analytically, statistically and logistically, with the first task falling primarily to the ECB's financial stability surveillance division. Its role thereby expanded from Euro-area analysis based on EU-wide aggregates – which since 2004 was documented in the ECB Financial Stability Review – toward country-specific analyses, with the need for such country-specific analysis seen as one lesson of the crisis (interview, ECB economist, May 9, 2016). In this context, the development of early warning models that take the specificities of each individual member state into account required the collaboration and coordination with national central banks regarding the available data and the appropriate way to understand country-level developments.

To support this process analytically, the leadership of the financial stability division decided in conjunction with the research department to start a Macroprudential Research Network (MaRS), which over the course of four years involved more than 130 central bank economists from all 27 central banks in a collaborative effort to generate models and metrics that could facilitate this system of European macro-prudential supervision. One of the three workstreams in the network was devoted to the development of EWS and systemic risk indicators, pursuing "relatively practical research which could be used – and, to some extent, already is being used – to strengthen the analytical toolkit for macro -prudential oversight in the EU" (ECB 2014, 49).

The very first practical outcome of this research effort was the construction of a historical database on banking and financial crises, which for the first time assembled data on periods of financial distress for all twenty-seven EU countries from 1970 onwards (Babecky et al. 2012; see also ECB 2014, 63). The goal of this dataset was to "provide a common basis for analysing the causes and effects of these crises and assessing the performance of early warning tools" (ECB 2014, 63). It provided researchers in the group and central bank staff in general with a dataset sufficiently large to test their EWS's capacity to predict crises, setting up an analytical competition over which central bank would generate the best predictive model.[1] These joint research efforts, seeking to set up well-performing EWS and engaging in comparative exercises, would prove to be an important building block for the set-up of a European system of macro-prudential supervision based on dialogue and collaboration between national central banks and the ECB.

The first instance in which this joint effort would prove useful in terms of practical results was during the work regarding the EU-wide framework for the possible calibration of the CCyB, wherein the ESRB as well as the ECB financial stability division would take a lead role. This work started in 2012, while the final version of the Capital Requirements Directive IV and the Capital Requirements Regulation, the European transposition of Basel III, was still negotiated in Brussels (interview, Bundesbank official, November 6, 2015). It was at that moment that the ESRB set up an instrument working group to test the capacity of the credit-to-GDP gap – the main indicator as proposed

---

[1] Emblematic of this friendly competition was the "horserace" of nine different EWS the researchers from the Macroprudential Research Network (MaRS) workstream conducted for the final conference of the network, in which the performance of EWS by seven central banks was compared (ECB 2014, 63f.).

by the Basel Committee – to detect pending financial distress in EU economies and function as a reliable indicator.

Composed of thirty economists delegated from different national European central banks, this group engaged in econometric studies that tested the suitability of the credit-to-GDP gap in light of historical country-specific evidence. The group met around every three months and exchanged the results of the first tests for different countries (interview, Bundesbank official, November 6, 2015). In its work, it encountered some problems with the credit-to-GDP gap due to data availability and unique historical pathways (interview, Bundesbank official, November 6, 2015; interview, BoE economist, February 13, 2020). Using the newly assembled European dataset on financial crisis as well as specific country-level data as the backdrop of its work, it was hence engaging in extensive econometric testing of different possible specifications and amendments.

Through its early start, the work of the ESRB working group was already well advanced when the European Directive 2013/36 in July 2013 implemented Basel III in Europe and with it the CCyB. Based on the econometric work of the working group, the ESRB published in the summer of 2014 its recommendation on guidance for setting counter-cyclical buffer rates (ESRB/2014/1–2014/C 293/01), where it explicitly tied the objective of the CCyB to "the sustainable provision of credit to the real economy throughout the financial cycle" and specified that the credit-to-GDP gap as described in the Basel III framework was the starting point for setting the CCyB in EU countries (ESRB/2014/1–2014/C 293/01, p. 5). At the same time, it acknowledged that for specific countries this measure could be ill adjusted due to the specificities of the structural features of these countries and that in general other non-specified variables should be taken into account (ESRB/2014/1–2014/C 293/01, p. 5).[2]

---

[2] This acknowledgment was based on a first finding of the working group that due to different historical paths in Europe, the credit-to-GDP gap was not a reliable indicator for Eastern European countries because they had experienced a very strong above trend growth of credit to GDP post-1989, which was due to "financial deepening." Hence for these countries, the credit-to-GDP gap was deemed an inadequate indicator (interview, Bundesbank official, November 6, 2015) and alternative and more appropriate indicators were chosen. This also held for countries that experienced a structural break in their credit expansion, an issue a simple Hodrick-Prescott (HP) filter cannot deal with (interview, ECB economist, May 9, 2016).

This convergence on the credit-to-GDP gap as a measure was based on the difficulties in generating more robust and reliable indicator guidance due to insufficient data availability for all countries (Detken et al. 2014). While testing different univariate and bivariate measures to detect the cyclical buildup of systemic risks in EU countries, the group found the credit-to-GDP gap to be the most robust and best-performing univariate indicator across all countries (Detken et al. 2014, 1). Alternatives, including indicators such as real estate prices that could improve upon the capacity of the credit-to-GDP gap (Detken et al. 2014, 23, 36), were discarded for the general EU-wide approach because these results were not robust enough, also due to data gaps (Detken et al. 2014, 36).[3] The decision to designate the credit-to-GDP gap as the best indicator at this point was hence driven by the desire to ensure comparability among countries, given that other specifications did not materially improve upon the Basel method (interview, Bundesbank economist, November 6, 2015).

At that moment in time, the group therefore recommended following an approach they themselves designated as the least costly path toward a calibration framework for the CCyB, "while leaving the framework open to future improvements, such as more sophisticated probabilistic approaches that included more variables, such as real estate, a calibration based on stress tests or cost-benefit analyses" (Detken et al. 2014, 51). Researchers at national central banks subsequently used this recommendation as input for their work to specify the best possible way of measuring the domestic financial cycle to calibrate the CCyB. In the end, most countries often directly relied on the credit-to-GDP gap as the central indicator, also due to the central position of the credit-to-GDP gap in the 2013 EU directive (for the case of Germany, see Tente et al. 2015; for the deviating case of the UK, see later in this chapter).

Within the Eurozone, this work of calibrating the metrics that would lead to an activation of the CCyB occurred in the context of an intensifying exchange between national competent authorities and the ECB, which with the advent of the Single Supervisory Mechanism in 2014 was granted co-decision-making powers regarding macro-prudential decisions (see Council Regulation (EU) No 1024/2013). These new

---

[3] These findings were in line with early work from the BoE, which indicated that augmenting this indicator through other variables would improve its performance (Giese et al. 2014). Giese herself was a member of the working group.

macro-prudential powers gave the ECB the possibility to top-up domestic macro-prudential buffers, based on the latter's analysis of cyclical developments in these countries, which in theory could justify raising national Ccybs if the ECB deemed it necessary (see last chapter). This shift in macro-prudential powers substantially upgraded the role of the ECB's financial stability division and its early warning models, which now became the starting point for debates between these two actors on the appropriate macro-prudential stance regarding the buildup of cyclical risks.

The European Central Bank: Negotiating an Appropriate Macro-Prudential Stance

Discussions regarding this stance were to take place in the Financial Stability Committee of the ESCB, a Committee that was founded in 2011 to support the ECB in its tasks related to financial stability.[4] While the decision-making set-up was asymmetric, in that the national authorities were to take the first decision, the role of the ECB being to evaluate the appropriateness of the stance, the ECB in the Committee sought a symmetric discussion on the "adequacy of the macroprudential stance across the SSM [Single Supervisory Mechanism] and not only in any one individual Member State" (ECB 2016a, 8). These discussions were to serve as a first step in the possible calibration of additional macro-prudential measures, a process characterized by coordination and consensus building between the ECB and the member states (ECB 2016a, 9). The ECB's goal in these discussions was to overcome an assumed "inaction bias" on the part of national authorities, which had to consider the political economy of possible anti-cyclical measures, for which the ECB instituted a process, which granted the ECB the right to request action if its early warning models indicated the need for it, or alternatively to receive an explanation for inaction.

The EWS of the ECB Financial Stability Surveillance division were hence to play a central role structuring this discussion. In addition to providing an overview of EU- and Euro-area wide developments, the division was now also tasked to conduct "analysis at country level, with

---

[4] In this forum, chaired by Vitor Constâncio, all the national central banks and relevant supervisory authorities were assembled in conjunction with the ECB's financial stability division.

the aim of identifying and monitoring risks that are specific to individual Member States" (ECB 2016a, 9). Working "in close cooperation with experts from the national authorities, exchanging data and analysis" as well as drawing "on material produced by members of the Eurosystem's Financial Stability Committee" (ECB 2016a, 9), these analyses were to trigger an early discussion of vulnerabilities. Because of this changed legal mandate and the new institutional set-up, the ECB division intensified its work on EWS. Paying attention to both the individual country-level specificities and the common trend, the goal of this work was to push for early national action to counter incipient systemic risks.

One direction of work pursued in this context was the refinement of financial cycle measurements for the Eurozone and individual countries at the same time (Schueler et al. 2015, 2017). During this work, Schueler – a postdoctoral researcher at the financial stability division of the ECB – detected severe shortcomings in the proposal of the Basel Committee to calibrate the CCyB, shortcomings that if not corrected would imply a delayed reaction function to a pickup in the credit cycle. This shortcoming emerged from the technical specifications as to how the credit-to-GDP gap was supposed to be measured according to the BCBS, in particular a faulty specification of the filter used to detect cyclical developments in the data.[5] Schueler and his senior colleagues at the ESRB therefore proposed a new measure, more sensitive to cyclical developments in the short term, which they found to outperform the credit-to-GDP gap as proposed by the Bank for International Settlements (Schueler et al. 2015, 3).[6] This new measure applied to the Eurozone showed a much earlier upswing in the financial cycle in several countries, such as Germany, allowing the ECB to make the case for early action[7] (see next chapter).

---

[5] Concretely, the work found that the specified setting of the HP filter to filter out the trend from random movement was too high, creating financial cycles at a spurious and excessive length. This misspecification implied that the credit-to-GDP gap would not show any rise of cyclical systemic risks for several years after a bust had occurred, independent of actual developments in the data, as the filter specifications would simply filter out any rise in the short term (see Schueler et al. 2015; Schueler 2018a, b; Constâncio et al. 2019, 54).

[6] Technically speaking, they proposed to use a multi-spectral approach instead, which used the co-movement of asset prices and credit growth jointly.

[7] As Schueler and colleagues put it, "Moreover, the distinct characteristics of financial cycles relative to business cycles within countries, as well as their divergences across countries, indicate that there is a potential scope for specialised country-level macroprudential policies targeted at the build-up of systemic risks" (Schueler et al. 2017, 3f.).

In addition to the attempt to develop better general indicators for cyclical systemic risks for both the Eurozone and individual countries, a second direction of work of the division was an increase in the individual country-level monitoring for cyclical upswings. To be able to accomplish these tasks, the division was strongly expanding, doubling its manpower between 2012 and 2014 (interview, ECB economist, May 9, 2016). And yet, it was clear to the management of the division that the ECB's analyses could not match the depth and sophistication of member-level central banks. In order to increase the validity and legitimacy of these analyses, researchers at the ECB also intensified their coordinating efforts with national central banks to agree upon commonly shared models and datasets to perform such country-level analysis of cyclical systemic risks.

In these negotiations, their goal was not necessarily to impose a unitary system of analysis due to possible individual country-level idiosyncrasies,[8] but to install a commonly agreed analytical frame and a commonly agreed set of data that could function as a basis of discussion. The leader of the financial stability surveillance division at the ECB deemed this agreement crucial to increase the reports' legitimacy. As an ECB official involved in the negotiations put it,

if we had not done this and a model would signal dangers, then they [national authority] would say, you have used the wrong data series on credit and you can always find one among the ten, where the results do not show up ... and so we have agreed on certain things to be reported ... and it was a necessary condition that such a model can have any role. (Interview, ECB economist, May 9, 2016, translation mine)

Using the "veil of ignorance" over dataset collection and models before the results were generated (interview, ECB economist, May 9, 2016), the ECB set out to agree ex ante with national central banks on a limited set of models and datasets in order to increase the legitimacy of future results.

This method of generating commonly accepted models and datasets was part of a strategy of the ECB to overcome the computing power advantages of the nationally competent authorities (interview, ECB economist, May 9, 2016). By agreeing ex ante on the appropriate

---

[8] These idiosyncrasies could be caused, for example, by the country-level specific aggregation of credit data, which would impact measures such as the credit-to-GDP gap (interview, French macro-prudential economist, April 8, 2021).

models and datasets, "the burden of proof is shifted to the national authorities" (interview, ECB manager, May 9, 2016), should any of these models indicate a pending problem. This configuration allowed the ECB team of about a dozen experts to match the computing power and expertise of national central banks, which might employ twenty or more persons each to assess financial stability risks in their countries. Rather than competing with these divisions on analytical prowess, the question in the discussion could now center on why the indicators of the ECB's model should or should not be discarded, given the particular country-level experience at this moment in time.

Once these EWS and the inversion of proof were introduced in 2014, these model-based measurements created some concern among economist in national central banks. They feared a degree of automaticity in terms of setting the CCyB that would leave no discretion to the national authorities (interview, Bundesbank economist, July 25, 2016). In particular, they were worried that a red flag by these models would automatically define the need to take action, in effect limiting the discretion of national authorities and their capacity to juggle political sensitivities in their countries. In the end, however, these fears turned out to be overblown, as these discussions were not driven by a singular models' detection of upcoming crises but instead by the subsequent expert discussions in the different fora of the Financial Stability Committee (ECB 2016a, 10; interview, ECB economist, May 9, 2016). As the ECB clarifies, "[m]odel-based inputs will serve as the ECB's starting point for calibration discussions within the Eurosystem, *in which expert judgement and knowledge about the sources of cyclical risks, as well as detailed information on the specificities of national financial sectors, will always be a key input*" (Constâncio et al. 2019, 42, emphasis mine).

While some of this expert judgment stems from the ECB, in the final analysis the decisive expertise resides in the financial stability departments in national central banks (interview, ECB economist, May 9, 2016). This fact is amplified by the information asymmetries that exist between them and the ECB (interview, German supervisor, January 10, 2020), allowing national authorities to undermine any analyses of the ECB (interview, French central bank economist, May 20, 2021). Despite a highly skilled expert group within the ECB (interview, German BaFin, January 17, 2020), the ECB can hence only structure the dialogue with national central banks through its models, but it cannot completely equalize the latter's manpower or information advantages (ECB manager, May 9, 2016). Instead, it needs to seek to persuade these divisions, slowly, generating the consensus for an increased level of macro-prudential vigilance should its models indicate the need for action. While this mode of governance did not pose a problem initially, as Europe was only slowly emerging from the trough of the cycle, this fragmented and negotiated form of the assessment of cyclical systemic risks was to pose severe challenges to the timely enactment of countercyclical measures in the subsequent upswing that developed from 2015 onwards (see Chapter 8).

As we will see in the following section, change agents at the Federal Reserve faced a different form of fragmentation, which, however, was also frustrating the immediate use of their measurement devices in terms of anti-cyclical action. In the USA, these pressures, which were linked to the incomplete financial stability mandate of the Federal Reserve and the expected political backlash by banks against discretionary measures, were pushing their efforts into the calibration of stress tests, which were less vulnerable to attack and delay by banks. This different origin would influence their set-up of the monitoring framework, which initially would focus on existing vulnerabilities in the system, which only over time would come to be complemented by a dynamic historical analysis that could inform the CCyB.

The Federal Reserve: Monitoring Financial Stability to Modify Stress Tests and Potentially Monetary Policy, but Not the Countercyclical Capital Buffer

At the Federal Reserve, the initial discussion of the "credit-to-GDP gap," the central measure for excessive credit growth suggested by the BCBS to calibrate the CCyB, was characterized by skepticism. In this vein, two economists from the financial stability division published a paper in 2011 (Edge and Meisenzahl 2011), which pointed to the risks of misspecification and measurement error, potentially imposing undue burdens on the financial system without providing beneficial results. This, in conjunction with the opposition by the higher echelon of the Federal Reserve Board members against openly discretionary time-varying measures (see Chapter 5), led to an initial rejection of the CCyB as a domestic policy tool. In this vein, the CCyB was only pro forma introduced into Regulation Q in 2013 to be officially compliant with Basel III, enabling the USA to reciprocate any CCyB buffers other jurisdictions might impose. This move gave the USA until 2016 to implement it domestically. Work on the CCyB hence did not play a large role in the initial formulation of the Federal Reserve's financial stability monitoring framework. Instead, in the context of the repositioning of the Federal Reserve as a systemic risk regulator (Bernanke 2012a, b), the Federal Reserve's EWS was developed for the purpose of calibrating the stress tests.

While the first stress tests contained no specific cyclical macro-prudential elements, the work of the financial stability division designing severely adverse scenarios initiated thinking about a framework that focused on the evolution of vulnerabilities in the financial system, which could be considered when designing these scenarios (interview, former Federal Reserve economist, January 9, 2018). Drawing upon the contacts established with the statistics department at the Federal Reserve New York and the Board in the context of designing the first stress test scenarios, the financial stability policy division Director Liang, together with Tobias Adrian (then Federal Reserve New York) and Daniel Covitz (the Board's statistics department), set out to develop such a monitoring framework. For this work, she had the explicit backing of Bernanke who chaired the financial stability discussions within the Federal Reserve until 2014 and who was worried that due to the restrictions imposed by the Dodd-Frank Act, it had become much more difficult for the Federal Reserve to provide liquidity in times of crisis (interview, former Federal Reserve economist, January 9, 2018; see Chapter 5). This to him implied the need for a forward-looking financial stability monitoring framework that could spot rising vulnerabilities in order to direct mitigating central bank actions (Adrian et al. 2013; Bernanke 2013), which is why the results of this framework were to be reported to the Board and the Federal Open Market Committee, in order to inform decision-making by the Board.

In line with the skepticism of the higher echelon of policymakers at the Federal Reserve to be able to spot the development of asset price bubbles (Bernanke 2012b), the framework abstained from a direct focus on asset bubbles and when they might burst, instead focusing on the underlying vulnerabilities, which might transform a shock into a system-wide crisis (Bernanke 2012b; Adrian et al. 2013, 1). Building such a framework, it was drawing on the new mainstream economic literature on frictions and vulnerabilities in the financial system that had emerged post-crisis (interview, former Federal Reserve economist,

January 9, 2018). This new work allowed for the identification of negative externalities market actors impose on non-involved third parties, externalities that could be remedied by regulation.[9] This "scientific" framework focused on the pricing of risk and its link to leverage in the financial system, seeking to capture what had come to be known as the "volatility paradox," the fact that the price of risk is lowest in the buildup phase of systemic risk (interview, former Federal Reserve economist, August 20, 2018). In line with work of one of the authors of the report (Adrian and Shin 2010), the framework linked this fact primarily to the increasing provision of liquidity by broker-dealers in good times, which sustained the increasing leverage of the system.

The framework, which was seeking to reorganize the expertise in the Federal Reserve to not only focus on financial conditions (monetary policy) but also financial vulnerabilities (interview, former Federal Reserve economist, January 9, 2018), became the basis for the permanent monitoring of the US financial system. One of its primary aims was to inform the discretionary macro-prudential element of stress tests by indicating which financial vulnerabilities should be considered and how their effects should be calibrated (Adrian et al. 2013, 42). Creating the concept of "salient risks" as a legally defined element of their annual stress tests in November 2013, the Federal Reserve created a venue for including this analysis in their scenario design (Federal Reserve System 2013, 27), making it the predominant venue through which cyclical analysis was included in the forward-looking supervision of the Federal Reserve (see Liang 2013, 6f.).[10]

In contrast, the same monitoring framework betrayed a certain distrust in the suitability of the CCyB for such countercyclical action, as it was seen to "raise notable challenges for the timing of the build-up and release. In particular, an early build-up of a buffer would risk imposing

---

[9] Both vulnerabilities as well as amplification mechanisms are derived from the concept of market failures. This market failure view allows the authors to assume the perfect rationality of agents, which, however, are confronted with coordination problems that produce negative externalities such as fire sales (Stein 2012), a central step to justify government interventions. They were thereby taking a stance that had already been taken in the mainstream New Keynesian literature pre-crisis to justify government interventions (Clift 2018, 70f.).

[10] In the subsequent stress tests, the Federal Reserve would include the possibility of "steeper yield curve and sharp corrections in corporate bond and real estate prices, risks arising from commercial real estate, negative interest rates and disruptions in bond market liquidity" (see Liang 2018).

unnecessary increases in the costs of credit" (Adrian et al. 2013, 28f.). While time-varying stress tests were seen to suffer from similar problems, their high frequency and the discretion granted to the Federal Reserve to adjust the severity of the scenarios annually, which allowed for the inclusion of newly identified cyclical risks, made this policy tool seem suppler and more fit for the purpose at hand (Adrian et al. 2013, 29). Underlying this assessment was a concern within the Federal Reserve (in particular by Tarullo) regarding the unavoidable time lags for raising the CCyB (twelve months from decision to implementation) as well as the difficulty of coordinating such a move with the Federal Deposit Insurance Corporation and the Office of the Currency of the Comptroller, which also needed to agree (interview, former Federal Reserve economist, January 9, 2018; see Chapter 5).

After the publication of the new framework, the first task for the financial stability division was to back test the framework with historical data in order to convince Board members of its usefulness.[11] To do so, they needed to show that the framework would have predicted prior crises sufficiently precise and ahead of time such that preemptive action could have been taken (interview, central bank economist involved in the exercise, January 13, 2020). The second, related task was to generate metrics that could be easily communicated to Board members, conveying the impending dangers that were building up to policymakers. These tasks structured the work by a team of Federal Reserve economists at the financial stability division, which jointly with economists from the research and statistics division sought to test the vulnerability framework using historical data and to visualize the results in terms of a heat map (Aikman et al. 2015; for a visualization, see 49f.).

To effectively back test the framework, the team used historical databases available at the Federal Reserve to match a range of forty-four indicators of developments in financial markets and of credit growth, with three categories of vulnerabilities identified in the framework.[12] For their econometric work, they could base themselves on prior efforts in the Federal Reserve System, which had expanded and

---

[11] In particular, Jeremy Stein, a former Harvard professor and himself a specialist on macro-prudential regulation (interview, central bank economist involved in the exercise, January 13, 2020), demanded this exercise.

[12] These three vulnerabilities were "investor risk appetite in asset markets, non-financial sector leverage and financial sector vulnerabilities linked to leverage and maturity transformation" (Aikman et al. 2015, 2).

updated the National Financing Condition Index database and experimented with attempts to weigh the data (Brave and Butters 2011). Using the past US experience as a de facto experimental playground to test the capability of the framework to predict future developments, the team was able to show the usefulness of the three vulnerabilities to signal the buildup of financial vulnerabilities in "pseudo-real-time" (Aikman et al. 2015, 28). In addition, the paper found that one of the vulnerabilities, namely investor risk appetite, was a good lead indicator, predicting developments both in the financial vulnerabilities' category and the non-financial imbalances category over time (Aikman et al. 2015, 26f.). However, the theoretical interpretations of these statistical findings were still tentative as overall the work suffered from the lack of a unified theoretical framework.[13]

This was particularly problematic in the context of their attempt to generate a meaningful aggregate indicator of evolving financial vulnerabilities, which they could present to policymakers. As they put it:

A central challenge to presenting a single summary statistic of vulnerability is the relatively unstructured approach we take: in the absence of a specific theory regarding how asset valuations, nonfinancial borrowing, and leverage and maturity transformation by the financial system interact to generate the vulnerability of the economy to financial stress, there is no clear direction to combining the indicators we consider into an overall assessment. (Aikman et al. 2015, 19)

This stance reflected the fact that the analytical framework to describe these relationships was still not robust and reliable enough at this time, as nothing like the "the Philipps curve to weigh the news that arrive" had emerged yet (interview, central bank economist involved in the effort, January 13, 2020). The research team hence decided to take a rather agnostic approach about how much to weigh individual variables, using

---

[13] The paper provided a tentative interpretation for this fact in line with Minsky's financial instability hypothesis, arguing that "[t]he credit cycle is triggered initially by an increase in investor willingness to bear risk, which is reflected in higher asset prices and a relaxation of lending standards. Households and businesses respond to these developments by taking on more debt, further supporting asset prices. While financial institutions are initially able to accommodate this credit expansion, as the boom continues, their balance sheets become stretched, and vulnerabilities increase" (Aikman et al. 2015, 26f.). This finding was as much political as it was economic, as it sought to establish the category of risk appetite as a firm element of the monitoring framework (interview, economist, January 13, 2020).

an arithmetic average of these indicators to calculate the evolving vulnerabilities (Aikman et al. 2015, 23). Based on these averages, they generated a heat map of vulnerabilities in the US system, which depicted the buildup of vulnerabilities before the financial crisis, as well as their subsequent cooling post-crisis (Aikman et al. 2015, 24f., 50).

Overall, the tentative evidence and the capacity to measure the persistent buildup of vulnerabilities before the financial crisis based on the aggregate indicators provided credibility for the framework and its visualization through the heat map, which since then has been an element that has informed the discussions of the Board over financial stability (interview, economist, January 13, 2020).

These results were also an important step toward the calibration of a possible CCyB framework, as they had shown that an efficient calibration of the CCyB could at least in theory be possible. Testing different ways of aggregating and normalizing the data (Aikman et al. 2015, 47ff.), the research team around Aikman had found that their proposed composite measure persistently outperformed the credit-to-GDP gap in terms of predictive capacities of impending dangers by more than a year (Aikman et al. 2015, 53), but also that it lowered itself much faster at the onset of the financial crisis, thereby allowing for a much faster release of the buffer, once a crisis hit (Aikman et al. 2015, 25). They hence suggested to use their summary measures for the calibration of the framework and developed two simple calibration rules for the USA modeled on the "Taylor rule" for monetary policy (interview, central bank economist, January 13, 2020). This rule suggested that the CCyB should be activated about one third of the time, standing at its maximum of 2.5 percent about 15 percent of the time (Aikman et al. 2015, 36). Their historical simulation of the calibration of the CCyB showed that the CCyB for US banks would have reached 2.5 percent by the second quarter of 2004, allowing for the full buildup of the buffer before the crisis.

These research results shifted the internal view of the financial stability division on the CCyB. While initially rejecting the CCyB as an uncertain and inefficient policy tool (Edge and Meisenzahl 2011), economists at the financial stability division had come to reconsider it due to this analytical work and in a change of mind had come to find it a rather useful tool (interview, former Federal Reserve economist, January 9, 2018). Thus, the same economists who had opposed it only years earlier were now involved in the effort of figuring out

when and how it should be activated (interview, central bank economist involved in the backtesting exercise, January 13, 2020). As a result
of this internal work, the financial stability division started to push for
the installation of an ambitious CCyB in the domestic US framework,
working on a proposal for rule-making, which was subsequently published in December 2015.

Simultaneously with the publication of the proposal, the financial
stability division published a Federal Reserve note in December 2015 in
which it revisited the credit-to-GDP gap (see Bassett et al. 2015). This
time it found it to be a useful tool but suggested that it should be
disaggregated and complemented with "financial-system vulnerabilities related to leverage, maturity transformation, asset-prices, and/or
underwriting standards" (Bassett et al. 2015). They were hence suggesting to either employ a multiple indicator approach as in Aikman et al.
(2015) or to employ qualitative considerations.[14] However, this work
by economists in the financial stability division was only one input
into the rule-making and their attempts to install a meaningful
framework was subsequently frustrated by political economy
considerations.

Having developed the framework outlining the objectives of the tool
and the factors that would influence the determination of its appropriate level, the proposal went through a period of public consultation
that had to be extended by a month due to wide interest for comment.[15]
Following this process, the Board aligned its final policy statement in
September 2016 with requests by industry to follow a much more
cautious approach to setting the CCyB, now including new wording
that refers to "excessive" credit growth, which had to be "meaningfully
above normal" to bring about action (Federal Reserve System 2016),
rather than the initial formulation of "somewhat above normal." It
furthermore assured industry that it would provide notice and seek
comments on measurements of credit risk before changing the CCyB,

---

[14] The paper ends by stating, "What seems most crucial is the consideration of
additional vulnerabilities, since, as the episode preceding the crisis suggests, a
persistent increase in the U.S. credit-to-GDP ratio should not automatically be
assumed to be a favorable, or even benign, financial deepening." Given the
generally positive view about finance and financial growth in the academic
economic mainstream pre- and post-crisis (for critical reviews, see Turner 2015;
Pagano 2014), this is a remarkable statement by the financial stability division.
[15] www.federalreserve.gov/newsevents/pressreleases/bcreg20160129a.htm.

reflecting the administrative procedures common in the USA, thereby substantially lengthening the implementation lag of the measure.[16]

The final CCyB regime in the USA, as established by the final policy statement and in contrast to the suggested rules by the financial stability division (Aikman et al. 2015, 36f.), was hence set such that the CCyB would be 0 percent most of the time.[17] This overall stance largely excluded discretionary anti-cyclical interventions based on the CCyB, as the experience of strong industry push back and the clumsiness of the measure due to long time lags led policymakers to abstain from the measure (interview, Federal Reserve economist, January 9, 2018; interview, central bank economist seconded to the Federal Reserve, January 13, 2020) and instead push for an increased use of stress tests to better capture the buildup of risk (see Chapter 5). This included the potential use of stress capital buffers, which would require higher capital requirements in times of anticipated greater stress, effectively replacing the CCyB (Tarullo 2016), a measure that, however, suffered from the problem of how to release such a measure in times of stress. While these debates would continue in the years to come (Quarles 2019a), they would not lead to any substantial shift in the policy framework for the CCyB.

Despite this blockage in terms of discretionary anti-cyclical policy actions, researchers within the Federal Reserve continued their work on the measurement of cyclical vulnerabilities developing in the financial sector, arguing now that it should be considered when conducting monetary policy (Adrian and Liang 2016). They took their lead from Board member Jeremy Stein, who from 2013 onwards had argued that given the weakness of the macro-prudential policy framework in the

---

[16] See www.federalreserve.gov/newsevents/pressreleases/files/bcreg20160908b1.pdf; www.federalreserve.gov/newsevents/pressreleases/bcreg20160908b.htm.

[17] The argument adopted by the Board was that the measures taken to increase the resilience of the system after the financial crisis would make anti-cyclical interventions largely unnecessary. In March 2019, Vice-Chairman for Supervision Quarles expressed this stance, when justifying the decision to keep the CCyB at 0 percent: "A notable feature of the Board's current framework is the *decision to maintain a 0 percent CCyB when vulnerabilities are within their normal range. Because we set high, through-the-cycle capital requirements in the United States that provide substantial resilience to normal fluctuations in economic and financial conditions*, it is appropriate to set the CCyB at zero in a normal risk environment. Thus, our presumption has been that the CCyB *would be zero most of the time*" (Quarles 2019a, emphasis mine).

USA, monetary policy with its capacity to "get in all the cracks" could serve as a "second best" policy tool in order to address financial stability concerns (Stein 2013a, 2014).[18] These works pointed out "that monetary policy impacts financial conditions as well as vulnerabilities, thus producing an intertemporal trade-off for monetary policy between present macroeconomic objectives and risks to objectives in the future" (Adrian et al. 2016, 20). Researchers at the Federal Reserve under the direction of Tobias Adrian developed the "Growth-at-Risk framework" (Adrian et al. 2016) to operationalize these concerns, seeking to quantify this trade-off by visualizing the downside growth vulnerabilities created by excessively loose monetary policy with respect to developments in financial markets (Adrian et al. 2016).

The development of this analytical framework was motivated by the desire to "provide *actionable knowledge* to the Federal Open Market Committee" (interview, former Federal Reserve economist, August 20, 2018, emphasis mine). The framework was a path-dependent outgrowth of the financial stability framework developed in 2013, placing at its center the volatility paradox and the underpricing of risk (Adrian et al. 2016). The researchers at the Federal Reserve used these insights to explore more in depth the possible impact the buildup of financial vulnerabilities could have upon GDP, thereby linking these developments to what matters most to policymakers, namely economic growth. Just like earlier work by Adrian (cf. Adrian and Brunnermeier 2008), the Growth-at-Risk framework was based on the technique of quantile regression, seeking to anticipate tail risks by focusing on the evolution of the tails of a distribution, in this case the distribution of growth, given developments in financial vulnerabilities. The researchers applied the longitudinal dataset build for the prior backtesting exercise and measured the effect of the buildup of endogenous vulnerabilities within the financial sector on the future distribution of growth to act as an EWS (Adrian et al. 2016, 1).

---

[18] Stein thereby opposed the decoupling view of macro-prudential and monetary policy which was held at the helm of the Federal Reserve (Bernanke and Yellen), which delegated the task of financial stability solely to macro-prudential tools. Instead, he argued that due to regulatory arbitrage and incomplete regulatory coverage, monetary policy could serve as a powerful possible tool to address the search for yield, which might occur as much outside of the banking sector as inside of it.

The investigation by Adrian and colleagues (2016) found that as financial vulnerabilities build up, tail risks to growth increase in an asymmetrical fashion, whereby positive surprises to growth do not increase but the possibility of recessions strongly does.[19] This stylized fact was seen as the basis to require preventative action by the FOMC to mitigate these effects, by taking these developments into account as they set monetary policy. The outstanding achievement of this work was to bundle all the different indicators assembled within the Federal Reserve's vulnerability framework into a simple number (interview, central bank economist, January 13, 2020), which could then be easily communicated to policymakers on a six-week to three-month basis.

Consciously designed to measure changes in financial markets and their impact on future growth on such a short time frame to provide "actionable knowledge" for the FOMC, this framework did not have much influence on monetary policy at the Federal Reserve (interview, former Federal Reserve economist, August 20, 2018). This was because the level of causal specifications of the model was deemed unsatisfactory (interview, Federal Reserve economist, as cited in Levingston 2021, 1477) and the trade-offs between uncertain long-term financial instability and the much more certain short-term impact on unemployment and inflation weighed in favor of the latter (interview, economist working at the Federal Reserve, December 8, 2021; see also Levingston 2021). Instead, the model would have an interesting career, both in the international realm, where it was adopted by the International Monetary Fund (IMF) as a central element for its Financial Sector Assessment Program in 2017, when Adrian himself moved to the IMF to become the director of the capital markets department. It was also to become one of the EWS that fed into the setting of countercyclical policies in the EU, with its most prominent role in the UK.

Negotiated Monitoring within the Bank of England: Disciplining Expert Judgment through Science

In the UK, the set-up of EWS was heavily influenced by the work of the financial stability division on measuring the credit cycle. Already the early work by the leader of the financial stability division Haldane,

---

[19] In technical terms, the right-hand tail of the distribution does not move following an increase in financial vulnerabilities, but the left-hand tail does.

jointly with Aikman and Nelson (Aikman et al. 2010), had set the tone in this regard. Based on a new longitudinal database on credit develop-ments from 1870s to 2010 (Schularick and Taylor 2009), they pro-nounced that credit cycles were both "clearly identifiable and regular," identifying research on "the sources and dynamics of the credit cycle" as an important intellectual task to complete the macro-prudential policy framework (Schularick and Taylor 2009, 2). This work on the identifi-cation of cyclical risks in the context of the credit cycle would quickly gain policy relevance in the BoE, as the CCyB was one of the two macro-prudential tools the BoE requested in January 2013 (BoE 2013a).

The approach to calibrating the CCyB was developed by the BoE's Financial Stability group in the context of the ESRB working group, basing itself on a newly formed database that contained data on finan-cial instability in the UK from 1969 onwards. A working paper, pro-duced in 2012 by five members of that group and a member of the Bank of Spain, conveys the underlying work and its link to the credit-to-GDP gap as an indicator (the paper was subsequently published in an aca-demic journal as Giese et al. 2014). In contrast to the intervention by the Federal Reserve economists Edge and Meisenzahl (2011), which argued that the credit-to-GDP gap was too unreliable, they found it to be a reasonably reliable indicator for the UK economy after having tested it as a predictor for the three crises in the UK since 1969 (Giese et al. 2014, 25f.).[20] They then set out to suggest complementing indi-cators for the signaling of rising credit risks in the UK that were likely to pose a threat to the financial system (Giese et al. 2014, 30–36), includ-ing the level of credit in the economy, the origin of that credit from stable or volatile (foreign) investors and the qualitative characteristics of credit (i.e. for what credit is granted and under which conditions). Testing these variables on their predictive capacity, they found real estate price gaps to be a very good predictor of impending crises,[21] although this was subject to type 2 errors (Giese et al. 2014, 40).[22]

These findings fed into the initial framework of the BoE for calibrat-ing the CCyB, which used the credit-to-GDP gap as the most important

---

[20] They argue that while there is statistical uncertainty due to the difference between real-time measurement and post-factum corrections of credit growth, these tend to be correlated with GDP growth corrections, implying that the ratio of credit to GDP is not negatively affected (Giese et al. 2014, 26).
[21] For the list of indicators tested, see Giese and colleagues (2014, 37).
[22] In other words, it was likely to signal a pending crisis when none was at hand.

measure (BoE 2014a, 23), carefully specifying the other measures used to complement it (BoE 2014a, 30f.). In setting up this framework, however, the BoE was careful to clarify that no mechanical link existed between these indicators and the setting of the CCyB (BoE 2014a, 23). Instead, these indicators were to serve "as the starting point of the analysis" (Giese et al. 2014, 40), to be complemented with market and supervisory intelligence to form an overall view of the positioning of the UK's financial system in the financial cycle. As the BoE (2014a) notes, "the greater the degree of imbalance as measured by the core indicators, the more homogeneous the picture that the different indicators convey, and the more consistent that picture is with market and supervisory intelligence, the more likely it is that the FPC will adjust the CCB and SCRs [Solvency Capital Requirements] in response."

The measurements thus produced were then fed into the discussion in the Financial Policy Committee, which frequently challenged the analyses of the financial stability division (interview, BoE officials, December 12, 2019). These debates allowed for the formation of an expert judgment, the prevalent mode of decision-making at the BoE,[23] with the input being subjected to intense scrutiny before any policy measure would be agreed (interview, former BoE economist, October 23, 2019). This intense scrutiny was linked to the initial stance regarding the CCyB, which as formulated by the BoE's policy statement was characterized by uncertainty over results to be expected from the use of this measure. This uncertainty not only concerned its effects for increasing the resilience of the system but also its short-term impact on credit provision when increasing the capital buffer (BoE 2014a, 16). The latter was seen as potentially impacting "growth and employment," which the BoE was not to endanger with its resiliency enhancing actions (BoE 2014a, 5), in particular as banks already were asked to have a lot of additional capital in the context of the phasing in of Basel III.[24]

---

[23] As Donald Kohn, the external member of the Financial Policy Committee (FPC), put it: "And in pursuit of that mandate we have made many judgments and taken quite a few actions based on a variety of indicators and techniques. Although identifying risks and gauging resilience poses significant challenges, we have found sufficient empirical regularities tied to financial instability in historical experience to justify taking action" (Kohn 2019a, 2).

[24] Because of the initially low recording of the credit-to-GDP gap and this uncertainty over possible consequences, the CCyB was set at 0 percent from May 2014 until December 2015 (for an example of this cautious stance, see BoE 2015c).

This cautious stance would successively give way to a more assertive use of this measure, as banks reached the specified levels of capital prescribed in Basel III and newly produced research of the financial stability division dispersed the doubts regarding its use. This shift in stance occurred in the context of a reshuffling of the financial stability division by Mark Carney, the new governor of the BoE from 2013, Andrew Haldane being replaced by Alex Brazier as the executive director for financial stability. The new director, impressed by the role stress tests had come to play in the USA both in detecting financial stability risks and their capacity to address it, pushed strongly for a heightened role of stress tests (interview, BoE economist, February 13, 2020).

Overall, the realignment of the policy framework for the CCyB sought to provide a greater role for economic analyses and stress tests to serve as a "check on the FPC's judgement and discretion" (BoE 2016a, 17). Limiting the judgment and discretion through models and forecasts, much as was the case for the Monetary Policy Committee (MPC), was a goal pursued by staff, who thought that a more explicit framework and model use might discipline the work of the Committee (interview, BoE economist, January 13, 2020; interview, BoE economist, February 13, 2020). In line with this, the goal in the new framework was to use the CCyB in an anti-cyclical manner, varying the resilience of the financial system in line with the movement along the stages of the financial cycle (BoE 2016a, 12f.).

The first step toward such a more active use guided by analysis occurred when the BoE published its medium-term capital framework (BoE 2015f), which announced the decision to install the CCyB permanently at the level of 1 percent, when risks were neither subdued nor elevated (BoE 2015f, 7),[25] thereby allowing for a more flexible use of the measure. The reason for that shift in policy resided at least partially in the research undertaken in the macro-prudential framework and policy strategy division of the BoE, which showed that building up CCyB in good times was not very costly, but that its release was very beneficial in the slump (Bahaj et al. 2016; interview, BoE officials, December 12, 2019). Based on that insight, the Financial Policy Committee deemed it beneficial to have at least 1 percent to be able to release in case of an

---

[25] At the same time, the BoE was reducing the permanent capital required by 1 percent. In April 2016, the BoE revised its CCyB framework accordingly; see BoE (2016b).

unexpected shock as well as being capable of raising it gradually if the need arises (see BoE 2015f.; also BoE 2016b).[26] Simultaneously with this more active role for the CCyB as an instrument, the importance of the stress test to inform its setting also increased (BoE 2016b, 15).

Increasing the role of stress tests, the BoE in October 2015 announced a new annual cyclical scenario, which was to stress test the banking system based on the analysis of the FPC as to where the financial system was positioned within the financial cycle. It announced that the

Bank of England's annual cyclical scenario will be calibrated to reflect policymakers' assessment of prevailing financial imbalances – the state of the financial cycle. The severity of this scenario will increase as risks build and decrease after those risks crystallise or abate. This systematic approach should mean that markets and banks will be better able to anticipate the broad shape and severity of the scenario over time. But the precise calibration will not be mechanical – it will reflect policymakers' judgements over the magnitude of prevailing imbalances. (BoE 2015d, 12)

Thereby, the FPC de facto inserted its assessment of the financial cycle into the calibration of the stress test, which in turn took an ever-increasing role informing the setting of the CCyB (BoE 2015d, 6).

To avoid surprises for banks, this scenario was supposed to evolve gradually, with the risk aversion of the policymakers staying constant and changes only occurring due to changes in observed indicators (see, e.g., BoE 2017a, point 10). To ensure this consistency, policymakers looked at the evolving distance of a certain specified set of variables (e.g. house prices) from what they assumed to be the equilibrium prices, and then assessed the likelihood of these prices falling (BoE 2015d, 16). They then developed a stress scenario in which a tail event occurs that could lead to such a fall and asked the banks to be able to withstand a shock to, for example, a fall in house prices. This should allow for banks to anticipate the stress test results, allowing them to build up capital gradually as the financial cycle accelerated (Brazier 2015, 6).

In this way, as Alex Brazier, the executive director of financial stability at the BoE, clarified, "systematic policymaking can shape the behaviour of the banking system, hardwiring into its DNA a capital strength that counters the cycle," generating beneficial effects much

---

[26] The FPC made immediate use of this option in spring 2016, setting the CCyB at 0.5 percent due to the risks to financial stability caused by the EU referendum (BoE 2016a).

like systematic policymaking had done for monetary policy (Brazier 2015, 6). And yet, to maintain flexibility and to also be able to react to changes in the financial system, a biennial exploratory scenario was supposed to explore new structural risks the UK financial system might be exposed to, including in the non-banking sector (see Chapter 8).

Concomitant with these changes, the BoE announced that it would increase its internal modeling capacities, to intensify its research efforts on stress-testing and to exchange with other central banks on their experiences (BoE 2015f, 28ff.), a task that directly affected the work of the financial stability division. The research of this division at that point in time was seeking to reduce the complexity of the large information set it was using to inform the FPC on the current position of the British economy within the financial cycle. Distilling a set of twenty-nine indicators for the cycle, indicators that were very close to the existing set of variables analyzed in the Financial Stability Report (interview, BoE officials, December 12, 2019), they were de facto struggling to generate easily interpretable results for the committee. Trying out heat maps and other devices to represent developments of interest (see, e.g., Aikman et al. 2015), they found it difficult to communicate those to policymakers (interview, BoE officials, December 12, 2019) and therefore abandoned those efforts.

In their search for indicators that could be easily communicated, the team then encountered the Growth-at-Risk framework at a joint IMF–BoE workshop in 2017, where Adrian himself presented his work (interview, BoE economist, January 13, 2020). To them, the framework was highly appealing as it combined several of the positive characteristics of EWS with an easily communicable number to policymakers, which presented to the policymaker both the likelihood and potential severity of a crisis, should it occur, impelling them to act. In this way, in contrast to other early warning measures, the Growth-at-Risk framework operated by using a continuous measurement, meaning that it was much better attuned to inform the gradual rise or reduction of the CCyB in the framework of the BoE (interview, BoE economists, December 12, 2019). Because of this appeal of the measure, the BoE team started to experiment with this framework, and after extensive backtesting[27] found it to

---

[27] Adapting the Growth-at-Risk framework to the task of setting the CCyB in the UK, however, still required work by the team at the BoE, as it was initially calibrated to influence monetary policy rather than the CCyB and thus had an outlook of three months rather than the three to five years ahead that are needed for the preemptive setting of the CCyB. From 2017 to

be operative. In that moment, the team praised the Growth-at-Risk framework as a great step forward, going so far as describing the "GDP-at-risk" measure as "a summary statistic of the ultimate objective of macroprudential policy" (Aikman et al. 2018, 27).[28]

In addition to this capacity of the GDP-at-Risk framework to inform discussions with policymakers, the team also found that it could use the GDP-at-Risk framework to engage in a tentative cost–benefit analysis by simulating the cushioning effects CCyBs could have had if activated before the great financial crisis (Aikman et al. 2019, 1). In other words, the Growth-at-Risk framework allowed them to generate a credible model-world (Braun 2014), in which such an alternative scenario could be credibly tested. They found that gradually raising the CCyB by 2.5 percent or 5 percent before the crisis of 2008, following the early warning signals by the Growth-at-Risk framework, would have reduced the probability and severity of the crisis, calculating a reduced impact of 21 percent and 42 percent, respectively (Aikman et al. 2019, 36f.). This counterfactual analysis allowed the team to make a strong case for raising the CCyB ahead of time, as it could bring about a reduction in

2018, the team was hence backtesting this framework, identifying twenty-nine variables from the academic literature that it grouped into three broader categories (private sector leverage, asset valuations and credit terms and conditions), which it used to measure financial vulnerabilities. It then built a database for these twenty-nine variables for sixteen Western countries for the years 1980–2016 (Q4), refining a data collection exercise at the ECB, which itself built on the first database build by Babecky and colleagues in 2012 (Lo Duca et al. 2017). They were then testing the framework's predictive capacities to capture rising crisis probabilities three to five years ahead of time. Using the full scale of data retrospectively as well as seeking to undertake pseudo-real time exercises (Do Luca et al. 2017), they found it to be operative.

[28] This endorsement by the team does not imply that the team was convinced that one could fully predict tail risks to growth or that this would ever be possible. Instead, it was the communicative aspect of this measure, capable of summarizing a host of indicators into a simple number, which generated the greatest appeal of this measure. As an economist of the team put it, making a comparison to the monetary policy framework: "we are not that good at predicting inflation either, but this is not a reason for us to abandon inflation forecasting, is it?" (interview, BoE economist, January 13, 2020). Instead, it is about the entire capacity to set up a clear framework that can guide policymakers' decision-making (see Aikman et al. 2018, 11 for such a discussion, showing how policymakers could seek to adjust their macro-prudential policy according to depictions by the GDP-at-Risk framework and their own risk preferences).

the crisis impact. This finding was furthermore supported by the fact that raising capital in good times was found to have little impact upon credit provisioning (Bahaj et al. 2016).

Based on this preparatory work by the financial stability division, the Growth-at-Risk framework was inserted as one element into the stress tests from 2019 onwards to determine the size of the CCyB (Brazier 2019; Kohn 2019a).[29] Concomitantly with this decision, the FPC decided to set the CCyB at 2 percent in a standard risk environment (BoE 2019e, 2), while announcing at the same time a search for a reduction in other elements of the capital requirements for a similar amount, allowing for the cyclical movements of the CCyB to become a more important element in the overall capital requirement framework. The reasoning that underlay this change was that by adjusting capital requirements in an anti-cyclical manner, policymakers could guarantee that capital requirements were at their highest at the peak of the cycle and hence the system safest, while not imposing such a high level throughout the entire cycle (BoE 2019e, 3).[30]

The executive director of financial stability at the BoE, Brazier, clarified this change in approach from crisis prediction to the building of resilience by using the metaphor of earthquake research and measures to prevent earthquakes. He points out that the

right approach, for building resilience to earthquakes into structures, and for building resilience to economic shocks into financial systems, is to focus not on tremors, but on the underlying vulnerability. By underlying vulnerability, I mean how serious a quake – real or economic – could be *if one occurred at any point*. Whether a quake seems likely to occur soon has no bearing on this. (Brazier 2019, 3, emphasis in original)

In this way, the Growth-at-Risk framework was used as a counter-cyclical element in maintaining the resilience of the system, in line with the mandate of the FPC (see Chapter 5).

---

[29] This adoption was helped by the fact that the Growth-at-Risk framework is observing the state of the financial system with respect to a posited "normal state" and assuming the larger the deviation, the larger the eventual correction in the system (Brazier 2019, 8). In this sense, it is very much a continuation of the use of stress tests for the CCyB right from 2016 (interview, BoE economist, January 13, 2020).

[30] A different reading of this change is to emphasize a de facto lowering of the overall capital requirements in times of crisis. Both of these readings are essentially correct, in that the anti-cyclical variations in the CCyB are primarily aimed at the downside.

And yet, in setting the CCyB, stress tests will not replace judgment by the FPC (interview, former BoE economist, October 23, 2019). As an external member of the FPC, Kohn, put it regarding the results from stress tests and the setting of the CCyB:

> But there is no mechanical link between the outputs of the stress test or the readings from a set of indicators and the setting of the CCyB. The FPC attempts to be systematic about our reactions to readings on risk and resilience, and we are transparent about what we are looking at and why we are or are not concerned about emerging phenomena in financial markets. (Kohn 2019a, 5f.)

In the case of the UK, we can then observe the most sophisticated evolution of the framework seeking to measure cyclical systemic risks and to translate them into discretionary action. Drawing on work in the other two jurisdictions, this evolution was driven by the desire to model the action of the FPC on its brethren committee, the Monetary Policy Committee. This led to the attempt to install a three-year forecast regarding the evolution of financial stability risks and an attempt to discipline the judgment and discretion of policymakers through the increased use of model-based inputs. The outcome of these attempts was the installation of a CCyB regime, which in line with the mandate of the FPC was seeking to maintain the resilience of the system in an anti-cyclical manner, based in the end on annual cyclical stress test exercises. These insertions of analytical economic models would not replace expert judgment but were installed to give coherence and expectability to their judgments, seeking to make financial stability decisions as predictable as monetary policy decisions.

Conclusion

The comparison of the development of different institutional set-ups of the CCyB and the intellectual work by applied economists underlying it reveals both substantial variation in terms of frameworks (see Table 6.1) and a joint intellectual effort that shapes the use of EWS and financial stability monitoring frameworks to inform policy. The different set-up of the CCyB framework installed in the three jurisdictions and their fine-tuning can be directly related to the legal capacities of the competent authorities to intervene, as well as the broader political economy within which it unfolds.

Table 6.1 *Comparison of the three different jurisdictions: European Central Bank, Federal Reserve and Bank of England*

	Federal Reserve	ECB/ESCB/NCAs*	BoE
Early warning models	Financial vulnerabilities and amplification framework	A variety of EWS (bank, asset valuation), aggregated in the composite systemic risk indicator in 2019 (see Lang et al. 2019)	Growth-at-Risk imputed into the stress test (2019)
Relation of stress test to CCyB	Macro-prudential vision of stress test from the beginning; currently considering in the context of the stress capital buffer legislation	Uploading macro-prudential elements (Constâncio et al. 2019), but still not relevant for CCyB	Using anti-cyclical stress tests to inform CCyB from 2014 onwards
CCyB	Set at 0% in 2016 and expected to be 0% for the foreseeable future (but pending reform for stress capital buffer)	Varied, 13 activations in 19 Eurozone countries until end 2019, first activation July 2016 (Slovakia)	Placed at 1% generally since 2017, at 2% from 2021, before some variance already

* NCA = nationally competent authorities.

As a general finding, expert judgment remains the decisive input within all of these discussions, while frameworks and models serve to structure the discussion (interview, ECB economist, August 15, 2016). The latter provide plenty of indicators regarding the buildup of aggregate systemic risk and it is only through an aggregated expert view, based on discussion, that a final decision is taken.[31] A general conviction among practitioners is that for many years to come, one is unlikely to find a simple measurement of cycles and systemic risk that would allow the agency to take clear decisions; instead, expert judgment will always be necessary. As the external member of the FPC, Kohn, has put it for the case of the BoE, "We are a ways from having a 'Taylor Rule' tied to a few right hand side variables to give us guidance; indeed one may doubt whether such a rule will ever be possible for as complex a phenomenon as 'financial stability'" (Kohn 2019a, 5f.).

And still, applied economists at the BoE and elsewhere push in such a direction, developing such simplifying indicators and rules for anti-cyclical interventions, such as the Growth-at-Risk framework. The appeal of this framework resides in the capacity to discipline an overflowing array of indicators, providing a single number to discipline the focus of policymakers. This framework and the data on which it is based are the outcome of a joint intellectual effort in the field of regulatory science by applied central bank economists regarding cyclical systemic risks that over the course of the last decade has considerably expanded the depth of knowledge about what causes these cyclical upswings and how to measure them (for an overview, see Stein 2021), establishing cyclical systemic risk as a "risk object."

This effort has first of all involved the construction of commonly shared databases that allowed researchers to test their EWS on ever longer time-series for ever more countries for an ever-larger list of variables. In this respect, the efforts within the ESCB and MaRS are particularly noteworthy, as they created a large, freely available database that included data on all European countries for a large list of variables (see Detken et al. 2014).[32] Researchers from other countries such as the UK could build and expand on this database to pursue their own research efforts. This newly established depth of data gave much wider credibility to the results generated, as it allowed to generate more

---

[31] In the case of the Eurozone, this expert judgment, supported by data and models, is further fed into a negotiation process between the European and national level, a process where one can actually see regulatory science at work as a negotiated process that involves not only the question of what science can say with certainty but also the political economy of the decisions to be taken.

[32] These efforts continued, leading to an even larger database including more time-series on different data (Lo Duca et al. 2017).

robust econometric findings that generalize findings over time and countries. Secondly, it involved the continuous evolution and refinement of EWS and frameworks to make sense of that vast amount data. Common to the UK, the ECB and the Federal Reserve is the move away from the simple credit-to-GDP gap as the guiding indicator, which was the initial foundation for the CCyB framework in Basel III, and instead a move toward a use of an amalgamated set of different variables.[33] Bringing in these different variables required careful testing by the applied economists of the causal impact they might have on financial instability, but it also posed the question of how to weigh them with respect to the ultimate policy goal of the CCyB, increasing the resilience of the system with respect to cyclical developments.

This became particularly important in the context of communicating the need for action to policymakers. This problem of easy and clear communication is one reason for the rise of the Growth-at-Risk framework, which was initially developed in the USA to provide actionable knowledge for monetary policy to now serve as a tool to calibrate the CCyB in the UK. Retooled by the financial stability team at the BoE, which came in touch with it both due to a seminar with the IMF but also due to staff exchanges between the BoE and the Federal Reserve, it now also arouses increasing interest in the Eurozone as a tool to detect the cyclical buildup of systemic risk (for the ECB, see ESRB 2019a; Lang et al. 2019; for the case of Germany, see Beutel 2019; Hartwig et al. 2019, as cited in Bundesbank 2019).[34] One reason for the appeal of this measure seems to be the capacity to move from predicting exactly when a crisis is supposed come and hence a 0/1 logic of action toward a continuous logic, one that does not seek to predict the timing of a crisis but, as Brazier puts it, presents to regulators the tensions that are building up in the financial system and builds resilience into the financial system as they grow.[35]

---

[33] The case of the USA is still pending, but the considerations undertaken under the Trump administration to connect the calibration of the CCyB with stress tests are an interesting emulation of UK practice – which, however, aims at reducing, not heightening, the overall capital buffers.

[34] One reason why the impact of the Growth-at-Risk is more muted in the Eurozone than in the UK might be the fact that the diversity of EWS currently still provides national authorities with sufficient wiggle room to debate the need for action with the ECB and that such wiggle room would be reduced by a uniform measure.

[35] One can even see the first attempts of a cost–benefit analysis using the Growth-at-Risk framework, the most sophisticated form of setting the CCyB according

Furthermore, rather surprisingly, the introduction of Growth-at-Risk in stress tests, and anti-cyclical stress tests in general, reveals stress tests as the new frontier for anti-cyclical regulation. These stress tests are generating the model worlds in which the need for anti-cyclical actions are increasingly simulated, bringing together cross-sectional considerations of systemic risk, such as contagion and feedback effects from initial shocks with a vulnerability framework that observes the buildup of risks over time. As the example of the UK shows, the financial cycle thinking is pushed into the stress tests: assuming a return to the mean of financial variables, they measure the amplitude of deviation from that mean to anticipate the height of the coming stress to the system. At the same time, we can also observe different relationships between CCyB frameworks and stress tests in the current calibrations of the CCyB, which might prevent a convergence around this practice.

While the UK uses stress tests to discipline its CCyB calibration and the USA is still considering a similar route, such a venue might be closed at the level of the Eurozone as a whole due to the fact that stress tests of the European Banking Authority, undertaken for the whole EU, do not have a macro-prudential focus and that ECB stress tests for the Eurozone are focusing on special problems to the Eurozone banking system rather than cyclical developments (interview, ECB manager, December 30, 2019). The splintered data landscape and the operation of national stress tests by only some national authorities in the Eurozone might imply that the road toward the more sophisticated institutional framework of calibrating the CCyB through stress tests might be foreclosed for these jurisdictions, unless every single country is willing to use its stress test for such purposes, a probability that seems extremely low in particular for small jurisdictions with limited manpower. This points to the fact that the diversity of national/European specificities will continue to shape the future evolution and use of EWS for anti-cyclical macro-prudential regulation.

An additional friction between these EWS and anti-cyclical macro-prudential regulation is the perimeter problem of regulation. While EWS today can detect buildups of risk in shadow banking, central banks cannot do much about it based on their tools, focusing mostly

to the ESRB working group (Detken et al. 2014), although the results are still pronounced very cautiously (interview, BoE economists, December 12, 2019).

on banks' capital requirements (see Adrian et al. 2015; see also Constâncio et al. 2019, 74). The next chapter will focus on the attempts by central banks' financial stability to expand their anti-cyclical powers to this system of non-bank credit intermediation immediately after the crisis, seeking to directly intervene in the repo-market. As we will see, attempts to install anti-cyclical tools to control the procyclical risks inherent in this market have largely failed. Yet, at the same time, these concerns over the procyclical risks inherent in the repo-markets led to the introduction of static penalizing measures on banks' broker-dealers, seeking to make them internalize the negative externalities of their procyclical liquidity provision in the upswing. The permanent frictions thus introduced in the market on the one hand somewhat limited provision of funding liquidity in the upswing, achieving the goals set. Yet, at the same time, they also increased the susceptibility of the repo-market to bouts of illiquidity, leading to a permanently larger footprint of central banks in that market.

7 | Taming Liquidity and Leverage in the Shadow Banking Sector

So I have a worry and I think this is something I haven't myself thought out, and I certainly think the world has not thought out, of theories of optimal liquidity which is: have we, by over-worrying about short-term liquidity in markets, a nice smooth operation of markets in a short term, do we end up with the official sector essentially underpinning too much trading in a way which creates a bigger risk?

(Former UK regulator involved in global liquidity regulation, February 27, 2015)

Introduction

Apart from setting up and operationalizing domestic macro-prudential frameworks for banks, central banks post-crisis also sought to extend macro-prudential regulation to the shadow banking system (see Box 7.1). In particular, they were eyeing the procyclical character of the wholesale financial markets upon which it was based. The crisis had brought into stark relief the fragile nature of this system of credit provision, which had developed in the wholesale finance market outside of banking regulation (Pozsar et al. 2012; see Chapter 4). Based on refinancing operations in the repo-market and private risk management systems, a system of credit intermediation involving non-bank financial entities such as hedge funds or open-ended bond funds, as well as larger dealer-banks, had developed that was prone both to cyclical exaggerations in the upswing (Adrian and Shin 2010) and to runs in case sufficiently bad news materialized (Gorton 2010). The central banking community hence deemed it urgent to address the fragile liquidity provision of this market through post-crisis regulation. And yet, no immediate consensus on regulatory measures to address its procyclical character could be reached in the immediate aftermath of the crisis, as was shown in Chapter 4.

This chapter traces the attempts by central bankers in the Financial Stability Board and the Basel Committee to install regulations to

165

Box 7.1 What Is Shadow Banking?

Shadow banking is a term used to designate non-banks, such as hedge funds and open-ended bond funds, which engage in the business of credit intermediation. The credit intermediation function of these non-banks is best understood in the context of a system of transactions (hence shadow banking system), which replicates the taking in of deposits and the granting of loans banks engage in through a series of steps, whereby most individual shadow banks do not undertake all functions, but the web of transactions achieves a similar outcome. Described as "money market funding of capital market lending" (Mehrling et al. 2013), these entities refinance in the short-term money market (most importantly the repo-market, a market for short-term collateralized loans) to purchase longer dated capital assets such as bonds.

What is peculiar about shadow banks in contrast to banks is that none of these entities, at least initially, had institutionalized access to central bank liquidity, but instead used the access to the short-term repo-market as an equivalent. The crisis of 2007–8 revealed two things. On the one hand, in times of financial booms, refinancing in these markets became extremely relaxed, allowing a procyclical rise in the leverage these shadow banks could take to realize their investment. In times of crisis, however, they could see their possibility for funding dramatically reduced, giving rise to the possibility of fire-sales and a systemic run on the shadow banking system, as materialized during the 2007–8 events. It was these two aspects central banks wanted to address. What complicated this regulation was the fact that central banks used the repo-market to implement their own monetary policy (Gabor 2016b; Braun 2020), making central banks engage in a delicate trade-off.

address the procyclical tendencies of repo-markets from 2011 to 2015, both through a specific set of policy initiatives to install anti-cyclical and through-the-cycle limits on the borrowing capacity in the repo-market (called margin requirements) and through specifying Basel III regulations regarding the business of extending liquidity by broker-dealers, most importantly the leverage ratio and the Net Stable Funding Ratio. It will show how the attempt to impose anti-cyclical haircut requirements failed, as central bankers were unable to coordinate around the concept of cyclical variations in the repo-market, which could justify such interventions. This failure was due to concerns over regulatory arbitrage, the exceeding demands of continuous coordination it required, the data requirements regarding evidence, which were seen as necessary, and the potential impact on central banks to execute monetary policy.

In contrast, attempts to coordinate around a structural measure constraining the behavior of broker-dealers in the repo-market in the context of specifications of Basel III liquidity regulations were successful, for several reasons. Based on a widely shared analysis of the procyclical behavior of broker-dealers in this market, implying a negative externality, this analysis did not require as extensive evidence, nor did it require continuous discretionary interventions by regulators. Most importantly, it was carried by macro-prudential change agents at the Federal Reserve Board in the USA, the most powerful central bank in the world.

An unintended side effect of this intervention, however, was to constrain the capacity of these private market-makers to provide liquidity during times of stress, initiating a process of repositioning of central banks with respect to the provision of liquidity to non-banks in the repo-market. The chapter concludes by addressing this repositioning, which occurred at around the same time (2012–15) and which was partially driven by the success of these regulatory initiatives. Using the case of the Bank of England as the vanguard example for the repositioning of central banks in this respect, I show how central banks were acting in an entrepreneurial spirit, accepting the role of market-maker of last resort and institutionalizing it in a way that would allow these central banks to provide such market-making function on a permanent basis.

To make these points, the chapter first introduces the reader to the repo-market and its central role in the shadow banking system, then traces the failed attempt to impose meaningful anti-cyclical or through-the-cycle haircuts by the Financial Stability Board (FSB) working groups. In a next step, the successful actions in the context of the Basel Committee are traced and their effects on the functioning of the market explained. Lastly, I shed light on the repositioning of collateral frameworks and intervention capacities of central banks to counter the reduced capacity to provide liquidity by broker-dealers this intervention provoked.

The Repo-Market and Its Endogenous Risk

Imagine a hedge fund that possesses a corporate bond generating 2 percent interest. The hedge fund might be happy with this, but can also turn to a market called the "repo-market" to leverage up its exposure. The fund can then enter in a so-called repo transaction with a broker-dealer, which involves providing the bond as collateral for a short-term secured loan by the dealer. The fund can use the loan to buy further corporate bonds, thereby leveraging up its position and increasing its returns. The broker-dealer in turn accepts to give the collateralized loan because of its low risk and because it can use the collateral it itself receives to lend out the bond to risk-averse non-banks, such as money market funds, which seek to invest their cash in a safe deposit-like manner that earns them a little extra.

In this way, the shadow banking system involves banks and non-banks in an intricate web of financial relationships. It allows these actors to finance long-term capital assets (such as bonds) with short-term money market funding. In a popular depiction of the shadow banking system, broker-dealers and derivative dealers are seen to be at the center of the shadow banking system. They link risk-averse cash-pools – that is, institutional investors with a preference for liquidity and security (pension funds, corporate cash of treasurers) – with risk-embracing actors, seeking financing to invest (such as hedge funds, open-ended bond funds). The system is characterized by chains of intermediation which constitute "money market funding for capital market lending" (see Mehrling et al. 2013; critical: Sissoko 2014, 2016), a business strategy often executed on the balance sheet of banks (Sissoko 2014) or by hedge funds and bond funds, levering their bond portfolios in order to deliver equity-like returns with bond-like volatility (Pozsar 2015).

The investment strategies of these investors are typically based on short-term money market funding, often through the use of repurchasing agreements (repos). The market for repos, a form of a collateralized loan, was often fostered by monetary authorities for the purpose of implementing monetary policy (for the case of the EU, see Gabor 2016b) and had doubled from 2002 to 2007 in the USA and the EU, making up more than 17 trillion dollars by the time of the crisis (Hoerdahl and King 2008, 39). In a repo transaction, one party sells an asset (collateral) to another party, combined with an agreement to buy this asset back in the (near) future. In this way, the seller gets cash without effectively selling the collateral (because there is an agreement to buy it back), while the buyer receives interest and a haircut, creating an in-substance securitized loan. As the buyer becomes the legal owner of this asset during the transaction, they can reuse the same asset in a repo agreement in turn, if they need short-term cash. This so-called re-hypothecation can lead to long repo-chains, increasing the interconnectedness of the financial system (Singh 2013). While repos represent an additional channel of liquidity for banks, it is the main source of refinancing for shadow banks (Pozsar 2015). Shadow banks, such as hedge funds, which otherwise face difficulties securing funding, use this instrument to further lever their portfolios. For this reason, the repo-market (cash against collateral) is at the heart of the shadow banking system, as depicted in Figure 7.1.

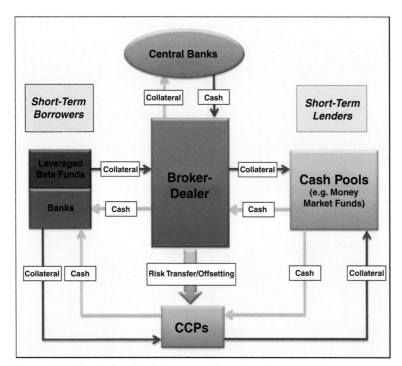

Figure 7.1 The shadow banking system (based on Singh 2014).

When entering a transaction, both parties agree on a haircut; that is, the difference between the current market price of the security and the money the lender is willing to lend against it (the lender is the seller of the repo-contract). This haircut is supposed to "provide a buffer against market fluctuations and incentivizes borrowers to adhere to their promise to buy securities back" (Gabor and Vestergaard 2016, 12) and is calculated by means of a value-at-risk calculation. If the value of the collateral decreases, the lender can claim additional collateral from the borrower (margin call) to compensate for the under-collateralization of the repo transaction.

While haircuts and margin calls provide "extra-ordinary security to lenders" (Sissoko 2016, 1), this private risk management system exposes the borrowers to funding risks, as it translates volatility in market prices for the underlying collateral into fluctuations in the lending conditions based on them (the margins and haircuts). It is here that the procyclical dangers of the repo-market reside, as they directly link prices in financial markets (based on market liquidity) to the availability of funding to financial market actors (funding liquidity) (Brunnermeier and Pedersen 2009). In the upswing, when volatility and credit-risk seem to be low while asset prices are rising, value-at-risk calculations indicate lower haircut requirements, incentivizing further risk-taking through additional leverage. This causal chain from increasing market value of assets toward the procyclical amplification of the repo-market on macro-prudential risks is illustrated in Figure 7.2, taken from the FSB's interim report

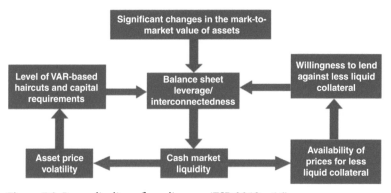

Figure 7.2 Procyclicality – flow diagram (FSB 2012a, 16).

on the risks inherent in the repo-market. However, when the cycle turns and volatility rises again, haircuts increase, and highly leveraged market participants need to deleverage quickly due to widely occurring margin calls. The crisis moment occurs when highly leveraged market participants are forced to sell off their assets in fire-sales, which put asset prices under increasing pressure. This, in turn, can cause additional fire-sales by other market actors, which fuels a further deterioration in market liquidity. This link creates the systemic risks inherent in this form of financing, as violently demonstrated during the financial crisis (Adrian and Shin 2008; Brunnermeier and Pedersen 2009), exposing all the hallmarks of the procyclical amplification of private risk management systems that macro-prudential critiques had criticized early on (Danielsson et al. 2001).

Tracing Post-Crisis Regulatory Efforts: The Macro-Prudential Critique of the Repo-Market

Against this backdrop, the repo-market and the private risk management systems it uses became a focal point of the macro-prudential regulatory discourse after the financial crisis. Already in the midst of the crisis, the former Financial Stability Forum (FSF) published a report linking risk measurements to the deterioration of the market in the run-up to and during the crisis (FSF 2008, 17; see Chapter 4). The Bank for International Settlements (BIS) followed up with a note to the FSF, arguing that one fundamental source of the system's procyclicality was the use of private risk measurement practices (BIS 2008, 2) and their linkages to margin requirements for collateral (BIS 2008, 9). The report argued that the short-term measurement of volatility, combined with a discretionary adjustment of the margins in times of stress, exacerbated the procyclicality of the system during the crisis. The report finished with different policy options, such as conservative and less market-value-oriented methods for valuation of collaterals, but also considering time-varying, countercyclical adjustments to margins (BIS 2008, 9; see also Kessler and Wilhelm 2013, 2014).

Similarly, in March 2009 the prominent Turner report by the British Financial Services Authority put the procyclical effects of collateral margin calls center stage in their analysis of the crisis, linking them directly to the procyclical effects of value-at-risk models (FSA 2009,

112). In April 2009, the Financial Stability Forum followed suit and published two reports, one jointly with the Committee for the Global Financial System (FSF 2009; FSF-CGFS 2009), criticizing margins as strongly procyclical and as important factors in the building up of leverage pre-crisis (FSF-CGFS 2009).

In the next year, the center of the regulatory discourse on the repo-market moved to the FSB, as the G20 in Seoul decided to task that body with developing an agenda for the regulation of shadow banking in general and of the repo-market in particular. In April 2011, the FSB published a first report laying out its ideas (FSB 2011a) and in October 2011 released its recommendations to dampen the procyclicality and other financial stability risks associated with securities financing and repo transactions. A close reading of these FSB reports from 2011 and of a follow-up from 2012 shows that securities markets' liquidity is linked to leverage cycles, and systemic instability is attributed to cyclical repo-collateral standards (FSB 2011a, 2012a; see also Gabor 2016b, 986 f.), which are lowered in the upswing and heightened in the downswing.

Concluding, the global regulatory discourse by the FSB, the BIS, and the CGFS displayed critical analyses of the procyclical effects of the repo-market, repeatedly calling for macro-prudential interventions. The crisis thus triggered a critical analysis of the financial stability risks inherent in the procyclical character of these markets, but, as I will show next, regulatory interventions to directly address the procyclical character on the global level have been much more timid and less interventionist than this analysis would call for. In the following, I focus on the regulatory dynamics that can explain this timidity, starting in 2009. I will show that besides a splintered policy field and lobbying, another reason for the missing transformation of macro-prudential ideas into action was the lack of data to justify regulatory interventions in the regulatory community, coupled with a fear of unintended consequences of these measures on market liquidity and monetary policy.

From Ideas to (Lacking) Action on the Global Level

Following up on its first report on the procyclical dynamics of valuation and leverage in the financial system (CGFS 2009), the Committee on the Global Financial System installed a working group in spring 2009. It was to record actual market practices in the repo-market and their impact during the crisis and to discuss the feasibility and desirability of the proposed policy options to limit their procyclical effects. The agenda of the working group points to the lack of knowledge on the side of regulators (interview, Bundesbank official, August 24, 2016), which regulators sought to overcome with the help of expert interviews and surveys. In fact, while academia had established a powerful narrative on the crisis as a run on the repo-market (Gorton 2009), the empirical evidence on which this narrative was based only demonstrated it for a very particular subsegment of the US market. Regulators had little further evidence for such dynamics and felt uneasy about imposing measures based on their limited knowledge. As has been argued by a German regulator, "it was difficult to assess what the side effects are because of the bad data" (interview, Bundesbank, July 25, 2016; similarly Bundesbank official, July 21, 2016; see also Commotto 2012; Hauser 2013, 8).

Amid these conversations, the lacking conviction of US regulators concerning the imposition of countercyclical haircuts became evident. While European regulators openly embraced through-the-cycle haircuts and even possibly anti-cyclical haircuts,[1] the British participants being the most vocal (interview, Bundesbank official, interview Bank of England official, September 22, 2016), US regulators were pointing to the possibilities for regulatory arbitrage by market agents (a powerful theme of American regulators since the 1990s; see, e.g., Jones 2000). In addition, US regulators doubted whether regulators could identify the right haircuts better than market agents (interview, Bundesbank official, July 25, 2016). As a result of this quarrel, the option of setting minimum haircuts as well as of countercyclical add-ons by regulators to dampen procyclical effects was not directly recommended in the final report of the group (CGFS 2010a), but only recommended "for consideration."[2] This initial opposition against interventions in private risk management systems by the USA and the subsequent emerging gridlock would prove decisive for the further regulation of risk

---

[1] Through-the-cycle haircuts refer to a permanent minimum haircut to be applied at all times. Anti-cyclical haircuts refer to a raising or lowering of haircuts by macro-prudential authorities in order to address repo-market developments deemed too expansionary in the upswing or too deflationary in the downswing.

[2] This recommendation applied both to direct bilateral repos, as well as to repos cleared through CCPs, whose increasing use should be seriously considered due to their mitigating effect on counterparty risk (CGFS 2010a, ix).

management practices in the repo-market, both for direct bilateral repos and for those cleared in central counterparties (CCPs) at the global level.

The task of considering such regulatory measures then fell to the Financial Stability Board, which was tasked by the G20 in Seoul to "develop recommendations to strengthen the oversight and regulation of the 'shadow banking system'" (FSB 2011a, 1). The FSB formed a task force on shadow banking by the end of 2010, co-chaired by Adair Turner, head of the Financial Services Authority (FSA) in the UK and chairman of the FSB Standing Committee on Supervisory and Regulatory Cooperation and Jaimie Caruana, manager of the BIS and chairman of the FSB Standing Committee on the Assessment of Vulnerabilities. Adair Turner, an outspoken proponent of macro-prudential regulation and critic of the procyclical character of the repo-market (FSA 2009), virtually assured a proactive stance regarding the need to regulate the shadow banking sector. Based on the analytical work of this task force, the Financial Stability Board then identified in October 2011 three main areas of possible direct intervention for regulators (FSB 2011b, 22):

a. Macro-prudential haircut requirements, "such as minimum margin or haircuts to mitigate procyclicality"
b. Possible limits for reuse and re-hypothecation
c. The improvement of market infrastructure for the settlement and clearing of repos, in particular through CCPs.[3]

By October 2012, these areas had further crystallized into a work program. On the one hand, this agenda included the task to calibrate minimum haircuts and to introduce minimum standards for collateral management in order to reduce the procyclicality of the system. On the other hand, they suggested that specific measures should be developed that ensure minimum standards of transparency and a set-up of private risk management regimes that reduce procyclicality. Most of these measures, however, did not involve material changes in market practices, rather benchmarking to best practices (such as extending the historical data based upon which these haircuts were to be calculated

---

[3] CCPs were recommended as they mitigate the risks of contagion and interconnectivity in the financial system in a straightforward, mechanical manner, substituting one bilateral trade with two trades with the CCP.

[FSB 2013b, 25]). In essence, those measures solely sought to improve market practices rather than fundamentally intervening in them. An eminent reason for this timid revision of current practices had been the fear of possible unintended consequences regarding market liquidity, as the Financial Stability Board pointed out at this moment (FSB 2012b, recommendation 7): a lower level of market liquidity could increase the fragility of the financial system.

Importantly, this pressure for restraint originated from an internal opposition within central banks, whereby those divisions within central banks responsible for the implementation of monetary policy through market operations were worried about a decline in repo-market liquidity (interview, former UK regulator involved in the negotiations, February 27, 2015). This fear was the most pronounced in the ECB, which was decisive as the policy work for this workstream of the FSB was under the mandate of the ECB DG Market Operations. Policymakers from this division not only shared those general concerns by the FSB but also feared additional market fragmentation in the Eurozone as well as the negative impact of these measures on monetary operations, which is why they opposed any stringent measures (interview, former ECB official, September 26, 2016). It was hence the entanglement of central banks with the repo-market to exercise their monetary policy operations that proved an important element in the restraint of regulatory interventions (Braun 2020). Given that this division's interventions in the repo-markets at that moment in time was literally holding the Eurozone together, the reduction of liquidity and market fragmentation was the outcome they least desired (interview, former ECB official, September 26, 2016).

It was these issues of lacking data and the fear of endangering the liquidity of markets and hence monetary policy efficiency that impeded stricter haircuts and margin requirements. Hence, when the idea of minimum haircuts materialized in 2013 into an official table of proposed numerical haircuts (FSB 2013b), these measures, both in terms of the actual minimum haircuts imposed and their coverage, were very limited. Therefore, this was a disappointing outcome for macro-prudential regulators (interview, London School of Economics economist and former Bank of England regulator, August 17, 2016; see also Tarullo 2013a, 15). In its final form, the regulation did not apply to government bonds, as regulators from Japan had insisted that no requirements be imposed in order not to raise the financing costs of the government (interview, UK regulator involved in the negotiations, February 27, 2015). Nor was the haircut applied to transactions that involved CCPs, which were subject to a different regulatory regime. Finally, all interventions in which banks borrowed in the repo-market from other banks and in which non-banks borrowed from non-banks were excluded. As a result, about 80 percent of repo transactions in Europe, which were backed by sovereign debt (ICMA 2015, 13) and all bilateral repo trades that involved CCPs had been excluded. Furthermore, the required minimum haircuts were much below average haircuts at that time and were thus not constraining for market actors (Tarullo 2013a interview, Dutch central banker, September 21, 2016).[4]

The timidity of these efforts, besides the ferocious lobbying of financial market actors, was caused by the very limited data available on repo-markets. This lack of data, itself a consequence of the largely unregulated nature of the repo-market pre-crisis (interview, Bundesbank economist, August 17, 2016), made it difficult to document the procyclicality of the repo-market and made the calibration of haircuts very difficult (interview, Dutch central banker, September 21, 2016). Repo-market lobbyists pointed exactly to this lack of knowledge and data in order to discredit any of these interventions, as they argued that regulators extrapolated limited data on one subsegment of the repo-market onto the global repo-market (Comotto 2012).

On the other hand, this timid intervention was also an outcome of concerns by regulators regarding the impacts these interventions might have on market liquidity. In particular, they were fearing unintentionally causing market disruptions (interview, former ECB economist, September 26, 2016; see also Global Investor 2013), a fear aggravated by limited data availability at this point in time.[5] Macro-prudential change agents hoped that these measures might function as an initial intervention that could be increased once the regulatory community achieved a better understanding of how these measures affect markets (interview, Dutch central banker, September 21, 2016). Particular hopes were pinned on a major data collection exercise on the procyclical

---

[4] They were set at approximately half the level deemed appropriate by macro-prudential change agents (interview, Dutch central banker, September 21, 2016; interview, former ECB economist, September 26, 2016).

[5] The calibration of the minimum haircuts in 2013, for example, was based on only three data points for seventeen large banks and broker-dealers (FSB 2015b, 14).

behavior of the repo-market, which was to start in 2018. A similar dynamic of regulatory self-restraint can be observed with respect to the possible limits for reuse and re-hypothecation, which were envisioned in 2012 by the FSB.

The Regulatory Attempt to Limit the Length of Repo-Chains

With the project on initial margins completed, the Financial Stability Board's main focus in 2013 shifted to re-hypothecation (FSB 2013a, recommendation 7 and 8), a practice whereby repo-market partici-pants were reusing the collateral pledged to them in exchange for a loan in order to take up a collateralized loan. This practice created chains of repo-loans, which linked many different market agents through the use of the same collateral in ever-shorter loan transactions, which created risks of contagion should any one member of the chain fail to return the collateral (Singh 2011).[6] Here, US and European regulators were "particularly keen to reduce the pro-cyclicality of repo markets by limiting the build-up of excessive leverage in the financial system resulting from re-hypothecation" (Euromoney 2013; Global Investor 2013). However, as I will show, these policy efforts once more only crystallized into three market-friendly recommenda-tions seeking to improve market discipline and transparency rather than fundamentally changing market practices.[7]

Based on its initial recommendations, the FSB installed a working group on re-hypothecation in 2014, which first undertook a stock-taking exercise of existing legal definitions of reuse and re-hypotheca-tion before examining their possible global harmonization (FSB 2015b, 10). It also undertook extensive interviews with market participants to get a better understanding of the market, while also seeking to gain knowledge of possible consequences and feasibility of certain

---

[6] This is called a repo-fail and can create serious problems for repo-market functioning. Regarding the repo-chain, imagine the first actor pledges collateral for three months; the receiving actor could then repledge the collateral for two months and so on and so forth, creating a potentially very long chain of repo-intermediated loans based on the same collateral.

[7] Concretely, these measures were asking intermediaries to provide sufficient disclosure to clients regarding reuse. The reuse of client assets (re-hypothecation) should exclude proprietary trading while "only entities subject to adequate regulation of liquidity risk should be allowed to engage in the re-hypothecation of client assets" (recommendation 9).

regulatory measures, such as data collection by industry (interview, Bundesbank economist, August 24, 2016). Despite an attempt by EU officials and certain European central banks within that working group to push for further measures,[8] these proposals could not overcome the resistance by the US representatives as well as by certain European central banks, which did not align with the EU position (interview, Bundesbank economist, August 24, 2016). While repo-chains were clearly perceived as a possible source of contagion and interconnectedness, the USA was reluctant to pursue further regulation as it had already installed the simple leverage ratio, which acted as a balance-sheet constraint for primary broker-dealers and was hence weary of any further measures constraining the repo-market (see later).

This internal gridlock, caused by the difficulties of international coordination and lacking data, meant that the statement by the Financial Stability Board that "[r]e-use of collateral may give rise to increased interconnectedness and contribute to the build-up of leverage" (FSB 2015b, 11) merely attained the status of a working hypothesis amidst a large-scale research program, rather than leading to direct action. As a regulator involved put it, "we have said that there are these risk for financial stability, leverage, pro-cyclicality, interconnectedness, etc. and when we will have the data we are supposed to verify in how far repos, in particular the reuse of collateral contributes to leverage" (interview, Bundesbank economist, August 24, 2016). So, the data that was to be collected from 2018 onwards should give a "feeling about the size of the market" (interview, Bundesbank economist, August 24, 2016) while the exact effects of these presumed mechanisms are to be discerned by the subsequent data analysis.

This stance explains the focus of the working group on how to measure cash collateral reuse and on how to exploit the data newly to be collected (FSB 2016), rather than exploring possible new measures. In this way, regulators now faced the daunting task of aggregating the data and providing meaningful results. The data collection exercise presented tremendous challenges to the ways this data could be aggregated and made available for statistical analysis, a fact further complicated by potential discrepancies between data collection efforts of the different private data repositories (interview, Bundesbank economist, July 25, 2016). In the end, the qualitative problematization of the

---

[8] Such as balance-sheet constraints imposed upon banks' balance sheets.

inherent procyclicality of the repo-market had been translated into a quantitatively-driven research project, rather than a project of regulatory intervention. However, faced with more than a million data points per month, the regulatory community was not sure how exactly to analyze the data.

This difficulty was aggravated by the ambiguity regarding how to properly conceptualize the cycle in analytical models (interview, Bundesbank official, July 25, 2016). Furthermore, and given that the data was to become available by 2018 at the earliest, it was unclear how much time was needed to generate sufficiently clear results from the data to convince the regulatory community of the need for action (interview, Bundesbank economist, September 23, 2016). Here, problems of exact causal specification in regressions were expected to pose severe challenges. As one interviewee put it, most likely the data that would proffer anti-cyclical action would only become available, if at all, once a full cycle was completed as only a new tail event, such as a financial crisis, would permit completing those calculations (interview, ESRB regulator, July 19, 2016).

Examining the regulatory agenda of the FSB on the procyclical aspects of the repo-market and its results, one can then state that the process itself was characterized by incremental, tepid reform steps, which hardly changed the way private risk management systems operate.[9] Regulatory efforts were hampered by US regulators, which acted as veto players with respect to new measures that challenged the predominance of private risk management system. Clinging to the pre-crisis notion of the private sectors' superior capacities to assess risks, they also pointed to a lack of data as a major impediment. In contrast, EU macro-prudential regulators, first and foremost the ECB (Constâncio 2014b, 2016a) and the ESRB (2015), have been vocal actors for more countercyclical interventions by public authorities. Accordingly, the EU was the first jurisdiction to fully implement the suggestions by the FSB from 2015, setting up a major data-collecting and transparency effort as well as the proposed limitations on re-hypothecation.

---

[9] Its challenge to procyclical risk management practices ended in minimum haircuts, which most of the time do not pose any constraint to the market. Limits to re-hypothecation and reuse of collateral, which builds the cornerstone of the private risk management system, have not been imposed.

Further to these projects, macro-prudential change agents within the EU were weighing additional steps, such as the imposition of macro-prudential anti-cyclical add-ons to the minimum haircuts as proposed by the FSB (see Constâncio 2014b; ESRB 2015). Yet, similar to the global level, they were not able to overcome the difficulties of coordination amid fears of regulatory arbitrage and the difficulties of who should calibrate such add-ons and in which manner. In these endeavors, the lack of scientific evidence for the procyclical character of the repo-market and the lack of a unifying conceptual framework was once more an important element in hindering such action (see Thiemann et al. 2018b). Whereas the project of anti-cyclical or meaningful through-the-cycle haircuts in repo-markets was thus weighed down by the disunity among central bankers, aggravated by a lack of conceptual clarity and lack of data needed to calibrate such interventions, structural measures to impinge upon the procyclical properties of the repo-market have been forthcoming, carried by macro-prudential change agents from the USA.

Regulatory Action by Stealth: The Calibration of Liquidity and Leverage Rules in Basel III

Executed as part of the final calibration of the leverage and liquidity regulation envisioned in Basel III, partly in stealth and outside of much public consultations, these measures aimed at the procyclical provision of liquidity by broker-dealers in the repo-market. This analysis, based on a market failure view that pointed to the incapacity of broker-dealers to internalize the negative externality of too much liquidity provisions in boom times, did not require ongoing data collection for calibration, nor did it evoke the measurement of a cycle. Instead, it based itself on a widely acknowledged form of economic analysis and most recent academic research, published by leading professors at Princeton University (Adrian and Shin 2008; Brunnermeier and Pedersen 2009). This research, which was undertaken in conjunction with staff of the US Federal Reserve, subsequently fed into the work by Federal Reserve Board governors and Federal Reserve presidents, who were increasingly worried about these tendencies. Thus substantiated, these worries could sway the community of regulators in the FSB to undertake last-minute changes in 2013/2014.

By 2013, the overreliance of the US financial system on short-term funding from wholesale financial markets became a substantial concern for these macro-prudential change agents at the Federal Reserve, as they identified it as a substantial contributor to the buildup of systemic risks (Rosengren 2013; Stein 2013b; Tarullo 2013a, b; see next chapter). In particular, their conviction had become that the post-crisis regulatory measures had insufficiently addressed the run-risks inherent in broker-dealer business.[10] This group of change agents therefore decided that measures to address these run-risks were of crucial importance in order to conclude the regulatory agenda post-crisis (Tarullo 2013a, 21). Their analyses, which were inspired by early analytical work that had documented the procyclical aspects of broker-dealer behavior (Adrian and Shin 2008), focused on the risks inherent in the matched repo-books of broker-dealers. While achieving such matched books were desired from a micro-prudential perspective, as it meant that each individual broker-dealer was safe from market disruptions, from a macro-prudential perspective the extensive provision of liquidity by broker-dealers through matched books in times of a cyclical upswing was identified as imposing a negative externality on the system as a whole (Tarullo 2013b).[11]

While the micro-prudential logic of the safety of individual institutions was pursued in the initial Basel III regulations (Tarullo 2013a, 11), this conviction in the community of macro-prudentially minded regulators in the USA led to a fine-tuning of liquidity measures within the Basel III framework to target the macro-prudential risks from the repo-market (interview, German regulator, August 17, 2016). In this vein, they pushed for a refinement of the leverage ratio in 2013 as well as the finalized Net Stable Funding Ratio in 2014 to disincentivize the activities of banks' broker-dealers in the repo-market. The revised version of the leverage ratio, proposed in June 2013 and finalized in January 2014, did so by consciously including almost all repo

---

[10] Federal Reserve Boston president Rosengren summed up this stance by saying: "Despite the central role that broker-dealers played in exacerbating the crisis, too little has changed to avoid a repeat of the problem, I am sorry to say" (Rosengren 2013, 5).

[11] Tarullo based his reasoning on recently published research on the link between funding and market liquidity by Princeton professor Brunnermeier (Brunnermeier and Pedersen 2009), as well as research by Federal Reserve economist Adrian and Princeton professor Shin (Adrian and Shin 2010), which documented the procyclical leverage behavior of broker-dealers.

transactions on the balance sheet of banks, a status they did not have pre-crisis, thereby imposing a limit to the expansion of repo-business.[12] The measure sought to constrain the buildup of leverage in the banking sector, thereby helping to avoid destabilizing deleveraging processes.

The second constraining regulatory measure was the Net Stable Funding Ratio (NSFR), which was part of the new liquidity framework, and which tried to reduce the reliance of the banking system on wholesale funding. Short-term repos as well as reverse repos were disincentivized in this framework, as they were perceived to be unstable forms of financing, contributing to the fragility of the financial system (second interview, Treasury Regulation European Bank, August 18, 2016). In imposing these changes, Tarullo, succeeding Adair Turner as chairman of the FSB's Standing Committee on Supervisory and Regulatory Cooperation in March 2013, took advantage of the fact that the NSFR was not yet finalized. The measure, which was supposed to ensure that large banks could withstand a reduction in funding liquidity for the length of one year, initially contained no macro-prudential ideas, instead being built on a mere micro-prudential focus on the liquidity position of each individual bank (for a critical review, see Claessen and Kondres 2014). Adding on a macro-prudential element, Tarullo used the fact that the measure was not yet finalized for his own purposes, seeking to force "firms to internalize the tail-event financial stability risks associated with SFT [securities financing transactions] matched books" (Tarullo 2013b, 12).[13]

He did so by convincing his fellow regulators to introduce a regulatory charge in terms of required stable funding both for repos (that is, short-term financing based on the provision of collateral) and reverse repos; that is, short-term lending based on the receipt of collateral, directly aiming at the business of broker-dealers (Tarullo 2014a, 13; for an explanation of the mechanics, see CGFS 2017, 61ff.). This counterintuitive regulatory charge, which penalized matched books of broker-dealers, was driven by the attempt to use this final calibration to capture an issue that up until

---

[12] The enhanced treatment of repo-transactions is explicitly mentioned by the Basel Committees as one of the five major revisions undertaken in the June 2013 revised version (see www.bis.org/publ/bcbs251.htm).

[13] Tarullo argued that because "broker-dealers generally do not internalize the externalities that arise in these cases [fire-sales, caused when a broker fails] they may use more than the economically efficient level of short-term funding" (Tarullo 2013b, 10).

then had gone unaddressed (Tarullo 2013b; interview, Federal Reserve economist, December 6, 2021). As Tarullo points out, a key concern regarding this revision of the NSFR was to address the systemic risks associated with matched books of broker-dealers, which stem from their short-term funding structure and which might create "liquidity squeezes" to the market as a whole (Tarullo 2014a). "To partially address these risks, the NSFR will require firms to hold some stable funding against short-term loans … to internalize the externalities produced" (Tarullo 2014a, 13) through the use of wholesale funding.[14]

These regulatory interventions into the repo-market were possible because they were based on a shared assessment by regulators in the UK and the Eurozone about the risks to financial stability the procyclical behavior of broker-dealers posed. By 2013, it had become accepted wisdom that there can be "too much repo," as the BoE manager responsible for market operations put it, leading the system to "overreach, straining asset valuations and ultimately leading to unravelling" and thereby exposing the financial system to run-risks (Hauser 2013, 3).[15] Similarly, Benoit Coeuré, responsible for market operations at the ECB, pointed to the risks of "fire sales spirals and various forms of contagion" (Coeuré 2013, 2; see also Coeuré 2017, 9f.) as reasons to impose liquidity regulations upon broker-dealers. This position was based on the insights generated by academic papers post-crisis that documented the procyclical leveraging behavior of broker-dealers at the height of the boom, based on the procyclical characteristics of the repo-market (Adrian and Shin 2010;

---

[14] Subsequently, US regulators would use these international agreements to impose even stricter rules in the USA, creating an extended Supplementary Leverage Ratio, which would force the eight Globally Systemically Important Banks in the USA to achieve a leverage ratio of 5 percent, rather than the 3 percent envisioned in Basel III (see www.federalreserve.gov/newsevents/pressreleases/bcre g20140903b.htm). In addition, they included the degree of wholesale funding as a ratio in the calculation of the Global-Systemically Important Bank (G-SIB) status in order to further disincentivize broker-dealer activities, or at least to insure that banks active in the broker-dealer market were sufficiently well capitalized in order to minimize the danger of runs on these Bank Holding Companies. This rule, suggested on December 9, 2014 and approved on July 20, 2015, marked a further deviation from Global Basel Rules in the pursuit of macro-prudential change agents in the USA to combat the wholesale funding risks large broker-dealers were exposed to and where themselves creating.

[15] The speech in which Hauser made these remarks was held at a lobbying event of the repo-industry. In the speech, he defended the regulatory measures taken as necessary and not contradictory to the increased need for collateral caused by regulation.

Adrian and Shin 2014).[16] Similarly, Mark Carney, governor of the Bank of England and head of the FSB, argued "much of the pre-crisis market making capacity among dealers was ephemeral" (Carney 2015) because they relied on short-term funding sources, which created a "tinder box" (see also Carney 2013).

Through the introduction of the leverage ratio and the NSFR, the business for broker-dealers in this market for the first time received a regulatory cost. Given its status as a low-margin business, this created a reluctance in the provision of liquidity by broker-dealers (interview, Treasury Regulation Large European Bank, August 18, 2016). Not surprisingly, in this new regulatory context, repo-market activities of broker-dealers have been reduced.[17] The decline in repo transactions can thus partially be explained through the new Basel III framework, which has altered the incentives of broker-dealers to engage in these transactions (interview, Treasury Regulation European Bank, July 21, 2016). Feared negative consequences were also projected by industry studies, such as PricewaterhouseCoopers (PwC 2015), which reported that "liquidity provision by broker-dealers has been reduced since the crisis, making this a subject of concern for market participants" (p. 7). Overall, these industry voices reflect the fact that post-crisis regulatory efforts were a push against market actors and their interests. These effects were indeed intended as "the people who wrote Basel knew exactly what they were trying to achieve" (ICMA 2015, 10).

Unintended Consequences of Basel Regulations: A Greater Central Bank Footprint in the Repo-Market

While macro-prudential change agents were in this way inserting frictions into the repo-market, this intervention created potential problems for central bankers working in the capital markets department, which

---

[16]   As Shin put it, summarizing this research, "dealer banks were taking on exposures in ways that proved to be unsustainable [which is why] there was too much liquidity ... in the broker-dealer sector" (Shin 2016, 3).

[17]   Although a lack of data impedes a distinct statement of whether and why repo transactions have declined, current reports estimate that repo transactions have been reduced because of the new regulatory costs or have altered the market structure (Fed 2015; Bank of England 2016c; ECB 2015b; ESRB 2016c). As Adrian and colleagues (2017b) argue, when actual trading behavior with regulatory balance-sheet constraints is measured, "post-crisis regulation has had an adverse impact on bond-level liquidity" (see also CGFS 2017).

used the repo-market extensively in order to transmit monetary policy decisions into markets (Gabor 2016b; Braun 2020). While these agents did agree with the attempt to reduce the funding liquidity risk to broker-dealers, they did not want to abandon the benefits vibrant repo-markets could provide, in particular in light of the increasing collateral demands imposed by regulatory changes and changing financial market practices (Coeuré 2012; Hauser 2013, 9). In their view, repo-market liquidity and the efficiency it provides should be safeguarded, also because it facilitated their own work in conducting monetary policy (Bindseil and Jablecki 2011).

In this context, the macro-prudential regulation of repo-markets posed a dilemma to monetary policymakers within central banks: on the one hand, they approved of regulatory interventions in the repo-market, which were seeking to curb the procyclical expansion of broker-dealer business in the upswing, emphasizing the need for prudentially sound repo-markets (Hauser 2013, 3). On the other hand, the contributions of well-functioning repo-markets to market liquidity and "collateral fluidity" were deemed essential for the creation of informationally "efficient" markets, which allowed for the transmission of monetary policy impulses (Hauser 2013, 3). Given this dilemma, central bank policymakers accompanied the post-crisis regulatory endeavor that tried to build more robust and resilient repo-markets (Hauser 2013, 9) with complementary measures to increase collateral fluidity and support the repo-market, in case broker-dealers were overwhelmed. Such provision of collateral to repo-market participants other than banks and broker-dealers, in particular Money Market Mutual Funds, became institutionalized in the USA and the UK in 2013, and in 2016 in the Eurozone.

The installation of such facilities in the USA occurred in a very low-key manner as a direct reaction to the anticipated consequences of the Basel III leverage ratio, which was to be implemented in the USA by 2014 (Frost et al. 2015, 5). More flamboyantly, the Bank of England in 2013 announced that it was "Open for Business," a statement that reflected the extensive broadening of the BoE's liquidity provision framework post-crisis. The Bank of England justified the broadening of its standing facilities as well as the formalization of the Market-Maker of Last Resort function with the new Basel regulations, which on the one hand made these interventions necessary, but also enabled them, as they reduced the risk of moral hazard (Shafik 2015, 7). Lastly, and somewhat belatedly, the ECB also adjusted its collateral framework to mitigate possible ructions in the repo-market. This happened in the aftermath of its own quantitative easing program, which began in March 2015 and soon led to industry complaints about a dearth of good collateral in the repo-market (Debnath and Harris 2016; Coeuré 2017, 6). As Chapters 8 and 9 will show, this institutionalized increased footprint of central banks would prove crucial for central banks' future encounters with financial instability.

Conclusion

This chapter has analyzed the attempts of macro-prudential change agents to gain greater control over the procyclical tendencies of the repo-market, which had been a main element in the crisis dynamics of 2007–8. It has shown how the initial efforts at the FSB to introduce countercyclical and/or through-the-cycle haircuts led to largely symbolic regulatory interventions. Impaired by the lack of reliable data on this market, the anxious state of central bankers responsible for monetary policy interventions in the repo-market as well as the opposition of US regulators regarding any such haircut requirements, change agents never could overcome the skeptical interventions by their counterparts. The measures this initiative produced were finally extremely limited in scope (excluding government securities and non-bank-to-non-bank transactions) and in calibration, not imposing any serious constraint on the procyclical tendencies of the market.

On the other hand, the chapter has shown how structural, non-discretionary measures in the context of the specification of Basel III rules, in particular the Leverage ratio and the NSFR, severely affected the intermediating role of broker-dealers in the repo-market, thereby impacting the price and availability of repo-funding liquidity. By imposing capital and funding regulations on this priorly unregulated activity, these measures reduced the willingness of market-makers to make markets, in particular for smaller agents (Gerba and Katsoulis 2021). These changes were consciously inserted into the final specifications of these rules by change agents from the USA concerned over the persistent run-risks of large broker-dealers and their procyclical provision of liquidity linked to their activities in the repo-market.

The consequence of this partial success, based on the regulatory control over the activities of broker-dealers but not the market as a whole, was an increasing footprint of central banks in the repo-market, seen as necessary to mitigate both the liquidity-reducing effects of the Basel regulations and the distorting effects introduced through quantitative easing. In this way, central banks, encouraged by the stricter liquidity regulations seen to reduce moral hazard, made their backstopping function for this market more explicit, seeking to ensure both the monetary policy transmission and financial stability.

Yet, as the repo-market shifted further away from broker-dealer intermediation, central banks had gained little to no control over the risk management practices by other market participants, such as open-ended investment funds or hedge funds. In the ensuing upswing from 2015 onwards, these actors that refinanced their holdings of bonds in the repo-market would grow substantially. As these actors were growing, their liquidity demands would pose increasing strains on broker-dealers, which would prove incapable of providing the repo-market with liquidity at all times. Instead, the repo-market would undergo several bouts of instability and unexpected volatility, which could be linked to the newly imposed balance-sheet constraints upon large broker-dealers and which required the ever-greater presence of central banks. Seeking to compensate for the unwillingness of broker-dealers to make markets, central banks came to backstop the shadow banking system, a backstop that became evident during the COVID-19 crisis. It is to this story of upswing and unexpected bust that we now turn.

8 | Into the Upswing

Introduction

In the last three chapters, I have focused on the installation, set-up and operationalization of anti-cyclical macro-prudential policies in the USA, the UK and the Eurozone. In this chapter, I will investigate the use and activation of these anti-cyclical tools in the context of the first sustained cyclical upswing, which materialized in these jurisdictions during the 2010s. While the exact timing differed between these three jurisdictions, with the Eurozone's emerging somewhat later from the financial trough due to the Eurozone crisis and subsequent austerity, by the late 2010s based on the common ultra-easy monetary policy and connected quantitative easing programs,[1] all three jurisdictions faced a notable upswing in the cyclical indicators that Chapter 6 has detailed. How have central banks been able to react? Did the signaling of macro-prudential risks according to the battery of early warning systems developed by applied central bank economists lead to preventive anti-cyclical measures, or was the signaling of impending dangers all that the new macro-prudential framework could achieve? Or did the inter-action of central banks with policymakers generate a more forceful reaction?

This chapter will show that central banks as central agents of macro-prudential supervision signaled the overheating of housing markets (Bank of England [BoE], European Central Bank [ECB]) and the growth of corporate indebtedness amidst the rise of leveraged loans (Federal Reserve, BoE and belatedly the ECB) as the most pressing problems in the period from 2013 to 2020. In line with these concerns, we see attempts on the one hand to activate discretionary tools to limit the growth of household debt for mortgages, involving first substantial

---

[1] Quantitative easing programs are programs in which central banks buy up financial assets in secondary markets, seeking "to loosen the monetary stance and combat low inflation" (van den End 2016).

debate and then interventions on the part of macro-prudential authorities. On the other hand, we see (largely unsuccessful) attempts to slow down the growth of corporate debt. This evoked in a second step the attempt to expand the perimeter of macro-prudential regulation into the shadow banking sector in order to control the systemic risks that might emanate from this accumulation of corporate debt, in particular related to the identified run-risks from mutual funds holding this debt.

Tracing these developments, this chapter proceeds as follows: it first traces the cyclical developments in the USA, which recovered the quickest from the transatlantic financial crisis, helped both by the massive quantitative easing programs executed by the Federal Reserve and a quickly expanding shadow banking sector. It shows how the Federal Reserve maintained on the one hand a separation principle, whereby macro-prudential policies would be capable to contain any negative side-effects such ultra-loose monetary policy might entail. On the other hand, it shows how the Federal Reserve failed in its attempt to engage in anti-cyclical action based on the diagnosis of an accelerating credit boom in the corporate sector, in particular in the high-risk segment. This incapacity is linked to the political resistance by banks, shadow banks and Congress it encountered, which can be linked to the limited macro-prudential mandate of the Federal Reserve, which saw itself accused of overreach. Similarly, these forces were the reasons for the difficulty it encountered when seeking to expand macro-prudential regulation to the open-ended investment fund sector, the fastest-growing element of the shadow banking system.

In the UK, we can similarly observe a concern over the accelerating credit expansion for corporate debt in the high-risk segment, a concern the BoE had few tools to address. Not only was its capacity to extend regulation beyond the banking sector very limited, it also faced the problem that most of the investment funds seen as fueling the boom were domiciled outside of the UK, granting British authorities little to no say over their behavior. Largely helpless regarding this concern, the British authorities also had to face a quickly accelerating housing boom from 2013 onwards. In this respect, the chapter shows how the BoE acted forcefully, which was facilitated by the fact that such anti-cyclical action was concentrated in the Financial Policy Committee, where the BoE negotiated with all actors regarding the necessary measures in-house in the context of an ex-post accountability framework. Political actors, while involved in the deliberations, had little capacity to stop the BoE from acting.

The third part of the chapter then details the policy reaction to the cyclical upswing in real estate markets in the European Union (EU), which occurred from 2015 onwards, conducting an analysis of which governance configurations affected how countries reacted to this overheating. Here, it details the role of central banks, technocrats and political actors enacting these measures. What will be documented is the slow but steady work of technocrats both at the national and the European level to convince political actors to enact discretionary tools to limit house price booms, in particular borrower-based measures, such as loan-to-value ratios. Such measures were opposed by political actors, such as ministries of finance, which feared the political repercussions of such measures. Only in governance contexts where these actors were muted or forced into a continued dialogue with central banks do we see action, which often took years to materialize. Overall, regulatory measures are analyzed as mostly weak, suggesting that the fragmented governance of anti-cyclical decisions in the Eurozone does not lend itself to enact forceful anti-cyclical action.

Out of the Trough

In the immediate aftermath of the financial crisis, from 2009 onwards anti-cyclical measures were needed to seek to halt the downswing in the financial cycle, as financial systems in all three jurisdictions were characterized by debt overhang and large uncertainty regarding future developments. As financial regulators at the same time were phasing in new capital requirements for banks based on the Basel III capital requirements, these measures could not operate through the anti-cyclical easing of capital requirements. Instead, central banks pushed interest rates to the zero lower bound and enacted large-scale quantitative easing programs to boost financial conditions (Reisenbichler 2020).

This process evolved gradually, as the emergency quantitative easing programs that were started in 2008 (USA) and 2009 (UK) were retooled not to stabilize financial markets but to revive them. These measures, which came belatedly and in a much more covert fashion in the Eurozone from 2010 onwards,[2] would reinflate financial markets,

---

[2] In the Eurozone, the ECB was constrained by a rigid interpretation of the European treaties, which prevented the ECB from engaging in monetary financing of public debt. It was only in 2015 that the ECB would officially launch their quantitative easing program.

thereby sustaining a debt-led recovery (Reisenbichler 2020). Inevitably, these highly accommodative monetary policies would also result in a turn-around in financial conditions, leading to a notable upswing by 2013 in financial conditions in the UK and the USA (FSOC 2013, 8; BoE 2014b, 7; BoE 2014e), and by 2015 in in the Eurozone, just in time to be picked up by the financial stability monitoring frameworks discussed in Chapter 6 (see ECB 2015a, 16).

However, these improvements were fragile and dependent on further market support in the form of quantitative easing, as the Federal Reserve was to find out when it sought to taper its bond purchasing program in 2013 and was forced to continue quantitative easing until October 2014.[3] In this context of buoyant financial markets, the growth of credit issuance and the ensuing search for yield by capital market investors fueled by quantitative easing, the anti-cyclical policies of these central banks, which were designated as the first line of defense, would face a grueling test, with the Federal Reserve first in line given that the upswing there occurred earlier than in the other two jurisdictions.

The Federal Reserve's Attempt to Tighten in Credit Provision amidst the Cyclical Upswing

Post-crisis, both the Financial Stability Oversight Council (FSOC) and the Federal Reserve Board were carefully analyzing the evolution of lending standards in the context of very low interest rates, which caused a search for yield among institutional investors (FSOC 2011). In the context of these analyses, the FSOC noted the issuance of more high-yielding and riskier bonds, which started to accelerate from 2010 onwards. In that regard, the growth in the market for leveraged loans – that is, loans extended to higher-risk corporate borrowers, which were carrying a much higher debt burden than the average borrower[4] – came to be of particular concern. These floating instruments, which provided

---

[3] This episode, named the taper tantrum, occurred after the announcement of a future reduction of bond purchases by the Federal Reserve chairman Bernanke at a congressional hearing in May 2013. The Federal Reserve quickly reversed course, assuring markets that tapering was still some way off, which would now only begin in October 2014.

[4] Leveraged loans are often used by these companies for leveraged buyouts or equity buy-backs.

a protection against possible raises of interest rates in the future at the same time that they provided high yields in the present, became particularly attractive to investors. Already in 2011, the Annual Report of FSOC pointed to the expansion of this segment amidst deteriorating credit standards (FSOC 2011, 104–106),[5] noting a growing "investor risk appetite" for these instruments. In conjunction with the rising issuance of high-yield bonds, these trends represented a cyclical upswing in credit-granting conditions, which the financial stability framework of the Federal Reserve was supposed to go against.

In response to these developments, the three national banking regulators, the Office of the Currency of the Comptroller (OCC), the Federal Deposit Insurance Corporation (FDIC) and the Federal Reserve, came together and collectively worked on revising the interagency guidance for the issuance of such leveraged loans, the prior one dating from 2001. In March 2012, they issued a proposal for Interagency Guidance on Leveraged Lending (Federal Register 77, pp. 19417–19424). In it, they proposed strict guidelines for risk management systems and policies related to the issuance and underwriting of these loans. They suggested to cap pro forma leverage for leveraged financings at six times earnings before interest, taxes, depreciation, and amortization and also required that a company be able to amortize at least 50 percent of its debt within five to seven years of closing the deal to qualify for such a loan (OCC et al. 2012). These restrictive guidelines were much more prescriptive than the 2001 ones, applying both to the issuance of loans and the underwriting of such loans by banks in syndicates.

Officially framed as addressing the safety and soundness of banking institutions, the proposed regulation had, however, more far-reaching macro-prudential goals, as they were seeking to act against a lowering of credit standards that might affect the financial stability of the system as a whole. The FSOC feared larger repercussions, as these loans, while dominantly being originated and/or underwritten by banks, were mostly sold on to institutional investors, such as bank loan funds (FSOC 2011, 105). As such, any regulatory intervention regarding the criteria according to which banks could issue or underwrite these loans would not only increase the safety of the banks but also affect the

[5] Meaning that these debt contracts increasingly also had less legal protection against risks.

quality of corporate debt held in the financial system at large (Nelson et al. 2017). Given the statutory limitations of the issuing parties, however, the proposal placed the emphasis on banks rather than the system as a whole, including both the procedures regarding the origination of these loans as well as their holding on banks' balance sheets.[6] The agencies followed the administrative due process, issuing the largely unchanged final guidelines a year later.

However, given the rather non-binding nature of interagency guidelines, the immediate effect of this guidance was rather limited (Calem et al. 2017). This was worrisome, as leading Federal Reserve Board members had declared such supervisory guidance as the main tool to address the risks stemming from a highly accommodative monetary policy (Tarullo 2014a), making the adjustment of quantitative easing and zero interest rates pursued for the goal of full employment and appropriate inflation unnecessary (Tarullo 2014a; see also Yellen 2014). Based on the principle of separation of monetary policy and financial instability, the hope expressed was that "pockets of risk taking" could be addressed through such more surgical interventions (Yellen 2014). Regulators hence persisted. To achieve constraining effects, they issued several clarifications on the guidance and increasingly enforced the guidelines as binding rules. Following this decision, the effect of the guidelines on the issuance of leveraged loans by banks was strong, as a working paper by the Federal Reserve documents (see Calem et al. 2017).

Yet, while this measure was limiting banks' issuance and underwriting business, it also clarified the limits of the anti-cyclical mandate of banking regulators in the context of a financial system characterized by a strong shadow banking system. As a different paper by the New York Federal Reserve documented (Kim et al. 2017), the diminished issuance by banks was almost 100 percent substituted for by non-banks, pointing to the dangers of migration of risks into shadow banking. Tarullo (2014a) had foreseen as much, when he presciently warned:

Third, and perhaps most important, the extent to which supervisory practice can either lean against the wind or increase the overall resiliency of the

---

[6] In order to extend beyond banks while staying within the mandate, the proposal also included "pipeline risks"; that is, risks originating from a sudden breakdown in market demand, which would expose banks to unplanned losses on their balance sheets, as they were preparing these assets for sale.

financial system is limited by the fact that it applies only to prudentially regulated firms. This circumstance creates an incentive for intermediation activities to migrate outside of the regulated sector. ... Indeed, it must be recognized that regular recourse to supervisory measures in response to nascent financial stability concerns would likely be perceived as increasing the payoff from this form of regulatory arbitrage. (Tarullo 2014a, 5)

Disadvantaging the banks, without overall changing the extent of the problem (Kim et al. 2017), this state of affairs angered banks even more (Nelson et al. 2017), which saw the interagency guidance as a broad overreach by the Federal Reserve. They were arguing, quite correctly, that the Federal Reserve was seeking to address systemic risks for the financial system as a whole when its mandate clearly limited it to the banking system (Nelson et al. 2017).

To instigate a revision to the rule, they used their contacts into the Republican Party, which just had come to power. In this vein, Republican Senator Pat Toomey submitted in March 2017 a request for clarification to the Government Accountability Office, enquiring whether the guidance was not de facto a rule and hence subject to the Congressional Review Act, allowing Congress to rescind it. In October 2017, the Government Accountability Office (GAO) issued its ruling, which against the opposition of the banking regulators decided that the guidance indeed was subject to the Comprehensive Capital Analysis and Review (CCAR). Shortly thereafter, and following pressure by Congress and the banks, the different banking regulators de facto rescinded the guidance, announcing that banks no longer must follow it and that it would not be subject to enforcement action (Leicht and Wall 2018).

The subsequent growth of the leveraged lending segment, in conjunction with the high-yield bond segment as well as the segment of collateralized loan obligations (CLOs), remained an issue of concern for the Federal Reserve (Federal Reserve 2019), as well as for the FSOC (FSOC 2019), yet it was clear that actions by the Federal Reserve would not be sufficient to address these issues. Too many were the actors issuing such leveraged loans, too large the ever-expanding investor base, which in the context of record low yields was searching for the extra return. Figure 8.1 displays the growth of high-yield and corporate bond funds, holding an ever-larger amount of corporate debt and of bank loans (i.e. leveraged loans).

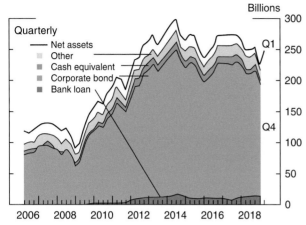

Figure 8.1 Growth of high-yield funds (Anadu and Cai 2019).

As the Financial Stability Report of the Federal Reserve put it in 2018, "Total assets under management in investment-grade and high-yield bond mutual funds and loan mutual funds have more than doubled in the past decade to over $2 trillion …. Bond mutual funds are estimated to hold about one-tenth of outstanding corporate bonds, and loan funds purchase about one-fifth of newly originated leveraged loans" (Federal Reserve Financial Stability Report 2018, 34).

These new actors in the asset management industry were fueling the demand for these debt products and were in this way seen as endangering financial stability. The greatest danger perceived by regulators at this moment in time were the run-risks these funds faced, holding highly illiquid assets while promising redemption at par. This, coupled with compressed yields on these debts and the fact that business were ever more indebted, caused concerns over the possibility of a sudden and large snap back in the prices of these debt and the expansion of this business segment (Federal Reserve Financial Stability Report 2018, 34).

These analyses and the difficulties of regulating these trends through guidance by banking regulators made it evident that to address this problem, a more holistic approach, seeking to encompass the entire shadow banking system and its contribution to the procyclical credit expansion, was needed (see also Tarullo 2014a). The FSOC, granted the mandate by the Dodd-Frank Act to address the overall financial stability risks through both an entity and activities-based approach, was the only player with the capacity to do so. These attempts by the FSOC to gain control over this part of the financial system, however, had run into substantial political problems, essentially failing by the mid-2010s, as we will see next.

The Failed Attempt to Expand the Regulatory Perimeter to the Shadow Banking System

In order to monitor and combat emerging risks to US financial stability, the Dodd-Frank Act in 2010 had given the capacity to the FSOC to expand the perimeter of regulation (Dodd-Frank Act, Sec. 112). In this vein, the FSOC could require the Board of Governors of the Federal Reserve System to "supervise designated nonbank financial companies that may pose risks to U.S. financial stability in the event of their material financial distress or failure or because of their activities" (Dodd-Frank Act, Sec. 112).[7] These FSOC powers regarding the expansion of the perimeter of regulation were codified in articles 113 and 120 of the Dodd-Frank Act and required an affirmative vote of no less than two thirds of the voting members of the Council, including an affirmative vote of the chair; that is, the treasury secretary of the USA for the designation of non-banks. These votes on the designation of non-bank financial companies to be supervised by the Federal Reserve Board were binding and not subject to a public consultation. Instead, in a deviation from the general rules of procedure for administrative decision-making, the concerned entity only had the right to appeal the decision after the fact (Dodd-Frank Act, Sec. 113), seeking to empower the Council to take such decisions (Bernanke et al. 2019a).

After its installation, the FSOC worked immediately on translating the abstract task of designing such non-bank entities deemed to pose systemic risks to the USA into an operational framework, issuing an advance notice of proposed rule-making for the Systemically Important

---

[7] In addition, the Dodd-Frank Act gave FSOC the power to recommend to the Federal Reserve Board heightened prudential standards for designated non-bank financial companies and provided it with the right to request "for more stringent regulation of a financial activity by issuing recommendations to the primary financial regulatory agencies to apply new or heightened standards and safeguards" (Dodd-Frank Act, Sec. 120).

Financial Institution (SIFI) designation process on October 6, 2010, six days after its inauguration (Cook 2011). Shortly thereafter, on January 26, 2011, it issued a notice of proposed rule-making (Cook 2011). After a lengthy consultation with industry and Congress, it published its final rule and interpretive guidance regarding such procedures in April 2012 (FSOC 2012), which involved a three-step process.[8] Based on this methodology, the FSOC proceeded to design four entities as non-bank Globally-Systemically Important Financial Institutions (G-SIFIs) in 2013 and 2014, three of which were insurers (AIG Group, Metlife and Prudential), one being a financial company (GE Capital). In all four cases, it deemed the size of these entities as well as their interconnections to the financial system at large to pose a systemic risk in case of their failure, thus justifying the decision. Importantly, in three of the four cases the issue of potential fire-sales was cited as an important reason as well (Braun 2019, 474–477), as such fire-sales could cause a reverberation of local difficulties into a system-wide crises.

It was in the context of these designation procedures and the concerns over potential fire-sales that the FSOC also came to consider the expansion of the regulatory perimeter to bond funds and other asset managers by designating them non-bank G-SIFIs. The FSOC began its analytical work on such investment funds in 2013, with the Office of Financial Research (OFR) publishing a first report on asset management and financial stability risks in September 2013 (OFR 2013).[9] The report notes the risks related to redemption risks (fire-sales) and leverage of investment funds linked to asset booms, risks, which were aggravated in the context of a general search for yield (OFR 2013, 9). It suggested following a mixed approach of activities and entities-based regulation, opening venues both for action under Sections 113 and 120 of the Dodd-Frank Act. These preliminary analytical works and the publicly announced consideration of designation of asset managers as G-SIFIs, while only at the initial stages already produced a strong

---

[8] In a first step, the FSOC would narrow the list of possible non-bank G-SIFIs based on size; second, they would investigate the possible systemic risks of an entity jointly with the responsible regulator; only in the third step would they announce the decision to consider such a designation to the concerned entity; that is shortly before the announcement (Braun 2019, 473ff.).

[9] The report was the outcome of a request by the FSOC, which was weighing whether – and how – to consider such firms for enhanced prudential standards and supervision under Section 113 of the Dodd-Frank Act (OFR 2013, 1).

backlash not only by industry, but also by the Securities Exchange Commission (SEC) as well as from House Republicans.

The industry attacked the report for its lacking knowledge of the industry and disqualified it as an insufficient basis for rule-making, where the greatest reproach to the report was that asset managers do not own funds, hence making prudential regulation entirely inappropriate (Loftchie 2014b). Lobbyists were hence framing these considerations by FSOC as an attempt by government seeking to interfere in the private decision-making of asset fund managers. Yet, the attacks stemmed not only from private actors but also from SEC commissioners. In an explicit show of disunity of regulators on the matter, one SEC Commissioner (Aguilar) pointed to the lack of expertise by the OFR and the FSOC and complained that the expertise of SEC commissioners and the SEC at large was not sufficiently taken into account (Loftchie 2014a). In addition, the fund industry also managed to sway political actors, such as the chair of the House Financial Services Committee Jeb Hensaerling to increase the pressure, calling on FSOC to "cease and desist" any further designations of non-banks as G-SIFI (Loftchie 2014c).

Reacting to this strong political opposition, the FSOC subsequently shifted its strategy and sought to engage the industry and the SEC on an activities-based approach to regulation. Focusing on the potential risks linked to liquidity and leverage (FSOC 2014, 1), the Council was pushing for regulation able to address the run-risks of funds invested in illiquid assets, which in the view of the Council could give rise to fire-sales. Outcome of the subsequent work by the FSOC was on the one hand a publication in 2016, in which it reaffirmed its view regarding the risks that stemmed from the continued growth of funds investing in illiquid corporate debt (FSOC 2016, 6f.); and on the other hand, the development of regulation by the SEC, which sought to control these liquidity risks (SEC 2016). And yet, the latter were largely self-regulatory, asking fund managers to assess the liquidity risks of their investment, but were not really constraining the expansion of investment by these funds into the asset class of high-risk corporate debt.[10]

While the FSOC was weighing further potentially constraining action, in particular with respect to the leverage of hedge funds, based on an interagency working group installed in 2016, political

---

[10]   The best evidence for it is the continued growth of this segment in the mutual fund industry (see Federal Reserve Financial Stability Report 2018, 34).

events meant that this regulatory agenda was premature. All of these preparatory works to initiate rule-making under Section 120 were torpedoed in November 2016 with the election of Donald Trump, substantially shifting the regulatory agenda toward deregulation (or in the words of the administration, "more efficient regulation"). With the new treasury secretary Mnuchin at its helm, FSOC would disband the interagency working group, stop collecting additional data and rescind the designation of any non-bank G-SIFI in the USA. Furthermore, through legislative proceedings completed on November 4, 2019, the designation procedures of FSOC for such entities were changed in such a way to make the designation of non-bank G-SIFIs largely impossible (Sullivan and Cromwell 2020), foreclosing any expansion of the regulatory perimeter for the time being.[11]

The UK

In the case of the UK, much like in the USA, the anti-cyclical macro-prudential framework faced a first test shortly after its installation. By 2013, and thus more quickly than in other European countries, the housing boom, which had gripped the country before the financial crisis, had returned, fueled by international investor inflows. Figure 8.2 depicts the annual house price changes, showing a strong growth pre-crisis, a crisis related trough from 2009 to 2013 and an acceleration of housing prices from 2013 onwards. This was particularly the case in London (BoE 2013c), raising the question for the Financial Policy Committee what to do about it.

In the case of the UK, the macro-prudential framework was set up in a way that allowed it to respond to these developments in a counter-cyclical manner. While the BoE in 2013 had only asked for three macro-prudential tools for itself (to limit the leverage of banks, to set the countercyclical capital buffer and to impose sectoral capital

---

[11] The text clarified that entity designation would only occur in "rare instances" (Sullivan and Cromwell 2020, 7) and only after all other options, including non-binding recommendations on activities, had been exhausted. When doing so, FSOC would "quantify reasonably estimable benefits and costs, using ranges, as appropriate, and based on empirical data when available," as well as considering costs and benefits qualitatively (Sullivan and Cromwell 2020, 11). By inverting the burden of proof, the new procedures effectively meant that any designation would take more than six years and hence largely lose its preventive character (Bernanke et al. 2019a).

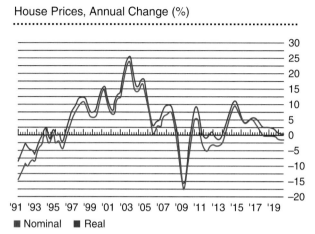

House Prices, Annual Change (%)

'91 '93 '95 '97 '99 '01 '03 '05 '07 '09 '11 '13 '15 '17 '19
■ Nominal   ■ Real

Figure 8.2 Annual change of house prices (Nationwide 2020).

requirements [BoE 2013a]), it nevertheless had from the beginning the right to issue recommendations to the in-house micro-prudential regulators for changes in credit regulation of real estate. It would use these powers of recommendations extensively as the housing market started to gain momentum again, while at the same time trying to expand its powers of direction. In this endeavor, what was most helpful was the fact that both the micro-prudential regulator and the Financial Conduct Authority were members of the Financial Policy Committee (FPC), allowing these agents to partake and shape these discussions and share their final outcomes in terms of recommendation (interview, former member FPC, April 21, 2021).

In September 2013, in its quarterly meeting, the FPC for the first time expressed worries about the risks that might arise if interest rates rose rapidly, starting an investigation into these matters (BoE 2013c). In November 2013, at the next meeting, the FPC found that while banks were resilient, highly indebted households were an area of concern. In particular, interest-rate risks for borrowers that had taken on too much debt were seen as great potential risks, leading the FPC to issue its first recommendation on the need to take interest-rate risks more into account when conducting affordability tests (BoE 2013e).[12]

[12] With this first recommendation, the FPC sought the right to set the appropriate interest rate for such affordability tests, a venue it would use shortly thereafter.

In January 2014, following a quickening pace of house price appreci-ations and a deterioration of lending standards (BoE 2013d, e), the BoE then shifted to a more active stance. Being worried about the debt-carrying capacity of indebted households (hearing Treasury Committee, January 14, 2014, as reported in Reuters 2014), the BoE requested new powers of direction regarding the borrower-based measures for mort-gages, in particular debt service to income measures. Based on its existing powers of recommendation, the FPC also issued in June 2014 a recom-mendation to the Financial Conduct Authority (FCA) to impose a loan-to-income ratio of no higher than 4.5 times as well as an interest-rate affordability test including a rise of 3 percent (BoE 2014c), effectively seeking to halt the accelerating dynamics in the housing market.

This shift, which was grounded in a worry about loosening credit standards, seen as the hallmark of a pending unsustainable boom, was facilitated by the change in leadership of the BoE from Mervyn King to Mark Carney on June 1, 2013. Carney, as the former governor of the Bank of Canada, already had some experience with anti-cyclical meas-ures, and was much more open to anti-cyclical thinking and measures than his predecessor (interview, BoE economist, January 13, 2020; see also Taylor 2019, 3). Furthermore, the close collaboration between the FCA and the micro-prudential regulator, which as active members of the FPC had also become convinced of the need to act, facilitated their action (interview, former member FPC, April 15, 2021).

In June 2014, the Treasury announced its intention to grant additional powers to the FPC, to which the FPC reacted by expressing the wish to gain powers over housing market developments and the leverage ratio (BoE 2014d). In the following year, the BoE would use these newly gained powers to formulate a strict framework for loan-to-value and loan-to-income ratios by 2015, based on its 2014 recommendation (BoE 2015b). These measures proved effective, constraining the capacity of home buyers to purchase homes (interview, former BoE economist involved in building the framework, October 23, 2019). In addition, after years of negotiations with the Treasury (Chan and Wallace 2015), the BoE would furthermore gain regulatory powers over the buy-to-let market in November 2016 (for a positive review of this measure, see IMF 2016), a market that was also seen to contribute to the overheating of the housing market (FPC Meeting Minutes March 2016).

All of these measures exerted some effect on the housing market, yet the real event that cooled the accelerating dynamics was the uncertainty provoked by the Brexit referendum, which was to be held in June 2016. In this vein, when the European Systemic Risk Board (ESRB) in 2016 issued a warning on medium-term vulnerabilities in the housing market in the UK (ESRB 2016f), it noted that the current house price dynamics were in doubt following the Brexit referendum. And in fact, house prices de facto cooled down post-Brexit, somewhat helped by the stringent measures of the BoE (interview, BoE economist, October 23, 2019), yet by no means due to these measures alone. Revisiting the issue of housing vulnerability in 2019, the ESRB then also found that the main measure to cool the housing boom was Brexit, leading the ESRB to deem the measures put in place by the BoE in line with cyclical developments (ESRB 2019f). While the Brexit referendum hence took care of the boom in residential real estate, much as it did in commercial real estate, a second issue that had come to preoccupy the FPC from 2013 onwards became ever more important, namely the evolution of corporate debt in the UK from November 2013 onwards (BoE 2013e) and its links to the growing investment fund sector.

The UK: An Island in an Ocean of Investment Fund Activity

In the UK, there were ample concerns in the FPC over the development of corporate debt from 2013 onwards. In particular, the above-trend growth of leveraged loans and loans for commercial real estate was a persistent worry for the FPC, who repeatedly pointed to the risks of these developments (BoE 2013e, 2015a, 2016a, 2017c, 2018a, b, c, 2019a, b). The problem with these cyclical developments was that the FPC largely lacked the tools to address them, as they were mostly driven by developments outside of the banking sector.

As the FPC noted, most of these new debts were not held on UK banks' balance sheets but rather were bought up by fixed-income investment funds. These funds, which grew rapidly, refinanced these assets through short-term repo-transactions, only aggravating the FPC's concerns regarding these developments. Observing that repo-market liquidity was reduced from 2014 onwards, the FPC feared that some market participants "may be underestimating the likelihood and severity of tail risks" (BoE 2014b, 22). In line with these concerns, the BoE started a review program to assess the risks from the changes in market liquidity and changes in the non-banking sector and to request an extension of the perimeter if it thought it necessary.

To do so, it had to collect data and interrogate the behavior of these entities in financial markets from a financial stability perspective. Such an exercise was initiated in the March 2015 meeting of the FPC, when these concerns, which linked the reduction of market liquidity to the growth of corporate indebtedness from a financial stability perspective, were jointly debated (BoE 2015a). At the end of this session, the FPC asked the Bank and the FCA to work together to contribute to the agenda of the Financial Stability Board (FSB) on asset managers and to analyze the exposure of the UK economy to financial stability risks emanating from the reduction in market liquidity, given the increasing reliance of corporations on market-based financing. This analysis was to be combined with an inquiry into both the reasons for the increased fragility of markets and the strategies of private investment managers to deal with the liquidity risks in stressed scenarios. This information should clarify the extent of any macro-prudential risks associated with market liquidity and allow the Committee to assess potential policy mitigants. The Committee asked for a full report at its meeting in September, the results of which were subsequently published in the December 2015 Financial Stability Report (BoE 2015e, 24f.).

From then onwards, the FPC would remain alert to the increasing risks posed by the growing investment fund industry and would seek to ensure that market liquidity was capable of accommodating the possibly volatile buying and selling behavior of the asset management industry (see Chapter 7).[13] In this context, they warily observed the reduction in bond premia in global markets, signs of a rising risk appetite of bond investors in the context of a low-yield environment (BoE 2016b, 7; BoE 2017d, 6; BoE 2018a, b). This reduction in risk premia was coupled in the UK with the persistent growth of open-ended bond funds (BoE 2017b, 2017d, 2018a, 2019a). This development meant that while the pricing dynamics in equity prices and home prices were dampened by the

---

[13] The FPC got a first taste of such procyclical behavior of funds in the context of the Brexit referendum. The vote for Brexit was surprising to international investors and led to redemption requests in funds devoted to commercial real estate, a sector priorly identified by the FPC as overheating (BoE 2016a). In response, these funds had to close for a while, as they were overwhelmed by requests for redemptions and could not sell assets quickly enough. While these periods of market turmoil were short-lived, they clarified to the BoE the risks the financial system of the UK was exposed to as a financial center with a large foreign investorship, based on the runnable liabilities of these funds and the connected fire-sale dangers (BoE 2016a).

Brexit decision in July 2016, the issuance of low-rated debt by highly leveraged firms in the UK continued, amidst a very compressed pricing of the risks inherent in these loans (BoE 2017d, 6). This deterioration was particularly marked in the leveraged loan market, with much of the loans being sold on and repackaged in collateralized loan obligations (see BoE 2018b, c, iii; Brazier 2019, 15). These developments increased the discomfort of the FPC regarding the growth of investment funds, which were doing so by buying up corporate debt that seemed to be of an increasingly diminished quality (BoE 2017d, 27). In essence, policymakers in the UK were facing a peaking credit cycle in the corporate sector, financed at least partly by open investment funds domiciled mostly abroad, which were prone to runs (BoE 2019a, 26f.).

These concerns were coming to a head in 2017, as investment inflows by foreign investors into the UK accelerated, in particular into "commercial real estate and UK leveraged loan markets" (BoE 2018a, 26), two markets seen as particularly overvalued by the FPC. Figure 8.3,

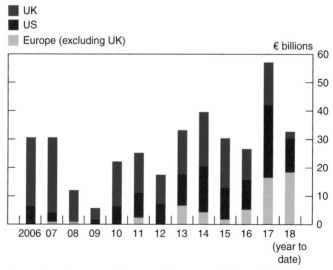

Figure 8.3 Issuance of leveraged loans and high-yield bonds (BoE 2018a, 28).

taken from the BoE's June 2018 financial stability report, documents these concerns, showing the acceleration in the issuance of high-risk debt as well as the fact that by 2017 more than 70 percent of this debt was subscribed by European and American financial institutions, a fact that is even more pronounced for the first half of 2018. These developments exposed the UK financial system to developments abroad, in particular those occurring in the USA (Carney 2019, 11f.), where as we saw before no regulatory measures were forthcoming.

Because of these developments, the FPC would increase its analytical work regarding the leveraged loan market and the market for collateralized loan obligations. In this work, the BoE sought to find out who held the leveraged loans originating in the UK, an attempt that took a large amount of time (interview, former BoE economist, October 23, 2019). As a result of this research, the BoE found that 40 percent of the global leveraged loan market was held by non-banks and that UK banks held a rather small share of the market (BoE 2019a, 27; see Figure 8.4). They furthermore found that non-banks account now for "56% of the stock of UK corporate debt" and that "*market-based debt has accounted for all of the growth in the stock of debt to UK businesses since end-2007*" (Brazier 2019, 15, emphasis mine).

Because such a large class of investors in the asset class of corporate bonds were not domestic banks, the anti-cyclical toolkit of the FPC hardly applied (BoE 2018c, iii). As such, all they could do was to collaborate with the FCA to install more stringent liquidity requirements for the domestic asset management industry to prevent investment into the most illiquid financial assets[14] and to support the international initiatives by the International Organization of Securities Commission (IOSCO) and the FSB (see BoE 2016b, 42), even if the results of the latter were not deemed fully satisfactory (BoE 2019a).[15]

---

[14] The FCA followed this request in September 2019 (FCA 2019).
[15] As the BoE notes in July 2019, the February 2018 recommendations by IOSCO are too vague to impose any meaningful liquidity regulation, leaving it up to the discretion of national regulators (BoE 2019a, 33). Given that international efforts largely returned the issue to national authorities, they hence installed a joint review with the FCA to inquire into the liquidity mismatches in open-ended investment funds in mid-2019, as they continued to judge "that the mismatch between redemption terms and the liquidity of some funds' assets has the potential to become a systemic issue" (BoE 2019a, 33). Their work focused on the matching of the liquidity of a fund's assets with the possibilities of investors to redeem their shares, including the costs and the frequency of such

A material share of the overall leveraged loan market
is held by global banks
Indicative estimate of leveraged loans and CLOs outstanding globally by
investor type[a][b][c][d][e][f][g][h]

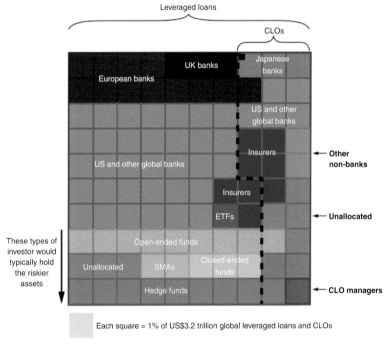

Figure 8.4 Who holds leveraged loans globally (BoE 2019d, 12).

In a second step, the FPC pushed for the development of stress-testing capabilities to include the risks of procyclical behavior of open-ended investment funds in the annual stress-test exercise. The macro-prudential support division, guided by Alexander Brazier, was making persistent progress on these issues, with several teams at the FPC working on these issues. A first simulation published in July 2017 (Baranova et al. 2017) was refined and fed with data in order to

redemptions (BoE 2019a, 74ff.), work that was to be concluded in 2020 and was to include new UK rules – important work that unfortunately was delayed by the COVID-19 events of March 2020.

investigate if and how far the correction of corporate debt prices, which were seen as stretched, could affect the financial stability of the UK financial system due to market developments (Brazier 2018, 6). These efforts culminated in the formulation of a biennial exploratory stress test in November 2019, which was supposed to stress-test the entire financial system to understand what would occur in the case of a severe disruption in market liquidity. This exercise, just as it was about to be implemented in spring 2020, was interrupted in March 2020 by the events surrounding the COVID-19 crisis. Overall, however, despite their attempts to take these risks into account in their outlook on financial markets, the FPC in the UK had little to no tools to act upon them.

The Eurozone

The Eurozone was the last of the three jurisdictions under study to experience a cyclical upswing. The Eurozone crisis from 2010 to 2012, which had escalated around the fear of a break-up of the Eurozone and which brought in its wake the application of austerity measures that crippled economic growth and financial risk-taking, meant that signs of cyclical upswings would only start to emerge from 2015 onwards (ECB 2015a, 16ff.; interview, ECB economist, May 9, 2016), sustained by the new quantitative easing program the ECB had begun to implement from April 2015 onwards. These cyclical upswings for different countries had different temporalities, with periphery countries affected by the Eurozone crisis experiencing a substantial delay. Amidst these temporally differentiated upswings, European macro-prudential authorities were expressing concerns over housing from 2016 onwards (cf. ESRB 2016e, 2019b), with the rising level of corporate debt only causing concern from 2019 onwards (see ECB 2019).

While the growth of the asset management industry was causing some macro-prudential concern (see Constâncio 2015), the initial focus was hence on the real estate booms in different countries and how the European authorities, both at the national and the European level, should react to it. As discussed in Chapter 6, the macro-prudential anti-cyclical apparatus in the Eurozone was highly fragmented, with the European level having a secondary role regarding anti-cyclical actions that had to be primarily taken at the national level. Amidst this fragmented nature of governance, we can witness the attempts to bring about action by the ECB and the ESRB in conjunction with the national central banks, seeking to convince national political actors of the need for action on housing.

Diagnosing the Cyclical Upswing and Pushing for Action on Housing

From 2015 onwards, the recovery in the Eurozone, which was further fueled by the recently initiated quantitative easing program, translated into rising credit growth, leading to both an expansion of corporate debt and rising investment in real estate markets (ECB 2016b, c). While these developments were initially seen as positive by the Financial Stability Division of the ECB, seeing no "no signs of the ongoing recovery of euro-area residential property markets translating into broad-based rapid housing loan growth in the Euro-area" (ECB 2016c, 42f.), this assessment would slowly change as the ECB noted the expansion of the boom to all countries, but Cyprus, Greece and Italy and saw the first "few signs" of this uptick translating into broad-based housing loan growth (ECB 2017a, 48). In this context, the ECB pointed to the need for country-level action to deal with these different stages of the cycle (ECB 2017a, 49f.). While the ECB was in theory given the right to top up national measures to face this upswing in the credit cycle, it preferred to use persuasion and the issuance of recommendations by the ESRB to get additional country-level action (ECB 2017a).

Among the twenty-seven countries within the EU, ten European countries reacted to this growth in credit by activating a capital buffer by 2019, with the Swedish being the first to announce its activation in October 2014, amidst signs of an overheating housing market (see Figure 8.5 below). As Figure 8.6 shows, most countercyclical capital buffer (CCyB) announcements came from 2017 onwards, with a strong prevalence among smaller northern and eastern European countries, a fact that can partially be explained for the latter by the greater acquaintance of these countries with macro-prudential measures during their transition period and partially by particularly strong housing cycles (Piroska et al. 2021).

In western European countries, however, the activation of the CCyB was much less numerous and extensive. This on the one hand can partially be explained by the fact that cyclical upswings there arrived later, in particular in the crisis-torn south (Italy, Spain, Portugal and

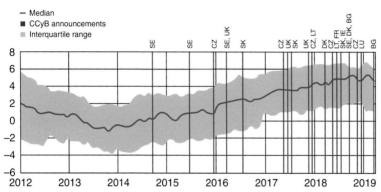

Figure 8.5 Credit growth and countercyclical capital buffer announcements (ESRB 2019b, 24).

Greece). Yet, more importantly, it is the fact that in most western European countries, it was not central banks but ministries of finance that were dominating the macro-prudential decision-making on the CCyB. They did so either as the sole macro-prudential authority or in financial stability councils, with central banks often playing only a subordinated role (see Arbatli-Saxegaard and Muneer 2020, 6; Lepers and Thiemann 2023). As political actors, these ministries were much more reluctant to impose frictions regarding the growth of credit, in particular for measures regarding access to the real estate market (Thiemann and Stellinga 2022).

This political economy issue of anti-cyclical policies interacted with the shortcomings of the credit-to-GDP gap as an early warning indicator, which did not detect the cyclical upswing sufficiently ahead of time (see Figure 8.7). This fact was exploited by countries, like Germany, in order to argue that no CCyB activation was necessary (interview, German central bank economist, October 16, 2019; interview, German central bank economist, July 9, 2021), as the credit-to-GDP gap had barely crossed into positive territory (see Figure 8.7). At the same time, all but the crisis countries had experienced substantial credit growth by 2018, which, however, did not lead to the credit-to-GDP gap showing any need for action.

The ESRB as well as the ECB were watching these developments with great concern (interview, ECB economist, May 9, 2016), being in constant touch with the national competent macro-prudential authorities

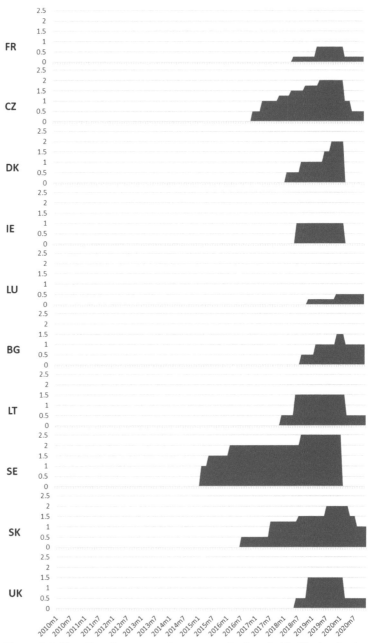

Figure 8.6 Timeline of announced countercyclical capital buffer (author's own presentation, based on ESRB data)

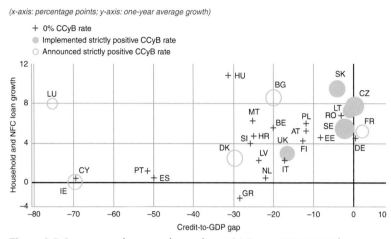

Figure 8.7 Loan growth versus the credit-to-GDP gap (ESRB 2019b, 24).

over the need for anti-cyclical macro-prudential action. In this context, the research endeavors at the financial stability division within the ECB and at the ESRB, which had focused their efforts on the refinement of the measurements of cyclical upswings, gained practical importance. This work, detailed in the last chapter, had shown that the credit-to-GDP gap was notoriously late in picking up cyclical upswings, which is why the ECB proposed a different measure, more sensitive to cyclical upswings (Schueler et al. 2017). Based on this new measure, Germany as well as other Western countries were seen to already have entered well in the upswing phase by 2015, a fact used by the ESRB and the financial stability division within the ECB to push for anti-cyclical action (interview, former ECB economist, October 16, 2019) (see Figure 8.8).

Yet getting these countries to enact anti-cyclical measures proved difficult, as these countries insisted on the credit-to-GDP gap as the measure enshrined in EU regulation (interview, former ECB economist, October 16, 2019; interview, German central bank economist, July 9, 2021). Getting them to act required lengthy and repeated discussions with national authorities and attempts of persuasion, involving both national and European central bankers as agents seeking to convince ministries of finance as well as prudential regulators. This can well be seen for the case of anti-cyclical action with respect to overheating residential real estate markets, which were the greatest cyclical concern of central bankers in the second half of the 2010s, on which we will focus next.

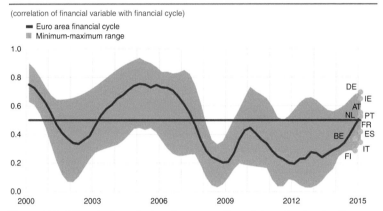

Figure 8.8 Historical analysis of country financial cycles in the Euro area (Constâncio et al. 2019, 54).

Getting Action on Real Estate: The Lengthy Process of Persuasion

Within the course of the cyclical upswing from 2015, macro-prudential authorities at the EU level had become increasingly concerned about the upswing in residential real estate markets across Europe (ECB 2016b). The EU-wide real estate price slowdown after the fallout of the 2008 crisis had reversed in 2013, after which prices surged and real estate price valuation metrics trended upward (Figure 8.9). House price growth remained strong at around 4 percent since 2016, a trend that did not show signs of weakening afterwards.

A first step for the European macro-prudential authorities to express their growing inquietude and issuing a first call for action regarding these developments in European housing markets occurred in 2016, when the ESRB laid out its analytical framework for analyzing medium-term vulnerabilities and applied it to individual European countries (ESRB 2016d). Based on this analysis, the ESRB issued eight warnings to member states regarding medium-term vulnerabilities in the residential real estate sector (ESRB 2016e).[16] In essence, in

---

[16] For the UK, these warnings were issued only for small countries (Sweden, Austria, Belgium, Denmark, the Netherlands, Luxembourg and Finland) amidst a sign that the real estate boom was not yet a widespread phenomenon.

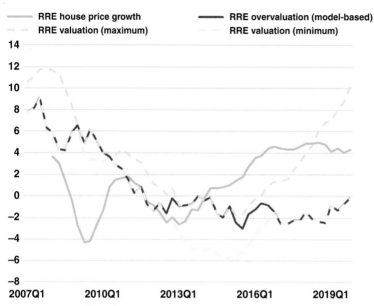

Figure 8.9 Residential real estate price developments (Euro area) (Lepers and Thiemann 2023).

issuing these warnings, the ESRB was simply seeking to point to trends that it thought required an answer and was asking for an official reaction by the competent national authorities. At the same time, these warnings had no legal implication other than allowing the ESRB to escalate to the next step of a recommendation, if no sufficient answer was formulated.

Accordingly, the answers by the corresponding national authorities, all eight ministers of finance, were largely defiant, pointing to the need to wait and see whether the measures taken, deemed insufficient by the ESRB, would nevertheless have the desired effects.[17] Having no capacity to coerce national authorities to act, little to no measures were effectively taken to address the issue. Given the persistent low-interest-rate environment, the housing boom could hence only accelerate. By 2019, the second wave of the issuance of warnings and recommendations, the ESRB now issued five additional warnings and six

---

[17] Only the British response letter pointed to the willingness to comply, which, however, was also made easier by the fact that Brexit had just let to a cooling of the housing market.

recommendations as a follow-up to the warnings issued in 2016.[18] The new warnings now also included France and Germany, two large Eurozone countries that had experienced a sustained upswing in residential real estate prices and household indebtedness since 2016, as the real estate boom had begun to engulf almost all of the Eurozone (ESRB 2019d, e).

At the moment these warnings were officially issued, both Germany and France enacted measures to react to this cyclical upswing, a fact they detailed in their response letters (see Ministry of Finance Germany 2019; Ministry of Finance France 2019). These actions, which particularly for the case of Germany were symbolic in nature rather than truly anti-cyclical (interview, German central bank economist/German financial market regulator, January 2020; interview, German ministry of finance, July 20, 2021),[19] occurred after years of debate in their respective financial stability councils. In these councils, macro-prudential analysts of the Banque de France and the Bundesbank had pushed for the need to act (interview, French Central Bank economist, April 4, 2021), but had faced stiff resistance from the ministries of finance, who were very sensitive to the political dangers of excluding people from the housing market. In this context, central bankers within these councils had come to collaborate with the ESRB, pushing for an ESRB warning to be issued (interview, French central bank economist, April 4, 2021, May 20, 2021; interview, German central bank economist, July 6, 2021) in order to increase the pressure domestically. Mediated through the organizational filter of financial stability councils, which forced these ministries of finance into repeated discussions, this intervention then proved the final tipping point, providing a push in the direction of anti-cyclical action (Thiemann and Stellinga 2022).

On the other hand, regarding the six countries that received a recommendation to act in 2019, only Luxembourg enacted change deemed sufficient for full compliance by the ESRB. All the others enacted little to no change with respect to anti-cyclical policies, insisting on the fact that the minimal measures they had agreed to needed

---

[18] Only the situation in the UK and Austria had sufficiently improved for the ESRB to not further escalate the procedures, now recommending action by the other six countries or requiring an explanation.

[19] Germany raised its CCyB from 0 percent to 0.25 percent, a move that was seen to de facto pose no friction for the housing market (interview, economist at the German financial market regulator, January 20, 2020).

further time for their effects to unfold, leading the ESRB in 2022 to rate five out of these six countries only partially compliant (ESRB 2022a). In four of these five countries, it was the ministries of finance that had the final say over stringent borrower-based measures, which were required to act against the overheating housing market (Sweden, Belgium, Denmark, the Netherlands), and these refused to enact any measures despite the national central banks and macro-prudential authorities pleading to the contrary (for the case of Belgium, see IMF 2020, 19; for the case of Sweden, see Riksbank 2021; interview, Danish member of the systemic risk council, March 25, 2022; for the case of the Netherlands, see Thiemann and Stellinga, 2022). In Finland, the last remaining country, even the introduction of a legal instrument for constraining borrowers to engage in risky borrowing proved impossible, as industry and political opposition prevented its realization (IMF 2022, 16).

In this vein, one can argue that the European regime for enacting anti-cyclical measures in the Eurozone, based on national decision-making supported by the comply-or-explain function of the ESRB, has proven largely ineffective to steer countries into action. In essence, only in countries with independent central banks in charge of anti-cyclical macro-prudential policies, such as Ireland, Slovakia or Malta, and with functional legal frameworks that provide the possibility to enact borrower-based measures could one observe meaningful anti-cyclical action (Lepers and Thiemann 2022). Yet, this was not the case for the majority of cases, with only ten out of twenty-seven countries in the EU having a fully functional legal framework by 2019 and only few central banks with a direct say over the enactment of these measures.[20] Political opposition to any such measures constraining access to the housing market proved repeatedly to be too big an obstacle for this governance framework to be overcome (for the paradigmatic case of the Netherlands, see Thiemann and Stellinga 2022). Fragmented as it was, knowledge of rising systemic risks was only translated into meaningful action in a limited number of cases, leading to growing concern among central bankers by 2019 (former BoE central banker, April 21, 2021).

---

[20] Post-COVID-19, the ESRB did pursue the harmonization agenda, pushing for an installation of functional frameworks for borrower-based measures in all of the EU (latest in ESRB 2022b). These attempts at harmonization do bear some fruits, allowing for some hope going forward.

Addressing the Procyclical Risks of the Asset Management Industry

To this concern over the procyclical tendencies in the EU housing market, a concern that slowly encroached upon almost all of the EU by the early 2020, a second concern was added from 2016 onwards. The ECB expressed an increasing worry about the growing segment of investment funds in the EU and globally (Constâncio 2016a), which from that moment onward was persistently mentioned by the ECB in its Financial Stability Review as the fourth stability risk threatening the Eurozone (ECB 2016b, c). Concerns were centering on the procyclical behavior of these funds, which in times of compressed yields would tend to take on too much credit risk, then in the downturn completely go into the reverse and sell these assets, causing the risk of fire-sales in the process (ESRB 2016b; ECB 2018, 18). These liquidity strains, emanating from the asset management industry, were seen to have the potential to amplify any existing downturn (ECB 2018), motivating in turn the attempts by macro-prudential change agents to gain control over their behavior.

In line with this reading of the procyclical behavior of mutual funds, the growth of the asset management industry was seen as partially responsible for feeding the corporate credit boom, as it unfolded, albeit at a much slower pace in the Eurozone than in the other jurisdictions (ECB 2019, 9). As the authors of the ECB Financial Stability Review put it, "The ongoing search for yield across non-banks may exacerbate the build-up of vulnerabilities, not least by lowering financing costs for riskier borrowers. ... Stress from an abrupt repricing of financial assets could be amplified by the behaviour of investment funds with high liquidity mismatches and elevated leverage" (ECB 2019, 9). Yet, just like their counterparts in the UK and the USA, macro-prudential change agents in the EU had little to no capacity to limit the expansionary behavior of these funds.

To address these issues, the ESRB had first issued a strategy paper in 2016 that sought to extend the macro-prudential frame beyond banking (ESRB 2016a), pointing to three main reasons that made such an expansion necessary. These were, first, excessive leverage; second, excessive liquidity and maturity mismatch that could lead to fire-sales; and third, interconnectedness with the banking system. Of these three, the first two were widely identified with the asset management industry (ECB FSR, November 2016). Secondly, the ESRB began a measurement exercise of the shadow banking system, which was also to be published from 2016 onwards (ESRB 2016b). These reports documented the size and composition of the fund industry as well as its accelerating growth. Collaborating closely with the European Securities Market Authority (ESMA) on these issues (interview, ECB economist, February 2022; ESMA economist, March 7, 2022; ESMA economist, May 16, 2022), in particular in the context of the Shadow Banking Working Group within the ESRB, the ESRB then sought to gauge the risks from this growth and potential measures to mitigate them.

Based on these preliminary works, in December 2017 the ESRB issued a recommendation, which asked the European Commission and ESMA to either develop new regulation that mitigated issues of leverage and liquidity risks linked to investment funds or explain why they failed to do so (ESRB 2018). ESMA followed up on these issues, providing studies about the risks emanating from the increased fund leverage and potential remedies (ESMA 2020d; Bouveret and Haferkorn 2022). Yet, these regulatory measures would be years in the making, coming to fruition only after the COVID-19 crisis. This meant that while being worried about the procyclical expansion of corporate credit, fueled at least in part by an expanding asset management industry, the macro-prudential regulatory framework in the EU provided the European authorities with no tools to act in a timely manner on these concerns.

Conclusion

This chapter has traced the main concerns of macro-prudential authorities in the UK, the USA and the Eurozone regarding cyclical upswings in financial markets occurring from 2011 to 2019 and how they sought to react to them. These concerns can be grouped around three main issues: housing, corporate debt and growth of the asset management industry, which was largely outside the regulatory perimeter of central banks and which was increasingly buying up the large issuance of ever-riskier corporate debt. With respect to the first issue of real estate booms in the residential real estate sector, the upswing encountered a resolute response in the case of the UK, which swiftly enacted a constraining framework of borrower-based measures based on recommendations and its own powers, thereby enacting anti-cyclical policies in the residential real estate sector. Yet, it was largely beyond its powers to stem the boom alone, also because of the global nature of the investment flows into real estate. Instead, this boom was de facto ended by Brexit.

In the Eurozone, we can observe a much more differentiated set of responses: some countries did enact constraining borrower-based measures; others did not, with the ESRB seeking to coordinate the response. While the ESRB here could indeed exert some influence, this influence was rather limited in that it could not fundamentally alter the domestic configurations of macro-prudential governance. While some anti-cyclical action is forthcoming in the Eurozone in the wake of the real estate boom setting in from 2015 onwards, this action was hence variegated and unevenly distributed. In those countries where central banks were solely in charge of national anti-cyclical policies, we do see a rather strong anti-cyclical reaction, much in line with the British experience.

However, in countries where political actors, such as ministries of finance, oversee this field of policy, such anti-cyclical action is largely blocked due to the political economy of intervening in real estate markets. There is a middle ground between these two extremes in the form of financial stability councils, wherein central banks and ministries of finance collaborate in order to generate a consensus on the need for macro-prudential action. Depending on the exact distribution of powers in the governance structure, such discussions might lead to meaningful (e.g. France) or less meaningful action (e.g. Germany), yet what characterizes all these councils is the slow-moving character of macro-prudential action, making swift anti-cyclical action largely impossible.

In the USA, given that up until the late 2010s there was no notable residential real estate bubble, and a very limited commercial real estate bubble, there is little to no attempt by the Federal Reserve or other agencies to undertake anti-cyclical action in this field. (Adrian et al. 2015 point out, however, that the Federal Reserve also has no tools to enact in case there is one, in particular if the boom is fueled by financing from the shadow banking system.) Instead, there the cyclical growth of corporate debt and in particular the leveraged loans segment worried the macro-prudential authorities, which, however, had little to no capacity to act on these concerns. On the one hand, this was due to a very limited financial stability mandate by the Federal Reserve, but more importantly it was due to its limited capacity to regulate the investment behavior beyond banks.

After the limited regulatory action of banking regulators, the activity of loan issuance migrated into the shadow banking system, for which the expansion of the perimeter of supervision proved to be impossible. Being unable to enact much anti-cyclical action on its own and seeing the procyclical tendencies mainly in the shadow banking system, macro-prudential change agents within the Federal Reserve started to focus on the latter. This lacking anti-cyclical regulation of leveraged loans in the USA then also led to worries in the UK, which saw itself as an island in an ocean of cheap liquidity. Observing the strong growth of collateralized loan obligations and leveraged loans, the UK authorities found themselves in the boom phase of a corporate credit cycle but had little to no capacity to properly interfere. Asset managers, who jointly with finance companies were an important investor group for the financing of leveraged loans, were largely outside of the FPC's perimeter of regulation, both in terms of domestic remit and most importantly in terms of geographical reach. In the EU, similarly, even if belatedly, corporate debt rose and fed into the growth of the asset management industry, which, however, was hardly controlled. All of this points to the shadow banking system as the main frontier for the anti-cyclical change agents, as they were seeking to rein in the procyclical tendencies of the financial system.

However, rather than a realization of these cyclical tendencies, the next crisis was to be caused by a liquidity event, which was to take the financial system by surprise. It was to reveal much of the fragilities the macro-prudential community had feared within the shadow banking system, as the latter is built on the persistent provision of liquidity. While banks were holding up unexpectedly well (Abboud et al. 2021), it was the shadow banking system that required a massive backstop in terms of liquidity. This sudden and unexpected intervention in spring 2020 would renew the attempts of regulators to gain a hold over the shadow banking system.

9 The Crisis That Wasn't
The COVID-19 Crisis and Its Regulatory Implications

When reports surfaced in the first month of 2020 about a spreading virus in China and its possible global propagation, there was little in terms of immediate reaction by Western financial markets. Rather than pricing in these risks immediately, financial markets instead continued their upward climb in January up until mid-February. By March 2020, when the increasingly global proportion of the ensuing pandemic began to disrupt the daily life of a large part of populations in the Western world, financial market reactions were all the harder. As envisioned by the macro-prudential change agents, a sudden re-evaluation of risks in financial markets occurred, leading to volatility in financial markets.

In particular, money market mutual funds (MMFs) as well as bond funds experienced large outflows as investors requested redemptions (FSB 2020), seeking to be redeemed at par. Just as the macro-prudential analysis of such developments in the sector had foreseen, these requests essentially overpowered the private provisions for liquidity management, forcing fund managers to sell liquid assets on a scale the private provision of market liquidity could not handle, in particular in the USA. Rather than stepping in to make markets, broker-dealers started to refrain from providing liquidity to fund managers (Vissing-Jorgensen 2021), leading to spiking interest rates that in turn threatened the transmission of monetary policy to the real economy.

Faced with this situation, the central banks in the USA, the UK and the Eurozone quickly reopened the emergency liquidity assistance programs they had installed in the wake of the transatlantic financial crisis in 2008 and supplemented them with massive quantitative easing, which directly sought to intervene in the markets for the provision of private liquidity (Schnabel 2020a, b; Mushtaq 2021). By mid-March 2020, these initiatives allowed central banks to engage in the direct buying of securities from the balance sheet of broker-dealers, interventions that in the end would place more than a trillion dollars' worth of securities on the balance sheet of the Federal Reserve alone (Vissing-Jorgensen 2021). Known as the "Dash for Cash" in the USA, these dislocations in financial markets and the central bank interventions they necessitated had several effects. On the one hand, they further inflated the balance sheet of central banks, which more than doubled in the course of the first year of the pandemic (Hauser 2021). On the other hand, they gave renewed urgency to the calls of macroprudential change agents to expand the perimeter of regulation to now also include fund managers and the systemic risks their business models of redemption at par carried.

This chapter will review these events and the subsequent regulatory initiatives, tracing the impact of this shock on the regulatory initiatives begun during the upswing (see Chapter 8). In the first section, it will detail the central bank interventions in the three jurisdictions under study, showing how it was the immediate liquidity infusions through quantitative easing that ended the run on MMFs and investment funds in general. In the second section, it will then review the impact of these events on regulatory initiatives, showing how, while massive regulatory change was initiated for the MMF industry, similar global dynamics for the fund industry are currently missing. This was despite the fact that macro-prudential change agents around the globe have pointed to the need to address the liquidity risks inherent in this sector (most prominently, Mark Carney [2019] in a hearing in front of Members of the European Parliament; see Rees 2019). Instead, what we can observe is a fragmented regulatory response, which on the one hand seeks to grant non-bank financial institutions the orderly access to the liquidity facilities of central banks, while also seeking to impose some control over their procyclical behavior. The latter initiatives proceed along the lines that became apparent in the decade before COVID-19, with regulators seeking to amass evidence of procyclical behavior in order to pass new regulations. Based on this work, the most forceful regulatory response to date is emerging from the European Union (EU), closely followed by the UK. In contrast, the USA, while having massively expanded the backstop for the shadow banking system in the wake of the COVID-19 crisis, has done little to nothing in terms of the macro-prudential regulation for investment funds.

The Financial Markets Turmoil during March 2020

The initial reverberations of the COVID-19 shock in global financial markets followed the usual script: as uncertainty increased, what could be observed was a "flight to safety" in a period that spanned from February to the first week of March. This period was characterized by falling prices in risky assets and stability in the core bond markets with small price increases (FSB 2020). But then, starting on March 9, the "Dash for Cash," the sudden increase in the demand for liquidity caused by the attempt of financial market agents to secure means of payment in a precautionary manner led to various disruptions in the financial markets, most remarkably severe disruptions in the core bond markets (Cunliffe 2022). Whereas before, bond prices had risen and yields fallen, these markets now experienced a snapback in yields and extreme volatility, especially for long-dated treasuries (Liang and Parkinson 2020). There were intense selling pressures, as investors sought to raise cash by liquidating treasury securities. These dynamics worsened as broker-dealers, the weak link in the provision of private liquidity, started to get overwhelmed and began to charge higher spreads, at some point completely stopping their intermediation activities (FSB 2020).

Financial market turmoil in the context of the COVID-19 crisis was then to a certain extent the same as central banks had experienced during the Great Financial Crisis, as in both cases the threat to the financial system emerged from the shadow banking system (Gorton 2010; FSB 2020). Yet it was also different as the shadow banking system itself, its composition and interconnections, had changed between 2008 and 2020 (FSB 2021b), which in turn implied the need for different and differently sized interventions by domestic central banks. In addition to this changed composition, with a much larger presence of investment funds (FSB 2021b), the originating cause of the crisis was also fundamentally different. While the crisis of 2008 was at its core a credit crisis that transformed into a liquidity crisis, the 2020 COVID-19 crisis was first and foremost a liquidity event (BoE 2021a) caused by the precautionary motive of accumulating cash in the face of a pandemic (FSB 2020). This motive led to a massive withdrawal of funds from MMFs, entities that promise daily redemption at par and who primarily serve the cash-management needs of large investment funds and other large investors. In light of the uncertainty surrounding these market developments and the margin calls they provoked, these investors engaged in a flight to liquidity and safe assets, massively withdrawing liquidity from those MMFs that were invested in private sector credit.[1]

This movement to security by investors became known as the "Dash for Cash" and unfolded from March 9, 2020 onwards. It expressed itself not only in strong redemption pressures for MMFs, which in turn sought to sell their most liquid assets (treasury bills) into financial markets, but also by a general sell-off of treasury bills and treasury bonds of large investors, including the mutual funds industry (FSB 2020, 21; Falato et al. 2021). The latter had also begun to come under pressure from redemption orders by clients in mid-March, as investors were adjusting to the probability of a looming recession, in turn implying potentially massive losses for the high-risk corporate debt these mutual funds had increasingly purchased. It was these high-yield corporate bond funds and mixed funds that macro-prudential change agents had been so worried about at the end of the last decade (FRB 2018; ECB 2019) that experienced the brunt of these redemption requests (Vissing-Joergensen 2021, 33). These redemption requests added further volume to the selling of treasury bills and bonds (Vissing-Joergensen 2021, 21), as fund managers also sought to service these requests by selling off their most liquid assets (Duffie 2020; Logan 2020). These large selling orders of treasury securities in turn put large pressure on the private liquidity provision by the broker-dealers, which broke down under this momentous pressure, confirming the worst fears of the macro-prudential thought collective (see Chapter 7).[2]

---

[1] In the worst two weeks of March, the net redemptions of institutional prime money market mutual funds reached 30 percent of assets under management (see Brainard 2021).

[2] In such moments of high selling pressure, market-making broker-dealers are expected to step in and make markets by purchasing the treasury bonds at the announced spreads and taking them onto their balance sheets. And yet, given the unexpectedly large selling orders, broker-dealers were simply unable/refused to make markets. Broker-dealers initially markedly increased their net-position in March (Clark et al. 2020; Duffie 2020, 6), yet were unable to accommodate all selling orders, leading to sudden declines in the value of T-bonds and sudden spikes of interest rates in mid-March (Vissing-Joergensen 2021, 20).

The Response by Central Banks: Quantitative Easing and Emergency Liquidity Assistance

This clogging of the system of private liquidity provision made an extraordinary intervention by the Federal Reserve necessary. In particular, the sudden decline of T-bonds and the rise in interest rates, a deeply counterintuitive development amidst a flight to safety, forced the hand of the Federal Reserve, announcing on March 15 a 500-billion-dollar asset-purchasing program, later to become unlimited, leading it to inject 1 trillion dollars in the next few weeks by purchasing treasury bonds (Vissing-Jorgensen 2021). These interventions, which exceeded in one quarter the total of either QE1, QE2 or QE3 as they were concluded in the prior years (Vissing-Jorgensen 2021, 24), aimed primarily at unclogging the balance sheets of broker-dealers, buying about 670 billion dollars' worth of inventories directly of broker-dealers' balance sheets (Schrimpf et al. 2020, 5f.). While the Federal Reserve also used its repo-facilities to support market liquidity for broker-dealers, reaching 441 billion on March 18, 2020 (calculation by author based on Federal Reserve balance-sheet operation), it was these direct purchases by the Federal Reserve that were seen as most effectual (Vissing-Joergensen 2021).

This now firmly assumed role of market-maker of last resort for treasury bonds and bills was accompanied by the reinstatement of primary and secondary market facilities for commercial paper (March 17, 2020), MMFs (MMLF, March 18) and primary and secondary corporate market facilities (March 23, 2020; see Clarida et al. 2021). These facilities, which were undergirded by treasury money to compensate for losses, allowed the Federal Reserve to stabilize the money market segment and ease the selling pressures by taking money market fund shares onto their balance sheet (reaching 54 billion dollars at its peak) (Brainard 2021).[3] With respect to the redemption requests for open-ended funds, the simple announcement that the Federal Reserve stood ready to purchase corporate debt on the secondary market already sufficed to stem the panic (Falato et al. 2021;

---

[3] "Following the announcement of these facilities (Commercial Paper Funding Facility on March 17 and the Money Market Mutual Fund Liquidity Facility on March 18, 2020, MT), prime MMF [money market mutual fund] redemptions slowed almost immediately, and other measures of stress in short-term funding markets began to ease" (Brainard 2021, 2f.).

Vissing-Joergensen 2021, 21), ending an incipient run on the open-end investment funds (Stein 2021, 15). The fact that it was the announcement of these two facilities that ended the run was highly consequential, as it would be fiercely contested by the lobbyists of the asset management industry, claiming instead that the crisis dynamics proved that the fund industry was resilient (interview, former Federal Reserve board member, December 2, 2021).

Similar dynamics, yet in an attenuated form, can be observed both for the Eurozone (Schnabel 2020b) and for the UK (Hauser 2020). In the latter case, the Bank of England (BoE) first eerily observed dynamics in the USA in the first two weeks of March, but then saw itself forced to announce on March 19 the purchase of an additional £200 billion treasury gilts amidst unusually high selling pressures in the gilt market (Hauser 2020; Cunliffe 2022). The latter was caused by an "increase in the net demand for liquidity from the NBFI [non-bank financial intermediation] sector" (Czech et al. 2021, 3), which the broker-dealers were not able to satisfy (BoE 2021a, 12).[4] In addition to this attempt to stabilize the gilt market, on March 24 the BoE opened its contingent term repo facility, declaring itself willing to provide repo funding against a broad set of collateral close to bank rate, somewhat normalizing the rates in this market (Hauser 2020, 8). It also opened a COVID-19 Corporate Credit Facility, a scheme to facilitate lending to corporations, undergirded by taxpayer money for eventual losses (Hauser 2020, 9). Yet again, here, much like in the case of the USA, it was the large-scale asset-purchasing programs that made the largest difference and restored liquidity.[5]

Lastly, in the case of the Eurozone, it was again the use of asset-purchasing programs in the context of quantitative easing that did the

---

[4] As the report put it, "Staff analysis suggests dealer constraints in supplying liquidity to the market might have accounted for around a third of March's increases in term gilt reverse repo spreads, with the rest attributed to the demand for liquidity by market participants" (BoE 2021a, 12).

[5] According to the literature, the renewed quantitative easing implemented by both the Federal Reserve and the UK has had a more substantial impact than the sizable expansion of the repo activities (Infante and Saravay 2020; Vissing Jorgensen 2021). In this vein, the report on quantitative easing, written for the House of Lords in the UK, concludes that "Quantitative easing is particularly effective as a tool to stabilise financial markets. There is strong evidence that shows it is an effective monetary policy tool when it is deployed at times of crisis, when financial markets are dysfunctional or in distress" (House of Lords Economic Affairs Committee, 1st Report of Session 2021–22, 19).

majority of the work (Altavilla et al. 2021).[6] In a first step, on March 12, 2020, the ECB increased the envelope of net assets purchases within the already existing quantitative easing (called the asset-purchasing program, APP) by €120 billion. However, the bulk of assets purchases have been implemented under the new Pandemic Emergency Purchasing Programme (PEPP), which was launched on March 18, 2020 with an initial overall envelope of €750 billion.[7] This money, which could be used in a discretionary manner, was used to stop the run on the money markets and upend the incipient run on the mutual fund sector. It also was used to directly intervene in the commercial paper market to uphold positive financing conditions for the "real economy" (Lane 2020; Schnabel 2021), as well as engaging in the purchase of sovereign bonds in secondary markets, seeking to halt any fragmentation of financial markets in the Eurozone.

The PEPP was able to do so as it was designed for and tasked with stabilizing purposes – a feature that distinguished it from prior ECB quantitative easing programs (Schnabel 2020a, b). Operationally, the market stabilization function of the program is associated with its flexibility, which also distinguishes it from the former asset purchase programs. It allows the ECB to intervene in a broad range of securities markets on short notice to a degree deemed necessary to resolve market impairment (Debrun et al. 2021, 66f.). The declared aim is to keep downward liquidity spirals from materializing and thus shielding the system from a "perilous macro-financial feedback loop" (Schnabel 2020a), which could have engulfed the Eurozone and impaired the monetary transmission mechanism. In particular, the ECB feared "adverse liquidity spirals and an overshooting of asset price corrections in many markets, impeding the transmission of monetary policy and endangering financial stability" (Lane 2020), showing the degree to which the risks for financial stability emanating from the shadow

---

[6] Overall, the interventions of the ECB were not as large as the Federal Reserve or the BoE in March, as the repo-markets held up in a better way, a fact that can largely be traced to the much larger importance of central counterparties (CCPs) in the repo-market in the Eurozone, which stabilized the latter. Overall, Altavilla et al., when reviewing its pandemic emergency purchasing program, assert that "PEPP averted an escalation of tail risks associated with pro-cyclical financial amplification mechanisms" (Altavilla et al. 2021, 29).

[7] This envelope was later extended to €1.35 trillion on June 4, 2020 and again increased by €500 billion on December 10, 2020, for a new total of €1,850 billion. At the end of October 2021, €1,480 trillion had already been used.

banking sector were factored in and taken seriously by the ECB management during the COVID-19 crisis.

This focus on the shadow banking sector, in particular on the investment fund sector by the ECB governing board in motivating the design of the PEPP, is further revealed in a speech by Schnabel in November 2020 (Schnabel 2020b). In the speech, she explicitly points to the procyclical behavior of the growing investment fund sector as substantially aggravating the liquidity crisis in March 2020. The problem with this sector, which was forced to sell €300 billion worth of assets in that month, with high-yield bond funds forced to sell more than 10 percent of their assets under management due to redemption requests, was that it had no access to emergency liquidity provision by central banks (Schnabel 2020b). In that situation, central banks according to her faced two choices: either "they expand their role as lender of last resort – or they purchase large quantities of illiquid assets" (Schnabel 2020b). Because of the emergency of the situation and the difficulty of setting up such liquidity provisions for non-banks, the purchase of illiquid assets through the large-scale PEPP was the only pragmatic solution in this challenging moment of an unfolding liquidity crisis.[8]

As she put it,

Allowing funds to become monetary policy counterparties, however, creates major operational, supervisory and regulatory challenges that cannot be solved overnight. For this reason, the Governing Council launched the pandemic emergency purchase programme (PEPP), which has been designed to serve two objectives: first, to stabilise financial markets and, second, to counter the negative shock to the economic and inflation outlook caused by the pandemic. (Schnabel 2020b)

These challenges that Schnabel refers to regard not only the questions at which rates and under which conditions investment funds could have access to central bank liquidity, but also at a more fundamental level the issue of private risk-taking and public backstops (see also BoE 2021a for a similar position by the BoE; Hauser and Logan 2022

---

[8] As later research by the ECB confirmed, the PEPP did indeed help alleviate the stress experienced by the asset management industry (Breckenfelder et al. 2021). One reason was that de facto, asset managers that were clients of banks were capable of handing over their assets to banks to offer them to the ECB in the context of the PEPP, a fact that de facto extended the emergency liquidity provision of the PEPP to non-banks (see Q4 at www.ecb.europa.eu/mopo/implement/pepp/html/ecb.faq_pepp.en.html).

for a shared analysis by the Federal Reserve and the BoE). This situation hence involved all the practical and theoretical questions central banks had grappled with during the 2010s, as they were deliberating if and how to backstop the repo-market (see Chapter 7), only this time operating at a much greater scale (see Hauser 2021).

Overall, as Schnabel points out, this situation was by no means satisfactory, as such central bank action invited even more risk-taking by investment funds, which to her required fundamental regulatory change. In this vein, she demanded that

[l]ooking forward, however, our regulatory landscape needs to better reflect the fact that credit intermediation increasingly takes place outside the banking sector. The current policy framework needs to be developed further with a view to strengthening the ability of authorities to limit the build-up of systemic risk in the non-bank financial sector and curb stress if and when it arises. (Schnabel 2020b)

This demand, postulated in the macro-prudential creed of the need for anti-cyclical action both during the buildup of risks and when they are realized, ironically would face its greatest impediment in the successful prevention of the crisis through the quantitative easing programs. Having prevented the shadow banking system from spiraling out of control in spring 2020, change agents were now lacking the political support needed to enact change, as the following months and years would reveal.

Fixing the Regulatory Fault Lines for Non-Banks: Revisiting Liquidity and Leverage Risks

The central bank interventions during March 2020 made evident to the central banking community the structural fault lines that continued to persist in the shadow banking sector.[9] It also showed that macro-prudential tools to deal with the risks of the investment fund sector at large were insufficient, both with respect to the liquidity

---

[9] As Schnabel put it, "All in all, and with this I would like to conclude, the market turmoil earlier this year suggests that structural fault lines in the non-bank financial sector continue to persist. These vulnerabilities have the potential to amplify procyclicality in the financial system, drain liquidity at a time when it is most needed and, ultimately, set in motion real-financial feedback loops that threaten the stability of our economies" (Schnabel 2020b).

risks and the leverage risks it accumulated (interview, ESMA regulator, March 7, 2022). This observation engendered an attempt at the level of the Financial Stability Board to revisit the regulation of the sector for non-bank financial intermediation, in particular the risks linked to liquidity and leverage (FSB 2020; interview, FSB economist, December 2021; interview, second FSB economist, February 14, 2022). This perceived need for action was driven by the fact that the new situation of a de facto liquidity backstop provided by the central banks invited a greater amount of risk-taking by the sector (interview, former Federal Reserve board member, December 2, 2021). In the words of Schnabel,

But the success of central bank interventions should not distract from the fact that the underlying vulnerabilities in the non-bank sector need a structural fix, not least to mitigate the risk of moral hazard. A large and growing sector that can systematically count on central banks absorbing large amounts of credit and duration risk on their balance sheets in periods of stress will create bad incentives. (Schnabel 2020b)

As a consequence of this delicate situation, Schnabel pointed to the need for a structural fix that aligned investment strategies of funds with their redemption policies, the need to limit leverage in the financial sector and the need to reform MMFs, which "includes a review of the liquidity requirements for MMFs and their portfolio composition" (Schnabel 2020b; see also Guindos 2020). In fact, the COVID-19 crisis demonstrated vividly the shortcomings of the regulations taken to date, which were operating at the micro-level and granting each fund manager the right to impose liquidity fees or gates, stopping runs at the individual fund level. Yet, as the vice-president of the ECB for financial stability pointed out in June 2020, the

rising levels of liquidity stress at the height of the crisis highlighted important weaknesses in the policy framework for non-banks. To date, the prudential policy framework for investment funds relies, to a large extent, *on ex post liquidity management tools in the hands of asset managers (redemption fees or the suspension of redemptions). But these tools are of limited use to prevent liquidity stress at the system level.* If applied in a period of wide-spread market stress, they could *limit the ability of firms and other financial institutions to raise cash*, undermining market confidence more broadly. (Guindos 2020, emphasis mine)

In other words, the COVID-19 crisis had shown that it was exactly the fear of such liquidity gates being activated at the individual fund level that instigated liquidity crunches at the systemic level (interview, ECB economist investigating liquidity dynamics in the investment fund sector, February 16, 2022; ESMA economist, March 7, 2022; interview, ESMA economist, May 16, 2022). This mismatch in levels of regulation (fund level) and dynamics (systemic) not only meant that the tools were inadequate or dull to combat the liquidity crunch but also that they were counter-productive.

Instead, de Guindos suggested that "[t]o reduce systemic risk in the investment fund sector, we need to ensure that *asset liquidity is closely aligned with fund redemption terms*. Additional macroprudential policy tools should be made available to authorities to *mitigate the build-up of systemic risk during times of financial exuberance*" (de Guindos 2020). These remarks reveal the consensus on the need for anti-cyclical macro-prudential policy at the ECB in summer 2020, and yet to achieve action on these issues would require substantial collaboration, both with the UK and the US authorities to achieve globally consistent regulation of the shadow banking sector, as well as domestically with market regulators and legislators in their own jurisdiction (interview, FSB economist, February 14, 2022). This collaboration across jurisdictions was helped by the fact that, but for a few minor deviations in terms of emphasis (see Brainard 2021; Hauser 2021), the analysis of the shortcomings revealed by the crisis was shared by both the Federal Reserve (Liang 2022) and the BoE (Bailey 2021). Based on this shared analysis, this community of central bankers placed the re-regulation of shadow banking once more on the agenda of the FSB, professing its willingness to get it right this time (Bailey 2021). The FSB, based on its existing working groups and expertise, which had built up over the last decade trying to generate regulations for the shadow banking sector (interview, FSB economist, February 14, 2022), put itself to work, bringing together securities markets regulators as well as central banks in order to analyze the COVID-19 events and draw the right regulatory lessons.

The Attempted Re-regulation of the Shadow Banking System at the Global Level

A first output of this work, published in November 2020, is the "Holistic Review of the March Market Turmoil" (FSB 2020). This report named both the rise of the investment fund sector (from $21 trillion to $53 trillion between 2008 and 2020 – FSB 2020, 12) and the surge in redemptions from private MMFs and from longer-term open-ended bond funds, both in Europe and the USA (FSB 2020, 21), as the two main factors explaining the propagation of stress during the March 2020 turmoil. Given this analysis, the FSB then outlined a regulatory work package, promising policy proposals for the regulation of MMFs by 2021 as well as an analysis of the availability and effectiveness of liquidity risk tools for open-ended funds, based on the March 2020 experience. In addition, it promised to also review margining practices as well as the functioning of core bond markets, including the role of highly leveraged funds (read hedge funds) in spreading dislocations in bond markets by the next year (see Table 9.1).

Table 9.1 *Work program of the Financial Stability Board in the aftermath of COVID-19 events (FSB 2020, 3)*

Topic	Brief description	Timing
1. Analytical and policy work on specific issues		
Money market mutual fund resilience	To make policy proposals, in light of the March experience, to enhance money market mutual fund resilience including with respect to the underlying short-term funding markets	2021, incl. report to the G20
Liquidity risk and its management in open-ended funds	To examine the availability and effectiveness of liquidity risk management tools for open-ended funds, including the experience of redemption pressures and use of tools in the March turmoil and their aggregate impact on the market	2021–2
Margining practices	To examine the frameworks and dynamics of margin calls in centrally cleared and uncleared derivatives markets and the liquidity	2021

Table 9.1 (*cont.*)

Topic	Brief description	Timing
	management preparedness of market participants to meet margin calls	
Liquidity, structure and resilience of core bond markets	To examine the structure and liquidity provision in core funding markets during stress, including the role of leveraged investors and factors that limit dealer capacity to intermediate	2021–2
2. Systemic risk assessments		
Strengthening the ongoing monitoring of non-bank financial intermediation risks	To assess non-bank financial intermediation risks in light of COVID-19 developments and lessons from the March turmoil	Ongoing
Advancing the understanding of systemic risks in non-bank financial intermediation and the financial system	To deepen the analysis of structural and interconnectedness issues in non-bank financial intermediation, including the interaction of USD funding pressures and fund outflows in emerging market economies, as input into enhanced risk monitoring and discussions on policies to address systemic risks in non-bank financial intermediation	Ongoing, incl. stakeholder workshop in 2021
3. Policies to address systemic risks in non-bank financial intermediation		
Policies to address systemic risks in non-bank financial intermediation	To examine policies to address systemic risks in non-bank financial	2022

Table 9.1 (*cont.*)

Topic	Brief description	Timing
	intermediation, including the adequacy of current policy tools and the concept and desired level of resilience in non-bank financial intermediation	

Overall, this initial work by the FSB can be characterized by its exploratory character, seeking to discern systemic risks arising from the sector of non-bank financial intermediation rather than proposing concrete steps for their regulation. The only concrete work on reform proposals was the one for MMFs, which should proceed surprisingly quickly, while all the other workstreams to date can best be described as an exercise in formulating the right kind of questions and seeking to identify possible ways forward, rather than pursuing any concrete regulatory proposals, as the following quote clarifies:

Work on the first area [MMFs] should proceed at pace to minimise the chances that similar vulnerabilities expose the real economy to unnecessary risks going forward. The second area of work will require more time *to develop a set of specific questions to answer as well as determining the preferred approach to doing so.* Finally, the analysis on policies to address systemic risks in the non-bank sector should *be flexible enough* so that any insights gained in the other two areas can be reflected in any future policy outcome. (FSB 2020, 43, emphasis mine)

In line with this vague language and the tepid appetite for reform it revealed, the only outcome of the coordinating efforts by the FSB to date has been a reform proposal for MMF reform, a first proposal for which was issued in March 2021, with a final proposal issued in October 2021. This work, which could draw on similar reform movements both in the USA and the Eurozone, assembled a list of options to address liquidity risks in MMFs, stemming from sudden redemption requests that in turn might lead to difficulties to sell assets. This list was an attempt to identify the structurally equivalent possible regulatory measures, which jurisdictions could choose from, seeking to clarify what each measure sought to achieve and how (interview, ESMA economist, May 16, 2022; interview, Federal Reserve economist, June 2, 2022).

The Attempted Regulation of Money Market Mutual Funds at the Global Level

MMFs as a regulatory object in a sense were both a surprise and the perfect rallying point for joint regulatory work by the financial market regulators thus assembled. They were a surprise in the sense that supervisory work leading up to the COVID-19 crisis had focused rather on the liquidity risk from open-ended investment funds (interview, ECB economist, February 16, 2022; ESMA economist, May 16, 2022). After the first round of reform proposals for MMFs, which had been agreed upon in 2014 in the USA and 2017 in the EU and their implementation in October 2016 and January 2019 respectively, the regulatory community had largely deemed the systemic liquidity risks inherent in that industry as fixed (FSOC 2017, 125), observing the reduction in the prime institutional investor segment it induced (the riskiest part) as signs of its effectiveness. While macro-prudential change agents had failed in their attempts to impose bank-like prudential regulation on these funds, despite a concerted effort in 2012 (interview, former SEC lawyer, June 9, 2022; Bouveret et al. 2022), final regulations in the USA in particular were seen by the majority of regulators as sufficiently stringent to reduce the regulatory advantages and reduce the run-risks (interview, Federal Reserve economist, June 2, 2022; for a critical view, see Cipriani et al. 2014).

Most importantly for the post 2020 reform agenda, these reforms brought about an enhanced monitoring of MMFs, with funds being forced into a much tighter regime of weekly reporting of their assets and liabilities. This new reporting regime allowed for a quick detection of the liquidity strains funds experienced during the COVID-19-crisis (interview, ESMA economist, May 16, 2022). Based on this data, a consensus among supervisors both at central banks and market regulators emerged, which identified MMFs as a major agent spreading and amplifying the liquidity strains. Worse still, the prior round of regulations, which had placed the possibility to deny redemption requests in the hands of fund managers, was seen as amplifying these dynamics, as institutional investors withdrew from funds they feared would be closed soon (ECB 2020; FRB 2020). These analyses clarified the need for action, with the industry holding little to no arguments to fend it off.

In the initial reform proposals by the FSB, then, measures were proposed to reduce the likelihood of large-scale redemptions at MMFs and/

or their impact on the system as a whole (FSB 2021a, 25). On the one hand, there was a list of potential liquidity management tools such as swing pricing or liquidity fees, which were seeking to force clients of MMFs asking for large-scale redemption to internalize parts of the negative externalities that they imposed on the financial system. These measures were suggested based on the observed failure of liquidity gates, which were the only liquidity management tool introduced in the round of reforms in the USA and the EU to stem massive liquidity withdrawals. On the other hand, the list of possible measures also included more structural measures such as limits on eligible assets or measures that would make MMFs more bank-like, such as capital buffers and/or a minimum balance at risk, which in essence would transform the cash-like status of MMF accounts into something like a savings account, limiting the immediately available liquidity to investors.

These reform proposals, which were very much favored by central bankers around the world as well as by independent academic economists (interview, academic economist in the USA involved with the regulatory debates, May 3, 2022; interview, Federal Reserve official, June 2, 2022), were, however, adamantly opposed by securities market regulators, both in the USA and the EU (interview, ESMA economist, March 7, 2022; interview, ESMA economist involved in the FSB negotiations, May 16, 2022). Much like in the initial round of reform efforts after the Great Financial Crisis, such measures were seen to endanger the economic rationale for the existence of these shadow banks, destroying a valuable source for the diversification of funding sources in the short-term money market (interview, Federal Reserve economist involved in the FSB negotiations, June 2, 2022). As such, reform efforts would again be limited to the degree that the existence of MMFs as an alternative to savings accounts would not be endangered, even if their status as attractive alternative primarily derived from their lighter regulation, a fact criticized by much of the academic community (interview, US academic, May 3, 2022; interview, ESMA economist, May 16, 2022).

The Final Regulation of Money Market Mutual Funds in the USA and EU

As a matter of fact, the final reform efforts that would be agreed both in the Eurozone (in the form of a final proposal by ESMA issued in February 2022) and in the USA would take some measures to limit the capacity of MMFs to invest in illiquid assets. Imposing stricter limits on the asset side by, for example, imposing a higher amount of very short-term debt liabilities MMFs need to invest into, these reforms aimed at limiting the likelihood of MMFs to be forced to engage into fire-sales should large-scale redemption requests arise. On the other hand, on the liability side, proposals aimed at the imposition of swing pricing (as per the SEC reform proposal) or the imposition of liquidity fees, thereby seeking to address the first mover advantage, which much of the regulatory literature post-COVID-19 identified as a major shortcoming of the set-up of MMFs (FSB 2021a; Bouveret et al. 2022; Grill et al. 2022).

These proposals, which were deemed rather powerful and courageous by the regulatory community overall (ESMA economist, May 16, 2022; interview, Federal Reserve economist, June 2, 2022), still face important implementation hurdles (interview, Federal Reserve New York economist, June 6, 2022). In particular, it is unclear how swing pricing – that is, the imposition of costs on redeeming investors based on the liquidity strains MMFs are experiencing – is supposed to be implemented (see, e.g., BNP Paribas 2021). At the same time, and even if such operational workarounds could be identified or less demanding versions, such as liquidity fees, are implemented, these measures fail to address the underlying problem of sudden liquidity demands, as revealed by the COVID-19 events. In this vein, even the FSB itself notes in its proposal for money market fund reforms (FSB 2021a), and that swing pricing as well as other measures proposed to remove the run-risks of funds would not be able to "prevent large redemptions due to an aggregate increase in demand for liquidity" (FSB 2021a, 29).

Rather, the enacted reforms, in particular in the USA, should be read as an attempt to make the MMF segment investing in private credit unattractive, transforming the sector into a cash investment tool based on investments in short-term government debt (interview, former Federal Reserve lawyer, May 20, 2022). In Europe, on the other hand, the dependence of large banks on refinancing via MMFs makes such developments less desirable, which is why the final proposal of ESMA is still very broad and open, awaiting the final compromises the European Commission and the European Council will agree upon (interview, ECB economist working on the reform proposals, February 16, 2022; interview, ESMA economist, March 7, 2022). These reform proposals, which are rather incremental than fundamental in nature, characterized by the desire to limit rather than eliminate these liquidity risks, are the greatest achievement of the FSB reform agenda to date.

On the other hand, while open-ended funds were clearly identified as an aggravating element in the "Dash for Cash" (FRB 2020; Guindos 2020; Schnabel 2020b), to date, more than two years after the "Dash for Cash," no additional initiatives have been undertaken on the level of the FSB, the strong lobbying power of asset managers such as BlackRock being an important impediment to regulatory action (interview, FSB official, March 23, 2022). Overall, with respect to the mutual funds, a much slower response can hence be observed, linked both to the fact that mutual funds did not experience a full run, a fact exploited by lobbyists (interview, former Federal Reserve board member, December 2, 2021), and that the industry itself is very powerful. However, this outcome is not for a lack of trying.

Initiatives to Limit the Liquidity Risks from Open-Ended Funds in the USA, UK and EU

The USA

Since coming into office as the new treasury secretary in 2021, Janet Yellen as the new head of the FSOC has made the liquidity risks arising from open-ended funds one of the three top priorities of FSOC (FSOC 2021), but this has not yet led to new regulatory proposals. What it did do was lead to the installation of an interagency task force on open-ended funds at the FSOC in March 2021, which reported to the Council in February 2022. Their work established the links between the redemption requests mutual funds experienced in March 2020 and their large-scale sale selling orders of treasuries, which in turn fed the market turmoil (FSOC 2022, 6), establishing the factual basis for regulations. These findings in turn led to the request to SEC staff to consider the possibility of amending existing regulations for open-ended investment funds, in particular "regarding the fund liquidity rule or through other reforms to enhance fund liquidity, pricing, and resiliency in possible future stress events" (Gensler 2022).[10] And yet, at

[10] Notable about this proposition is that the SEC and its expertise is again in the driver's seat of reforms, placing the capability and willingness of SEC economists to include systemic considerations in their analysis at the heart of regulatory initiatives.

the time of writing (summer 2022), no new proposals have been forthcoming.

Instead, the regulation of liquidity risks continues to rely on the liquidity risk management strategies of fund managers, which since the latest reform of liquidity rules by the SEC in 2017 are forced to divide their assets into three liquidity risk buckets, based on the depth of the markets within which they trade. These new rules, themselves the outcome of an intense collaboration between FSOC and the SEC between 2014 and 2016 (see White 2014), still rely upon the classification of these assets by fund managers, with no supervisory capacity for the SEC to direct the assignment to these liquidity risk buckets. Rather than acting upon developments in the investment fund sector that are deemed to procyclically raise systemic risks, these regulations leave the final decision-making to fund managers, asking them to determine a justifiable position regarding their assumptions of liquidity in times of market stress. While these measures hence discipline fund managers, forcing them to consider the possibility of severe liquidity disruptions, they do not foresee a macro-prudential intervention by the authorities.

Initiatives at the EU Level

Somewhat more far-reaching developments can be observed in the case of the EU's regulation of liquidity risks, even though there too no final decision-making power over the investment decisions of private investment funds has been allocated to authorities. Regulatory action there was catalyzed by the collaboration between the European Systemic Risk Board (ESRB) and ESMA that developed from 2015 onwards (interview, ESMA economist, May 16, 2022), which ensured that regulatory initiatives and supervisory action were well advanced by the time the COVID-19 crisis led to market disruptions. The most fortuitous outcome of this collaboration, which was driven by shared concerns regarding the growing investment fund sector, was the common supervisory action by national competent authorities and ESMA that began on January 30, 2020 (ESMA 2020a). In this exercise, ESMA set out to investigate the liquidity risk management practices of collective investment funds in the EU, and jointly with national competent authorities (NCAs) came to request data from these funds at exactly the time COVID-19 put these management practices under severe strain. The ESRB followed up on this fortuitous coincidence with a recommendation on May 6, 2020 on liquidity risks in investment funds, whereby it singled out those funds holding corporate debt and real estate for an in-depth investigation by ESMA, as these funds were seen to pose particular financial stability risks (ESRB 2020).

In a follow-up to this ESRB recommendation, ESMA presented its first results of the common supervisory action in November 2020, finding that funds overall held up well, but that this resilience was facilitated by central bank intervention (ESMA 2020c, 5f.). A second finding was that liquidity risk management tools were often not installed or insufficiently adjusted to the specificity of the business model, with several funds being overly optimistic regarding their capacity to sell assets in times of crises (ESMA 2020c, 6). These findings revealed the fallacy of composition emanating from these individual-level liquidity emergency plans, as many individual funds were applying overly optimistic scenarios, not taking into account the effects of a sudden general demand for liquidity.[11] Based on this finding, ESMA on the one hand derived recommendations for supervisory practices of NCAs, seeking to push for a renewed dialogue with the fund industry on liquidity risks. On the other hand, it derived the need to introduce more liquidity management tools into EU regulation, closing ranks with the ESRB, explicitly supporting the recommendations of the ESRB on liquidity and leverage risks from December 2017 (ESRB 2018).

In particular, it was insisting on the harmonization of liquidity management tools across the EU (ESMA 2020c, 8; see also ESMA 2020b), which could provide national supervisors with the capacity to discipline fund managers' liquidity risk profiles and liquidity risk strategies. These suggestions applied both the regulation of Alternative Investment Fund in the Alternative Investment Fund Management Directive (AIFMD), as well as the broader regulation of Undertakings for Collective Investment in Transferable Securities funds (UCITS), which was much more principles-based and hence much less prescriptive (interview, ESMA economist, May 16, 2022). The goal of these regulatory initiatives was to push the European Commission to initiate a clear format for

---

[11] This finding is very much in line with the initial findings of the stress testing exercise in the USA in 2009, when the supervisors found that all banks assumed that they would be able to sell off their assets without great costs, despite the general turmoil (interview, former Federal Reserve official, January 9, 2018). Such a position evidently is not tenable at the systemic level.

reporting liquidity profiles for funds, based upon which supervisors would have more leverage to force fund managers to align their liquidity management plans with their actual exposure.

The European Commission followed up on these proposals on November 25, 2021, suggesting the expansion of liquidity reporting requirements for both AIFMs and UCITS, whereas before, regulation simply stipulated that UCITS could only be invested in liquid assets without defining what that meant (interview, ESMA economist, May 16, 2022). It further suggested the introduction of at least one additional liquidity management tools both for UCITS and AIFs, as well as granting NCAs the capacity to intervene and order the use of these tools in times of crisis. It thereby followed up on the suggestion both by ESRB (2020) and ESMA (2020a) to increase the amount of liquidity management tools available to funds and their possible mandatory use through direction by NCAs. Importantly, this regulation was not only to be introduced both in AIFMD and the UCITS regulation but also to apply to funds that were domiciled outside of the EU, but that were marketing their services within the EU (EC 2021, 35).

While these rule changes would be a major step forward in the EU, their implementation, if at all occurring, can only be expected by 2025 at the earliest (Société Générale 2022).[12] In addition, much of the future regulation, such as the classification of what liquid assets are, based on an assessment of underlying liquidity of markets is supposed to be delegated to ESMA, which can then seek to impose common liquidity standards in the EU. Yet, the specification of such liquidity profiles by ESMA through delegated regulation can only begin by 2023, making 2025 look very optimistic as a first application date. ESMA will have to develop a classification of the liquidity of markets for assets in stressed conditions in order to direct fund managers investment strategies. While these issues are not new to ESMA, and hence pose few intellectual problems, the actual operationalization of these issues and the agreement with industry and NCAs poses challenges, which most likely will require lengthy negotiations (interview, ESMA economist, May 16, 2022). These delays then are not the

---

[12] For now, the proposal is sent to the European Parliament, which jointly with the Commission and the European Council will have to find a common position in trilogue negotiations, the results of which are expected at the earliest by 2023. After that, individual countries still have two years to implement the Directive, which regards the tools.

expression of an intellectually new terrain but rather an expression of the intricate regulatory pathways such initiatives must travel.

Going beyond this immediate regulatory work, there is a clear macro-prudential perspective on these issues emerging, which could allow for a macro-prudential authority such as ESMA to set these liquidity requirements in an anti-cyclical fashion. Such an approach could be based on the system-wide stress simulations for the investment fund sector, performed by ESMA since 2019. Such simulations, subject to further improvement, could very well indicate systemic fragilities in the investment fund sector, pointing to an overinvestment in particularly illiquid asset classes, which in turn could permit an intervention by the securities market authority, which could require either higher liquidity buffers to permit such holdings of assets or a gradual disinvestment (interview, ESMA economist, May 16, 2022). Yet, such ideas are still years if not decades from implementation, simply because they first would require a massive expansion of capacities of supervisors to intervene, based on a rather new set of stress tests; and second because they very likely would require a centralization of supervisory powers at ESMA, requiring a disempowerment of NCAs. As such, these countercyclical ideas for the regulation of liquidity risks posed by open-ended bond funds, which are also developed at the Bank for International Settlements (BIS) (see Claessens and Lewrick 2021), are a far cry from becoming a regulatory reality.

Regulatory Endeavors in the UK

In the UK, the regulatory situation with respect to liquidity risks emanating from open-ended funds was even more complicated. With almost all open-ended funds in the UK operating under the UCITS directive of the EU, regulatory authorities in the UK, including both the Financial Conduct Authority (FCA) and the BoE, had little regulatory leeway, despite their urgent awareness of the problem (cf. Carney 2019, as documented in Rees 2019).[13] Given that the Financial Policy Committee in particular was preoccupied with these liquidity risks, it started in June 2019 a review into the liquidity risk management

---

[13] In June 2019, Carney had warned publicly in an FPC meeting with the Members of the European Parliament that the offering of quasi-daily redemption by open-ended funds was a lie and could very well be the trigger of the next financial crisis.

practices of open-ended funds, which meant that it was looking into these practices right when the COVID-19 crisis occurred. Publishing its results in a report in 2021, the BoE FCA noted the fact that overall individual managers had severely misjudged their capacity to deal with liquidity risks. In this context, it noted the need for an "effective liquidity classification framework would capture the full spectrum of liquid and illiquid assets, and consider both normal and stressed conditions," which could help to design a fund and in determining appropriate redemption terms and could inform the appropriate liquidity management tools as regards redemptions (BoE 2021a, 31f.). And yet, none of these suggestions are placed into a regulatory framework, as the UK is largely dependent on regulatory decisions in the USA and the EU, where more than 95 percent of investment funds investing into UK assets are domiciled.[14]

Unfinished Business: The Regulation of the Leverage of Hedge Funds

The initiatives regarding the regulation of leverage of hedge funds are even more in their infancy, and this even though researchers at the BIS clearly identified the use of leveraged trading strategies by hedge funds as a major cause of the crisis (Schrimpf et al. 2020; similarly FRB 2020). However, this finding by central bankers was contested by securities markets regulators, which pointed to the lack of data and contradictory evidence (IOSCO 2022). Disqualifying the intervention by these BIS authors as the speculation of some commentators (IOSCO 2022, 22),[15] the report points to a host of other studies,

---

[14] The only local initiative in this respect is the creation of a regime to enable UK-authorized open-ended funds to invest more efficiently in long-term, illiquid assets through a Long-Term Asset Fund (LTAF) structure. These LTAFs will be expected to be set up with notice periods and other liquidity management features that take account of the liquidity profile of the underlying assets (FCA 2021). Yet, these regulations only apply to non-UCITS.

[15] IOSCO writes: "In the initial period directly after the COVID-19 related volatility, *some commentators speculated* that hedge funds were the main cause for the market volatility. For example, Schimpft et al. suggest that relative value hedge funds were a major source of the dislocation. Specifically, they posit that the unrolling of large, leveraged positions in US treasuries was a source of dislocation that also amplified through margin effects to other funds that, they assume (correctly or incorrectly), are required to systematically adjust their portfolios with no discretion in allocation" (IOSCO 2022, 22, emphasis mine).

which provide a much more nuanced picture, essentially acquitting the hedge fund industry from this charge (IOSCO 2022). This defense by IOSCO clarifies that market regulators, and in particular the SEC, were unwilling to entertain the idea of further leverage restrictions given the existing evidence.

This state of play would prove crucial for the unfolding initiatives, which in turn were focusing mostly on data and evidence generation, rather than regulation, which can be well seen for the case of the USA, home to the largest hedge fund sector in the world. While it was placed high up on the agenda in 2021 in the USA, with the arrival of Janet Yellen at the helm of FSOC, this initiative only led to the formation of an interagency task force investigating the role of the leverage of hedge funds in transmitting liquidity shocks in the bond market during the "Dash for Cash" (FSOC 2021). By now, this group has established the link between these two, while being careful not to characterize them as the sole cause (FSOC 2022). Yet, other than highlighting existing data gaps and seeking their closure and seeking to amend them through additional reporting requirements (FSOC 2022, 1f.; Liang 2022), no other regulatory initiatives are planned.

Similarly, in the UK, which regulates its hedge funds based on the AIFM Directive of the EU, there has been no limitation of leverage by hedge funds. This inaction can be linked to competitiveness consider-ations as well as the current state of evidence available on hedge funds' contributions to the March 2020 dynamics. This tentative evidence and its implication for the position of the BoE is well summarized in a speech by Jon Cunliffe, the deputy governor of financial stability of the BoE, in November 2020. He first traces the increasing role of leveraged hedge funds in bond markets and their likely contribution to the March 2020 turmoil, based on an unwinding of their leveraged positions (Cunliffe 2020, 9). This strong argument, which implies the need to limit the leverage of such position taking in order to limit the amplification of stress in the financial system, is, however, followed up by the qualification that clear evidence is missing regarding the extent to which these dynamics moved market liquidity.

Cunliffe thereby transforms the issue from a call to action to a call for research, which would allow weighing the right degree of regulation. Drawing upon the analogy to broker-dealers' contribution to financial market liquidity in normal versus stressed times (see Chapter 7), he opens up the possibility of a trade-off of extensive liquidity provision

by leveraged hedge funds in good times, masking underlying vulnerabilities that unfold in times of stress (Cunliffe 2020, 11). Making the
link between the regulation of hedge funds and the regulation of
broker-dealers, he emphasizes at the end of the speech:

> And to the extent that such vulnerabilities arise from market activity that aids
> liquidity in good times but is fragile and damages liquidity in stress, we have, as
> I have said, to assess whether we have got *the balance right between efficiency
> in the short term and resilience through time*. This is not a new question for
> those of us in the financial stability trade. We faced a very similar question in
> relation to banks after the global financial crisis ten years ago. To be sure, the
> answers on market liquidity will not be the same. Market-based finance and
> banking are very different. The right balance and the way of achieving it may
> well lie in a different place. (Cunliffe 2020, 14, emphasis mine)

And yet, while Cunliffe points to the need to consider this trade-off, his
hopes are placed on the work at the transnational FSB, which to date
has not published any additional guidance on the leverage of hedge
funds, in turn leading to inaction by the financial authorities in the UK.
UK authorities on their own, simply given their limited reach, will not
act on their own.

The only jurisdiction in which regulatory developments that place
potential limits on the leverage of hedge funds have unfolded is the EU,
aided by the fact that the initial hedge fund regulation of 2011 (the
AIFMD) already envisioned such a limit in paragraph 25. Based on the
long-term collaboration between the ESRB and ESMA since 2015, facilitated by the direct financial stability mandate of ESMA, a much more
pronounced pro-regulation stance had developed already pre-COVID-19
events. In this vein, following up on the ESRB recommendation of
December 2017 regarding the regulation of the leverage of hedge funds
(ESRB 2018), ESMA had published in March 2020 Draft Guidelines on
how to collect data on leverage of Alternative Investment Fund Managers
in the EU and how to impose limits on them, thereby operationalizing
paragraph 25 in the Alternative Investment Fund Manager Directive.[16]

---

[16] The latter was passed in 2011 and already contained a paragraph that tasked
national competent authorities with "identifying the extent to which the use of
leverage contributes to the build-up of systemic risk in the financial system."
However, up until 2021 this paragraph had received no operationalization in
terms of metrics or in terms of definition of systemic risks such leverage could
cause, thereby making the harmonized application of this Directive in the EU
and its coordination by ESMA impossible.

Setting out to operationalize this framework, ESMA could base itself on the preparatory work of the FSB, which in 2017 had published an initial suggestion as to how to measure such leverage, an issue subsequently delegated to the International Organization of Securities Commissions (IOSCO), which had proposed such metrics in December 2019 (IOSCO 2019). The final guidelines were then published by ESMA on June 23, 2021 (ESMA 2021), with NCAs implementing the framework from July 2021 onwards. In this way, this work by ESMA, which built on the preparatory work of the FSB and IOSCO, established an operational framework both for assessing and limiting the leverage of hedge funds by NCAs in the EU. And yet, its implementation resides at the national level, where it still faces the difficulty of overcoming supervisory competition, as no NCA has an incentive to limit the leverage of domiciled hedge funds. In line with this problematic constellation, since July 2021 no leverage limits for any hedge funds have been imposed in the EU.

The Recession That Wasn't: The Resilience of the Banking System and Anti-Cyclical Measures

These overall very weak regulatory effects of the COVID-19 events on the investment fund sector are puzzling when one considers the extent of central bank interventions in March 2020. Yet, at the same time, they can be explained by the successful limitation of the fall-out of these events these interventions made possible, with little to no repercussions for the real economy.

This lackluster regulatory reaction after what was truly a massive central bank intervention during the COVID-19 March 2020 events thus can at least be partially explained by the fact that the COVID-19 crisis did not transform into the worst economic recession since World War II, as many official forecasters had foreseen (see, e.g., World Bank 2020). Instead, the COVID-19 crisis recessionary impact was surprisingly short-lived, also due to the massive policy stimulus engineered by governments and central banks, with the recession officially ending in the USA in April 2020, only two months after it had begun (NBER 2021).

An important supporting factor in this respect was the resilience of the banking system in both Europe and the USA, a fact that gave much cause for self-praise in the international regulatory community (FSB

2020). Indeed, in contrast to the substantial financial turmoil caused by the endogenous amplification of the external COVID-19 shock through the shadow banking system, this resilience of the banking sector in the wake of the shock and its continued capacity to provide credit to the real economy was a pleasant surprise for the central banking community. Whereas initial assessments of the situation by central banks had predicted the possibility of a credit crunch (ECB 2020), in fact the well-capitalized banks were able to withstand the shock and continue lending. Buoyed by all the support measures taken by governments in terms of countercyclical spending but also directly guaranteeing the lending of banks, often channeled through national development banks (Massoc 2022) and central banks,[17] they were even able to expand the credit supply (Budnik et al. 2021).

This expansion was furthermore made possible by a host of counter-cyclical measures national macro-prudential authorities took in light of the expected cyclical downswing. In this moment, the countercyclical action was swift, much to the contrary of the anti-cyclical action in the upswing (see Chapter 8), and occurred both in countries that had priorly activated anti-cyclical measures (Liang 2022) and in those that did not, for in those countries where no anti-cyclical measures were activated, supervisors chose the path of regulatory forbearance, announcing the exceptional exemption from certain micro-prudential rules such as the Pillar 2 guidance (Galhau 2021, 14). As a result of these measures, including the large-scale interventions by central banks and the extensive use of the anti-cyclical macro-prudential toolkit, the predicted recession following the COVID-19 events was only short-lived (NBER 2021).

Instead of a long and hard downturn, economies in the USA, the UK and the Eurozone were approaching quasi-full employment by the end of 2021, with inflationary pressures building up.[18] In line with this unexpected turn of events, the dominant narratives of the financial stability reports, as they were issued by the International Monetary Fund, the ECB, the BoE and the Federal Reserve, slowly changed. Whereas initially these reports were highlighting the uncertainty and

[17] Most notably, the Federal Reserve set up a Main Street facility, seeking to directly support the credit supply to businesses in the USA. For a full description and a critical take on these programs, see Menand (2022).

[18] These inflationary pressures were also caused by interrupted supply chains due to COVID-19 restrictions in China.

the downside risks for the economy and the financial system with it (ECB 2020; FRB 2020), such gloomy immediate outlooks slowly gave way to reports on the continued expansion of house price increases (ECB 2021; FRB 2021), deemed unsustainable in many countries in the EU (ESRB 2022b), and of the continued expansion of corporate credit (BoE 2021b; ECB 2021), which had already been major concerns for macro-prudential authorities pre-COVID-19.

Two years after the pandemic, rather than finding themselves in the midst of a downturn, macro-prudential authorities faced once more an accelerating financial boom, now accompanied by inflationary pressures. In this sense, the great resilience of the financial system, which expressed itself in the continued lending to households and corporations alike, was a mixed blessing, as leveraged loans and high-risk bonds continued their expansion amidst ultra-loose financial conditions. This boom in high-risk corporate debt was sustained by the increased risk-taking by asset managers, which had begun immediately after the worst of the COVID-19 liquidity turmoil had abated (Stein 2021). This increase in risk-taking was coupled with a notable rise in inflation from 2021 onwards, which created pressure upon central banks to reverse a decade of ultra-low inflation and raise interest rates. However, doing so could lead to a sell-off of securities, both corporate and government, and in turn test once more the financial infrastructure that underlay the new market-based system of credit provision, with all the lurking dangers to financial stability.

Conclusion

The COVID-19 crisis, which erupted in March 2020 in Western economies, functioned like a test of the macro-prudential set-up of the banking system and the shadow banking system. Given this test, a first finding, which caused much pride and optimism in the community of central bankers, was that the banking system proved largely resilient to this shock (Schnabel 2020b). Instead of drastically cutting the credit provision, banks continued lending to the "real economy," as well as households, further fueling the asset price bubbles identified by central bank analysts pre-COVID-19. On the other hand, with respect to the shadow banking system, a system of credit intermediation based on the private provision of liquidity through broker-dealers, the central bank community experienced a debacle. The regulation of this system, which the FSB had announced in 2014 as an important step to engineer a "resilient system of market-based finance" (FSB 2014), had not only broken down but actually threatened to take the entire financial system with it. Instead of resilience, amplification mechanisms were on full display, which threatened to lead to a meltdown of the financial system.

Fully aware of the dangers inherent in an unstable shadow banking system and fearing a repeat of the 2008 financial crisis, central bankers engaged in massive emergency liquidity interventions, which this time were even larger than the interventions in 2008. Retooling their quantitative easing programs to prevent macro-financial feedback loops (Schnabel 2020b), as well as refitting emergency liquidity assistance programs provided in 2008, central banks were able to stop the run on both MMFs and open-ended funds and support the recovery. However, by doing so, central bankers became the victims of their own success. Having successfully halted a run on the shadow banking system, they now faced the problem of limited public outrage over the costs of this rescue. With public attention focused on the COVID-19 pandemic, few if any realized the tremors that went through the financial system in 2020, and once halted, the limited attention it drew quickly moved elsewhere.

Yet, without such public attention, how were the central bankers to overcome the political lobby of the asset management industry? How were they to push market regulators to regulate the liquidity risks, so blatantly revealed by the crisis, if their limited data was uncapable of proving beyond a doubt that the fund industry was responsible for the amplification? In a system of public regulation built on incontestable evidence of runs, which their own interventions had undone before they came to be fully realized, how were they to push through the regulations needed to address these risks caused by the offer of daily liquidity redemptions by the fund industry and the risks by the largely unlimited leverage of hedge funds, which based on the repo-market could basically lever up their carry trades to a system-threatening dimension?

It is an irony of history that the successful "firefighters" (Bernanke et al. 2019b), the metaphor in which central bankers have come to clothe themselves since the Great Financial Crisis, were unable to remove the structural fault lines the COVID-19 crisis revealed. Instead, they were asked to safeguard a financial system whose crisis-proneness stemmed from internal, not external, reasons, which central bankers are aware of but have little to no tools to address other than through the "firepower" of their own balance sheets. As a consequence of their actions, these balance sheets have expanded to unprecedented proportions (Hauser 2021), with central banks in the USA, the UK and the Eurozone owning assets worth more than 12 percent of GDP by year end 2020 (Hauser 2021, 8). Thus caught in the position of stabilizing a system they can do little to reform, their position is probably best described as tragic, propping up a financial system without any capacity to undo the financial fault lines that caused these interventions in the first place. These developments pose the question of the role of central banks in the newly configured financial system and the role of the macro-prudential regime to stabilize financial systems, which seems to be operating swiftly in downturns but hardly at all in the upswing. It is to these issues that we now turn.

10 | *Conclusion*
The Asymmetric Application of Financial Stability Concerns

This book set out to investigate the development of so-called macro-prudential policy frameworks after the Global Financial Crisis of 2007–9, which would allow policymakers to tame the cycles of finance. It did so based on a nuanced historical analysis of the creation, implementation and use of policy devices for that purpose; that is, tools for monitoring, supervising and intervening the financial system from an anti-cyclical macro-prudential perspective. Rather than operating on a binary view of post-crisis financial reform – either a paradigm change or no change – which has been the primary political science approach to the issue, I instead sought to understand the fragmented policy change these regulatory reforms have brought about. Doing justice to the set-up of an entirely new policy program, which was very much in its infancy when the financial crisis hit, I used Peter Hall's (1989b) viabilities-framework regarding the political power of economic ideas. I thus placed the evolution of these frameworks in three different jurisdictions (the USA, the UK and the Eurozone) in the context of their economic, administrative and political viability, so as to understand their differential embrace and adoption in different countries over time.

In this final chapter of the book, I will discuss the study's main findings. In brief, the analysis revealed a substantial evolution of the economic analysis underlying the way central banks observe the financial system. Since the financial crisis, a cyclical view of financial systems took hold in economics, which was mostly developed by central bank economists themselves. These efforts increased the *economic viability* of the proposition that financial systems behave cyclically and that they require anti-cyclical interventions. In the administrative realm, the analysis also showed how in the wake of the financial crisis, reflexive central bank leaders sought to depoliticize the new duties bestowed upon them, so as to ensure the *administrative viability* of anti-cyclical macro-prudential ideas. They therefore carefully calibrated anti-cyclical macro-prudential policies in line with their capacity for implementation. The development of stress tests proved crucial here, as they allowed central bankers to intervene anti-cyclically while avoiding politicization. The *political viability* of these anti-cyclical ideas, however, proved to be the weakest element, as there are few politicians supporting intervention during an upswing, instead delaying or obstructing such measures (see Table 10.1).

I will place these findings in the longer-term historical trajectory of the macro-prudential thought collective's attempts to develop an anti-cyclical financial regulatory regime since the breakdown of Bretton Woods. Doing so, we can unearth both the manifold obstacles that this thought collective had to overcome and its incremental accumulation of power, however small it may seem in light of the continued expansion of a cyclical financial system. Tracing this process allows us

Table 10.1 *Variegated change in the three fields of viability*

Economic viability	Administrative viability	Political viability
Big change in the perception of financial markets as potentially dangerous, including the endogenous buildup of systemic risks. New models of cyclical risk in the financial system are published in academic flagship journals, often published by applied economists in central banks in conjunction with allied academics.	Some change, with reflexive agency leaders seeking depoliticization and mandate driving action. Countercyclical action, if taken, is often based on stress tests, as stress tests act as the reliable model worlds that permit depoliticization.	No change. Few politicians directly go against finance and financialization, as it is too important for the current growth models in the European Union and USA. Rather than embracing anti-cyclical action, politicians push for "more resilient finance."

to gain further insights into the factors that drive the incremental process of fragmented change, with important feedback loops occurring between the political field, the administrative field and the transnational field of economics shaping the viability of the idea of a cyclical financial system. This process has been driven by the ways that this thought collective has managed to take advantage of financial crises to push its ideas in different realms, gaining additional allies in central banks and academia and solidifying its notions of financial instability into "robust facts."

The following section traces the rise of macro-prudential thinking amidst a group of central bankers' pre-crisis and how they managed to slowly raise the power of their arguments before 2007. It shows how their still rather embryonic ideas about financial cycles were picked up by the political field as the discursive answer to the crisis, but then experienced a very selective and limited embrace in the context of immediate post-crisis regulation. The subsequent section analyzes the national implementation of macro-prudential regulation for the banking sector, tracing the interaction between efforts to operationalize a viable macro-prudential framework and the economic viability of the idea of a cyclical financial system. Here I discuss the varied embrace of anti-cyclical policies in the installation of macro-prudential programs for the European Central Bank (ECB), the Federal Reserve and the Bank of England.

I then turn to the attempted anti-cyclical regulation of the shadow banking system, which can be deemed the greatest shortcoming of post-crisis macro-prudential reform. In this area, all viabilities are shown to have been particularly low, thereby impinging upon the attempts of central bankers to impose anti-cyclical limits. To achieve regulatory reform, central bankers had to coordinate with market regulators operating on a very different economic mindset and face opposition both from powerful capital market actors and politicians. This explains why the only meaningful regulatory limitation of the procyclical tendencies of the shadow banking system occurred through stealth, with central bankers using their regulatory control over broker-dealers to that end. This regulatory intervention, which fragilized the liquidity provision by these actors, in turn led central banks to institutionalize their market-maker-of-last-resort function, a very important unintended consequence.

The penultimate section reviews the anti-cyclical efforts of central banks in the boom that unfolded from 2015 onwards. It shows that both administrative and political factors limited central banks' interventions, which, however, were clearly indicated as necessary by the newly installed early warning systems. This discrepancy between the results of regulatory science and regulatory action were particularly visible with respect to the growth of corporate debt and, linked to it, the growth of shadow banking. With little to no traction over corporate debt growth or asset managers, central banks were helplessly facing a financial boom that they themselves were fueling with massive quantitative easing programs. The analysis then contrasts these very limited countercyclical action in the upswing with the resolute and quick liquidity interventions during the COVID-19 crisis, which occurred in particular in the shadow banking sector. Sensitized to the run-risks inherent in this system and its potential for procyclical amplifications in the downswing, central bankers intervened massively, using quantitative easing programs for financial stability purposes.

This highly asymmetric enactment of anti-cyclical interventions – quick and decisive in the downswing, hesitant and slow in the upswing – is the starting point of the concluding discussion, which points to a dismal situation within which central banks find themselves. Having gained full awareness over the highly unstable financial structure they govern, they can intervene quickly when things fall apart but face limited capacity to intervene in the upswing. This tragic state of the macro-prudential program can be linked directly to the uneven development of the different viabilities this book has traced.

The Pre-crisis Development of Macro-prudential Ideas

The historical analysis has shown how macro-prudential ideas first surfaced in the 1980s in the Euro-Currency Standing Committee at the Bank for International Settlements. Concerned over the financial innovations that were linking capital markets and banking business since the breakdown of Bretton Woods, this group of central bankers was deeply worried about their implications for the lender-of-last-resort function of central banks. It hence sought to formulate a systemic perspective on these developments, arguing that they made the macro-prudential regulation of the system as a whole necessary. It was, however, hindered from spreading these concerns in the transnational realm by its sister organization, the Basel Committee for Banking Supervision, which embraced these financial innovations and the private risk management systems designed to control it. Because of its organizational set-up – besides central banks, it also included micro-prudential regulators – this body excluded the macro-prudential concerns and did its best to suppress their expression in the transnational realm, forcing these concerns into a somewhat subterranean existence.

While this view was hence persistently minimized by the Basel Committee for Banking Supervision, the increasing number and intensity of financial crises from the 1990s onwards empowered these agents in the Euro-Currency Standing Committee, forming an active program of research on systemic risks linked to the lender-of-last-resort function of banks. This de facto constituted a new space of regulatory science, in which academics and concerned central bankers exchanged their assessments of recent financial market developments before the Great Financial Crisis. This group, which sought to generate robust theories of systemic risks, included a faction at the Bank of International Settlement (BIS) that was concerned with the cyclical properties of financial systems, arguing that this was amplified by recent financial innovations. The work of this group thereby increased the economic viability of systemic risk ideas.

These recurring bouts of financial instability, in particular the East Asian financial crisis (1997–8), also led to a first empowerment of the macro-prudential thought collective on the transnational level. The Financial Stability Forum (FSF), founded in 1999, was a prominent (although weaker than envisioned by its designers) transnational outlet for the concerns over systemic risk, joining the Euro-Currency Standing Committee (now renamed the Committee for the Global Financial System – CGFS) and the BIS. The then president of the BIS and the FSF, Andrew Crockett, used this newfound prominence in the early 2000s to push for a macro-prudential vision of financial regulation. This vision clearly emphasized the endogenous capacity of financial systems to accumulate systemic risks in a cyclical fashion and hence the need for a systemic anti-cyclical component of financial regulation.

While all this implied a strengthening of the economic and bureaucratic viability of macro-prudential ideas, this agenda did not manage to sway the broader central bank community. This community was instead pursuing the proposals developed by the Basel Committee, which was based on private risk management systems. Not only did this regulatory approach find a strong foundation in mainstream financial academic thinking, it was also pushed by private interests (big banks) and US regulators in particular. Politically, this approach was thus much more viable than the macro-prudential ideas. Nevertheless, this clear exposition of these contrarian cyclical views, in conjunction with a persistent critique of private risk management systems and a first operationalization of anti-cyclical tools, would prove beneficial during the Great Financial Crisis, when policymakers were seeking new approaches.

The Post-Crisis Rise of Macro-prudential Banking Regulation

This crisis began as a local subprime mortgage crisis in 2007 but quickly transformed into a transatlantic run on the shadow banking system. It shattered several of the tenets of the dominant policy paradigm. Financial markets were neither self-regulating nor did the recent financial innovations, in particular those allowing for credit risk sharing between financial agents, contribute to the financial system's resilience. By creating new linkages between banks and capital markets, these innovations were instead seen to aggravate the crisis and accelerate its expansion. Much like the macro-prudential thought collective had warned, these innovations had spurred a cyclical upswing in financial market conditions, which now was unloading its full devastating potential on the economy. In this moment of high epistemic uncertainty and political contestation, the macro-prudential idea set gained an unexpected influence on global banking regulation, even though it was still largely underdeveloped in terms of its underlying economics and the toolkit.

A group of BIS policymakers played a key role. Already before the crisis these BIS economists had stressed the cyclical properties of financial systems, which this group argued was amplified by recent financial innovations. At the moment of the financial crisis of 2008, these concepts, although still rather embryonic in terms of econometric testing and economic model building, gained new prominence, largely based on the political need for the G20 to present a regulatory answer to the financial crisis. This political viability thus helped them to insert, albeit marginally, their concerns over the cyclical nature of financial systems into the global regulatory agenda post-crisis, with the countercyclical capital buffer as the most visible anchoring of this view in terms of new regulatory instruments.

Thus enshrined in the global banking regulation post-crisis, this global consensus on the need for macro-prudential banking regulation empowered central banks in many jurisdictions to take a much more active role in this domain, in particular regarding its anti-cyclical component. This empowerment was seen as both a capacity to exert greater influence and a threat to independent central banking, as macro-prudential action clearly implied distributional consequences and hence the potential for politicization. Weighing these advantages and disadvantages, different central banks developed unique macro-prudential strategies.

These tools were embraced or muted by central bank leaders based on their assessment of the practicality of these tools, given administrative and political constraints as well as the effects of these tools on central bank's reputation. Tracing the interaction of these strategic considerations on the one hand and the developments in the realm of regulatory science on the other, we observed the ECB fully embracing the anti-cyclical element of the macro-prudential reform agenda and the Bank of England finding a pragmatic approach to the enactment of anti-cyclical policies as a subordinated policy aim to the overarching goal of financial system resilience, whereas in the USA we find few to almost no explicit anti-cyclical tools, with the Federal Reserve instead using their annual stress test to act in a covert countercyclical fashion. In this way, this analysis revealed how anti-cyclical tools today have gained some administrative viability but are still hindered by decentralized decision-making (Eurozone and the Federal Reserve) and a limited mandate (Federal Reserve), which slows their implementation.

This newly found role went hand in hand with the creation and/or expansion of central banks' financial stability departments, which engaged in a hiring spree to accumulate the manpower and economic expertise to operationalize and implement the macro-prudential program of anti-cyclical regulatory action. These departments engaged in a decade-long applied research endeavor, seeking to generate the early warning systems that could inform central banks sufficiently ahead of time to engage in anti-cyclical action, as well as particular elements of financial cycles that required particular attention. Over the course of this decade, they assembled the historical datasets on credit and banking crises and engaged in econometric exercises to test the capacity of the newly developing early warning systems to perform their function. In this way, they managed to make the data speak and provide their superiors with robust knowledge regarding the cyclical properties of the financial system they were tasked to regulate. In this quest, they also produced stylized facts that shifted the economic discourse, including the academic discipline, thereby providing a much greater legitimacy to possible anti-cyclical central bank interventions.

I linked these developments to the installation of a research program from 2008 onwards that sought to produce actionable knowledge, which was primarily carried by financial stability departments that were newly installed or expanded within central banks after the financial crisis. As academia was slow or unwilling to pick up on these themes, it was the collaborative exercise of data assemblage and hypothesis testing by this group of applied economists working across central banks that led to important advances both in what regards the stylized facts about the cyclical characteristics of the financial system and the connected proper calibration of potential anti-cyclical tools in order to act against them. The economic viability of macro-prudential ideas was raised significantly by the work of these applied central bank economists.

Yet as to the political viability regarding the use of these new tools, I showed that the enactment of anti-cyclical measures must contend with the strong opposition of politicians regarding any measures that might limit the access of the population to homeownership. Here, governance arrangements are crucial with respect to the question of which actors hold the legal prerogative over the activation of these anti-cyclical measures, be they the countercyclical capital buffer or more direct interventions into the capacity of aspiring homeowners to take up mortgages, such as loan-to-income or debt-to-income ratios. The enactment of these measures often involves the interaction of technocrats and politicians, with technocrats leading a long and arduous fight to convince politicians to enact such measures. Political actors, such as ministries of finance or ministries of the economy, are wary of intervening in these markets as they are deemed highly contentious. These actions were more forthcoming when central banks were the sole agents, embedded in an accountability framework, within which they were to justify their actions post-factum, such as was the case for the Bank of England. Overall, the limited political viability of anti-cyclical action, which did not improve post-crisis, is the biggest obstacle to an active anti-cyclical policy program for the banking sector.

The Failure to Extend Macro-prudential Regulation to the Shadow Banking System

While post-crisis reforms led to the emergence of elaborate macro-prudential frameworks for banks, the same cannot be said for the shadow banking sector. Here, macro-prudential thinking clearly encountered its limits, as establishing the three viabilities of macro-prudential ideas proved particularly challenging. In their endeavors to insert anti-cyclical ideas, macro-prudential change agents were facing the opposition of politicians and the financial industry, first and fore-most the asset management industry, providing low political viability to these proposals. They also had to face skeptical market regulators, which often were unwilling to cooperate, diminishing their bureau-cratic viability. Furthermore, they had to convince market regulators and academia of the economic need for macro-prudential interven-tions, expressing the limited economic viability of their proposals. Central bankers' attempts for "prudential market regulation" (Tarullo 2015c) thus faced mutually reinforcing obstacles in the eco-nomic, administrative and political field.

These obstacles would thwart change agents' efforts to expand macro-prudential regulation beyond the banking sector and into the realm of capital markets. Pointing to the systemic connections between liquidity and leverage in the buildup of systemic risks pre-crisis, these interventions encountered from the beginning the concentrated oppos-ition by accounting and securities markets regulators. These actors opposed any regulatory interventions in their realm, requesting add-itional evidence and research instead. This difficulty to expand macro-prudential regulation beyond banking and into capital markets was a harbinger of problems to come, as the coordination with market regu-lators, predominantly adhering to an efficient market framework, would prove to be a major stumbling block over the course of the next decade.

One of the key issues was the attempt to impose anti-cyclical haircuts in the repo-market from 2011 onwards. Facing stiff resistance by securities markets regulators, but also (at least initially) by the Federal Reserve, this endeavor merely generated symbolic regulation as it was not constraining the provision of private liquidity in good times at all. Hindered by a lack of evidence of the procyclical behavior of the repo-market, this attempt was transformed into a large-scale data collection and research exercise, with little to no implications for financial market behavior. While this improved the economic viability of cyclical ideas with respect to the shadow banking sector, it was unable to overcome the administrative difficulties to agree on joint measures in a fragmented system of governance.

Constrained by the need for international coordination across regulatory boundaries, key agents in the macro-prudential thought collective used a window of opportunity in 2014 (during the final implementation phase of Basel III) to insert anti-cyclical regulation of the repo-market through the regulation of broker-dealers. Concerned over these private actors' excessive liquidity provision in good times, these regulations imposed a regulatory charge on their repo-activities. This intervention, while well intended, would subsequently fragilize broker-dealers' liquidity provision, making the capacity of the repo-market to provide uninterrupted liquidity a constant concern in the central banking community and requiring central banks to extend emergency liquidity backstops to the repo-market when selling volumes extended beyond their capacities. This open acknowledgment of central banks' role as market makers of last resort was also made necessary by the growth of market-based finance, which had become an ever-larger element of the credit provision both in the European Union and the USA.

The Consequences of Limited Anti-Cyclical Reforms

This limited installment of anti-cyclical tools for shadow banks caught central banks in a double bind, as they welcomed the growth of market-based finance but feared the procyclical exaggerations to which it might give rise. In this vein, I documented how central bankers, which through their aggressive quantitative easing programs were seeking to engender a growth dynamic, were at the same time observing the emergence of cyclical excesses in the system. In particular, they focused on the growth of high-risk corporate debt, driven by the search for yield of investors as well as the real estate boom, which unfolded at different pace in the Eurozone and in the UK. In this context, central bankers often had to face political actors unwilling to engage in countercyclical action, which they hence engaged in a long process of persuasion. They also had to face financial market actors in the shadow banking system, which fiercely opposed any expansion of prudential regulation. Seeking to expand the perimeter of macro-prudential regulation, they faced substantial difficulties both in the administrative and the political realm, creating a chasm between knowing about the procyclical risks building up in the system and acting upon them.

These limited anti-cyclical efforts amidst simultaneously developing central bank backstops of the shadow banking system were put to the test by the liquidity events in March 2020, caused by the eruption of the COVID-19 crisis (FSB 2020). During these events, the resilience of market-based finance was found wanting (BoE 2021a) and central banks had to intervene. They did so using the newly established direct links through the repo-market facilities, by reinstating the emergency liquidity facilities of the 2008 crisis and by engaging in new rounds of quantitative easing. Fully aware of the potentially disastrous effects a meltdown of the shadow banking system could have on their economies, central banks reacted more quickly and more extensively than they had during the Great Financial Crisis, substantially expanding their balance sheets in the process.

These events confirmed once more the seeming inevitability of central banks providing liquidity backstops for the shadow banking system in crisis times, enshrining their role as market makers of last resort. They subsequently also led to institutional reforms of central banks' links to the shadow banking system as well as a debate for broader regulatory reforms (see FSB 2021a). Yet central banks' highly successful intervention during the COVID-19 crisis has stymied their capacity to engender an expansion of the regulatory perimeter and their control over the procyclical tendencies of the shadow banking system. In contrast to the unfolding of regulatory dynamics after the Great Financial Crisis, the massive interventions by central banks to safeguard the system have hence not translated into an empowerment of the macro-prudential thought collective.

Conclusion: Central Banks at the Apex of a Fragile Financial System

The COVID-19 crisis starkly revealed the asymmetry in central banks' enaction of the policy program to prevent and contain financial instability, which strongly diverges from the initial macro-prudential vision as espoused post-crisis (see, e.g., IMF 2011, 10). Quick and resolute in moments of crisis (from the Great Financial Crisis to the

COVID-19 crisis, including both quantitative easing and emergency liquidity facilities), it is slow and hesitant, if not ineffective, in moments of financial booms. This was the case from 2015 onwards, when anti-cyclical macro-prudential policy instruments proved largely ineffective, were hardly used or were non-existent (Thiemann 2019; Edge and Liang 2020). This asymmetric set-up invites us to shortly reflect upon the present situation and the possible future pathways the macro-prudential regulation of the financial system might take.

Central banks' actions during the March 2020 events manifest their awareness that they currently sit at the top of a very fragile and volatile financial system, which at the same time has become the centerpiece of a debt-led growth regime. With no or very little control over the procyclical aspects of this system in the upswing, they act as its back-stop when disturbances occur, acting not only as bankers' lender of last resort but also as the market maker of last resort and the investor of last resort for financial markets as a whole (Mehrling 2010). This asymmetric relationship is based on the fact that there is no need for evidence to justify anti-cyclical action in times of crisis, whereas there is extensive need for evidence to justify anti-cyclical interventions in times of booms. This need for evidence is coupled with the only very limited control central banks can exert over the behavior of actors in the shadow banking sector, a sector of credit intermediation that is largely outside of the prudential control of central banks. At the same time, central banks have come to explicitly backstop the system of market-based financing, providing liquidity and thereby "unclogging" the system of private liquidity provision when a "tail risk liquidity event" (BoE 2021a) materializes.

The present situation is thus characterized by the persistent discrepancy between regulatory science and regulatory action regarding cyclical financial stability risks emanating from the financial system, in particular the shadow banking sector. This discrepancy can be linked to a lack of explicit mandates, as in the case of the USA. It can also be linked to coordination issues, both transnationally and between central banks and securities regulators and between central banks and political actors, such as ministries of finance. These difficulties are furthermore linked to the political economy of financial regulation as well as the fact that research into financial stability issues, in particular with respect to liquidity risks, is often deemed immature. As central banks engage in such research to generate the arguments for regulatory interventions, however, the growth of market-based finance continues, further aggravating the dangers postulated by this line of research. While central bankers are hence not able to shift the regulatory apparatus regarding the control of the shadow banking system in their favor, they are nevertheless fully aware of the risks inherent in this new infrastructure of markets, which in turn motivates their decisive interventions in times of crisis.

As a consequence of this asymmetric set-up of financial stability policies, central banks today find themselves in a most unenviable situation (for a similar conclusion, based on different approaches, Moschella 2023, Wansleben 2023). They are bound to see their balance sheets increase ever further as financial instabilities reoccur, in the process validating the procyclical decisions of private investors (Minsky 1986, 106). This dynamic, which backstops and stabilizes an otherwise unstable system of private liquidity provision, leads to an uninterrupted expansion of private credit and sows the seeds of future instabilities, which will have to be backstopped by central banks again. Central banks' growing balance sheets, the outcome of this attempt to quell financial instabilities, furthermore lead to growing demands of societal stakeholders to use central bank balance sheets for other purposes than rescuing the financial system, as systemic risks are arguably extending beyond the financial system (such as climate change). Central banks hence find themselves at a crossroads in terms of their institutional evolution. To address this problem, central banks either need to gain larger control over the shadow banking system's procyclical behavior before a crisis or, on the contrary, to reduce the backstop of the system of market-based financing.

Central banks' continued reliance on market-based banking and wholesale financial markets for the implementation of their monetary policy, bestowing infrastructural power on the financial industry (Braun 2020), means that any radical clamp-down on the shadow banking system is virtually excluded. This means that reforms (if any) will be incremental, and most likely too timid to fundamentally change the growth dynamics the sector has experienced since the Great Financial Crisis. This continued need for the provision of public liquidity, in case unexpected events occur, is baked into a path-dependent decision to continue with the private calculation of risk after the financial crisis (Pagliari 2012; Thiemann 2021). The continued use of private risk management systems of shadow banks, calculating the risks portfolios are exposed to and adjusting their positions accordingly, can only work if liquidity in financial markets is present. In order to ensure these private risk management strategies, but also to ensure the short-term financing of the economy, central banks remain in a situation of financial dominance (Diessner and Lisi 2020).

Only time will tell whether and to what extent central banks will manage to move beyond this disastrous institutional equilibrium. As it stands, this equilibrium embeds within itself the mechanism for an ever-repeated cyclical upswing, which will be cushioned by central bank liquidity interventions in the moment of a downswing, cyclical or otherwise (similarly Gabor 2021). In this vein, central banks' interventions themselves become a fundamental element of financial system behavior, as they shape the expectations of market participants (cf. Stellinga 2019). To escape from this equilibrium, increased coordination with securities market regulators is necessary, an increased regulation that is underway and developing in all three jurisdictions under study.

Yet, even if this leads to a macro-prudential tool set for market-based finance that is acceptable for both central banks and market regulators, this does not mean immediate success. Instead, shifting the regulatory perimeter to implement these measures will have to overcome the concentrated opposition by the financial industry as well as the political class in favor of the increased production of credit. This means that even if the economic and administrative viability of these measures can be secured, the political viability is hardly given, thereby likely enabling these administrative agents to enact only minimal measures.

Tragically, a rise in political viability might only come about if there is another financial crisis, which could be construed as unfolding along the lines of a procyclical upswing turning into a financial bust. Macro-prudential change agents within central banks and securities regulators could then frame events in this way in front of an outraged public, allowing them to channel the public anger into a fundamental restructuring of the financial system. Yet, it is highly questionable (and undesirable) that central bankers would allow for such a cataclysmic event to unfold on their watch. It is rather likelier that they would instead intervene with the full firepower of their central banks' balance sheet. Having learned their lessons regarding the scarring effects of financial crises on economic growth all too well, they will most likely choose the latter path, just as they did during the COVID-19 events, thereby entrapping their institutions into a potentially self-destroying equilibrium. If so, this would be a particular irony for a thought collective that had sought to tame the cycles of finance: rather than mitigating the amplitude of these cyclical up- and downswings, it would essentially do so only one-sidedly, addressing only the downturn while keeping the procyclical tendencies in the upswing unchecked.

Appendix: List of Interviews Conducted

1. August 19, 2014: academic economist, formerly Bundesbank
2. September 4, 2014: European Central Bank (ECB) economist
3. September 22, 2014: former Financial Services Authority regulator
4. October 22, 2014: Bundesbank economists
5. May 18, 2015: International Monetary Fund (IMF) economist
6. May 30, 2015: academic economist, UK
7. August 7, 2015: academic economist, formerly Federal Reserve Boston
8. August 26, 2015: employee, large German bank, formerly Banque de France
9. November 6, 2015: Bundesbank economist
10. April 21, 2016: ECB economist
11. April 29, 2016: academic, USA
12. May 9, 2016: ECB economist
13. June 9, 2016: Bundesbank economist
14. July 9, 2016: Bundesbank economists
15. July 19, 2016: European Systemic Risk Board (ESRB) economists
16. July 21, 2016: Bundesbank economist
17. July 22, 2016: interview, economists, large German bank, Frankfurt
18. July 25, 2016: Bundesbank economists
19. July 27, 2016: Bundesbank economist
20. August 15, 2016: interview, ECB economist
21. August 17, 2016: interview, academic economist, UK, formerly Bank of England
22. August 17, 2016: interview, economists at large private bank, UK
23. August 24, 2016: Bundesbank economist
24. September 21, 2016: economist, Dutch Central Bank
25. September 22, 2016: interview, Bank of England economist
26. September 23, 2016: interview, Bundesbank economist

27. September 26, 2016: formerly ECB economist, now Lithuanian Central Bank
28. October 11, 2016: Bank for International Settlements (BIS) economist
29. October 12, 2016: ECB supervisor
30. October 28, 2016: employee, large central counterparty, London
31. April 6, 2017: Federal Reserve economist
32. April 6, 2017: ECB research economist
33. December 20, 2017: interview, economist, formerly Bank of England
34. January 9, 2018: economist, think tank, formerly Federal Reserve board
35. January 19, 2018: academic economist, USA
36. March 12, 2018: interview, Italian economist
37. March 13, 2018: interview, academic economist, formerly Banque de France
38. March 27, 2018: academic economist, Germany
39. August 20, 2018: interview, IMF economist, formerly Federal Reserve
40. August 20, 2018: interview, BIS economist
41. September 11, 2019: former ECB economist
42. September 25, 2019: academic economist, Spain, consultant for the Banco de Espana
43. October 16, 2019: Bundesbank economist
44. October 23, 2019: ECB supervisor, formerly Bank of England
45. October 25, 2019: academic, Spain, consultant for ESRB
46. December 12, 2019: Bank of England economists
47. December 30, 2019: ECB economist, formerly Bundesbank
48. January 6, 2020: second interview, Bundesbank economist
49. January 10, 2020 and January 17, 2020: interviews, German banking supervisors
50. January 13, 2020: Bank of England economist
51. February 13, 2020: interview, applied economist, Bank of England
52. April 4, 2021: interview, Banque de France economist, financial stability division
53. April 15, 2021: interview, former Federal Reserve economist/ former UK Financial Policy Committee member
54. May 11, 2021: interview, Banque de France, financial stability division

55. May 20, 2021: interview, Banque de France, financial stability division
56. June 11, 2021: interview, Banque de France, financial stability division, prior work at the treasury
57. June 18, 2021: interview, Bundesbank economist, financial stability division
58. July 6, 2021: interview, Bundesbank economist, member of the Financial Stability Council
59. July 20, 2021: interview, former secretary, ministry of finance, Germany
60. August 3, 2021: interview, two Bundesbank economists
61. October 29, 2021: interview, former high-ranking official, Banque de France, member of the Committee for the Global Financial System
62. November 9, 2021: interview, former Dutch central banker, member of the CGFS
63. December 2, 2021: interview, former Federal Reserve board member
64. December 7, 2021: interview, FSB economist
65. December 9, 2021: interview, academic economist working with central banks
66. February 14, 2022: interview, Financial Stability Board economist
67. February 16, 2022: interview, ECB economist
68. March 7, 2022: interview, European Securities and Markets Authority (ESMA) economist
69. March 23, 2022: second interview, FSB economist
70. March 25, 2022: interview, member of the Danish Systemic Risk Council
71. April 27, 2022: interview, academic economist, USA, working on financial stability risks
72. May 3, 2022: interview, second academic economist, USA, working on financial stability risks
73. May 16, 2022: interview, ESMA economist
74. May 20, 2022: interview, former Federal Reserve lawyer
75. June 2, 2022: interview, Federal Reserve board economist
76. June 6, 2022: interview, Federal Reserve New York economist
77. June 9, 2022: interview, former Securities and Exchange Commission lawyer, working on money market mutual fund reforms

References

Abbott, A. (1988). *The System of Professions*. Chicago, IL: University of Chicago Press.

Abbott, A. (2001). *The Chaos of Disciplines*. Chicago, IL: University of Chicago Press.

Abbott, A. (2005). "Linked Ecologies: States and Universities As Environments for Professions," *Sociological Theory*, 23(3): 245–274.

Abboud, A., Duncan, E., Horvath, A. et al. (2021). "COVID-19 As a Stress Test: Assessing the Bank Regulatory Framework," Finance and Economics Discussion Series 2021–024. Washington, DC: Board of Governors of the Federal Reserve System, https://doi.org/10.17016/FEDS.2021.024.

Abolafia, M. Y. (2001). *Making Markets: Opportunism and Restraint on Wall Street*. Cambridge, MA: Harvard University Press.

Abolafia, M. Y. (2012). "Central Banking and the Triumph of Technical Rationality," in K. Knorr-Cetina and A. Preda (eds.), *Oxford Handbook of the Sociology of Finance*, pp. 94–114. Oxford: Oxford University Press.

Abolafia, M. Y. (2020). *Stewards of the Market: How the Federal Reserve Made Sense of the Financial Crisis*. Cambridge, MA: Harvard University Press.

Acharya, V. V. (2009). "A Theory of Systemic Risk and Design of Prudential Bank Regulation," *Journal of Financial Stability*, 5(3): 224–255.

Acharya, V. V. and Schnabl, P. (2010). "Do Global Banks Spread Global Imbalances? Asset-Backed Commercial Paper during the Financial Crisis of 2007–2009," *IMF Economic Review*, 58(1): 37–73.

Acharya, V. V., Engle, R. and Richardson, M. (2012). "Capital Shortfall: A New Approach to Ranking and Regulating Systemic Risks," *American Economic Review*, 102(3): 59–64.

Acharya, V. V., Pedersen, L. H., Philippon, T. and Richardson, M. (2010). "Measuring Systemic Risk." Federal Reserve Bank of Cleveland Working Paper 10–02.

Acharya, V. V., Pedersen, L. H., Philippon, T. et al. (2017). "Measuring Systemic Risk," *Review of Financial Studies*, 30(1): 2–47.

Acosta, J., Cherrier, B., Claveau, F. et al. (2020). "A History of Economic Research at the Bank of England (1960–2019)." Working Paper presented to the Financial Stability Research Group.

Adenbaum, J., Hubbs, D., Martin, A. et al. (2016). "What's Up with GCF Repo® May 2." Federal Reserve Bank of New York, Liberty Street Economics.

Adrian, T. (2018). *Risk Management and Regulation*. Washington, DC: International Monetary Fund.

Adrian, T. and Boyarchenko, N. (2015). "Intermediary Leverage Cycles and Financial Stability." Federal Reserve Bank of New York Staff Report 794. www.newyorkfed.org/medialibrary/media/research/staff_reports/sr567 .pdf.

Adrian, T. and Brunnermeier, M. (2008). "CoVaR." Federal Reserve Bank of New York Staff Report 348.

Adrian, T. and Brunnermeier, M. (2011). "CoVaR." Federal Reserve Bank of New York Staff Report 348, revised version.

Adrian, T. and Brunnermeier, M. (2016). "CoVaR," *American Economic Review*, 106(7): 1705.

Adrian, T. and Liang, N. (2016). "Monetary Policy, Financial Conditions, and Financial Stability." CEPR Discussion Paper No. DP11394.

Adrian, T. and Shin, H. S. (2008). "Liquidity and Leverage." Paper presented at the Financial Cycles, Liquidity, and Securitization Conference hosted by the International Monetary Fund, Washington, DC, April 18.

Adrian, T. and Shin, H. S. (2010). "Liquidity and Leverage," *Journal of Financial Intermediation*, 19(3): 418–437.

Adrian, T. and Shin, H. S. (2014). "Procyclical Leverage and Value-at-Risk," *The Review of Financial Studies*, 27(2): 373–403.

Adrian, T., Boyarchenko, N. and Giannone, D. (2016). "Vulnerable Growth." Federal Reserve Bank of New York Staff Report 794.

Adrian, T., Boyarchenko, N. and Giannone, D. (2019). "Vulnerable Growth," *American Economic Review*, 109(4): 1263–1289.

Adrian, T., Boyarchenko, N. and Shachar, O. (2017). "Dealer Balance Sheets and Bond Liquidity Provision." Federal Reserve Bank of New York Staff Report 803.

Adrian, T., Covitz, D. and Liang, N. (2013). "Financial Stability Monitoring." Federal Reserve Bank of New York Staff Reports 601.

Adrian, T., Covitz, D. and Liang, N. (2015). "Financial Stability Monitoring," *Annual Review of Financial Economics*, 7(1): 357–395.

Adrian, T., de Fontnouvelle, P., Yang, E. and Zlate, A. (2015). "Macroprudential Policy: Case Study from a Tabletop Exercise." Federal Reserve Bank of New York Staff Reports 742.

Adrian, T., Begalle, B., Copeland, A. et al. (2013). "Repo and Securities Lending." Federal Reserve Bank of New York Staff Report 529.

Adrian, T., Fontnouvelle, P. de, Yang, E. et al. (2017). "Macroprudential Policy: A Case Study from a Tabletop Exercise," *Economic Policy Review*, 23(1): 1–30.

Aggarwal, N., Arora, S., Behl, A. et al. (2013). "A Systematic Approach to Identify Systemically Important Firms." Indira Gandhi Institute of Development Research, Mumbai, Working Paper 2013–021.

Aglietta, M. (2018). *Money: 5,000 Years of Debt and Power*. London: Verso.

Aikman, D., Haldane, A. and Nelson, B. (2010). "Curbing the Credit Cycle." Speech given at Columbia University Center on Capitalism and Society, www.bankofengland.co.uk/-/media/boe/files/speech/2010/curbing-the-credit-cycle-speech.pdf?la=en&hash=AB55B58EB5678AE8589FED8F 24DC618E13962317.

Aikman, D., Bridges, J., Kashyap, A. and Siegert, C. (2019). "Would Macroprudential Regulation Have Prevented the Last Crisis?" *Journal of Economic Perspectives*, 33(1): 107–130.

Aikman, D., Bridges, J., Hacioglu Hoke, S., O'Neill, C. and Raja, A. (2019). "Credit, Capital and Crises: A GDP-at-Risk Approach." Staff Working Paper No. 824.

Aikman, D., Kiley, M. T., Lee, S. J., Palumbo, M. G., and Warusawitharana, M. N. (2015). "Mapping Heat in the U.S. Financial System," Finance and Economics Discussion Series 2015–059. Washington, DC: Board of Governors of the Federal Reserve System.

Aikman, D., Alessandri, P., Eklund, B. et al. (2009). "Funding Liquidity Risk in a Quantitative Model of Systemic Stability." Bank of England Working Paper No. 372.

Aikman, D., Haldane, A. G., Hinterschweiger, M. et al. (2018). "Rethinking Financial Stability." Bank of England Financial Stability Paper No. 712.

Aikman, D., Bridges, J., Burgess, S. et al. (2018). "Measuring Risks to UK Financial Stability." Bank of England Staff Working Paper No. 738.

Alessi, L., Antunes, A., Babecký, J. et al. (2015). "Comparing Different Early Warning Systems: Results from a Horse Race Competition among Members of the Macro-Prudential Research Network." MPRA Paper 62194.

Alexander, K. (2017). "The European Central Bank's Supervisory Powers: The Need for Enhanced Macro-Prudential Supervision." Frankfurt: European Central Bank.

Allen, F. and Gale, D. (1998). "Optimal Financial Crises," *Journal of Finance*, 53: 1245–1284.

Allen, F. and Gale, D. (2000). "Financial Contagion," *Journal of Political Economy*, 108(1): 1–33.

Allen, F., Carletti, E., Goldstein, I. et al. (2015). "Moral Hazard and Government Guarantees in the Banking Industry," *Journal of Financial Regulation*, 1(1): 30–50.

Altavilla, C. Lemke, W., Linzert, T. et al. (2021). "Assessing the Efficacy, Efficiency and Potential Side Effects of the ECB's Monetary Policy Instruments since 2014." ECB Occasional Paper Series No. 278.

Anadu, K. and Cai, F. (2019). "Liquidity Transformation Risks in U.S. Bank Loan and High-Yield Mutual Funds," www.federalreserve.gov/econres/notes/feds-notes/liquidity-transformation-risks-in-US-bank-loan-and-high-yield-mutual-funds-20190809.htm.

Anderson, N., Webber, L., Noss, J. et al. (2015). "The Resilience of Financial Market Liquidity." Bank of England Financial Stability Paper 34.

Arbatli-Saxegaard, E. and Muneer, M. A. (2020). "The Countercyclical Capital Buffer: A Cross-Country Overview of Policy Frameworks." Norges Bank, Oslo.

Argitis, G. (2013). "The Illusions of the 'New Consensus' in Macroeconomics: A Minskian Analysis," *Journal of Post Keynesian Economics*, 35(3): 483–505.

Arsov, I., Canetti, E., Kodres, M. L. E. et al. (2013). "Near-Coincident Indicators of Systemic Stress." IMF Working Paper No. 13–115.

Arthur, W. B. (2013). "Complexity Economics: A Different Framework for Economic Thought." Santa Fe Institute: Santa Fe Working Paper 2013–04–012.

Asensio, A. (2013). "The Achilles' Heel of the Mainstream Explanations of the Crisis and a Post Keynesian Alternative," *Journal of Post Keynesian Economics*, 36(2): 355–380.

Avinash D. (ed.) (2003a). *Liquidity Black Holes: Understanding, Quantifying and Managing Liquidity Risk*. London: Risk Books.

Aymanns, C., Doyne Farmer, J., Kleinnijenhuis, A. M. and Wetzer, T. (2018). "Models of Financial Stability and Their Application in Stress Tests," in C. Hommes and B. LeBaron (eds.), *Handbook of Computational Economics*, pp. 329–391. Amsterdam: North Holland.

Babb, S. (2002). *Managing Mexico: Economists from Nationalism to Neoliberalism*. Princeton, NJ: Princeton University Press.

Babb, S. (2013). "The Washington Consensus As Transnational Policy Paradigm: Its Origins, Trajectory and Likely Successor," *Review of International Political Economy*, 20(2): 268–297.

Babecký, J., Havranek, T., Matějů, J. et al. (2011). "Early Warning Indicators of Economic Crises: Evidence from a Panel of 40 Developed Countries." CNB Working Paper 8–2011.

Babecky, J., Havranek, T., Matěju, J. et al. (2012). "Banking, Debt and Currency Crises: Early Warning Indicators for Developed Countries." ECB Working Paper Series No. 1485/October 2012.

Backhouse, R. E. (1998). "If Mathematics Is Informal, Then Perhaps We Should Accept That Economics Must Be Informal Too," *The Economic Journal*, 108(451): 1848–1858.

Backhouse, R. E. (2010). *The Puzzle of Modern Economics: Science or Ideology*. Cambridge: Cambridge University Press.

Bahaj, S., Bridges, J., Malherbe, F. and O'Neill, C. (2016). "What Determines How Banks Respond to Changes in Capital Requirements?" Bank of England Working Paper No. 593 15, April.

Bailey, A. (2021). "Taking Our Second Chance to Make MMFs More Resilient." Speech given at the ISDA 35th Annual General Meeting, published on May 12. www.bankofengland.co.uk/speech/2021/may/and rew-bailey-international-swaps-and-derivatives-association.

Baker, A. (2013a). "The New Political Economy of the Macroprudential Ideational Shift," *New Political Economy*, 18(1): 112–139.

Baker, A. (2013b). "When New Ideas Meet Existing Institutions: Why Macroprudential Regulatory Change Is a Gradual Process," in M. Moschella and E. Tsingou (eds.), *Transformations: Incremental Change in Post-Crisis Regulation*, p. 35. Colchester: ECPR Press.

Baker, A. (2013c). "When New Ideas Meet Existing Institutions: Why Macroprudential Regulatory Change Is a Gradual Process," in M. Moschella and E. Tsingou (eds.), *Great Expectations, Slow Transformation Incremental Change in Financial Governance*, pp. 35–56. Colchester: ECPR Press.

Baker, A. (2014). "Macroprudential Regulation," in D. Muegge (ed.), *Europe and the Governance of Global Finance*, pp. 172–187. Oxford: Oxford University Press.

Baker, A. (2015). "Varieties of Economic Crisis, Varieties of Ideational Change: How and Why Financial Regulation and Macroeconomic Policy Differ," *New Political Economy*, 20(3): 342–366.

Baker, A. (2017). "Political Economy and the Paradoxes of Macroprudential Regulation." SPERI Working Paper 40.

Baker, A. (2018). "Macroprudential Regimes and the Politics of Social Purpose," *Review of International Political Economy*, 25(3): 293–316.

Baker, A. (2020). "Tower of Contrarian Thinking: How the BIS Helped Reframe Understandings of Financial Stability," in C. Borio, S. Claessens, P. Clement, R. McCauley and H. Shin (eds.), *Promoting Global Monetary and Financial Stability: The Bank for International Settlements after Bretton Woods, 1973–2020*, pp. 134–167. Cambridge: Cambridge University Press.

Baker, A. and Widmaier, W. (2015). "Macroprudential Ideas and Contested Social Purpose: A Response to Terrence Casey," *British Journal of Politics and International Relations*, 17(2): 371–380.

Ban, C. (2015). "Austerity versus Stimulus? Understanding Fiscal Policy Change at the International Monetary Fund since the Great Recession," *Governance*, 28(2): 167–183.

Ban, C. (2016). *Ruling Ideas: How Global Neoliberalism Goes Local*. Oxford: Oxford University Press.

Ban, C. and Patenaude, B. (2019). "The Professional Politics of the Austerity Debate: A Comparative Field Analysis of the European Central Bank and the International Monetary Fund," *Public Administration*, 97(3): 530–545.

Ban, C., Seabrooke, L. and Freitas, S. (2016). "Grey Matter in Shadow Banking: International Organizations and Expert Strategies in Global Financial Governance," *Review of International Political Economy*, 23 (6): 1001–1033.

Bandt, O. de and Hartmann, P (2000). "Systemic Risk: A Survey." November 2000: ECB Working Paper No. 35.

Bandt, O. de, Héam, J. C., Labonne, C. et al. (2013). "Measuring Systemic Risk in a Post-Crisis World." Banque de France Working Paper No. 6.

Bank for International Settlement. (BIS). (2001). "Marrying the Macro- and Microprudential Dimensions of Financial Stability." BIS Papers No. 1. www.bis.org/publ/bppdf/bispap01.pdf.

Bank for International Settlement. (BIS). (2002). "Risk Measurement and Systemic Risk: Proceedings of the Third Joint Central Bank Research Conference." October.

Bank for International Settlement. (BIS). (2008). "Addressing Financial System Procyclicality: A Possible Framework." Note for the FSF Working Group on Market and Institutional Resilience. www.fsb.org/wp-content/uploads/r_0904e.pdf.

Bank for International Settlement-International Organization of Securities Commissions (BIS-IOSCO). (2012). "Principles for Financial Market Infrastructures."

Bank of England. (2009). "The Role of Macroprudential Policy." Bank of England Discussion Paper.

Bank of England. (2012). "Record of the Interim Financial Policy Committee Meeting 22nd of June 2012." www.bankofengland.co.uk//media/boe/file s/record/2012/financial-policy-committee-meeting-june-2012.

Bank of England. (2013a). "The Financial Policy Committee's Powers to Supplement Capital Requirements: A Draft Policy Statement." January www .bankofengland.co.uk/news/2013/january/financial-policy-committees-powers-to-supplement-capital-requirements.

Bank of England. (2013b). "Financial Policy Committee Statement," March 19. www.bankofengland.co.uk/statement/fpc/2013/financial-policy-committee-statement-march-2013.

Bank of England. (2013c). "Record of the Financial Policy Committee Meeting on 18th of September 2013." www.bankofengland.co.uk/-/medi a/boe/files/record/2013/financial-policy-committee-meeting-september-2 013.pdf.

Bank of England. (2013d). "Financial Stability Report November 2013."

Bank of England. (2013e). "Record of the Financial Policy Committee meeting November 20th 2013." www.bankofengland.co.uk/-/media/boe/ files/record/2013/financial-policy-committee-meeting-november-2013.pd f?la=enandhash=52E109E5915E7B709C3C48654278D4B116CC957E.

Bank of England. (2014a). "The Financial Policy Committee's Powers to Supplement Capital Requirements: A Policy Statement." January. www .bankofengland.co.uk/-/media/boe/files/statement/2014/fpc-powers-to-supplement-capital-requirements-policy-statement.

Bank of England. (2014b). "Financial Stability Report," June (Issue No. 35).

Bank of England. (2014c). "Record of the Financial Policy Committee Meetings – 17 and 25 June 2014." www.bankofengland.co.uk/-/media/b oe/files/record/2014/financial-policy-committee-meeting-june-2014.pdf.

Bank of England. (2014d). "Financial Policy Committee Statement," September 26. www.bankofengland.co.uk/statement/fpc/2014/financial-policy-committee-statement-september-2014.

Bank of England. (2014e). "Financial Stability Report December 2014" (Issue No. 36).

Bank of England. (2015a). "Records of the Financial Policy Committee meeting on 24th of March 2015." www.bankofengland.co.uk/record/20 15/financial-policy-committee-march-2015.

Bank of England. (2015b). "The PRA's Intended Implementation Approach to FPC Directions on Loan to Value and Debt to Income Ratio Limits." www.bankofengland.co.uk/-/media/boe/files/prudential-regulation/publi cation/pra-statement-on-housing-tools-10-july-2015.pdf.

Bank of England. (2015c). "Financial Policy Committee Statement." September 23.

Bank of England. (2015d). "The Bank of England's Approach to Stress Testing the UK Banking System." October.

Bank of England. (2015e). "Financial Stability Report December 2015."

Bank of England. (2015f). "Supplement to the December 2015 Financial Stability Report: The Framework of Capital Requirements for UK Banks."

Bank of England. (2015g). "Red Book 2015: The Bank of England's Sterling Monetary Framework."

Bank of England. (2016a). "Financial Policy Committee Statement," March 23. www.bankofengland.co.uk/statement/fpc/2016/financial-policy-committee-statement-march-2016.

Bank of England. (2016b). "The Financial Policy Committee's Approach to Setting the Countercyclical Capital Buffer: A Policy Statement." April.

Bank of England. (2016c). "Financial Stability Report July 2016."

Bank of England. (2017a). "Financial Policy Committee Statement," March 22. www.bankofengland.co.uk/statement/fpc/2017/financial-policy-committee-statement-march-2017.

Bank of England. (2017b). "Financial Stability Report June 2017."

Bank of England. (2017c). "Record of the Financial Policy Committee Meeting on 20 September 2017." www.bankofengland.co.uk/-/media/boe/files/record/2017/financial-policy-committee-meeting-september-2017.pdf?la=enandhash=D6EDEB7BAE687E9E419782ACBEE2E1437569B2BE.

Bank of England. (2017d). "Financial Stability Report November 2017."

Bank of England. (2018a). "Financial Stability Report June 2018."

Bank of England. (2018b). "Record of the Financial Policy Committee Meeting 2018: October 3rd 2018." www.bankofengland.co.uk/record/2018/financial-policy-committee-october-2018.

Bank of England. (2018c). "Financial Stability Report November 2018."

Bank of England. (2019a). "Financial Stability Report July 2019."

Bank of England. (2019b). "Financial Policy Summary and Record of the Financial Policy Committee Meeting on October 2nd 2019." www.bankofengland.co.uk/-/media/boe/files/financial-policy-summary-and-record/2019/october-2019.pdf?la=enandhash=5AC2F4CC658151FCFA3B4BA438CDAA37D5996310.

Bank of England. (2019c). "Financial Policy Summary and Record of the Financial Policy Committee Meeting on 13 December 2019." www.bankofengland.co.uk/-/media/boe/files/financial-policy-summary-and-record/2019/december-2019.pdf?la=enandhash=FE3C4D2A51C505571C756D49FC08E5CD3A456560.

Bank of England. (2019d). "Financial Stability Report December 2019."

Bank of England. (2019e). "Financial Policy Summary and Record of the Financial Policy Committee Meeting on 13 December 2019." www.bankofengland.co.uk/-/media/boe/files/financial-policy-summary-and-record/2019/december-2019.pdf.

Bank of England. (2021a). "Assessing the Resilience of Market-Based Finance." www.bankofengland.co.uk/report/2021/assessing-the-resilience-of-market-based-finance.

Bank of England. (2021b). "Financial Stability Report December 2021."

Bank of Japan. (1998). "Summary of The Second Joint Central Bank Research Conference on Risk Measurement and Systemic Risk Toward a Better Understanding of Market Dynamics during Periods of Stress."

Banulescu, G.-D. and Dumitrescu, E.-I. (2015). "Which Are the SIFIs? A Component Expected Shortfall Approach to Systemic Risk," *Journal of Banking and Finance*, 50: 575–588.

Baranova, Y., Coen, J., Lowe, P., Noss, J. and Silvestri, L. (2017). "Simulating Stress across the Financial System: The Resilience of Corporate Bond Markets and the Role of Investment Funds." Bank of England Financial Stability Paper No. 42.

Barth, J. R., Caprio Jr, G. and Levined, R. (2004). "Bank Regulation and Supervision: What Works Best?" *Journal of Financial Intermediation*, 13: 205–248.

Barwell, R. (2013). *Macroprudential Policy: Taming the Wild Gyrations of Credit Flows, Debt Stocks and Asset Prices*. New York: Springer.

Basel Committee on Banking Supervision (BCBS). (2008). "Addressing Financial System Procyclicality: A Possible Framework." Note for the FSF Working Group on Market and Institutional Resilience: Bank for International Settlements.

Basel Committee on Banking Supervision (BCBS). (2009). "Strengthening the Resilience of the Banking Sector." www.bis.org/publ/bcbs164.pdf.

Basel Committee on Banking Supervision (BCBS). (2010). "Basel III: A Global Regulatory Framework for More Resilient Banks and Banking Systems." www.bis.org/publ/bcbs189.pdf.

Basel Committee on Banking Supervision (BCBS). (2014a). "Basel III Leverage Ratio Framework and Disclosure Requirements." Bank for International Settlements.

Basel Committee on Banking Supervision (BCBS). (2014b). "Basel III: The Net Stable Funding Ratio." Bank for International Settlements.

Basel Committee on Banking Supervision (BCBS). (2015). "Frequently Asked Questions on the Basel III Countercyclical Capital Buffer." Bank for International Settlements.

Bassett, W. F., Daigle, A., Edge, R. M. and Kara, G. (2015). "Credit-to-GDP Trends and Gaps by Lender- and Credit-Type," FEDS Notes 2015–12–03, Board of Governors of the Federal Reserve System (US).

Baud, C. and Chiapello, E. (2014). "Disciplining the Neoliberal Bank: Credit Risk Regulation and the Financialization of Loan Management." Working Paper SSRN 2417396.

Bell, S. and Hindmoor, A. (2015). *Masters of the Universe, Slaves of the Market*. Cambridge, MA: Harvard University Press.

Bennani, T., Couaillier, C., Devulder, A. et al. (2017). "An Analytical Framework to Calibrate Macroprudential Policy." Banque de France Working Paper No. 648.

Benoit, S., Colletaz, G., Hurlin, C. et al. (2013). "A Theoretical and Empirical Comparison of Systemic Risk Measures." HEC Paris Research Paper No. FIN-2014-1030.

Berger, A. N., Herring, R. J. and Szegö, G. P. (1995). "The Role of Capital in Financial Institutions," *Journal of Banking and Finance*, 19(3–4): 393–430.

Berman, S. (2013). "Ideational Theorizing in the Social Sciences since 'Policy Paradigms, Social Learning, and the State'," *Governance*, 26(2): 217–237.

Bernanke, B. (2004). "The Great Moderation." Remarks by Governor Ben S. Bernanke at the meetings of the Eastern Economic Association, Washington, DC.

Bernanke, B. (2008). "Reducing Systemic Risk." Speech at the Federal Reserve Bank of Kansas City's Annual Economic Symposium, Jackson Hole, Wyoming, August 22.

Bernanke, B. (2011). "Implementing a Macroprudential Approach to Supervision and Regulation." Speech at the 47th Annual Conference on Bank Structure and Competition, Chicago, IL.

Bernanke, B. (2012). "Some Reflections on the Crisis and the Policy Response." Remarks by Ben S. Bernanke, Chairman Board of Governors of the Federal Reserve System, at the Conference on "Rethinking Finance: Perspectives on the Crisis." Presented by the Russell Sage Foundation and The Century Foundation. New York.

Bernanke, B. (2013). "Monitoring the Financial System." Speech at the Federal Reserve Bank of Chicago, IL, May 10.

Bernanke, B. (2015). *The Courage to Act: A Memoir of a Crisis and Its Aftermath*. New York: Norton.

Bernanke, B. and Gertler, M. (1990). "Financial Fragility and Economic Performance," *The Quarterly Journal of Economics*, 105(1): 87–114.

Bernanke, B., Geithner, T., Lew, J. and Yellen, J. (2019a). "Comment from Former Chairs of the Financial Stability Oversight Council and Two Previous Chairs of the Federal Reserve Board." www.regulations.gov/comment/FSOC-2019-0001-0010.

Bernanke, B., Geithner, T. and Paulson, H. (2019b). *Firefighting: The Financial Crisis and Its Lessons*. New York: Penguin Books.

Bernard, C. and Czado, C. (2015). "Conditional Quantiles and Tail Dependence," *Journal of Multivariate Analysis*, 138: 104–126.

Berrospide, J. M. and Edge, R. M. (2019). "The Effects of Bank Capital Buffers on Bank Lending and Firm Activity: What Can We Learn from Five

Years of Stress Test Results?" Finance and Economics Discussion Series 2019–050. Washington, DC.

Best, J. (2020). "The Quiet Failures of Early Neoliberalism: From Rational Expectations to Keynesianism in Reverse," *Review of International Studies*, 46(5): 594–612. Doi: 10.1017/S0260210520000169.

Best, J. and Widmaier, W. (2006). "Micro- or Macro-Moralities? Economic Discourses and Policy Possibilities," *Review of International Political Economy*, 13(4): 609–631.

Beutel, J. (2019). "Forecasting Growth at Risk," mimeo.

Bezemer, D. J. (2016). "Towards an 'Accounting View' on Money, Banking and the Macroeconomy: History, Empirics, Theory," *Cambridge Journal of Economics*, 40(5): 1275–1295.

Biebricher, T. (2012). *Neoliberalismus zur Einführung*. Hamburg: Junius Verlag.

Bieling, H.-J. (2014). "Shattered Expectations: The Defeat of European Ambitions of Global Financial Reform," *Journal of European Public Policy*, 21(3): 346–366.

Bindseil, U. and Jabłecki, J. (2011). "The Optimal Width of the Central Bank Standing Facilities Corridor and Banks' Day-to-Day Liquidity Management." Working Paper series 1350, June.

Birk, M. and Thiemann, M. (2020). "Open for Business: Entrepreneurial Central Banks and the Cultivation of Market Liquidity," *New Political Economy* 25(2).

Bischof, J. and Airoldi, E. M. (2012). "Summarizing Topical Content with Word Frequency and Exclusivity," *Proceedings of the 29th International Conference on Machine Learning*, 201–208.

Bisias, D., Flood, M., Lo, A. W. et al. (2012). "A Survey of Systemic Risk Analytics," *Annual Review of Financial Economics*, 4(1): 255–296.

Black, J. (2013). "Seeing, Knowing, and Regulating Financial Markets: Moving the Cognitive Framework from the Economic to the Social." LSE Legal Studies Working Paper No. 24/2013.

Blancher, N. R., Mitra, S., Morsy, H. et al. (2013). "Systemic Risk Monitoring ('SysMo') Toolkit: A User Guide." International Monetary Fund Working Paper No. 13/168.

Blaug, M. (2009). "The Trade-Off between Rigor and Relevance: Sraffian Economics As a Case in Point," *History of Political Economy*, 41(2): 219–247.

Blei, D. M. (2012). "Probabilistic Topic Models," *Communications of the ACM*, 55(4): 77–84.

Blei, D. M. and Lafferty, J. (2006). "Correlated Topic Models," *Advances in Neural Information Processing Systems*, 18: 147.

Blei, D. M. and Lafferty, J. D. (2007). "A Correlated Topic Model of Science," *The Annals of Applied Statistics*, 1(1): 17–35.

Blei, D. M., Ng, A. Y. and Jordan, M. I. (2003). "Latent Dirichlet Allocation," *Journal of Machine Learning Research*, 3(Jan.): 993–1022.

Blustein, P. (2012). "How Global Watchdogs Missed a World of Trouble." CIGI Papers No. 5, July. Waterloo: Centre for International Governance Innovation.

Blyth, M. (2002). *Great Transformations: Economic Ideas and Institutional Change in the Twentieth Century*. Cambridge: Cambridge University Press.

Blyth, M. (2008). "The Politics of Compounding Bubbles: The Global Housing Bubble in Comparative Perspective," *Comparative European Politics*, Fall: 387–406.

Blyth, M. (2013). "Paradigms and Paradox: The Politics of Economic Ideas in Two Moments of Crisis," *Governance*, 26(2): 197–215.

Blyth, M. and Mark, B. (2002). *Great Transformations: Economic Ideas and Institutional Change in the Twentieth Century*. Cambridge: Cambridge University Press.

BNP Paribas. (2021). "FSB Policy Proposals to Enhance Money Market Fund Resilience BNP PARIBAS Response to the Consultative Report 22 July 2021." https://cdn-group.bnpparibas.com/uploads/file/policy_pro posals_to_enhance_mmf_bnp_paribas_fsb_consultation_july_2021.pdf.

Board of Governors of the Federal Reserve System (U.S.). (1996). "Risk Measurement and Systemic Risk: Proceedings of a Joint Central Bank Research Conference, November 16–17, 1995." Board of Governors of the Federal Reserve System (US), November.

Boehmer-Christiansen, S. (1995). "Reflections on Scientific Advice and EC Transboundary Pollution policy," *Science and Public Policy*, 22(3): 195–203.

Borio, C. (2000). "Market Liquidity and Stress: Selected Issues and Policy Implications." *BIS Quarterly Review*. November 2000.

Borio, C. (2003a). "Market Distress and Vanishing Liquidity: Anatomy and Policy Options," in D. Avinash (ed.), *Liquidity Black Holes: Understanding, Quantifying and Managing Liquidity Risk*, pp. 213–248. London: Risk Books.

Borio, C. (2003b). "Towards a Macroprudential Framework for Financial Supervision and Regulation?" BIS Working Papers No. 128.

Borio, C. (2009). "Implementing the Macroprudential Approach to Financial Regulation and Supervision," *Financial Stability Review*, 13: 31–41.

Borio, C. (2012). "The Financial Cycle and Macroeconomics: What Have We Learnt?" BIS Working Paper No. 395.

Borio, C. E. V. and Lowe, P. W. (2002). "Asset Prices, Financial and Monetary Stability: Exploring the Nexus." BIS Working Papers No. 114.

Borio, C. and Drehmann, M. (2009). "Towards an Operational Framework for Financial Stability: 'Fuzzy' Measurement and Its Consequences." BIS Working Papers No. 284.

Borio, C. and Zhu, H. (2012). "Capital Regulation, Risk-Taking and Monetary Policy: A Missing Link in the Transmission Mechanism?" *Journal of Financial Stability*, 8(4): 236–251.

Borio, C., Furfine, C. and Lowe, P. (2001). "Procyclicality of the Financial System and Financial Stability: Issues and Policy Options." *Marrying the Macro- and Microprudential Dimensions of Financial Stability*, BIS Papers, No. 1, pp. 1–57.

Bouveret, A. and Haferkorn, M. (2022). "Leverage and Derivatives: The Case of Archegos (May 18, 2022)." Working Paper.

Bouveret, A., Martin, A. and McCabe, P. (2022). "Money Market Fund Vulnerabilities: A Global Perspective." FEDS Working Paper No. 2022–12.

Bowman, A., Erturk, I., Froud, J. et al. (2013). "Central Bank-Led Capitalism?" *Seattle Law Review*, 36(2): 455–487.

Bradshaw, G. A. and Borchers, J. G. (2000). "Uncertainty As Information: Narrowing the Science-Policy Gap," *Conservation Ecology*, 4(1).

Brainard, L. (2021). "Some Preliminary Financial Stability Lessons from the COVID-19 Shock." Speech given on March 1 at the 2021 Annual Washington Conference, Institute of International Bankers (via webcast), www.federalreserve.gov/newsevents/speech/brainard20210301a.htm.

Braun, B. (2014). "Why Models Matter: The Making and Unmaking of Governability in Macroeconomic Discourse," *Journal of Critical Globalisation Studies*, 7: 48–79.

Braun, B. (2016a). "The Financial Consequences of Mr Draghi? Infrastructural Power and the Rise of Market-Based (Central) Banking." FEPS Working Paper.

Braun, B. (2016b). "Speaking to the People? Money, Trust, and Central Bank Legitimacy in the Age of Quantitative Easing," *Review of International Political Economy*, 23(6): 1064–1092.

Braun, B. (2020). "Central Banking and the Infrastructural Power of Finance: The Case of ECB Support for Repo and Securitization Markets," *Socio-Economic Review*, 18(2): 395–418.

Braun, B. and Downey, L. (2020). "Against Amnesia: Re-imagining Central Banking." Council on Economic Policies Working Paper. www.cepweb.org/wp-content/uploads/2020/01/CEP-DN-Against-Amnesia.-Re-Imagining-Central-Banking.pdf.

Braun, B., Krampf, A. and Murau, S. (2021). "Financial Globalization As Positive Integration: Monetary Technocrats and the Eurodollar Market in the 1970s," *Review of International Political Economy*, 28(4): 794–819.

Braun, M. (2019). "Designation and De-designation of Systemically Important Financial Institutions," *Review of Banking and Financial Law*, 38: 470–481.

Brave, S. and Butters, A. (2011). "Monitoring Financial Stability: A Financial Conditions Index Approach," *Economic Perspectives*, 35(1).

Brazier, A. (2015). "The Bank of England's Approach to Stress Testing the UK Banking System." Speech given at the London School of Economics Systemic Risk Centre. October 30.

Brazier, A. (2018). "Market Finance and Financial Stability: Will the Stretch Cause a Strain?" Speech given at Imperial College Business School, February 1.

Brazier, A. (2019). "Financial Resilience and Economic Earthquakes." Speech given at University of Warwick, June 13.

Breckenfelder, J., Grimm, N. and Hoerova, M. (2021). "Do Non-Banks Need Access to the Lender of Last Resort? Evidence from Fund Runs (November 15, 2020)." Proceedings of Paris December 2021 Finance Meeting EUROFIDAI – ESSEC, SSRN: https://ssrn.com/abstract=3843356.

Breslau, D. (1997a). "Contract Shop Epistemology: Credibility and Problem Construction in Applied Social Science," *Social Studies of Science*, 27(3): 363–394.

Breslau, D. (1997b). "The Political Power of Research Methods: Knowledge Regimes in US Labor-Market Policy," *Theory and Society*, 26(6): 869–902.

Breslau, D. (2003). "Economics Invents the Economy: Mathematics, Statistics, and Models in the Work of Irving Fisher and Wesley Mitchell," *Theory and Society*, 32(3): 379–411.

Breslau, D. and Yonay, Y. (1999). "Beyond Metaphor: Mathematical Models in Economics As Empirical Research," *Science in Context*, 12(2): 317–332.

Brigo, D., Garcia, J. and Pede, N. (2015). "CoCo Bonds Pricing with Credit and Equity Calibrated First-Passage Firm Value Models," *International Journal of Theoretical and Applied Finance*, 18(3): 1550015.

Brimmer, A. F. (1989). "Distinguished Lecture on Economics in Government: Central Banking and Systemic Risks in Capital Markets," *Journal of Economic Perspectives*, 3(2): 3–16.

Brownlees, C. and Engle, R. F. (2017). "SRISK: A Conditional Capital Shortfall Measure of Systemic Risk," *Review of Financial Studies*, 30(1): 48–79.

Brunnermeier, M. K. (2009). "Deciphering the Liquidity and Credit Crunch 2007-2008," *Journal of Economic Perspectives*, 23(1): 77–100.

Brunnermeier, M. K. and Pedersen, L. H. (2009). "Market Liquidity and Funding Liquidity," *Review of Financial Studies*, 22(6): 2201–2238.

Brunnermeier, M. K. and Sannikov, Y. (2014). "A Macroeconomic Model with a Financial Sector," *American Economic Review*, 104(2): 379–421.

Brunnermeier, M., Crockett, A., Goodhart, C. A. E. et al. (2009). "The Fundamental Principles of Financial Regulation." ICMB, International Center for Monetary and Banking Studies.

Budnik, K. B. and Kleibl, J. (2018). "Macroprudential Regulation in the European Union in 1995–2014: Introducing a New Data Set on Policy Actions of a Macroprudential Nature." ECB Working Paper 2123.

Budnik, K., Dimitrov, I., Gross, K. et al. (2021). "Policies in Support of Lending Following the Coronavirus (COVID-19) Pandemic." ECB Occasional Paper Series 257.

Burchell, G., Davidson, A. and Foucault, M. (2010). *The Birth of Biopolitics: Lectures at the Collège de France, 1978–1979*. New York: Palgrave Macmillan.

Busuioc, M. and Lodge, M. (2017). "Reputation and Accountability Relationships: Managing Accountability Expectations through Reputation," *Public Administration Review*, 77(1): 91–100.

Calem, P., Correa, R. and Lee, S.-J. (2017). "Federal Prudential Policies and Their Impact on Credit in the United States." BIS Working Papers No. 635.

Callon, M. (1986). "Some Elements of a Sociology of Translation: Domestication of the Scallops and the Fishermen of St Brieuc Bay," in J. Law (ed.), *Power, Action and Belief: A New Sociology of Knowledge?*, pp. 196–233. London: Routledge.

Callon, M. (1998a). "An Essay on Framing and Overflowing: Economic Externalities Revisited by Sociology," in M. Callon (ed.), *The Laws of the Market*, pp. 244–269. Oxford: Blackwell.

Callon, M. (1998b). "Introduction: The Embeddedness of Economic Markets in Economics," in M. Callon (ed.), *The Laws of the Market*, pp. 1–57. Oxford: Blackwell.

Callon, M. (ed.). (1998c). *The Laws of the Market*. Oxford: Blackwell.

Callon, M. (2007). "What Does It Mean to Say That Economics Is Performative?" in M. F. MacKenzie and L. Siu (eds.), *Do Economists Make Markets? On the Performativity of Economics*, pp. 311–357. Princeton, NJ: Princeton University Press.

Callon, M. (2009). *Acting in an Uncertain World: An Essay on Technical Democracy*. Cambridge, MA: MIT Press.

Callon, M., Millo, Y. and Muniesa, F. (eds.). (2007). *Market Devices*. Oxford: Blackwell Publishing.

Calomiris, C. W. and Gorton, G. (1991). "The Origins of Banking Panics: Models, Facts, and Bank Regulation," in R. G. Hubbard (ed.), *Financial Markets and Financial Crises*, pp. 109–174. Chicago, IL: University of Chicago Press.

Camic, C., Gross N. and Lamont, M. (eds.). (2011). *Social Knowledge in the Making*. Chicago, IL: Chicago University Press.

Campbell, J. L. (1998). "Institutional Analysis and the Role of Ideas in Political Economy," *Theory and Society*, 27(3): 377–409.

Campbell, J. L. and Pedersen, O. K. (eds.). (2001). *The Rise of Neoliberalism and Institutional Analysis*. Princeton, NJ: Princeton University Press.

Campbell, J. and Pedersen, O. K. (2014). *The National Origins of Policy Ideas*. Princeton, NJ: Princeton University Press.

Carney, M. (2013). "The UK at the Heart of a Renewed Globalisation." Speech given at an event to celebrate the 125th anniversary of the *Financial Times*, London.

Carney, M. (2015). "Building Real Markets for the Good of the People." Speech given at the Lord Mayor's Banquet for Bankers and Merchants of the City of London at the Mansion House, London.

Carney, M. (2019.) "Pull, Push, Pipes: Sustainable Capital Flows for a New World Order." Speech given at the Institute of International Finance Spring Membership Meeting, Tokyo, June 6.

Carpenter, D. (2014). *Reputation and Power: Organizational Image and Pharmaceutical Regulation at the FDA*. Princeton, NJ: Princeton University Press.

Carruthers, B. (1996). *City of Capital: Politics and Markets in the English Financial Revolution*. Princeton, NJ: Princeton University Press.

Carruthers, B. G. and Babb, S. (1996). "The Color of Money and the Nature of Value: Greenbacks and Gold in Postbellum America," *American Journal of Sociology*, 101(6): 1556–1591.

Carruthers, B. G. and Ariovich, L. (2010). *Money and Credit: A Sociological Approach*. Cambridge: Polity Press.

Carstensen, M. B. (2011). "Paradigm Man vs. the Bricoleur: Bricolage As an Alternative Vision of Agency in Ideational Change," *European Political Science Review*, 3(1): 147–167.

Carstensen, M. B. and Schmidt, V. A. (2016). "Power through, over and in Ideas: Conceptualizing Ideational Power in Discursive Institutionalism," *Journal of European Public Policy*, 23(3): 318–337.

Casey, T. (2015). "How Macroprudential Financial Regulation Can Save Neoliberalism," *The British Journal of Politics and International Relations*, 17(2): 351–370.

Cecchetti, S. G. and Tucker, P. (2015). "Is There Macroprudential Policy without International Cooperation?" Paper prepared for the 2015 biennial Asia Economic Policy Conference (AEPC) on Policy Challenges in a Diverging Global Economy at the Federal Reserve Bank of San Francisco on November 19–20.

Cerutti, E., Claessens, S. and Laeven, L. (2017). "The Use and Effectiveness of Macroprudential Policies: New Evidence," *Journal of Financial Stability*, 28: 203–224.

Chan, S. P. and Wallace, T. (2015). "Bank of England Warns Buy-to-Let Is the Next Big Threat to UK Financial Stability." *Telegraph*, September 25. www.telegraph.co.uk/finance/bank-of-england/11890392/Buy-to-Let-economic-stability-Carney-Bank-of-England.html.

Chang, J., Gerrish S. Wang, C., Boyd-Graber, J. L. and Blei, D. M. (2009). "Reading Tea Leaves: How Humans Interpret Topic Models," *Advances in Neural Information Processing Systems*, 22: 288–296.

Christensen, J. (2017). *The Power of Economists within the State*. Stanford, CA: Stanford University Press.

Christensen, T. and Laegreid, P. (eds.). (2006). *Autonomy and Regulation*. Northampton, MA: Edward Elgar.

Christensen, T. and Laegreid, P. (eds.). (2011). *The Ashgate Research Companion to New Public Management*. Farnham: Ashgate.

Christophers, B. (2011). "Making Finance Productive," *Economy and Society*, 40(1): 112–140.

Christophers, B. (2013). *Banking across Boundaries: Placing Finance in Capitalism*. Oxford: John Wiley and Sons.

Chwieroth, J. M. (2010). *Capital Ideas: The IMF and the Rise of Financial Liberalization*. Princeton, NJ: Princeton University Press.

Cipriani, M., Antoine, M., McCabe, P. and Parigi, B. M. (2014). "Gates, Fees, and Preemptive Runs." Federal Reserve Bank of New York Staff Reports.

Claessens, S. and Kodres, M. L. E. (2014). "The Regulatory Responses to the Global Financial Crises: Some Uncomfortable Questions." IMF Working Paper No. 14/46.

Claessens, S. and Ratnovski, L. (2015). "What Is Shadow Banking?" IMF Working Paper No. 14/25.

Claessens, S. and Lewrick, U. (2021). "Open-Ended Bond Funds: Systemic Risks and Policy Implications." *BIS Quarterly Review*, December, pp. 37–51.

Clarida, R. H., Duygan-Bump, B. and Scotti, C. (2021). "The COVID-19 Crisis and the Federal Reserve's Policy Response," Finance and Economics Discussion Series 2021–035. Washington, DC: Board of Governors of the Federal Reserve System.

Clark, K., Martin, A. and Wessel, T. (2020). "The Federal Reserve's Large-Scale Repo Program," *Liberty Street Economics*, August 3.

Clark, W. (2014). "Creating the Financial Stability Forum: What Role for Existing Institutions?" *Global Society*, 28(2): 195–216.

Claveau, F. and Dion, J. (2018). "Quantifying Central Banks' Scientization: Why and How to Do a Quantified Organizational History of Economics," *Journal of Economic Methodology*, 25(4): 349–366.

Clement, P. (2010). "The Term 'Macroprudential': Origins and Evolution," *BIS Quarterly Review*, March, pp. 59–68.

Clerc, L., Derviz, A., Mendicino, C. et al. (2015). "Capital Regulation in a Macroeconomic Model with Three Layers of Default." ECB Working Paper Series No. 1827/July.

Clift, B. (2018). *The IMF and the Politics of Austerity in the Wake of the Global Financial Crisis*. Oxford: Oxford University Press.

Clift, B. (2019). "Contingent Keynesianism: The IMF's Model Answer to the Post-Crash Fiscal Policy Efficacy Question in Advanced Economies." *Review of International Political Economy*, 26(6).

Coeuré, B. (2012). "Collateral Scarcity: A Gone or a Going Concern?" Speech at the ECB-DNB Joint central bank seminar on collateral and liquidity, Amsterdam, October 1.

Coeuré, B. (2013). "Ensuring the Smooth Functioning of Money Markets." Speech at the 17th Global Securities Financing Summit, Luxembourg.

Coeuré, B. (2017). "Asset Purchases, Financial Regulation and Repo Market Activity." Speech at the ERCC General Meeting on "The Repo Market: Market Conditions and Operational Challenges." Brussels, November 14.

Coffee, J. (2003). "Gatekeeper Failure and Reform: The Challenge of Fashioning Relevant Reforms." Columbia Law and Economics Working Paper No. 237.

Coffey, A. (2014). "Analysing Documents," in *The SAGE Handbook of Qualitative Data Analysis*, pp. 367–380. London: Sage.

Cohan, W. D. (2017). "In Farewell, Daniel Tarullo Offers Fixes on Bank Regulation," *New York Times*, April 14.

Colander, D. (2004). "From Muddling through to the Economics of Control: View of Applied Policy from J. N. Keynes to Abba Lerne." Middlebury College Economics Discussion Paper No. 04–21.

Committee on Financial Services. (2009). "Systemic Regulation, Prudential Matters, Resolution Authority, and Securitization." Hearing before the Committee on Financial Services/US House of Representatives One Hundred Eleventh Congress First Session, October 29.

Committee on the Global Financial System (CGFS). (1986). "Recent Innovations in International Banking."

Committee on the Global Financial System (CGFS). (1992). "Recent Developments in International Interbank Relations" (Promisel Report).

Committee on the Global Financial System (CGFS). (1994a). "A Discussion Paper on Public Disclosure of Market and Credit Risks by Financial Intermediaries" (Fisher Report). CGFS Paper Number 3.

Committee on the Global Financial System (CGFS). (1994b). "Macroeconomic and Monetary Policy Issues Raised by the Growth of Derivatives Markets" (Hannoun Report). CGFS Paper Number 4.

Committee on the Global Financial System (CGFS). (1995). "Issues of Measurement Related to Market Size and Macroprudential Risks in Derivatives Markets" (Brockmeijer Report). CGFS Paper Number 5.

Committee on the Global Financial System (CGFS). (2003). "Credit Risk Transfer." CGFS Paper 20.

Committee on the Global Financial System (CGFS). (2006). "Housing Finance in the Global Financial Market." CGFS Paper 26.

Committee on the Global Financial System (CGFS). (2009). "The Role of Valuation and Leverage in Procyclicality." CGFS Papers No. 34.

Committee on the Global Financial System (CGFS). (2010a). "The Role of Margin Requirements and Haircuts in Procyclicality." CGFS Paper 36. March.

Committee on the Global Financial System (CGFS). (2010b). "Macroprudential Instruments and Frameworks: A Stocktaking of Issues and Experiences." CGFS Paper 38. May.

Committee for the Global Financial System (CGFS). (2011). "Central Bank Governance and Financial Stability."

Committee on the Global Financial System (CGFS). (2017). "Repo Market Functioning." CGFS Papers No. 59.

Commotto, R. (2012). "Repo: Guilty Notwithstanding the Evidence?" International Capital Market Association. www.icmagroup.org/assets/do cuments/Maket-Practice/Regulatory-Policy/Repo-Markets/Comotto–rep o-haircuts-April-2.pdf.

Constâncio, V. (2010). "Macro-Prudential Supervision in Europe." Speech at the ECB-CFS-CEPR conference on "Macro-Prudential Regulation As an Approach to Containing Systemic Risk: Economic Foundations, Diagnostic Tools and Policy Instruments" at Frankfurt, September 27.

Constâncio, V. (2012a). "How Can Macro-Prudential Regulation Be Effective?" CFS Colloquium "Mission Completed? Consequences of Regulatory Change on the Financial Industry," Frankfurt.

Constâncio, V. (2012b). "Shadow Banking: The ECB Perspective." Speech given at the European Commission Conference, Brussels.

Constâncio, V. (2014a). "Making Macro-Prudential Policy Work." Speech given at high-level seminar organized by De Nederlandsche Bank.

Constâncio, V. (2014b). "The ECB and Macro-Prudential Policy: From Research to Implementation." Speech given at the Third Conference of the Macro-Prudential Research Network, Frankfurt.

Constâncio, V. (2014c). "Where to from Here?" Remarks at the Federal Reserve Bank of Chicago 17th Annual International Banking Conference, Chicago, IL.

Constâncio, V. (2015). "Financial Stability Risks, Monetary Policy and the Need for Macro-Prudential Policy." Speech at the Warwick Economics Summit, February 13.

Constâncio, V. (2016a). "Capital Markets Union and the European Monetary and Financial Framework." Keynote speech at Chatham House, London, March 21.

Constâncio, V. (2016b). "Margins and Haircuts As a Macroprudential Tool." Remarks at the ESRB international conference, Frankfurt.

Constâncio, V. (2016c). "Principles of Macroprudential Policy." Speech given at the ECB-IMF Conference on Macroprudential Policy, Frankfurt.

Constâncio, V. (2018). "Completing the Odyssean Journey of the European Monetary Union." Remarks at the European Central Bank Colloquium on "The Future of Central Banking," Frankfurt, May 16–17.

Constâncio V. (ed.), I. Cabral, C. Detken et al. (2019). "Macroprudential Policy at the ECB: Institutional Framework, Strategy, Analytical Tools and Policies." ECB Occasional Paper Series 227.

Conti-Brown, P. (2017). *The Power and Independence of the Federal Reserve*. Princeton, NJ: Princeton University Press.

Cook, R. (2011). "Testimony on the Financial Stability Oversight Council before the United States House of Representatives Committee on Financial Services Subcommittee on Oversight and Investigations." Thursday, April 14. www.sec.gov/news/testimony/2011/ts041411rc.htm#P42_11669.

Coombs, N. (2020). "What do Stress Tests Test? Experimentation, Demonstration and the Sociotechnical Performance of Regulatory Science," *The British Journal of Sociology*, 71(3): 520–536.

Coombs, N. (2022). "Narrating Imagined Crises: How Central Bank Storytelling Exerts Infrastructural Power," *Economy and Society*, 51(4): 679–702.

Coombs, N. and Thiemann, M. (2022). "Recentering Central Banks: Theorizing State-Economy Boundaries as Central Bank Effects," *Economy and Society*, 51(4): 535–558.

Council Regulation (EU) No. 1096/2010 of 17 November 2010 conferring specific tasks on the European Central Bank concerning the functioning of the European Systemic Risk Board (OJ L 331, 15.12.2010, p. 162).

Council Regulation (EU) No 1024/2013 of 15 October 2013 conferring specific tasks on the European Central Bank concerning policies relating to the prudential supervision of credit institutions.

Cozzi, G., Newman, S. and Toporowski, J. (eds.). (2016c). *Finance and Industrial Policy*. Oxford: Oxford University Press.

Crockett, A. (2000). "Marrying the Micro- and Macro-Prudential Dimensions of Financial Stability." BIS Review 76/2000.

Crockett, A. (2002). *Introductory Remarks at the 3rd Triannual Conference on Risk Measurement and Systemic Risk*. Basel: Bank for International Settlements.

Crombie, A. C. (1994). *Styles of Scientific Thinking in the European Tradition*. 3 vols. London: Duckworth.

Cunliffe, J. (2015). "The Outlook for Countercyclical Macroprudential Policy." Speech by Sir Jon Cunliffe, deputy governor for financial stability of the Bank of England, at The Graduate Institute, Geneva.

Cunliffe, J. (2020). "The Impact of Leveraged Investors on Market Liquidity and Financial Stability." Speech given at the Managed Funds Association Global Summit 2020, November 12. www.bis.org/review/r201117g.pdf.

Cunliffe, J. (2022). "Learning from the Dash for Cash: Findings and Next Steps for Margining Practices." Keynote address at the FIA and SIFMA Asset Management Derivatives Forum 2022, February 9.

Czech, R., Gual-Ricart, B., Lillis, J. and Worlidge, J. (2021). "The Role of Non-bank Financial Intermediaries in the 'Dash for Cash' in Sterling Markets." Bank of England Financial Stability Paper No. 47.

Danielsson, I. (2000). "The Emperor Has No Clothes: Limits to Risk Modelling." LSE Financial Markets Group Special Papers.

Danielsson, J. (2013). *Global Financial Systems: Stability and Risk*. Harlow: Pearson.

Danielsson, J., Shin, H. S. and Zigrand, J.-P. (2012). "Endogenous and Systemic Risk." NBER Chapters No. 12054.

Danielsson, J., Embrechts, P., Goodhart, C. et al. (2001). "An Academic Response to Basel II." Special Paper-LSE Financial Markets Group.

Debnath, A. and Harris A. (2016). "ECB Bond Lending to Spur Liquidity But May Not Ease Repo Squeeze." *Bloomberg*.

Debrun, X., Ferrero, G., Masuch, K. et al. (2021). "Monetary-Fiscal Policy Interactions in the Euro Area." ECB Occasional Paper Series ECB Strategy Review.

De Goede, M. (2001). *Virtue, Fortune and Faith: A Genealogy of Finance*. Minnesota: Minnesota University Press.

De Goede, M. (2004). "Repoliticizing Financial Risk," *Economy and Society*, 33(2): 197–217.

De Larosiere, J., Balcerowicz, L., Issing, O. et al. (2009). *The High Level Group on Financial Supervision in the EU Report.* Brussels: European Commission.

Demirguec-Kunt, A. and Detragiache, E. (1998a). "The Determinants of Banking Crises in Developing and Developed Countries: IMF Staff Papers," *IMF Staff Papers*, 45(1): 29.

Demirguec-Kunt, A. and Detragiache, E. (1998b). "Financial Liberalization and Financial Fragility." Annual World Bank Conference Development Economics.

Desrosières, A. (2003). "Managing the Economy," *The Cambridge History of Science*, 7: 553–564.

Desrosières, A. (2015). "Retroaction: How Indicators Feed Back onto Quantified Actors," in R. Rottenburg, S. E. Merry, S.-J. Park and J. Mugler (eds.), *A World of Indicators: The Making of Governmental Knowledge through Quantification*, pp. 329–353. Cambridge: Cambridge University Press.

Detken, C., Weeken, O., Alessi, L. et al. (2014). "Operationalising the Countercyclical Capital Buffer: Indicator Selection, Threshold Identification and Calibration." ESRB Occasional Paper Series No. 5.

Deutsche Bundesbank. (2013a). "Macroprudential Oversight in Germany: Framework, Institutions and Tools." Monthly Report April.

Deutsche Bundesbank. (2013b). "Monatsbericht Dezember 2013." www .bundesbank.de/Redaktion/DE/Downloads/Veroeffentlichungen/Monats berichte/2013/2013_12_monatsbericht.pdf?__blob=publicationFile.

Deutsche Bundesbank. (2014). "Financial Stability Review 2014." www .bundesbank.de/en/tasks/topics/financial-stability-review-2014-666622.

Deutsche Bundesbank. (2015). "Financial Stability Review 2015." www .bundesbank.de/en/tasks/topics/financial-stability-review-2015-666976.

Deutsche Bundesbank. (2016). "Financial Stability Review 2016." www .bundesbank.de/en/publications/reports/financial-stability-reviews/finan cial-stability-review-2016-667246.

Deutsche Bundesbank. (2017). "Financial Stability Review 2017." www .bundesbank.de/en/publications/reports/financial-stability-reviews/finan cial-stability-review-2017-667536.

Deutsche Bundesbank. (2018a). "Monthly Report Bundesbank 02/2018."

Deutsche Bundesbank. (2018b). "Financial Stability Review 2018." www .bundesbank.de/en/publications/reports/financial-stability-reviews/finan cial-stability-review-2018-766586.

Deutsche Bundesbank. (2019). "Financial Stability Review 2019." www .bundesbank.de/en/publications/reports/financial-stability-reviews/finan cial-stability-review-2019-814946.

Dewatripont, M. and Tirole, J. (1994). *The Prudential Regulation of Banks.* Cambridge: MIT Press.

Diamond, D. W. and Dybvig, P. H. (1983). "Bank Runs, Deposit Insurance, and Liquidity," *Journal of Political Economy*, 91(3): 401–419.

Diessner, S. and Lisi, G. (2020). "Masters of the 'Masters of the Universe'? Monetary, Fiscal and Financial Dominance in the Eurozone," *Socio-Economic Review*, 18(2): 315–335.

Dietsch, P., Claveau, F. and Fontan, C. (2018). *Do Central Banks Serve the People?* Cambridge: Polity Press.

DiMaggio, P., Nag, M. and Blei, D. (2013). "Exploiting Affinities between Topic Modeling and the Sociological Perspective on Culture: Application to Newspaper Coverage of US Government Arts Funding," *Poetics*, 41(6): 570–606.

Dombret, A. and Tucker, P. (2012). "Blueprint for Resolving Regulation," *Financial Times*, May 20.

Dow, S. C. (2014). "The Relationship between Central Banks and Governments: What Are Central Banks For?" in C. Goodhart, D. Gabor, J. Vestergaard and I. Ertürk (eds.), *Central Banking at a Crossroads: Europe and Beyond*, pp. 229–244. London: Anthem Press.

Drehmann, M. and Juselius, M. (2014). "Evaluating Early Warning Indicators of Banking Crises: Satisfying Policy Requirements," *International Journal of Forecasting*, 30(3): 759–780.

Drehmann, M. and Tsatsaronis, K. (2014). "The Credit-to-GDP Gap and Countercyclical Capital Buffers: Questions and Answers." *BIS Quarterly Review*, Bank for International Settlements, March.

Drehmann, M., Borio, C. and Tsatsaronis, K. (2011). "Anchoring Countercyclical Capital Buffers: The Role of Credit Aggregates," *International Journal of Central Banking, International Journal of Central Banking*, 7(4): 189–240.

Drehmann, M., Borio, C., Gambacorta, L., Jiminez, G. and Trucharte, C. (2010). "Countercyclical Capital Buffers: Exploring Options." BIS Working Papers, No. 317, www.bis.org/publ/work317.pdf.

Dudley, W. C. (2016). "Market and Funding Liquidity: An Overview." Remarks at the Federal Reserve Bank of Atlanta 2016 Financial Markets Conference, Fernandina Beach, Florida.

Duffie, D. (2018). "Financial Regulatory Reform after the Crisis: An Assessment," *Management Science*, 64(10): 4835–4857.

Duffie, D. (2020). "Still the World's Safe Haven? Redesigning the U.S. Treasury Market after the Covid19 Crisis." Hutchins Working Paper 62.

Dyson, K. and Featherstone, K. (1999). *The Road to Maastricht: Negotiating Economic and Monetary Union.* Oxford: Oxford University Press.

Dyson, K. and Marcussen, M. (eds.). (2009). *Central Banks in the Age of the Euro-Europeanization, Convergence and Power.* Oxford: Oxford University Press.

Edge, R. M. and Meisenzahl, R. R. (2011). "The Unreliability of Credit-to-GDP Ratio Gaps in Real Time: Implications for Countercyclical Capital Buffers," *Journal of International Central Banking*, 7(4): 261–298.

Edge, R. M. and Liang, N. (2017). "New Financial Stability Governance Structures and Central Banks." Hutchins Center Working Paper No. 32.

Edge, R. M. and Liang, J. N. (2020). "Financial Stability Committees and Basel III Macroprudential Capital Buffers." Finance and Economics Discussion Series No. 2020-016, Washington, DC: Board of Governors of the Federal Reserve System, https://doi.org/10.17016/FEDS.2020.016.

Eichengreen, B. (2014). *Hall of Mirrors: The Great Depression, the Great Recession, and the Uses and Misuses of History.* Oxford: Oxford University Press.

Ekholm, K. (2014). "What Should Be the Ambition Level of Macroprudential Policy?" in A. Houben, R. Nijskens and M. Teunissen (eds.), *Putting Macro-Prudential Policy to Work.* De Nederlandsche Bank, Occasional Studies vol. 12.

Elliott, D. J., Feldberg, G. and Lehnert, A. (2013). "The History of Cyclical Macroprudential Policy in the United States," Office of Financial Research Working Paper No. 8. Washington, DC: US Department of the Treasury.

EMIR (European Market Infrastructure Regulation). (2012). Regulation (EU) No 648/2012 of the European Parliament and the Council of 4 July 2012 on OTC derivatives, central counterparties and trade repositories.

Endrejat, V. and Thiemann, M. (2018). "Reviving the Shadow Banking Chain in Europe: Regulatory Agency, Technical Complexity and the Dynamics of Co-habitation." Research Center SAFE Working Paper.

Endrejat, V. and Thiemann, M. (2019). "Balancing Market Liquidity: Bank Structural Reform Caught between growth and stability," *Journal of Economic Policy Reform*, 22(3): 226–241.

Endrejat, V. and Thiemann, M. (2020). "When Brussels Meets Shadow Banking: Technical Complexity, Regulatory Agency and the Reconstruction of the Shadow Banking Chain," *Competition & Change*, 24(3–4): 225–247.

Esposito, E. (2011). *The Future of Futures: The Time of Money in Financing and Society.* London: Edward Elgar Publishing.

Euromoney. (2013). "Hangover from Banks' Use of Short-Term Funding Refuses to Go Away."

European Central Bank (ECB). (2007). "Risk Measurement and Systemic Risk." Report from the Fourth Joint Central Bank Research Conference

8–9 November 2005 in Cooperation with the Committee on the Global Financial System. Frankfurt.

European Central Bank (ECB). (2014). "ESCB Heads of Research Report on the Macro-prudential Research Network (MARS)." Frankfurt. www .ecb.europa.eu/pub/pdf/other/macroprudentialresearchnetworkrepor t201406en.pdf.

European Central Bank (ECB). (2015a). "Financial Stability Review, May 2015." Frankfurt: ECB Press.

European Central Bank (ECB). (2015b). "Euro Money Market Survey, September 2015." Frankfurt: ECB Press.

European Central Bank (ECB). (2016a). "Macroprudential Bulletin Issue 1/ 2016." www.ecb.europa.eu/pub/pdf/other/ecbmpbu201603.en.pdf.

European Central Bank (ECB). (2016b). "Financial Stability Review, May 2016." Frankfurt: ECB Press.

European Central Bank (ECB). (2016c). "Financial Stability Review, November 2016." Frankfurt: ECB Press.

European Central Bank (ECB). (2017a). "Financial Stability Review, May 2017." Frankfurt: ECB Press.

European Central Bank (ECB). (2017b). "Financial Stability Review, November 2017." Frankfurt: ECB Press.

European Central Bank (ECB). (2018). "Financial Stability Review, November 2018." Frankfurt: ECB Press.

European Central Bank (ECB). (2019). "Financial Stability Review, November 2019." Frankfurt: ECB Press.

European Central Bank (ECB). (2020). "Financial Stability Review, May 2020." Frankfurt: ECB Press.

European Central Bank. (2021). "Financial Stability Review, November 2021." www.ecb.europa.eu/pub/pdf/fsr/ecb.fsr202111~8b0aebc817.en.pdf.

European Commission. (2011). "Proposal for a Directive of the European Parliament and of the Council on the access to the activity of credit institutions and the prudential supervision of credit institutions and investment firms and amending Directive 2002/87/EC of the European Parliament and of the Council on the supplementary supervision of credit institutions, insurance undertakings and investment firms in a financial conglomerate." www.europarl.europa.eu/RegData/docs_autres_institutions/ commission_europeenne/com/2011/0453/COM_COM(2011)0453_EN.pdf.

European Commission. (2021). "Proposal for a Directive of the European Parliament and of the Council amending Directives 2011/61/EU and 2009/65/EC as regards delegation arrangements, liquidity risk management, supervisory reporting, provision of depositary and custody services and loan origination by alternative investment funds." Brussels, November 25.

European Securities Market Authority (ESMA). (2020a). "ESMA Launches a Common Supervisory Action with NCAS on UCITS Liquidity Risk Management." www.esma.europa.eu/press-news/esma-news/esma-launc hes-common-supervisory-action-ncas-ucits-liquidity-risk-management.

European Securities Market Authority (ESMA). (2020b). "Letter to the European Commission Regarding the Review of the Alternative Investment Fund Managers Directive." August 18. www.esma.europa.e u/sites/default/files/library/esma34-32-551_esma_letter_on_aifmd_review .pdf.

European Securities Market Authority (ESMA). (2020c). "Report on the Recommendation of the European Systemic Risk Board (ESRB) on Liquidity Risk in Investment Funds." November 12. www.esma.europa .eu/sites/default/files/library/esma34-39-1119-report_on_the_esrb_recom mendation_on_liquidity_risks_in_funds.pdf.

European Securities Market Authority (ESMA). (2020c). "Report on the Recommendation of the European Systemic Risk Board (ESRB) on Liquidity Risk in Investment Funds." November 12. www.esma.europa .eu/sites/default/files/library/esma34-39-1119-report_on_the_esrb_recom mendation_on_liquidity_risks_in_funds.pdf.

European Securities Market Authority (ESMA). (2020d). "EU Alternative Investment Funds ESMA Annual Statistical Report." www.esma.europa .eu/sites/default/files/library/esma50-165-1734_asr_aif_2021.pdf.

European Securities Market Authority (ESMA). (2021). "Guidelines on Article 25 of Directive 2011/61/EU." www.esma.europa.eu/sites/default/ files/library/esma34-32-701_guidelines_on_article_25_aifmd.pdf.

European Systemic Risk Board (ESRB). (2012). "Advices of the European Systemic Risk Board of 31 July 2012, C268/13 on EMIR."

European Systemic Risk Board (ESRB). (2013). "Recommendations of the European Systemic Risk Board of April 2013 on Intermediate Objectives and Instruments of Macro-Prudential Policy." ESRB/ 2013/1.

European Systemic Risk Board (ESRB). (2014). "Flagship Report on Macro-Prudential Policy in the Banking Sector."

European Systemic Risk Board (ESRB). (2015). "Report on the Efficiency of Margining Requirements to Limit Pro-cyclicality and the Need to Define Additional Intervention Capacity in This Area."

European Systemic Risk Board (ESRB). (2016a). "Macroprudential Policy beyond Banking: An ESRB Strategy Paper." www.esrb.europa.eu/pub/pd f/reports/20160718_strategy_paper_beyond_banking.en.pdf.

European Systemic Risk Board (ESRB). (2016b). "Shadow Banking Monitor." www.esrb.europa.eu/pub/pdf/reports/nbfi_monitor/20160727_shadow_ban king_report.en.pdf?0855f207ed48eb36954071e2b8740195.

European Systemic Risk Board (ESRB). (2016c). "Market Liquidity and Market-Making." October.

European Systemic Risk Board (ESRB). (2016d). *Vulnerabilities in the EU Residential Real Estate Sector*. Frankfurt: ESRB Press, November.

European Systemic Risk Board (ESRB). (2016e). "The ESRB Issues Eight Warnings on Medium-Term Residential Real Estate Vulnerabilities and a Recommendation on Closing Real Estate Data Gaps." www .esrb.europa.eu/news/pr/date/2016/html/pr161128.en.html.

European Systemic Risk Board (ESRB). (2016f). "Warning of the European Systemic Risk Board of 22nd of September 2016 on Medium Term Vulnerabilities in the Residential Real Estate Sector of the United Kingdom." www.esrb.europa.eu/pub/pdf/warnings/2016/161128_ESR B_UK_warning.en.pdf?62da3406e05239bb957357388c9b4ac8.

European Systemic Risk Board (ESRB). (2018). "Recommendation of the European Systemic Risk Board of 7 December 2017 on Liquidity and Leverage Risks in Investment Funds." ESRB/2017/6, 2018/C 151/01.

European Systemic Risk Board (ESRB). (2019a). "Features of a Macroprudential Stance: Initial Considerations." April.

European Systemic Risk Board (ESRB). (2019b). "A Review of Macroprudential Policy in the EU in 2018." www.esrb.europa.eu/pub/pdf/ reports/review_macroprudential_policy/esrb.report190430_reviewofmacro prudentialpolicy~32aae4bd95.en.pdf?0b21e4503cb0a97287bf4a5 397dec754.

European Systemic Risk Board (ESRB). (2019c). "ESRB Annual Report 2018." www.esrb.europa.eu/pub/pdf/ar/2019/esrb.ar2018~d69ff774ac.en.pdf.

European Systemic Risk Board (ESRB). (2019d). "Warning of the European Systemic Risk Board of 27 June 2019 on Medium-Term Vulnerabilities in the Residential Real Estate Sector in Germany." www.esrb.europa.eu/pub/ pdf/warnings/esrb.warning190923_de_warning~6e31e93446.en.pdf.

European Systemic Risk Board (ESRB). (2019e). "Vulnerabilities in the Residential Real Estate Sectors of the EEA countries." September. www .esrb.europa.eu/pub/pdf/reports/esrb.report190923_vulnerabilities_eea_ countries~a4864b42bf.en.pdf.

European Systemic Risk Board (ESRB). (2019f). "Follow-Up Report on Countries That Received ESRB Warnings in 2016 on Medium Medium-Term Vulnerabilities in the Residential Real Estate Sector." http://bitly .ws/Kjf5.

European Systemic Risk Board (ESRB). (2020). "Recommendation on Liquidity Risks in Investment Funds." http://bitly.ws/Kjfn.

European Systemic Risk Board (ESRB). (2022a). "Compliance Report February 2022." www.esrb.europa.eu/pub/pdf/recommendations/esrb .Country-specific_Recommendations202201~816f54bbf7.en.pdf.

European Systemic Risk Board (ESRB). (2022b). "ESRB Issues New Warnings and Recommendations on Medium-Term Residential Real Estate Vulnerabilities." http://bitly.ws/KjfA.

Ewald, F. (1991). "Insurance and Risk," in G. Burchell, C. Gordon and P. Miller (eds.), *The Foucault Effect: Studies in Governmentality*, pp. 197–210. Chicago, IL: University of Chicago Press.

Eyal, G. and Buchholz, I. (2010). "From the Sociology of Intellectuals to the Sociology of Interventions," *Annual Review of Sociology*, 36(1): 117–137.

Eyal, G. and Pok, G. (2015). "What Is Security Expertise? From the Sociology of Professions to the Analysis of Networks of Expertise," in T. V. Berling and C. Bueger (eds.), *Security Expertise: Practice, Power, Responsibility*, pp. 37–59. London: Routledge.

Eyal, G. (2013). "The Spaces between Fields," in P. Gorski (ed.), *Bourdieusian Theory and Historical Analysis*, pp. 158–182. Durham, NC: Duke University Press.

Falato, A., Goldstein, I. and Hortaçsu, A. (2021). "Financial Fragility in the COVID-19 Crisis: The Case of Investment Funds in Corporate Bond Markets," *Journal of Monetary Economics*, 123: 35–52.

Fama, E. (1970), "Efficient Capital Markets: A Review of Theory and Empirical Work," *The Journal of Finance*, 25(2): 383–417.

Federal Reserve Bank of New York. (2015). "Reference Guide to U.S. Repo and Securities Lending Markets: Federal Reserve Bank of New York Staff Reports 2015."

Federal Reserve Board. (2005). "92nd Annual Report."

Federal Reserve Board. (2018). "Financial Stability Report November 2018." www.federalreserve.gov/publications/files/financial-stability-report-20201 109.pdf.

Federal Reserve Board. (2019). "Financial Stability Report November 2019." www.federalreserve.gov/publications/files/financial-stability-report-20191 115.pdf.

Federal Reserve Board. (2020). "Financial Stability Report November 2020." www.federalreserve.gov/publications/files/financial-stability-report-20201 109.pdf.

Federal Reserve Board. (2021). "Financial Stability Report November 2021." www.federalreserve.gov/publications/files/financial-stability-report-20211 108.pdf.

Federal Reserve System. (2013). "Policy Statement on the Scenario Design Framework for Stress Testing." www.federalreserve.gov/bankinforeg/bcr eg20131107a1.pdf.

Federal Reserve System. (2016). "12 CFR Part 217, Appendix A Docket No. R-1529; RIN 7100 AE-43. Regulatory Capital Rules: The Federal Reserve Board's Framework for Implementing the U.S. Basel III Countercyclical

Capital Buffer." www.federalreserve.gov/newsevents/pressreleases/files/b
creg20160908b1.pdf.
Financial Conduct Authority. (2019). "PS19/24: Illiquid Assets and Open-
Ended Funds and Feedback to Consultation Paper CP18/27." www
.fca.org.uk/publications/policy-statements/ps19-24-illiquid-assets-and-
open-ended-funds-and-feedback-consultation-paper-cp18-27.
Financial Conduct Authority. (2021). "A New Authorised Fund Regime for
Investing in Long Term Assets." Policy Statement PS21/October 14. www
.fca.org.uk/publication/policy/ps21-14.pdf.uk.
Financial Services Authority (FSA). (2009). "The Turner Review:
A Regulatory Response to the Global Banking Crisis."
Financial Stability Board (FSB). (2009). "Guidance to Assess the Systemic
Importance of Financial Institutions, Markets and Instruments: Initial
Considerations." Report to G20 finance ministers and governors.
Financial Stability Board (FSB). (2011a). "Shadow Banking: Scoping the
Issues." A Background Note of the Financial Stability Board.
Financial Stability Board (FSB). (2011b). "Shadow Banking: Strengthening
Oversight and Regulation." Recommendations of the Financial Stability
Board.
Financial Stability Board (FSB). (2012a). "Securities Lending and Repos:
Market Overview and Financial Stability Issues." Interim Report of the
FSB Workstream on Securities Lending and Repos.
Financial Stability Board (FSB). (2012b). "Consultative Document:
Strengthening Oversight and Regulation of Shadow Banking." A Policy
Framework for Addressing Shadow Banking Risks in Securities Lending
and Repos.
Financial Stability Board (FSB). (2013a). "Strengthening Oversight and
Regulation of Shadow Banking." Policy Framework for Addressing
Shadow Banking Risks in Securities Lending and Repos.
Financial Stability Board (FSB). (2013b). "Strengthening Oversight and
Regulation of Shadow Banking: An Overview of Policy Recommendation."
Financial Stability Board (FSB). (2014). "Progress Report on Transforming
Shadow Banking into Resilient Market-Based Financing."
Financial Stability Board (FSB). (2015a). "Transforming Shadow Banking
into Resilient Market-Based Finance." Regulatory framework for haircuts
on non-centrally cleared securities financing transactions.
Financial Stability Board (FSB). (2015b). "Transforming Shadow Banking
into Resilient Market-Based Finance: An Overview of Progress."
Financial Stability Board (FSB). (2016). "Transforming Shadow Banking
into Resilient Market-Based Finance: Possible Measures of Non-cash
Collateral Re-use."

Financial Stability Board (FSB). (2017). "Implementation and Effects of the G20 Financial Regulatory Reforms," 3rd Annual Report.

Financial Stability Board (FSB). (2020). "Holistic Review of the March Market Turmoil."

Financial Stability Board (FSB). (2021a). "Policy Proposals to Enhance Money Market Fund Resilience."

Financial Stability Board (FSB). (2021b). "Non-Bank Monitoring Report."

Financial Stability Board (FSB). (2022). "Global Monitoring Report on Non-Bank Financial Intermediation."

Financial Stability Forum (FSF). (2007). "Preliminary Report to the G7 Finance Ministers and Central Bank Governors." FSF Working Group on Market and Institutional Resilience, October 15. www.fsb.org/wp-content/uploads/r_0710a.pdf.

Financial Stability Forum (FSF). (2008). "Report of the Financial Stability Forum on Enhancing Market and Institutional Resilience." April.

Financial Stability Forum (FSF). (2009). "Report of the Financial Stability Forum on Addressing Procyclicality in the Financial System."

Financial Stability Oversight Council (FSOC). (2011). "Annual Report."

Financial Stability Oversight Council (FSOC). (2012). 12 CFR Part 1310 RIN 4030–AA00. Authority to Require Supervision and Regulation of Certain Nonbank Financial Companies. Federal Register, vol. 77, no. 70. Rules and Regulations, pp. 21637–21662. www.govinfo.gov/content/pkg/FR-2012-04-11/pdf/2012-8627.pdf.

Financial Stability Oversight Council (FSOC). (2013). "Annual Report."

Financial Stability Oversight Council (FSOC). (2014). "Notice Seeking Comment on Asset Management Products and Activities." https://home.treasury.gov/system/files/261/Notice-Seeking-Comment-on-Asset-Management-Products-and-Activities.pdf.

Financial Stability Oversight Council (FSOC). (2016). "Update on Review of Asset Management Products and Activities."

Financial Stability Oversight Council (FSOC). (2017). "Annual Report."

Financial Stability Oversight Council (FSOC). (2019). "Annual Report."

Financial Stability Oversight Council (FSOC). (2021). "Meeting Minutes 31st of March 2021." https://home.treasury.gov/system/files/261/FSOC_Minutes_6-11-21.pdf.

Financial Stability Oversight Council (FSOC). (2022). "Meeting Minutes February 2022." https://home.treasury.gov/system/files/261/February-4-2022-FSOC-Meeting-Minutes.pdf.

Finn, E. Kydland and Prescott, E. C. (1977). "Rules Rather Than Discretion: The Inconsistency of Optimal Plans," *Journal of Political Economy*, 85(3): 473–492.

Fischer, F., Torgerson, D., Durnová, A. et al. (eds.). (2015). *Handbook of Critical Policy Studies*. Cheltenham: Edward Elgar Publishing.

Fleck, L. (1935). *Entstehung und Entwicklung einer wissenschaftlichen Tatsache – Einführung in die Lehre vom Denkstil und Denkkollektiv*. Frankfurt: Suhrkamp.

Fligstein, N., Stuart Brundage, J. and Schultz, M. (2017). "Seeing Like the Fed: Culture, Cognition, and Framing in the Failure to Anticipate the Financial Crisis of 2008," *American Sociological Review*, 82(5): 879–909.

Fourcade, M. (2006). "The Construction of a Global Profession: The Transnationalization of Economics," *American Journal of Sociology*, 112(1): 145–194.

Fourcade, M. (2009). *Economists and Societies: Discipline and Profession in the United States, Britain, and France, 1890s to 1990s*. Princeton, NJ: Princeton University Press.

Fourcade, M., Ollion, E. and Algan, Y. (2015). "The Superiority of Economists," *Journal of Economic Perspectives*, 29(1): 89–114.

Fourcade-Gourinchas, M. (2001). "Politics, Institutional Structures, and the Rise of Economics: A Comparative Study," *Theory and Society*, 30(3): 397–447.

Fourcade-Gourinchas, M. and Babb, S. L. (2002). "The Rebirth of the Liberal Creed: Paths to Neoliberalism in Four Countries," *American Journal of Sociology*, 108(3): 533–579.

Freixas, X. and Rochet, J.-C. (2008). *Microeconomics of Banking*. Cambridge, MA: MIT Press.

Freixas, X., Parigi, B. M. and Rochet, J.-C. (2000). "Systemic Risk, Interbank Relations, and Liquidity Provision by the Central Bank," *Journal of Money, Credit and Banking*, 32(3): 611–638.

Frost, J., Logan, L., Martin, A. et al. (2015). "Overnight RRP Operations As a Monetary Policy Tool: Some Design Considerations." Finance and Economics Discussion Series 2015–010. Washington, DC: Board of Governors of the Federal Reserve System.

FSB, IMF and BIS. (2009a). "Report to G20 Finance Ministers and Governors Guidance to Assess the Systemic Importance of Financial Institutions, Markets and Instruments: Initial Considerations."

FSB, IMF and BIS. (2009b). "Report to G20 Finance Ministers and Governors Guidance to Assess the Systemic Importance of Financial Institutions, Markets and Instruments: Initial Considerations, Background Paper."

FSB, IMF and BIS. (2011). "Macroprudential Policy Tools and Frameworks: Update to G20 Finance Ministers and Central Bank Governors." Report. www.imf.org/external/np/g20/pdf/021411.pdf.

Funk, R. J. and Hirschman, D. (2014). "Derivatives and Deregulation: Financial Innovation and the Demise of Glass–Steagall," *Administrative Science Quarterly*, 59(4): 669–704.

G20. (2008). "Declaration of the Summit on Financial Markets and the World Economy." Washington, DC, November 15.

G20. (2009a). "London Summit – Leaders' Statement, 2 April 2009." www .imf.org/external/np/sec/pr/2009/pdf/g20_040209.pdf.

G20. (2009b). "Global Plan Annex: Declaration on Strengthening the Financial System, London, 2 April 2009." www.g20.utoronto.ca/2009/2 009ifi.html.

G20. (2009c). "G20 Leaders Statement: The Pittsburgh Summit." www .g20.utoronto.ca/2009/2009communique0925.html.

G20. (2010a). "The G20 Toronto Summit Declaration." www .g20.utoronto.ca/2010/to-communique.html.

G20. (2010b). "Declaration Seoul Meeting." www.g20.utoronto.ca/2010/g 20seoul.html.

Gabor, D. (2015). "The IMF's Rethink of Global Banks: Critical in Theory, Orthodox in Practice," *Governance*, 28(2): 199–218.

Gabor, D. (2016a). "A Step Too Far? The European Financial Transactions Tax on Shadow Banking," *Journal of European Public Policy*, 23(6): 925–945.

Gabor, D. (2016b). "The (Impossible) Repo Trinity: The Political Economy of Repo Markets," *Review of International Political Economy*, 23(6): 967–1000.

Gabor, D. (2016c). "Rethinking Financialization in European Banking," in G. Cozzi, S. Newman and J. Toporowski (eds.), *Finance and Industrial Policy*, pp. 81–100. Oxford: Oxford University Press.

Gabor, D. (2021). *Revolution without Revolutionaries: Interrogating the Return of Monetary Financing*. Berlin: Heinrich Böll Foundation.

Gabor, D. and Ban, C. (2016). "Banking on Bonds: The New Links between States and Markets," *JCMS: Journal of Common Market Studies*, 54(3): 617–635.

Gabor, D. and Vestergaard, J. (2016). "Towards a Theory of Shadow Money." Institute for New Economic Thinking, INET Working Paper.

Gai, P. and Kapadia, S. (2010). "Contagion in Financial Networks," *Proceedings of the Royal Society A: Mathematical, Physical and Engineering Sciences*, 466(2120): 2401–2423.

Galati, G. and Moessner, R. (2013). "Macroprudential Policy: A Literature Review," *Journal of Economic Surveys*, 27(5): 846–878.

Galhau, F. V. de. (2021). "Financial Stability at the Nexus of Monetary and Macroprudential Policies." *Financial Stability Review* 24 (March 2021), pp. 7–16.

Gallagher, K. P. (2016), *Ruling Capital: Emerging Markets and the Reregulation of Cross-Border Finance*. Ithaca, NY: Cornell University Press.

Gamble, A. (1994). *The Free Economy and the Strong State: The Politics of Thatcherism*. Basingstoke: Macmillan International Higher Education.

Geithner, T. (2014). *Stress-Test: Reflections on Financial Crises*. London: Random House Business Books.

Gensler, G. (2022). "Statement before the Financial Stability Oversight Council on Money Market Funds, Open-End Bond Funds, and Hedge Funds." www.sec.gov/news/statement/genseler-fsoc-statement-020422.

George, A. L., Bennett, A., Lynn-Jones, S. M. et al. (2005). *Case Studies and Theory Development in the Social Sciences*. Cambridge, MA: MIT Press.

Gerba, E. and Katsoulis, P. (2021). "The Repo Market under Basel III." Bank of England Working Paper No. 954.

Gerring, J. (2008). *Case Study Research: Principles and Practices*. Cambridge: Cambridge University Press.

Gertenbach, L. (2010). *Die Kultivierung des Marktes: Foucault und die Gouvernementalität des Neoliberalismus*. Berlin: Parodos Verlag.

Gieryn, T. F. (1983). "Boundary-Work and the Demarcation of Science from Non-Science: Strains and Interests in Professional Ideologies of Scientists," *American Sociological Review*, 48(6): 781–795.

Gieryn, T. F. (1995). "Boundaries of Science," in S. Jasanoff, G. E. Markle, J. C. Peterson and T. Pinch (eds.), *The Handbook of Science and Technology Studies*, pp. 393–443. Thousand Oaks, CA: Sage Publications.

Gieryn, T. (1999). *Cultural Boundaries of Science: Credibility on the Line*. Chicago, IL: University of Chicago Press.

Giese, J., Andersen, H., Bush, O., Castro, C., Farag, F. and Kapadia, S. (2014). "The Credit-to-GDP Gap and Complementary Indicators for Macroprudential Policy: Evidence from the UK," *International Journal of Finance Economics*, 19: 25–47.

Gigliobianco, A. and Giordano, C. (2012). "Does Economic Theory Matter in Shaping Banking Regulation? A Case-Study of Italy (1861–1936)," *Accounting, Economics, and Law*, 2(1).

Gilardi, F. (2006). *Delegation in the Regulatory State: Independent Regulatory Agencies in Western Europe*. Cheltenham: Edward Elgar Publishing.

Glasserman, P., Kang, C. and Kang, W. (2015). "Stress Scenario Selection by Empirical Likelihood," *Quantitative Finance*, 15(1): 25–41.

Global Investor. (2013) "Analysis: FSB Shifts Focus to Rehypothecation."

Goede, M. de (2004). "Repoliticizing Financial Risk," *Economy and Society*, 33(2): 197–217.

Goede, M. de (2005). *Virtue, Fortune, and Faith: A Genealogy of Finance.* Minneapolis: Minnesota University Press.

Golub, S., Kaya, A. and Reay, M. (2015). "What Were They Thinking? The Federal Reserve in the Run-Up to the 2008 Financial Crisis," *Review of International Political Economy*, 22(4): 657–692.

Goodhart, C. (2011). *The Basel Committee on Banking Supervision: A History of the Early Years 1974–1997.* Cambridge: Cambridge University Press.

Goodhart, C., Gabor, D., Vestergaard, J. et al. (eds.). (2014) *Central Banking at a Crossroads: Europe and Beyond.* London: Anthem Press.

Goodhart, C., Hartmann, P., Llewellyn, D. T. et al. (1998). *Financial Regulation: Why, How and Where Now?* New York: Routledge.

Goodhart, C. A. E., Basurto, M. A. S. and Hofmann, B. (2006). "Default, Credit Growth, and Asset Prices." IMF Working Paper No. 06–223.

Goodhart, L. M. (2015). "Brave New World? Macro-Prudential Policy and the New Political Economy of the Federal Reserve," *Review of International Political Economy*, 22(2): 280–310.

Gorton, G. (2010). *Slapped by the Invisible Hand: The Panic of 2007.* Oxford: Oxford University Press.

Gorton, G. and Metrick, A. (2012). "Securitized Banking and the Run on Repo," *Journal of Financial Economics*, 104(3): 425–451.

Grabel, I. (2018). *When Things Don't Fall Apart: Global Financial Governance and Developmental Finance in an Age of Productive Incoherence.* Cambridge, MA: MIT Press.

Gravelle, T. and Li, F. (2013). "Measuring Systemic Importance of Financial Institutions: An Extreme Value Theory Approach," *Journal of Banking and Finance*, 37(7): 2196–2209.

Greenspan, A. (1996). "Luncheon Address: Remarks on Systemic Risk and Risk Measurement." Board of Governors of the Federal Reserve System (US), 1995. Proceedings, November, pp. 11–16.

Greenspan, A. (2008). "Prepared Statement in Testimony in front of the House of Representatives."

Greenwood, R., Shleifer, A. and You, Y. (2019). "Bubbles for Fama," *Journal of Financial Economics*, 131(1): 20–43.

Greenwood, R., Hanson, S., Shleifer, A. and Soerensen, J. (2020). "Predictable Financial Crises." NBER Working Paper Series 27396.

Grill, M., Molestina Vivar, L., Mücke, C. et al. (2022). "Mind the Liquidity Gap: A Discussion of Money Market Fund Reform Proposals," *Macroprudential Bulletin*, 16.

Guindos, L. de (2020). "Financial Stability and the Pandemic Crisis." Speech given on June 22. www.ecb.europa.eu/press/key/date/2020/html/ecb.sp200622~422531a969.en.html.

Haar, B. (2015). "Organizing Regional Systems: The EU Example," in N. Moloney, E. Ferran and J. Payne (eds.), *The Oxford Handbook of Financial Regulation*, pp. 156–191. Oxford: Oxford University Press.

Haas, P. M. (1992). "Introduction: Epistemic Communities and International Policy Coordination," *International Organization*, 46(1): 1–35.

Haldane, A. G. and May, R. M. (2011). "Systemic Risk in Banking Ecosystems," *Nature*, 469(7330): 351–355.

Hall, P. A. (1986). *Governing the Economy: The Politics of State Intervention in Britain and France.* Oxford: Oxford University Press.

Hall, P. A. (ed.). (1989a). *The Political Power of Economic Ideas: Keynesianism across Nations.* Princeton, NJ: Princeton University Press.

Hall, P. A. (1989b). "Conclusion: The Politics of Keynesian Ideas," in P. Hall (ed.), *The Political Power of Economic Ideas: Keynesianism across Nations*, pp. 361–392. Princeton, NJ: Princeton University Press.

Hall, P. A. (1992). "The Movement from Keynesianism to Monetarism: Institutional Analysis and British Economic Policy in the 1970s," in S. Steinmo, K. Thelen and F. Longstreth (eds.), *Structuring Politics: Historical Institutionalism in Comparative Analysis*, pp. 90–113. Cambridge: Cambridge University Press.

Hall, P. A. (1993). "Policy Paradigms, Social Learning, and the State: The Case of Economic Policymaking in Britain," *Comparative Politics*, 25: 275–296.

Hanson, S. G., Kashyap, A. K. and Stein, J. C. (2011). "A Macroprudential Approach to Financial Regulation," *Journal of Economic Perspectives*, 25 (1): 3–28.

Hardie, I. and Howarth, D. (2013). *Market-Based Banking and the International Financial Crisis.* Oxford: Oxford University Press.

Harnay, S. and Scialom, L. (2016). "The Influence of the Economic Approaches to Regulation on Banking Regulations: A Short History of Banking Regulations," *Cambridge Journal of Economics*, 40(2): 401–426.

Hartwig, B., Meinerding, C. and Schüler, Y. (2019). "Identifying Indicators of Systemic Risk." https://ssrn.com/abstract=3437285.

Harvey, D. (2005). *Neoliberalism: A Brief History.* Oxford: Oxford University Press.

Hauser, A. (2013). "The Future of Repo: 'Too Much' or 'Too Little'?" Speech given at the ICMA Conference on the Future of the Repo Market, London. www.bankofengland.co.uk/-/media/boe/files/speech/20 13/the-future-of-repo-too-much-or-too-little.pdf.

Hauser, A. (2020). "Seven Moments in Spring: Covid-19, Financial Markets and the Bank of England's Balance Sheet Operations." Speech given on June 4, Bloomberg.

Hauser, A. (2021). "From Lender of Last Resort to Market Maker of Last Resort via the Dash for Cash: Why Central Banks Need New Tools for Dealing with Market Dysfunction." Speech in London, January 7. http://bitly.ws/KjEm.

Hauser, A. and Logan, L. (2022). "Market Dysfunction and Central Bank Tools: Insights from a Markets Committee Working Group chaired by Andrew Hauser (Bank of England) and Lorie Logan (Federal Reserve Bank of New York)." www.bis.org/publ/mc_insights.pdf.

Hay, C. (2001). "The 'Crisis' of Keynesianism and the Rise of Neoliberalism in Britain: An Ideational Approach," in J. L. Campbell and O. K. Pedersen (eds.), *The Rise of Neoliberalism and Institutional Analysis*, pp. 193–218. Princeton, NJ: Princeton University Press.

Hay, C. (2004). "Ideas, Interests and Institutions in the Comparative Political Economy of Great Transformations," *Review of International Political Economy*, 11(1): 204–226.

Hay, C. (2016). "Good in a Crisis: The Ontological Institutionalism of Social Constructivism," *New Political Economy*, 21(6): 520–535.

Heires, M. and Nölke, A. (eds.). (2014). *Politische Ökonomie der Finanzialisierung*. Wiesbaden: Springer.

Helgadóttir, O. (2021). "How to Make a Super-Model: Professional Incentives and the Birth of Contemporary Macroeconomics," *Review of International Political Economy*, DOI: 10.1080/09692290.2021.1997786.

Helleiner, E. (1994). *States and the Reemergence of Global Finance: From Bretton Woods to the 1990s*. Ithaca, NY: Cornell University Press.

Helleiner, E. (2010). "A Bretton Woods Moment? The 2007–08 Crisis and the Future of Global Finance," *International Affairs*, 86(3)(May): 619–636.

Helleiner, E. (2011). "Understanding the 2007–2008 Global Financial Crisis: Lessons for Scholars of International Political Economy (June)," *Annual Review of Political Science*, 14: 67–87.

Helleiner, E. (2014). *The Status Quo Crisis: Global Financial Governance after the 2008 Meltdown*. Oxford: Oxford University Press.

Hellwig, M. (2014). "Financial Stability, Monetary Policy, Banking Supervision, and Central Banking." Discussion Paper Series of the Max Planck Institute for Research on Collective Goods 2014_09.

Hennessy, A (2014). "Redesigning Financial Supervision in the European Union (2009–2013)," *Journal of European Public Policy*, 21(2): 151–168.

Henriksen, L. F. (2013). "Economic Models As Devices of Policy Change: Policy Paradigms, Paradigm Shift, and Performativity," *Regulation and Governance*, 7(4): 481–495.

Hilgartner, S. (1992). "The Social Construction of Risk Objects: Or, How to Pry Open Networks of Risk," in James F. Short and L. Clarke (eds.), *Organizations, Uncertainties, and Risk*, pp. 39–55. Boulder, CO: Westview.

Hirschman, D. and Berman, E. P. (2014). "Do Economists Make Policies? On the Political Effects of Economics," *Socio-Economic Review*, 12(4): 779–811.

Hoerdahl, P. and King, M. (2008). "Developments in Repo Markets during the Financial Turmoil." *BIS Quarterly Review* December, pp. 37–53.

Holm, P. (2007). "Which Way Is Up on Callon," in M. F. MacKenzie and L. Siu (eds.), *Do Economists Make Markets? On the Performativity of Economics*, pp. 190–224. Princeton, NJ: Princeton University Press.

Holmes, D. R. (2013). *Economy of Words: Communicative Imperatives in Central Banks*. Chicago, IL: University of Chicago Press.

Hood, C. (2011). *The Blame Game: Spin, Bureaucracy, and Self-Preservation in Government*. Princeton, NJ: Princeton University Press.

Hood, C. and Lodge, M. (2006). *The Politics of Public Service Bargains*. Oxford: Oxford University Press.

Houben, A., Nijskens, R. and Teunissen, M. (eds.). (2014). "Putting Macro-Prudential Policy to Work." De Nederlandsche Bank, Occasional Studies vol. 12 (7).

House of Lords. (2021). "Economic Affairs Committee 1st Report of Session 2021–22."

Hubbard R. G. (ed.). (1991). *Financial Markets and Financial Crises*. Chicago, IL: University of Chicago Press.

Huebner, M. (2018). *Wenn der Markt regiert: Die Politische Oekonomie der Europaeischen Kapitalmarktunion*. Frankfurt Campus Verlag.

Hungin, H. and James, S. (2019). "Central Bank Reform and the Politics of Blame Avoidance in the UK," *New Political Economy*, 24(3): 334–349.

Ibrocevic, E. (2022). "Independence without Purpose? Macroprudential Regulation at the Bundesbank," *Economy and Society*, 51(4): 655–678.

Ibrocevic, E. and Thiemann, M. (2018). "All Economic Ideas Are Equal, but Some Are More Equal Than Others: A Differentiated Perspective on Macroprudential Ideas and Their Implementation." SAFE Working Paper 214.

Icard, A. (2005). "Dinner Speech on the Occasion of the Fourth Joint Central Bank Research Conference on Risk Measurement and Systemic Risk." European Central Bank, Frankfurt, November 8.

Infante, S. and Saravay, Z. (2020). "Treasury Market Functioning during the COVID-19 Outbreak: Evidence from Collateral Re-use," Federal Reserve notes. Washington, DC: Board of Governors of the Federal Reserve System, December 4. https://libertystreeteconomics.newyorkfed.org/202 0/08/the-federal-reserves-large-scale-repo-program.html.

IMF, FSB and BIS. (2016). *Elements of Effective Macroprudential Policies: Lessons from International Experience*. Washington, DC: IMF Press.

International Capital Market Association (ICMA). (2015). "European Repo Market Survey." Number 30 – conducted December 2015.

International Capital Market Association (ICMA). (2015). "Perspectives from the Eye of the Storm: The Current State and Future Evolution of the European Repo Market" (November).

International Monetary Fund (IMF). (2007). "Global Financial Stability Report Market Developments and Issues" (April).

International Monetary Fund (IMF). (2011). "Macroprudential Policy: An Organizing Framework." Prepared by the Monetary and Capital Markets Department. www.imf.org/external/np/pp/eng/2011/031411.pdf.

International Monetary Fund (IMF). (2016). "United Kingdom: Financial Sector Assessment Program–Financial System Stability Assessment." IMF Country Report 16/167; June 1. www.imf.org/external/pubs/ft/scr/2016/cr16167.pdf.

International Monetary Fund (IMF). (2020). "Belgium:2020 Article IV Consultation-Press Release; Staff Report; Staff Supplement; and Statement by the Executive Director for Belgium." www.imf.org/en/Publ ications/CR/Issues/2020/03/30/Belgium-2020-Article-IV-Consultation-Press-Release-Staff-Report-Staff-Supplement-and-49299.

International Monetary Fund (IMF). (2022). "Finland: 2021 Article IV Consultation-Press Release; Staff Report; and Statement by the Executive Director for Finland." www.imf.org/en/Publications/CR/Issues/2022/01/ 28/Finland-2021-Article-IV-Consultation-Press-Release-Staff-Report-and-Statement-by-the-512330.

IOSCO. (2019). "Recommendations for a Framework Assessing Leverage in Investment Funds (December 2019)." www.iosco.org/library/pubdocs/p df/IOSCOPD645.pdf.

IOSCO. (2022). "IOSCO Investment Funds Statistics Report." www .iosco.org/library/pubdocs/pdf/IOSCOPD693.pdf.

Issing, O. (2016). "Central Banks: From Overburdening to Decline?" SAFE White Paper No. 42.

Jabko, N. (2009). "Transparency and Accountability," in K. Dyson and M. Marcussen (eds.), *Central Banks in the Age of the Euro-Europeanization, Convergence and Power*, pp. 391–406. Oxford: Oxford University Press.

Jacobs, L. R. and King, D. S. (2016). *Fed Power: How Finance Wins*. Oxford: Oxford University Press.

Jasanoff, S. (1987). "Contested Boundaries in Policy-Relevant Science," *Social Studies of Science*, 17(2): 195–230.

Jasanoff, S. (1990). *The Fifth Branch: Science Advisers As Policymakers*. Cambridge, MA: Harvard University Press.

Jasanoff, S. (2004). "Afterword," in S. Jasanoff (ed.), *States of Knowledge: The Co-production of Science and the Social Order*, pp. 274–282. London: Routledge.

Jasanoff, S. (2005). *Designs on Nature: Science and Democracy in Europe and the United States*. Princeton, NJ: Princeton University Press.

Jasanoff, S. (2011a). "The Practices of Objectivity in Regulatory Science," in C. Camic, N. Gross and M. Lamont (eds.), *Social Knowledge in the Making*, pp. 307–337. Chicago, IL: Chicago University Press.

Jasanoff, S. (2011b). "Quality Control and Peer Review in Advisory Science," in J. Weingart and P. Lentsch (eds.), *The Politics of Scientific Advice: Institutional Design for Quality Assurance*, pp. 19–35. Cambridge: Cambridge University Press.

Jasanoff, S. (2012). *Science and Public Reason*. London: Routledge.

Jasanoff, S., Markle, G. E., Peterson, J. C. et al. (eds.). (1995). *The Handbook of Science and Technology Studies*. Thousand Oaks, CA: Sage Publications.

Johnson, J. (2016). *Priests of Prosperity: How Central Bankers Transformed the Postcommunist World*. Ithaca, NY: Cornell University Press.

Johnson, J., Arel-Bundock, V. and Portniaguine, V. (2019). "Adding Rooms onto a House We Love: Central Banking after the Global Financial Crisis," *Public Administration*, 97(3): 546–560.

Jones, D. (2000). "Emerging Problems with the Basel Capital Accord: Regulatory Capital Arbitrage and Related Issues," *Journal of Banking and Finance*, 24(1–2): 35–58.

Jordà, Ò., Richter, B., Schularick, M. et al. (2017a). *Bank Capital Redux: Solvency, Liquidity, and Crisis*. Cambridge, MA: National Bureau of Economic Research.

Jordà, Ò., Schularick, M. and Taylor, A. M. (2015). "Leveraged Bubbles," *Journal of Monetary Economics*, 76: 1–20.

Jordà, Ò., Schularick, M. and Taylor, A. M. (2017b). "Macrofinancial History and the New Business Cycle Facts," *NBER Macroeconomics Annual*, 31(1): 213–263.

Jovanovic, F. (2012). "Finance in Modern Economic Thought," in K. Knorr-Cetina and A. Preda (eds.), *Oxford Handbook of the Sociology of Finance*, pp. 546–566. Oxford: Oxford University Press.

JP Morgan. (2014). "Leveraging the Leverage Ratio Basel III: Leverage and the Hedge Fund-Prime Broker Relationship through 2014 and Beyond – Post Keynesians and the Global Financial Crisis."

Kaltwasser, A. (2016). *A Sociological Inquiry into the Performance of Economic Paradigms.* Saarbrucken: AV Akademikerverlag.

Kaminsky, G. L. and Reinhart, C. M. (1999). "The Twin Crises: The Causes of Banking and Balance-of-Payments Problems," *American Economic Review*, 89(3): 473–500.

Kapstein, E. (1992). "Between Power and Purpose: Central Bankers and the Politics of Regulatory Convergence," *International Organization*, 46(1): 265–287.

Kaufman, G. G. (1994). "Bank Contagion: A Review of the Theory and Evidence," *Journal of Financial Services Research*, 8(2): 123–150.

Kauppi, N. and Madsen, M. R. (eds.). (2013). *Transnational Power Elites: The New Professionals of Governance, Law and Security.* London: Routledge.

Kaya, A. and Reay, M. (2019). "How Did the Washington Consensus Move within the IMF? Fragmented Change from the 1980s to the Aftermath of the 2008 Crisis," *Review of International Political Economy*, 26(3): 384–409.

Keeley, M. C. (1990). "Deposit Insurance, Risk, and Market Power in Banking," *American Economic Review*, 80(5): 1183–1200.

Kentikelenis, A. E. and Babb, S. (2019). "The Making of Neoliberal Globalization: Norm Substitution and the Politics of Clandestine Institutional Change," *American Journal of Sociology*, 124(6): 1720–1762.

Kentikelenis, A. E. and Seabrooke, L. (2017). "The Politics of World Polity: Script-Writing in International Organizations," *American Sociological Review*, 82(5): 1065–1092.

Kessler, O. (2012). "Sleeping with the Enemy? On Hayek, Constructivist Thought, and the Current Economic Crisis," *Review of International Studies*, 38(2): 275–299.

Kessler, O. and Wilhelm, B. (2013). "Financialization and the Three Utopias of Shadow Banking," *Competition and Change*, 17(3): 248–264.

Kessler, O. and Wilhelm, B. (2014). "Finanzialisierung und die Performativität des Schattenbanksystems," in M. Heires and A. Nölke (eds.), *Politische Ökonomie der Finanzialisierung*, pp. 97–113. Wiesbaden: Springer.

Keynes, J. M. (1936). *The General Theory of Employment, Interest and Money.* New York: Harcourt, Brace and Company.

Kim, D. and Santomero, A. M. (1988). "Risk in Banking and Capital Regulation," *The Journal of Finance*, 43(5): 1219–1233.

Kim, S., Plosser, M. C. and Santos, J. A. C. (2017). "Macroprudential Policy and the Revolving Door of Risk: Lessons from Leveraged Lending." Federal Reserve Bank of New York Staff Reports No. 815.

Kindleberger, C. P. (1988). *The International Economic Order: Essays on Financial Crisis and International Public Goods.* Hempstead: Harvester Wheatsheaf.

King, M. (2005). "Epistemic Communities and the Diffusion of Ideas: Central Bank Reform in the United Kingdom," *West European Politics*, 28(1): 94–123.

King, M. (2016). *The End of Alchemy: Money, Banking and the Future of the Global Economy.* London: Little, Brown.

Kjaer, P. and Pedersen, O. (2001). "Translating Liberalization-Neoliberalism in the Danish Negotiated Economy," in J. Campbell and O. K. Pedersen (eds.), *The Rise of Neoliberalism and Institutional Analysis*, pp. 219–248. Princeton, NJ: Princeton University Press.

Kleinberg, J. M. (1999). "Authoritative Sources in a Hyperlinked Environment," *Journal of the ACM*, 46(5): 604–632.

Knaack, P. (2015). "Innovation and Deadlock in Global Financial Governance: Transatlantic Coordination Failure in OTC Derivatives Regulation," *Review of International Political Economy*, 22(6): 1217–1248.

Knoll, K., Schularick, M. and Steger, T. (2017). "No Price Like Home: Global House Prices, 1870–2012," *American Economic Review*, 107(2): 331–353.

Knorr-Cetina, K. and Preda, A. (eds.). (2012). *Oxford Handbook of the Sociology of Finance.* Oxford: Oxford University Press.

Kohn, D. (2014). "Institutions for Macroprudential Regulation: The UK and the US." Speech given at the Kennedy School of Government, Harvard University, April 17.

Kohn, D. (2016). "Macroprudential Policy: Implementation and Effectiveness." Keynote speech, first annual ECB macroprudential policy and research conference.

Kohn, D. (2019a). "How Can the Objective of Macroprudential Policy Be Operationalised, Given the High Uncertainty about the State of the Financial System?" Speech given at the Joint Bundesbank–ECB Spring Conference 2019, Frankfurt, May 15.

Kohn, D. (2019b). "Stress Tests and the Countercyclical Capital Buffer: The U.K. Experience." Speech given at the London School of Economics, Money Macro and Finance 50th Anniversary Conference, Wednesday September 4.

Konings, M. (2009). "Rethinking Neoliberalism and the Subprime Crisis: Beyond the Re-regulation Agenda," *Competition and Change*, 13(2): 108–127.

Konings, M. (2011). *The Development of American Finance.* Cambridge: Cambridge University Press.

Konings, M. (2016). "Governing the System: Risk, Finance, and Neoliberal Reason," *European Journal of International Relations*, 22(2): 268–288.

Konings, M. (2018). *Capital and Time: For a New Critique of Neoliberal Reason*. Stanford, CA: Stanford University Press.

Koo, R. (2009). *The Holy Grail of Macroeconomics: Lessons from Japan's Great Recession*. Chichester: John Wiley and Sons.

Kotz, D. M. (2015). *The Rise and Fall of Neoliberal Capitalism*. Cambridge, MA: Harvard University Press.

Krahnen, J. P. and Wilde, C. (2006). *Risk Transfer with CDOs and Systemic Risk in Banking*. Frankfurt: Goethe-University.

Krainer, J. and Lopez, J. A. (2008). "Using Securities Market Information for Bank Supervisory Monitoring," *International Journal of Central Banking*, 4(1): 125–164.

Kranke, M. and Yarrow, D. (2019). "The Global Governance of Systemic Risk: How Measurement Practices Tame Macroprudential Politics," *New Political Economy*, 24(6): 816–832.

Krippner, G. (2011). *Capitalizing on Crises: The Political Origins of the Rise of Finance*. Cambridge, MA: Harvard University Press.

Kuhn, T. S. (1962). *The Structure of Scientific Revolutions*. Chicago, IL: University of Chicago Press.

Lane, P. R. (2020). "Pandemic Central Banking: The Monetary Stance, Market Stabilisation and Liquidity." Remarks at the Institute for Monetary and Financial Stability Policy Webinar, May 19.

Lang, J. H., Izzo, C., Fahr, S. and Ruzicka, J. (2019). "Anticipating the Bust: A New Cyclical Systemic Risk Indicator to Assess the Likelihood and Severity of Financial Crises." ECB Occasional Paper Series No. 219, February.

Langley, P. (2013). "Anticipating Uncertainty, Reviving Risk? On the Stress Testing of Finance in Crisis," *Economy and Society*, 42(1): 51–73.

Langley, P. (2014). *Liquidity Lost: The Governance of the Global Financial Crisis*. Oxford: Oxford University Press.

Large, A. (2005). "A Framework for Financial Stability." Bank of England – Financial Stability Review Number 18: June, pp. 135–141.

Latour, B. (1987). *Science in Action: How to Follow Scientists and Engineers through Society*. Cambridge, MA: Harvard University Press.

Latour, B. (1999). *Pandora's Hope: Essays on the Reality of Science Studies*. Cambridge, MA: Harvard University Press.

Latour, B. and Woolgar, S. (1986). *Laboratory Life: The Construction of Scientific Facts*. Princeton, NJ: Princeton University Press.

Law, J. (ed.). (1986) *Power, Action and Belief: A New Sociology of Knowledge?* London: Routledge.

Lee, J. H., Ryu, J. and Tsomocos, D. P. (2013). "Measures of Systemic Risk and Financial Fragility in Korea," *Annals of Finance*, 9(4): 757–786.

Leicht, E. and Wall, D. (2018). "Banking Regulators Signal Movement Away from Leveraged Lending Guidance." www.whitecase.com/publications/alert/banking-regulators-signal-movement-away-leveraged-lending-guidance.

Lemke, T. (2001). "'The Birth of Bio-politics': Michel Foucault's Lecture at the Collège de France on Neo-Liberal Governmentality," *Economy and Society*, 30(2): 190–207.

Lenza, M. and Slacalek, J. (2019). "Quantitative Easing Did Not Increase Inequality in the Euro Area." ECB Research Bulletin No. 54.

Lepers, E. and Thiemann, M. (2023). "Taming the Real Estate Boom in the EU: Pathways to Macroprudential (In)action," *Regulation & Governance*. https://doi.org/10.1111/rego.12529.

Levieuge, G. (2009). "The Bank Capital Channel and Counter-Cyclical Prudential Regulation in a DSGE Model," *Recherches Économiques de Louvain/Louvain Economic Review*, 75(4): 425–460.

Levi-Faur, D. (2005). "The Global Diffusion of Regulatory Capitalism," *The Annals of the American Academy of Political and Social Science*, 598(1): 12–32.

Levingston, O. (2021). "Minsky's Moment? The Rise of Depoliticised Keynesianism and Ideational Change at the Federal Reserve after the Financial Crisis of 2007/08," *Review of International Political Economy*, 28(6): 1459–1486.

Levy, J. D. (ed.). (2006). *The State after Statism: New State Activities in the Age of Liberalization*. Cambridge, MA: Harvard University Press.

Liang, N. (2013). "Implementing Macroprudential Policies." Remarks given at Conference on "Financial Stability Analysis: Using the Tools, Finding the Data." Federal Reserve, Cleveland, May 31.

Liang, N. (2018). "Well-Designed Stress Test Scenarios Are Important for Financial Stability." Brookings Institute Research Note, February 2. www.brookings.edu/articles/well-designed-stress-test-scenarios-are-important-for-financial-stability.

Liang, N. (2022). "Remarks by Under Secretary for Domestic Finance Nellie Liang at King's College London's Global Banking and Finance Conference July 5, 2022."

Liang, N. and Parkinson, P. (2020). "Enhancing Liquidity of the U.S. Treasury Market Under Stress." Hutchins Working Paper 72.

Lim, C., Krznar, I., Lipinsky, F. et al. (2013). "The Macroprudential Framework: Policy Responsiveness, and Institutional Arrangements." IMF Working Papers 13/166.

Lockwood, E. (2015). "Predicting the Unpredictable: Value-at-Risk, Performativity, and the Politics of Financial Uncertainty," *Review of International Political Economy*, 22(4): 719–756.

Lo Duca, M., Koban, A., Basten, M. et al. (2017). "A new database for financial crises in European countries – ECB/ESRB EU crises database." ECB Occasional Paper Series 194, July.

Löffler, G. and Raupach, P. (2013). "Robustness and Informativeness of Systemic Risk Measures." Bundesbank Discussion Paper No. 04/2013.

Loftchie, S. (2014a). "SEC Commissioner Aguilar Gives FSOC Thumbs-Down on Mutual Funds, Discusses Cybersecurity and Reg. NMS." http://centerfor financialstability.org/wp/2014/04/03/sec-commissioner-aguilar-gives-fsoc-thumbs-down-on-mutual-funds-discusses-cybersecurity-and-reg-nms.

Loftchie, S. (2014b). "House Financial Services Subcommittee Chairman Introduces Legislation to Reform FSOC." centerforfinancialstability.org/wp/2014/04/04/house-financial-services-subcommittee-chairman-introduces-legislation-to-reform-fsoc.

Loftchie, S. (2014c). "House Financial Services Committee Chairman Calls on FSOC to Cease and Desist." http://centerforfinancialstability.org/wp/2014/05/21/house-financial-services-committee-chairman-calls-on-fsoc-to-cease-and-desist.

Logan, L. (2020). "Treasury Market Liquidity and Early Lessons from the Pandemic Shock." Remarks at Brookings-Chicago Booth Task Force on Financial Stability (TFFS) meeting, panel on market liquidity (delivered via videoconference). As prepared for delivery October 23. www .newyorkfed.org/newsevents/speeches/2020/log201023.

Lombardi, D. and Moschella, M. (2017). "The Symbolic Politics of Delegation: Macroprudential Policy and Independent Regulatory Authorities," *New Political Economy*, 22(1): 92–108.

Lombardi, D. and Siklos, P. L. (2016). "Benchmarking Macroprudential Policies: An Initial Assessment," *Journal of Financial Stability*, 27: 35–49.

Lucas, R. (1972). "Expectations and the Neutrality of Money," *Journal of Economic Theory*, 4: 103–124.

Lucas, R. and Sargent, T. J (1979). "After Keynesian Macroeconomics," *Federal Reserve Bank of Minneapolis Quarterly Review*, 3(2): 295–319.

Luhmann, N. (1984). *Soziale Systeme. Grundriß einer allgemeinen Theorie.* Frankfurt: Suhrkamp.

Luhmann, N. (1994). *Die Wirtschaft der Gesellschaft.* Frankfurt: Suhrkamp.

Lysandrou, P. and Nesvetailova, A. (2015). "The Role of Shadow Banking Entities in the Financial Crisis: A Disaggregated View," *Review of International Political Economy*, 22(2): 257–279.

Mabbett, D. and Schelkle, W. (2019). "Independent or Lonely? Central Banking in Crisis," *Review of International Political Economy*, 26(3): 436–460.

MacKenzie, D. (ed.). (2006). *An Engine, Not a Camera.* Princeton, NJ: Princeton University Press.

MacKenzie, D. and Millo, Y. (2003). "Constructing a Market, Performing Theory: The Historical Sociology of a Financial Derivatives Exchange," *American Journal of Sociology*, 109(1): 107–145.

MacKenzie, M. F. and Siu, L (eds.). (2007). *Do Economists Make Markets? On the Performativity of Economics*. Princeton, NJ: Princeton University Press.

Maes, I. (2009). "On the Origins of the BIS Macro-Prudential Approach to Financial Stability: Alexandre Lamfalussy and Financial Fragility." National Bank of Belgium Working Paper No. 176.

Mainik, G. and Schaanning, E. (2014). "On Dependence Consistency of CoVaR and Some Other Systemic Risk Measures," *Statistics and Risk Modeling*, 31(1): 49–77.

Majone, G. (1997). "From the Positive to the Regulatory State: Causes and Consequences of Changes in the Mode of Governance," *Journal of Public Policy*, 17(2): 139–167.

Mallard, A. (1998). "Compare, Standardize and Settle Agreement: On Some Usual Metrological Problems," *Social Studies of Science*, 28(4): 571–601.

Malone, S., Rodriguez, A. and ter Horst, E. (2009). "What Executives Should Know about Structural Credit Risk Models and Their Limitations: A Primer with Examples," *Journal of Financial Transformation*, 27: 58–62.

Mandelkern, R. (2021). "Neoliberal Ideas of Government and the Political Empowerment of Economists in Advanced Nation-States: The Case of Israel," *Socio-Economic Review*, 19(2): 659–679.

Mandelkern, R. and Shalev, M. (2010). "Power and the Ascendance of New Economic Policy Ideas: Lessons from the 1980s Crisis in Israel," *World Politics*, 62(3): 459–495.

Mandis, S. G. (2013). *What Happened to Goldman Sachs?* Cambridge, MA: Harvard University Press.

Mankiw, N. G. (1986). "The Allocation of Credit and Financial Collapse," *The Quarterly Journal of Economics*, 101(3): 455–470.

Marcussen, M. (2006). "The Fifth Age of Central Banking in the Global Economy." Conference "Frontiers of Regulation," University of Bath.

Marcussen, M. (2009a). "Scientization of Central Banking: The Politics of A-Politization," in K. Dyson and M. Marcussen (eds.), *Central Banks in the Age of the Euro-Europeanization, Convergence and Power*, pp. 373–391. Oxford: Oxford University Press.

Marcussen, M. (2009b). "The Transnational Governance Network of Central Bankers," in M.-L. Djelic and K. Sahlin-Andersson (eds.), *Transnational Governance: Institutional Dynamics of Regulation*, pp. 373–390. Cambridge: Cambridge University Press.

Marcussen, M. (2011). "Scientization," in T. Christensen and P. Laegreid (eds.), *The Ashgate Research Companion to New Public Management*, pp. 321–334. Farnham: Ashgate.

Marcussen, M. (2013). "The Triumph and Despair of Central Banking," in N. Kauppi and M. R. Madsen (eds.), *Transnational Power Elites: The New Professionals of Governance, Law and Security*, pp. 19–35. London: Routledge.

Masciandaro, D. and Volpicella, A. (2016). "Macro Prudential Governance and Central Banks: Facts and Drivers," *Journal of International Money and Finance*, 61: 101–119.

Massoc, E. (2022). "Having Banks 'Play Along': State-Bank Coordination and State-Guaranteed Credit Programs during the COVID-19 Crisis in France and Germany," *Journal of European Public Policy*, 29(7): 1135–1152.

Masters, B. and Braithwaite, T. (2011). "Tighter Rules on Capital: Bankers versus Basel," *Financial Times*, October 2.

Mayntz, R. (2010). "Die transnationale Ordnung globalisierter Finanzmaerkte: Was lehrt uns die Krise." MPIFG Working Paper No. 10/8.

Mayring, P. (2010). *Qualitative Inhaltsanalyse*. Wiesbaden: VS Verlag für Sozialwissenschaften.

McNamara, K. R. (1998). *The Currency of ideas: Monetary Politics in the European Union*. Ithaca, NY: Cornell University Press.

McNamara, K. (2002). "Rational Fictions: Central Bank Independence and the Social Logic of Delegation," *West European Politics*, 25(1): 47–76.

McPhilemy, S. (2015). "Financial Stability and Central Bank Power: A Comparative Perspective," University of Warwick.

McPhilemy, S. (2016). "Integrating Macro-Prudential Policy: Central Banks As the 'Third Force' in EU Financial Reform," *West European Politics*, 39 (3): 526–544.

McPhilemy, S. and Roche, J. (2013). "Review of the New European System of Financial Supervision (ESFS), Part 2: The Work of the European Systemic Risk Board – The ESFS'S Macro-Prudential Pillar." Brussels: European Parliament.

Mehrling, P. (2010). *The New Lombard Street: How the Fed Became the Market-Maker of Last Resort*. Princeton, NJ: Princeton University Press.

Mehrling, P. (2012). "The Inherent Hierarchy of Money." Prepared for Duncan Foley Festschrift Volume and Conference, April 20–21.

Mehrling, P. (2014). "Why Central Banking Should Be Re-imagined." BIS Paper No. 79.

Mehrling, P., Pozsar, Z. and Sweeney, J. (2013). "Bagehot Was a Shadow Banker: Shadow Banking, Central Banking, and the Future of Global Finance." Social Science Research Network. https://ssrn.com/abstrac t=2232016 or http://dx.doi.org/10.2139/ssrn.2232016.

Menand, L. (2022). "Fed Unbound: Central Banking in a Time of Crisis." Columbia Global Reports.

Merton, R. K. (1945) "Role of the intellectual in public bureaucracy," *Social Forces*: 405–415.

Mian, A. and Sufi, A. (2011). "House Prices, Home Equity-Based Borrowing, and the US Household Leverage Crisis," *American Economic Review*, 101 (5): 2132–2156.

Mian, A. and Sufi, A. (2018). "Finance and Business Cycles: The Credit-Driven Household Demand Channel," *Journal of Economic Perspectives*, 32(3): 31–58.

Mian, A., Sufi, A. and Verner, E. (2017). "Household Debt and Business Cycles Worldwide," *The Quarterly Journal of Economics*, 132(4): 1755–1817.

Miller, P. and Rose, N. (1990). "Governing Economic Life," *Economy and Society*, 19(1): 1–31.

Millo, Y. (2007). "Making Things Deliverable: The Origins of Index-Based Derivatives," in M. Callon, Y. Millo and F. Muniesa (eds.), *Market Devices*, pp. 196–214. Oxford: Blackwell Publishing.

Millo, Y. and MacKenzie, D. (2009). "The Usefulness of Inaccurate Models: Towards an Understanding of the Emergence of Financial Risk Management," *Accounting, Organizations and Society*, 34(5): 638–653.

Ministry of Finance France. (2019). "Response Letter to the ESRB Regarding the Warning on Housing Market Developments." November.

Ministry of Finance Germany. (2019). "Response Letter to the ESRB Regarding the Warning on Housing Market Developments." November.

Minsky, H. P. (1977). "The Financial Instability Hypothesis: An Interpretation of Keynes and an Alternative to 'Standard' Theory," *Nebraska Journal of Economics and Business*, 16(1) (Winter 1977): 5–16.

Minsky, H. P. (1986). *Stabilizing an Unstable Economy*. New Haven, CT: Yale University Press.

Miranda-Agrippino, S. and Rey, H. (2015). "US Monetary Policy and the Global Financial Cycle." NBER Working Paper No. 21722.

Mirowski, P. (1989). *More Heat Than Light: Economics As Social Physics, Physics As Nature's Economics*. Cambridge: Cambridge University Press.

Mirowski, P. (2013). *Never Let a Serious Crisis Go to Waste: How Neoliberalism Survived the Financial Meltdown*. New York: Verso Books.

Mirowski, P. and Plehwe, D. (eds.). (2015). *The Road from Mont Pèlerin: The Making of the Neoliberal Thought Collective, with a New Preface.* Cambridge, MA: Harvard University Press.

Mitchell, T. (2002). *The Rule of Experts: Egypt, Techno-Politics, Modernity.* Berkeley: University of California Press.

Mitchell, T. (2005). "The Work of Economics: How a Discipline Makes Its World," *European Journal of Sociology*, 46(2): 297–320.

Monnet, E. (2018). *Controlling Credit: Central Banking and the Planned Economy in Postwar France, 1948–1973.* Cambridge: Cambridge University Press.

Morgan, M. S. (2012). *The World in the Model: How Economists Work and Think.* Cambridge: Cambridge University Press.

Morris, S. and Shin, H. S. (2003). "Global Games: Theory and Applications," *Advances in Economics and Econometrics* (Proceedings of the Eighth World Congress of the Econometric Society), ed. M. Dewatripont, L. Hansen and S. Turnovsky. Cambridge: Cambridge University Press.

Moschella, M. (2015). "The Institutional Roots of Incremental Ideational Change: The IMF and Capital Controls after the Global Financial Crisis," *British Journal of Politics and International Relations*, 17(3): 442–460.

Moschella, M. (2023). *Banking on Orthodoxy: Central Banks and the Unmaking of Monetary Orthodoxy.* Ithaca, NY: Cornell University Press.

Moschella, M. and Tsingou, E. (2013a). "Introduction: The Financial Crisis and the Politics of Reform – Explaining Incremental Change," in M. Moschella and E. Tsingou (eds.), *Transformations: Incremental Change in Post-Crisis Regulation*, pp. 1–45. Colchester: ECPR Press.

Moschella, M. and Tsingou, E. (eds.). (2013b). *Transformations: Incremental Change in Post-Crisis Regulation.* Colchester: ECPR Press.

Mudge, S. L. (2008) "What Is Neo-Liberalism?" *Socio-Economic Review*, 6 (4): 703–731.

Mudge, S. L. (2018). *Leftism Reinvented.* Cambridge, MA: Harvard University Press.

Mudge, S. L. and Vauchez, A. (2012). "Building Europe on a Weak Field: Law, Economics, and Scholarly Avatars in Transnational Politics," *American Journal of Sociology*, 118(2): 449–492.

Mudge, S. L. and Vauchez, A. (2016). "Fielding Supranationalism: The European Central Bank As a Field Effect," *The Sociological Review*, 64 (2, suppl.): 146–169.

Muegge, D. (2013). "Resilient Neo-Liberalism in European Financial Regulation," in V. A. Schmidt and M. Thatcher (eds.), *Resilient Liberalism in Europe's Political Economy*, pp. 201–225. Cambridge: Cambridge University Press.

Muegge, D. (ed.). (2014). *Europe and the Governance of Global Finance*. Oxford: Oxford University Press.

Muegge, D. (2016). "Studying Macroeconomic Indicators As Powerful Ideas," *Journal of European Public Policy*, 23(3): 410–427.

Muegge, D. and Perry, J. (2014). "The Flaws of Fragmented Financial Standard Setting: Why Substantive Economic Debates Matter for the Architecture of Global Governance," *Politics and Society*, 42(2): 194–222.

Muegge, D. and Stellinga, B. (2015). "The Unstable Core of Global Finance: Contingent Valuation and Governance of International Accounting Standards," *Regulation and Governance*, 9(1): 47–62. https://doi.org/10.1111/rego.12052.

Musthaq, F. (2021). "Unconventional Central Banking and the Politics of Liquidity," *Review of International Political Economy*, DOI: 10.1080/09692290.2021.1997785.

Nagel, M. and Thiemann, M. (2019). "Shifting Frames of the Expert Debate: Quantitative Easing, International Macro-Finance and the Potential Impact of Post-Keynesian Scholarship," in L. P. Rochon and V. Monvoisin (eds.), *Finance, Growth and Inequality: Post-Keynesian Perspectives*, pp. 238–257. London: Edward Elgar Publishing.

National Bureau of Economic Research (NBER). 2021. "Business Cycle Dating Committee Announcement," July 19. www.nber.org/news/business-cycle-dating-committee-announcement-july-19-2021021.

Nationwide. (2020). "Global Property Guide 2020." www.globalpropertyguide.com.

Nelson, B. and Newell, J. (2017). "Why Leveraged Lending Guidance Is Far More Important, and Far More Misguided, Than Advertised." November 14. https://bpi.com/why-leveraged-lending-guidance-is-far-more-important-and-far-more-misguided-than-advertised.

Nesvetailova, A. (2015). "A Crisis of the Overcrowded Future: Shadow Banking and the Political Economy of Financial Innovation," *New Political Economy*, 20(3): 431–453.

Nesvetailova, A. (ed.). (2017). *Shadow Banking. Scope, Origins and Theories*. New York: Routledge.

OCC, FDIC and Federal Reserve Board. (2012). "A Proposal for Interagency Guidance on Leveraged Lending." Federal Register 77, pp. 19417–19424.

Office of Financial Research (OFR). (2013). "Asset Management and Financial Stability." www.financialresearch.gov/reports/files/ofr_asset_management_and_financial_stability.pdf.

Ohnsorge, F. L. and Yu, S. (2016). "Recent Credit Surge in Historical Context." Policy Research Working Paper Series 7704, The World Bank.

Orlean, A. (2011). *L'Empire de la valeur. Refonder l'économie*. Seuil: Paris.

Osterloo S., de Haan J., Jong-A-Pin, R. (2007). "Financial Stability Reviews: A First Empirical Analysis," *Journal of Financial Stability*, 2: 337–355.

Ozgode, O. (2022). "The Emergence of Systemic Risk: The Federal Reserve, Bailouts, and Monetary Government at the Limits," *Socio-Economic Review*, 20(4) (October): 2041–2071.

Padoa-Schioppa, T. (2003). "Central Banks and Financial Stability: Exploring a Land in Between," in V. Gaspar et al. (eds.), *The Transformation of the European Financial System: Second ECB Central Banking Conference*, pp. 269–310. Frankfurt: European Central Bank.

Pagano, M. (2014). "Dealing with Financial Crises: How Much Help from Research?" CSEF Working Papers 361, Centre for Studies in Economics and Finance (CSEF), University of Naples, Italy.

Pagliari, S. (2012). "Who Governs Finance? The Shifting Public–Private Divide in the Regulation of Derivatives, Rating Agencies and Hedge Funds," *European Law Journal*, 18(1): 44–61.

Pagliari, S. (2013). "Governing Financial Stability: The Financial Stability Board As the Emerging Pillar in Global Economic Governance," in M. Moschella and K. Weaver (eds.), *Routledge Handbook of Global Economic Governance*, pp. 143–155. London: Routledge.

Pagliari, S. and Wilf, M. (2021). "Regulatory Novelty after Financial Crises: Evidence from International Banking and Securities Standards, 1975–2016," *Regulation and Governance*, 15: 933–951. https://doi.org/10.1111/rego.12346.

Pagliari, S. and Young, K. L. (2014). "Leveraged Interests: Financial Industry Power and the Role of Private Sector Coalitions," *Review of International Political Economy*, 21(3): 575–610.

Papadia, F. and Välimäki, T. (2018). *Central Banking in Turbulent Times*. Oxford: Oxford University Press.

Papadopoulos, S., Stavroulias, P. and Sager, T. (2016). "Systemic Early Warning Systems for EU15 Based on the 2008 Crisis." Bank of Greece, Working Paper No. 202.

Peck, J. (2010). *Constructions of Neoliberal Reason*. Oxford: Oxford University Press.

Persaud, A. (2001). "Sending the Herd Off the Cliff Edge: The Disturbing Interaction between Herding and Market-Sensitive Risk Management Practices." BIS Papers 02.

Persaud, A. (2010). "The Locus of Financial Regulation: Home versus Host," *International Affairs*, 86(3): 637–646.

Persaud, A. (2014). "Central Banks, Monetary Policy and the New Macro-Prudential Tools," in A. Houben, R. Nijskens and M. Teunissen (eds.), *Putting Macro-Prudential Policy to Work*. De Nederlandsche Bank, Occasional Studies Vol. 12 (7).

Piroska, D., Gorelkina, Y. and Johnson, J. (2021). "Macroprudential Policy on an Uneven Playing Field: Supranational Regulation and Domestic Politics in the EU's Dependent Market Economies," *JCMS: Journal of Common Market Studies*, 59: 497–517.

Pixley, J. (2018). *Central Banks, Democratic States and Financial Power*. Cambridge: Cambridge University Press.

Porter, T. M. (1996). *Trust in Numbers: The Pursuit of Objectivity in Science and Public Life*. Princeton, NJ: Princeton University Press.

Power, M. (2007). *Organizing Uncertainty: Designing a World of Risk Management*. Oxford: Oxford University Press.

Pozsar, Z. (2015). "A Macro View of Shadow Banking. Levered Betas and Wholesale Funding in the Context of Secular Stagnation." Draft as of January 31.

Pozsar, Z., Adrian, A., Ashcraft, A. and Boesky, H. (2012). "Shadow Banking." Federal Reserve Bank of New York Staff Reports Staff Report No. 458, revised February.

Price, D. A. and Walter, J. R. (2011). "Identifying Systemically Important Financial Institutions," *Richmond Fed Economic Brief* (April).

PWC. (2015). *Global Financial Markets Liquidity Study*. Price Waterhouse Coopers.

Quarles, R. (2019a). "Frameworks for the Countercyclical Capital Buffer." Spring 2019 Meeting of the Manhattan Institute's Shadow Open Market Committee, New York.

Quarles, R. (2019b). "Refining the Stress Capital Buffer." Remarks at Program on International Financial Systems Conference Frankfurt, Germany, September 5.

Reay, M. J. (2012). "The Flexible Unity of Economics," *American Journal of Sociology*, 118(1): 45–87.

Rees, T. (2019). "Mark Carney Blasts Investment Funds with Liquidity Mismatch As 'Built on a Lie'." *The Telegraph*. www.telegraph.co.uk/busi ness/2019/06/26/markets-latest-news-pound-euro-ftse-100-bitcoin-rallies-towards.

Reichlin, L. (2007). "Closing Remarks." Risk Measurement and Systemic Risk. Report from the Fourth Joint Central Bank Research Conference November 8–9 in Cooperation with the Committee on the Global Financial System. Frankfurt. ECB, pp. 31–35.

Reisenbichler, A. (2015). "The Domestic Sources and Power Dynamics of Regulatory Networks: Evidence from the Financial Stability Forum," *Review of International Political Economy*, 22(5): 996–1024.

Reisenbichler, A. (2020). "The Politics of Quantitative Easing and Housing Stimulus by the Federal Reserve and European Central Bank, 2008–2018," *West European Politics*, 43(2): 464–484.

Repullo, R. and Saurina, J. (2011). "The Countercyclical Capital Buffer of Basel III: A Critical Assessment." Working Papers wp2011_1102, CEMFI, revised June.

Reuters. (2014). "BoE's Carney Speaks on Financial Policy in Parliament." www.reuters.com/article/britain-boe-highlights-idUSL5N0KP1YO20 140115.

Rey, H. (2013). "Dilemma Not Trilemma: The Global Financial Cycle and Monetary Policy Independence." Presentation at Jackson Hole, August.

Riksbank. (2021). *Financial Stability Report 2021:2*. Stockholm: Riksbank Press.

Riles, A. (2011). *Collateral Knowledge: Legal Reasoning in the Global Financial Markets*. Chicago, IL: Chicago University Press.

Rimkutė, D. (2018). "Organizational Reputation and Risk Regulation: The Effect of Reputational Threats on Agency Scientific Outputs," *Public Administration*, 96(1): 70–83.

Rixen, T. (2013). "Offshore Financial Centres, Shadow Banking and Jurisdictional Competition: Incrementalism and Feeble Re-regulation," in M. Moschella and E. Tsingou (eds.), *Transformations: Incremental Change in Post-Crisis Regulation*, pp. 95–124. Colchester: ECPR Press.

Roberts, M. E., Stewart, B. M., Tingley, D. et al. (2014). "Structural Topic Models for Open-Ended Survey Responses," *American Journal of Political Science*, 58(4): 1064–1082.

Rocco, M. (2014). "Extreme Value Theory in Finance: A Survey," *Journal of Economic Surveys*, 28(1): 82–108.

Rochet, J.-C. and Tirole, J. (1996). "Interbank Lending and SYSTEMIC RISK," *Journal of Money, Credit and Banking*, 28(4): 733–762.

Rochon, L. P. and Monvoisin, V. (eds.). (2019). *Finance, Growth and Inequality: Post-Keynesian Perspectives*. London: Edward Elgar Publishing.

Romer, P. (2016). "The Trouble with Macroeconomics," *The American Economist*, 20: 1–20.

Rosengren, E. S. (2013). "Risk of Financial Runs – Implications for Financial Stability." Remarks at "Building a Financial Structure for a More Stable and Equitable Economy." 22nd Annual Hyman P. Minsky Conference on the State of the U.S. and World Economies.

Rosen-Zvi, M., Griffiths, T., Steyvers, M. et al. (2004). "The Author-Topic Model for Authors and Documents." Proceedings of the 20th Conference on Uncertainty in Artificial Intelligence, pp. 487–494.

Rosen-Zvi, M., Chemudugunta, C., Griffiths, T. et al. (2010). "Learning Author-Topic Models from Text Corpora," *ACM Transactions on Information Systems (TOIS)*, 28(1): 1–38.

Rottenburg, R., Merry, S. E., Park, S.-J. et al. (eds.). (2015). *A World of Indicators: The Making of Governmental Knowledge through Quantification.* Cambridge: Cambridge University Press.

Santos, J. A. C. (2001). "Bank Capital Regulation in Contemporary Banking Theory: A Review of the Literature," *Financial Markets, Institutions and Instruments,* 10(2): 41–84.

Saurina, J. (2009). "Loan Loss Provisioning: A Working Macroprudential Tool." Estabilidad Financiera No. 17, 11/2009, pp. 9–26.

Schelkle, W. (2017). "The Political Economy of Monetary Solidarity," in W. Schelkle (ed.), *The Political Economy of Monetary Solidarity: Understanding the Euro Experiment.* Oxford: Oxford University Press.

Schinasi, G. (2004). "Defining Financial Stability." IMF Working Paper 04/187.

Schmidt, V. A. (2002). "Does Discourse Matter in the Politics of Welfare State Adjustment?" *Comparative Political Studies,* 35(2): 168–193.

Schmidt, V. A. (2008). "Discursive Institutionalism: The Explanatory Power of Ideas and Discourse," *Annual Review of Political Science,* 11: 303–326.

Schmidt, V. A. (2011). "Speaking of Change: Why Discourse Is Key to the Dynamics of Policy Transformation," *Critical Policy Studies,* 5(2): 106–126.

Schmidt, V. A. and Thatcher, M. (eds.). (2013). *Resilient Liberalism in Europe's Political Economy.* Cambridge: Cambridge University Press.

Schnabel, I. (2020a). "The ECB's Response to the COVID-19 Pandemic." Remarks at a 24-Hour Global Webinar co-organized by the SAFE Policy Center on "The COVID-19 Crisis and Its Aftermath: Corporate Governance Implications and Policy Challenges." Frankfurt, April 16.

Schnabel, I. (2020b). "COVID-19 and the Liquidity Crisis of Non-Banks: Lessons for the Future." Speech given at the Financial Stability Conference on "Stress, Contagion, and Transmission" organized by the Federal Reserve Bank of Cleveland and the Office of Financial Research, Frankfurt, November 19.

Schnabel, I. (2021). "Asset Purchases: From Crisis to Recovery." September 20. www.ecb.europa.eu/press/key/date/2021/html/ecb.sp210920~ae2c7412dc .en.html.

Schrimpf, A. Shin, H. and Sushko, V. (2020). "Leverage and Margin Spirals in Fixed Income Markets during the Covid-19 Crisis." BIS Bulletin No. 2.

Schularick, M. and Taylor, A. M. (2012). "Credit Booms Gone Bust: Monetary Policy, Leverage Cycles, and Financial Crises, 1870-2008," *American Economic Review,* 102(2): 1029–1061.

Schueler, Y. (2018a). "On the Cyclical Properties of Hamilton's Regression Filter." Deutsche Bundesbank Discussion Paper No. 03/2018.

Schueler, Y. (2018b). "Detrending and Financial Cycle Facts across G7 Countries: Mind a Spurious Medium Term!" ECB Working Paper Series No. 2138/March.

Schueler, Y. S., Hiebert, P. and Peltonen, T. A. (2015). "Characterising the Financial Cycle: A Multivariate and Time-Varying Approach." ECB Working Paper Series 184.

Schueler, Y. S., Hiebert, P. and Peltonen, T. A. (2017). "Coherent Financial Cycles for G-7 Countries: Why Extending Credit Can Be an Asset." ESRB Working Paper Series No. 43/May.

Seabrooke, L. and Tsingou, E. (2009). "Revolving Doors and Linked Ecologies in the World Economy." Working Paper: 260/09, Centre for the Study of Globalisation and Regionalisation.

Seabrooke, L. and Tsingou, E. (2014). "Distinctions, Affiliations, and Professional Knowledge in Financial Reform Expert Groups," *Journal of European Public Policy*, 21(3): 389–407.

Seabrooke, L. and Tsingou, E. (2015). "Professional Emergence on Transnational Issues: Linked Ecologies on Demographic Change," *Journal of Professions and Organization*, 2(1): 1–18.

Seabrooke, L. and Tsingou, E. (2021). "Revolving Doors in International Financial Governance," *Global Networks*, 21(2): 294–319.

Seawright, J. and Gerring, J. (2008). "Case Selection Techniques in Case Study Research: A Menu of Qualitative and Quantitative Options," *Political Research Quarterly*, 61(2): 294–308.

Seabrooke, L. and Henriksen, L. F. (2017). "Issue Control in Transnational Professional and Organizational Networks," in L. Seabrooke and L. Henriksen (eds.), *Professional Networks in Transnational Governance*, pp. 3–24. Cambridge: Cambridge University Press.

Securities Exchange Commission (SEC). (2016). "Liquidity Risk Management Rule (Rule 22e-4)." October 13. www.law.cornell.edu/cfr/text/17/270.22e-4.

Seung, J. L, Li, D., Meisenzahl, R. and Sicilian, M. (2019). "The U.S. Syndicated Term Loan Market: Who Holds What and When?" Federal Reserve.

Shafik, M. (2015). "Goodbye Ambiguity, Hello Clarity: The Bank of England's Relationship with Financial Markets." Speech given at the University of Warwick.

Shin, H. S. (2011). *Risk and Liquidity*. Oxford: Oxford University Press.

Shin, H. S. (2016). "Market Liquidity and Bank Capital." Speech at the Bank for International Settlements.

Singh, M. (2011). "Velocity of Pledged Collateral." IMF Working Paper 11/256.

Singh, M. (2013). "The Changing Collateral Space." IMF Working Paper.

Singh, M. (2014). "Financial Plumbing and Monetary Policy." IMF Working Paper 14/111.

Sissoko, C. (2014). "Shadow Banking: Why Modern Money Markets Are Less Stable Than 19th c. Money Markets but Shouldn't Be Stabilized by a 'Dealer of Last Resort'." USC Law Legal Studies Paper No. 14–21.

Sissoko, C. (2016). "How to Stabilize the Banking System: Lessons from the Pre-1914 London Money Market," *Financial History Review*, 23(1): 1–20.

Skidelksy, R. (2010). *Keynes: The Return of the Master*. London: Penguin Books.

Slobodian, Q. (2018). *Globalists: The End of Empire and the Birth of Neoliberalism*. Cambridge, MA: Harvard University Press.

Smaga, P. (2014). "The Concept of Systemic Risk." Systemic Risk Centre Special Paper 5, London School of Economics and Political Science.

Societe Generale. (2022). "Revision of the AIFM and UCITS Directives: European Commission Proposal." www.securities-services.societegenerale .com/en/insights/views/news/revision-aifm-ucits-directives-european-commission-proposal.

Spillman, L. (2014). "Mixed Methods and the Logic of Qualitative Inference," *Qualitative Sociology*, 37(2): 189–205.

Spruijt, P., Knol, A. B., Vasileiadou, E. et al. (2014). "Roles of Scientists As Policy Advisers on Complex Issues: A Literature Review," *Environmental Science and Policy*, 40: 16–25.

Star, S. L. and Griesemer, J. R. (1989). "Institutional Ecology, Translations and Boundary Objects: Amateurs and Professionals in Berkeley's Museum of Vertebrate Zoology, 1907-39," *Social Studies of Science*, 19(3): 387–420.

Stein, J. (2012). "Monetary Policy As Financial-Stability Regulation," *Quarterly Journal of Economics*, 127(1): 57–95.

Stein, J. (2013a). "Overheating in Credit Markets: Origins, Measurement, and Policy Responses." Speech at "Restoring Household Financial Stability after the Great Recession: Why Household Balance Sheets Matter," research symposium sponsored by the Federal Reserve Bank of St. Louis, St. Louis, MO.

Stein, J. (2013b). "The Fire Sales Problem and Securities Financing Transactions." Speech on November 7 at the Federal Reserve Bank of Chicago and International Monetary Fund Conference, Chicago, IL.

Stein, J. (2014). "Incorporating Financial Stability Considerations into a Monetary Policy Framework." Remarks at the International Research Forum on Monetary Policy Sponsored by the European Central Bank, the Federal Reserve Board, the Center for Financial Studies at the Goethe University, and the Georgetown Center for Economic Research at Georgetown University, Washington, DC, March 21.

Stein, J. (2021). "Can Policy Tame the Credit Cycle?" *IMF Economic Review*, 69(1): 5–22.

Stellinga, B. (2019). "The Open-Endedness of Macroprudential Policy: Endogenous Risks As an Obstacle to Countercyclical Financial Regulation," *Business and Politics*, 22(1): 224–251.

Stellinga, B. (2021). "The Rise and Stall of EU Macro-Prudential Policy: An Empirical Analysis of Policy Conflicts over Financial Stability, Market Integration, and National Discretion," *Journal of Common Market Studies*, 59(6): 1438–1457.

Stellinga, B. and Muegge, D. (2017). "The Regulator's Conundrum: How Market Reflexivity Limits Fundamental Financial Reform," *Review of International Political Economy*, 24(3): 393–423.

Steyvers, M. and Griffiths, T. (2007). "Probabilistic Topic Models," *Handbook of Latent Semantic Analysis*, 427(7): 424–440.

Strassheim, H. (2015). "Politics and Policy Expertise: Towards a Political Epistemology," in F. Fischer, D. Torgerson, A. Durnová and M. Orsini (eds.), *Handbook of Critical Policy Studies*, pp. 319–340. Cheltenham: Edward Elgar Publishing.

Suh, S., Jang, I. and Ahn, M. (2013). "A Simple Method for Measuring Systemic Risk Using Credit Default Swap Market Data," *Journal of Economic Development*, 38(4): 75.

Sullivan and Cromwell. (2020). "FSOC Finalizes Changes to Nonbank SIFI Designation Guidance." www.sullcrom.com/files/upload/SC-Publication-FSOC-Finalizes-Nonbank-SIFI-Designation-Guidance.pdf.

Sundarajan, V., Enoch, C., San José, A. et al. (2002). "Financial Soundness Indicators: Analytical Aspects and Country Practices." IMF Occasional Paper 212, Washington, DC: IMF Press.

Swedberg, R. (2012). "The Role of Confidence in Finance," in K. Knorr-Cetina and A. Preda (eds.), *Oxford Handbook of the Sociology of Finance*, pp. 529–566. Oxford: Oxford University Press.

Tarullo, D. (2008). *Banking on Basel: The Future of International Financial Regulation*. Washington, DC: Peterson Institute for International Economics.

Tarullo, D. K. (2012). "Developing Tools for Dynamic Capital Supervision." Remarks to the Federal Reserve Bank of Chicago Annual Risk Conference, Chicago, IL, April 10.

Tarullo, D. K. (2013a). "Shadow Banking and Systemic Risk Regulation." Speech given at the Americans for Financial Reform and Economic Policy Institute Conference, Washington, DC, November 22.

Tarullo, D. K. (2013b). "Macroprudential Regulation." Speech at Yale Law School Conference on Challenges in Global Financial Services, New Haven, CT.

Tarullo, D. K. (2014a). "Monetary Policy and Financial Stability." Speech at the 30th Annual National Association for Business Economics Economic Policy Conference, Arlington, VA, February 25.

Tarullo, D. K. (2014b). "Stress Testing after Five Years." Speech given at the Federal Reserve Third Annual Stress Test Modeling Symposium, Boston, MA.

Tarullo, D. K. (2014c). "Liquidity Regulation." Speech given at The Clearing House 2014 Annual Conference, New York.

Tarullo, D. K. (2015a). "Advancing Macroprudential Policy Objectives." Office of Financial Research and Financial Stability Oversight Council's 4th Annual Conference, January 30, Arlington, VA.

Tarullo, D. K. (2015b). "Systemic Risk and Macroprudential Stress Testing." [Video file].

Tarullo, D. K. (2015c). "Thinking Critically about Nonbank Financial Intermediation." Speech at the Brookings Institution, Washington, DC, November 17.

Tarullo, D. K. (2016). "Next Steps in the Evolution of Stress Testing." Speech given at the Yale University School of Management Leaders Forum, New Haven, CT, September 26.

Tarullo, D. K. (2020). "Time-Varying Measures in Financial Regulation," *Law and Contemporary Problems*, 83: 1–20.

Tavolaro, S. and Visnovsky, F. (2014). "What Is the Information Content of the SRISK Measure As a Supervisory Tool?" Debats Economique et Financiers 10.

Taylor, C. (1996). "Risk Measurement and Systemic Risk: Proceedings of a Joint Central Bank Research Conference, November 16–17, 1995." Proceedings, Board of Governors of the Federal Reserve System (US), pp. 17–27.

Taylor, J. B. (2009). "The Financial Crisis and the Policy Responses: An Empirical Analysis of What Went Wrong." National Bureau of Economic Research No. w14631.

Taylor, L. and O'Connell, S. A. (1985). "A Minsky Crisis," *The Quarterly Journal of Economics*, 100(Supplement): 871–885.

Taylor, M. (2019). "Overcoming Macroprudential Inertia: An Ambush, and the Votes That Never Were." Speech given at the 5th Annual Macroprudential Conference, Frankfurt, June 21.

Tente, N., Stein, I., Silbermann, L. and Deckers, T. (2015). "The Countercyclical Capital Buffer in Germany." Analytical framework for the assessment of an appropriate domestic buffer rate, Deutsche Bundesbank, November.

Thiemann, M. (2018). *The Growth of Shadow Banking: A Comparative Institutional Analysis*. Cambridge: Cambridge University Press.

Thiemann, M. (2019). "Is Resilience Enough? The Macroprudential Reform Agenda and the Lack of Smoothing of the Cycle," *Public Administration*, 97(3): 561–575.

Thiemann, M. (2021). "The Asymmetric Relationship of Central Banks to Market-Based Finance: Weighing Financial Stability Implications in the Light of Covid Events," *Revue d'economie financiere*, 144(4): 191–201.

Thiemann, M. (2022). "Growth at Risk: Boundary Walkers, Stylized Facts and the Legitimacy of Countercyclical Interventions," *Economy and Society*, DOI: 10.1080/03085147.2022.2117341.

Thiemann, M. and Stellinga, B. (2023). "Between Technocracy and Politics: How Financial Stability Committees Shape Precautionary Interventions in Real Estate Markets," *Regulation and Governance*, 17: 531–548.

Thiemann, M., Aldegwy, M. and Ibrocevic, E. (2018a). "Understanding the Shift from Micro-to Macro-Prudential Thinking: A Discursive Network Analysis," *Cambridge Journal of Economics*, 42(4): 935–962.

Thiemann, M., Birk, M. and Friedrich, J. (2018b). "Much Ado about Nothing? Macro-Prudential Ideas and the Post-crisis Regulation of Shadow Banking," *KZfSS Kölner Zeitschrift für Soziologie und Sozialpsychologie*, 70(1): 259–286.

Thiemann, M., Melches, C. R. and Ibrocevic, E. (2021). "Measuring and Mitigating Systemic Risks: How the Forging of New Alliances between Central Bank and Academic Economists Legitimize the Transnational Macroprudential Agenda," *Review of International Political Economy*, 28 (6) 1433–1458.

Tietmeyer, H. (1999). "International Cooperation and Coordination in the area of Financial Market Supervision and Surveillance." February 11. www.fsb.org/wp-content/uploads/r_9902.pdf.

Toporowski, J. (2014). "Debt, Class and Asset Inflation," in R. Bellofiore and G. Vertova (eds.), *The Great Recession and the Contradictions of Contemporary Capitalism*, pp. 100–111. Cheltenham: Edward Elgar Publishing.

Tooze, A. (2018). *Crashed: How a Decade of Financial Crises Changed the World*. New York: Viking.

Tooze, A. (2022). "Welcome to the World of the Polycrisis." *Financial Times*, October 22.

Trampusch, C. and Palier, B. (2016). "Between X and Y: How Process Tracing Contributes to Opening the Black Box of Causality," *New Political Economy*, 21(5): 437–454.

Tsingou, E. (2004). "Policy Preferences in Financial Governance: Public-Private Dynamics and the Prevalence of Market-Based Arrangements in the Banking Industry." CSGR Working Paper 131/04.

Tsingou, E. (2015a). "Club Governance and the Making of Global Financial Rules," *Review of International Political Economy*, 22(2): 225–256.

Tsingou, E. (2015b). "Transnational Veto Players and the Practice of Financial Reform," *The British Journal of Politics and International Relations*, 17(2): 318–334.

Tucker, P. (2009). "The Debate on Financial System Resilience: Macroprudential Instruments." Barclays Annual Lecture, London.

Tucker, P. (2011). "Macroprudential Policy – Building Financial Stability Institutions." Remarks at the 20th Annual Hyman P. Minsky Conference, New York.

Tucker, P. (2012). "Competition, the Pressure for Returns, and Stability." Speech at the British Bankers' Association Annual Banking Conference, London.

Tucker, P. (2013a). "A New Regulatory Relationship – The Bank, the Financial System and the Wider Economy." Speech at the Institute for Government, London.

Tucker, P. (2013b). "Banking Reform and Macroprudential Regulation – Implications for Banks' Capital Structure and Credit Conditions." SUERF/ Bank of Finland Conference, "Banking after Regulatory Reform – Business As Usual," Helsinki.

Tucker, P. (2014a). "The Lender of Last Resort and Modern Central Banking: Principles and Reconstruction." Bank for International Settlements.

Tucker, P. (2014b). *Regulatory Reform, Stability and Central Banking*. Washington, DC: Brookings Institution.

Tucker, P. (2015). "The Pressing Need for More Complete Central Bank Policy Regimes." Bank for International Settlements Research Conference, Lucerne.

Tucker, P. (2016). "The Design and Governance of Financial Stability Regimes: A Common Resource Problem That Challenges Technical Know-How, Democratic Accountability and International Coordination." CIGI Essays on International Finance, volume 3.

Tucker, P. (2018). *Unelected Power: The Quest for Legitimacy in Central Banking and the Regulatory State*. Princeton, NJ: Princeton University Press.

Tucker, P. and Cecchetti, S. (2021). "Understanding How Central Banks Use Their Balance Sheets: A Critical Categorization." VoxEU column. https://cepr.org/voxeu/columns/understanding-how-central-banks-use-their-balance-sheets-critical-categorisation.

Turner, A. (2011). *Leverage, Maturity Transformation and Financial Stability: Challenges beyond Basel III*. Cass Business School.

Turner, A. (2012). *Economics after the Crisis: Objectives and Means.* Cambridge, MA: MIT Press.

Turner, A. (2015). *Between Debt and the Devil: Money, Credit, and Fixing Global Finance.* Princeton, NJ: Princeton University Press.

Ueno, Y. and Baba, N. (2006). "Default Intensity and Expected Recovery of Japanese Banks and 'Government'." Working Paper No. 06–E–04. Bank of Japan.

Underhill, G. R. D. (2015). "The Emerging Post-Crisis Financial Architecture: The Path-Dependency of Ideational Adverse Selection," *The British Journal of Politics and International Relations,* 17(3): 461–493.

van den End, J. W. (2016). "Quantitative Easing Tilts the Balance between Monetary and Macroprudential Policy," *Applied Economics Letters,* 23 (10): 743–746.

Vissing-Jorgensen, A. (2021). "The Treasury Market in Spring 2020 and the Response of the Federal Reserve," *Journal of Monetary Economics,* 124: 19–47.

Vogel, S. K. (1996). *Freer Markets, More Rules: Regulatory Reform in Advanced Industrial Countries.* Ithaca, NY: Cornell University Press.

Volcker, P. (1994). *American Economic Policy in the 1980s.* Chicago, IL: University of Chicago Press.

Vollmer, H. (2007). "How to Do More with Numbers: Elementary Stakes, Framing, Keying, and the Three-Dimensional Character of Numerical Signs," *Accounting, Organizations and Society,* 32 (6): 577–600.

Walker, J. and Cooper, M. (2011). "Genealogies of Resilience: From Systems Ecology to the Political Economy of Crisis Adaptation," *Security Dialogue,* 42(2): 143–160.

Wang, Y.-C., Wu, J.-L. and Lai, Y.-H. (2013). "A Revisit to the Dependence Structure between the Stock and Foreign Exchange Markets: A Dependence-Switching Copula Approach," *Journal of Banking and Finance,* 37(5): 1706–1719.

Wansleben, L. (2021). "Divisions of Regulatory Labor, Institutional Closure, and Structural Secrecy in New Regulatory States: The Case of Neglected Liquidity Risks in Market-Based Banking," *Regulation and Governance,* 15(3): 909–932.

Wansleben, L. (2023). *The Rise of Central Banks: State Power in Financial Capitalism.* Cambridge, MA: Harvard University Press.

Watson, M. (2002). "The Institutional Paradoxes of Monetary Orthodoxy: Reflections on the Political Economy of Central Bank Independence," *Review of International Political Economy,* 9(1): 183–196.

Weingart, J. and Lentsch, P. (eds.). (2011). *The Politics of Scientific Advice: Institutional Design for Quality Assurance.* Cambridge: Cambridge University Press.

Weingart, P. (1999). "Scientific Expertise and Political Accountability: Paradoxes of Science in Politics," *Science and Public Policy*, 26(3): 151–161.

Weir, M. (1989). "Ideas and Politics: The Acceptance of Keynesianism in Britain and the United States," in P. A. Hall (ed.), *The Political Power of Economic Ideas: Keynesianism across Nations*, pp. 53–86. Princeton, NJ: Princeton University Press.

Weiss, R. (1995). *Learning from Strangers*. New York: Free Press.

Werner, R. (2014). "Can Banks Individually Create Money Out of Nothing? The Theories and the Empirical Evidence," *International Review of Financial Analysis*, 36: 1–19.

Westermeier, C. (2018). "The Bank for International Settlements As a Think Tank for Financial Policy-Making," *Policy and Society*, 37(2): 170–187.

Weyl, E. G. (2017). "Finance and the Common Good," in E. L. Glaeser, T. Santos and E. G. Weyl (eds.), *After the Flood: How the Great Recession Changed Economic Thought*, pp. 277–301. Chicago, IL: Chicago University Press.

White, M. J. (2014). "Enhancing Risk Monitoring and Regulatory Safeguards for the Asset Management Industry." Speech given at the *New York Times* DealBook Opportunities for Tomorrow Conference held at One World Trade Center, New York, December 11.

Whitley, R. (1986). "The Transformation of Business Finance into Financial Economics: The Roles of Academic Expansion and Changes in US Capital Markets," *Accounting, Organizations and Society*, 11(2): 171–192.

Whitley, R. (2000). *The Intellectual and Social Organization of the Sciences*. Oxford: Oxford University Press.

Widmaier, W. (2016). *Economic Ideas in Political Time*. Cambridge: Cambridge University Press.

Widmaier, W., Blyth, M. and Seabrooke, L. (2007). "Exogenous Shocks or Endogenous Constructions? The Meanings of Wars and Crises," *International Studies Quarterly*, 51(4): 747–759.

Wilder, M. and Howlett, M. (2014). "The Politics of Policy Anomalies: Bricolage and the Hermeneutics of Paradigms," *Critical Policy Studies*, 8 (2): 183–202.

Wilf, M. (2016). "Credibility and Distributional Effects of International Banking Regulations: Evidence from US Bank Stock Returns," *International Organization*, 70(4): 763–796.

Wilkins, C. A. (2018). "Financial Stability: Taking Care of Unfinished Business." Remarks at "Are We Ready For the Next Financial Crisis?" Toronto, Ontario.

Willke, H., Becker, E. and Rostásy, C. (2013). *Systemic Risk: The Myth of Rational Finance and the Crisis of Democracy*. Frankfurt: Campus Verlag.

Winters, B. (2012). "Review of the Bank of England's Framework for Providing Liquidity to the Banking System."

Woll, C. (2014). *The Power of Inaction: Bank Bailouts in Comparison.* Ithaca, NY: Cornell University Press.

Wood, M. (2015). "Puzzling and Powering in Policy Paradigm Shifts: Politicization, Depoliticization and Social Learning," *Critical Policy Studies*, 9(1): 2–21.

World Bank. (2020). "COVID-19 to Plunge Global Economy into Worst Recession since World War II." www.worldbank.org/en/news/press-release/2020/06/08/covid-19-to-plunge-global-economy-into-worst-recession-since-world-war-ii#:.

Yamaguchi, Y. (2002). "Triangular View of Systemic Risk and Central Bank Responsibility." www.bis.org/cgfs/conf/mar02.htm.

Yardeni, E. (2023). "Central Banks: Monthly Balance Sheets." www.yardeni.com/pub/peacockfedecbassets.pdf.

Yellen, J. L. (2014). "Monetary Policy and Financial Stability." 2014 Michel Camdessus Central Banking Lecture, International Monetary Fund, Washington, DC, July 2.

Young, K. (2013). "Financial Industry Groups' Adaptation to the Post-Crisis Regulatory Environment: Changing Approaches to the Policy Cycle," *Regulation and Governance*, 7(4): 460–480.

Zigraiova, D. and Jakubík, P. (2014). "Systemic Event Prediction by Early Warning System." IES Working Paper No. 01/2014.

Index

Printed in the United States
by Baker & Taylor Publisher Services